World Literature:

EARLY ORIGINS TO 1800

Arthur H. Bell, Vincent F. Hopper, and Bernard D.N. Grebanier

BARRON'S

All inquiries should be addressed to:
Barron's Educational Series, Inc.
250 Wireless Boulevard
Hauppauge, New York 11788

Library of Congress Catalog Card No.: 94-6600
International Standard Book No. 0-8120-1811-7

Library of Congress Cataloging-in-Publication Data

Bell, Arthur, H., 1946–
    World literature / by Arthur H. Bell, Vincent F. Hopper, and Bernard
D.N. Grebanier. — 2nd [rev.] ed.
        p.   cm. — (College review series)
    Rev. ed of: Essentials of European literature. 1952.
    Includes bibliographical references and indexes.
    Contents: 1. Early origins to 1800 — 2. 1800 to the present.
    ISBN 0-8120-1811-7 (v. 1). — ISBN 0-8120-1812-5 (v. 2)
    1. Literature—History and criticism. I. Hopper, Vincent Foster, 1906–   II.
Grebanier, Bernard D.N., 1903– . III. Bell, Arthur H. (Arthur Henry), 1946–
Essentials of European literature. IV. Title. V. Series.
PN524.H6   1994
809—dc20   94-6600
                                                                              CIP

PRINTED IN THE UNITED STATES OF AMERICA
4567 9770 987654321

PREFACE

The task of writing meaningfully about more than two thousand years of world literature within the constraints of one volume has proven challenging. It has been our goal to provide readers with more than a roadmap of the thoroughfares and byways of world literature, however. Wherever possible, we have endeavored to pause for reflective and appreciative consideration of the works themselves, with their many and various characters, themes, and settings.

For many years, world literature was synonymous with Western European literature. That has changed. This new edition has provided an opportunity to explore that change as well as others. Significant additional material has been added on non-European literatures, women writers, classical and bibli cal literary influences, historical and philosophical background, theatrical history, and other topics. Reader's aids and study features have been placed throughout the work. These include Works at a Glance pages that provide convenient overviews of authors, works, and dates; a Chronology that places major works in their historical context; Review Questions that highlight important factual and interpretative information; a Glossary of useful literary terms an concepts; and Suggested Readings for further in-depth study of authors, works, and periods. The entire volume has been fine-tuned to reflect contemporary scholarship pertaining to the interpretations and dating of works, cultural perspectives, and relevant details of authors' lives. The rich panorama of imagination and history found within this work invites and rewards the reader's exploration.

> *Arthur Bell*
> *San Francisco, California*
> *May 1994*

PREFACE
TO THE FIRST EDITION

This book was written with the express intention of filling the long-felt need for a dependable and comprehensive guide to Continental European Literature. It is hoped that herein will be found the answers to the many questions that inevitably plague the reader who adventures into an unfamiliar literary realm.

There was a time when our teaching of literature was confined exclusively to the study of English and American authors, because it was then believed that advanced study of a foreign language was necessary for the reading of non-English men of letters. But, gradually, educators have come to realize the absurdity of turning out college graduates who had studied works of minor English writers but who had never even read such masterpieces as Dante's *Divine Comedy* or Goethe's *Faust*. Even in the traditional survey course in English literature, the relationship of English to continental literatures soon became apparent; the English Renaissance, for example, must be understood as much more an outgrowth of continental literary trends than a development of its Anglo-Saxon and Middle English predecessors.

Considerations such as these prompted the gradual introduction into college curricula of literature courses which would more nearly than in the past approximate Matthew Arnold's conception of literature as "the best that has been thought and said in the world." Under such titles as "Comparative Literature," "General Literature," "Humanities," and "Great Books," many new courses have accordingly been devised in which translations of foreign books are studied as texts either exclusively or in conjunction with English works.

Concurrently, several excellent new anthologies and many new translations and inexpensive reprints of good earlier translations have been published or are in the process of being prepared. The attractiveness of these translations, together with the popularity of a few excellent radio programs which range far and wide in their discussions of great books, has disclosed to many literate adults the hitherto-unsuspected treasures which exist outside of the strictly "Anglo-Saxon" world.

Having all these things in mind, the authors have tried to put together a book which will be as readily available as the translations themselves, which will acquaint the reader with the outstanding European authors, which will relate these authors to the cultural patterns of their respective milieux, and which will heighten the reader's understanding and enjoyment of the books themselves. In order to bring into focus the many historical trends, aesthetic developments, national tendencies, and highly individualized artistic talents, the authors have adopted what they believe to be a sensible plan of organization. A total view of the history of European literature is conveyed by the chapter divisions, beginning with the early Middle Ages. The guide to the different national literatures will be of assistance to those who are interested particularly in the literary history of a single country.

Since the general aim of these volumes has been to examine European literature as a whole, each chapter is concerned with a single phase of continental literature, opening with a comprehensive description of the period in question. The ensuing subdivisions of most of the chapters then concentrate on the national literatures which were outstanding during that period, beginning with general discussion and then turning to the examination of individual authors. Major authors are given extended treatment; lesser authors are touched on briefly. The first volume covers the Christian era up to the end of the neoclassic period. The second volume opens with the Romantic Movement and carries the literary history well through the end of the nineteenth century. An index is added at the end of each volume to provide ready reference for those seeking information on a specific author, book, literary trend, or historical period.

A third volume provides an extensive bibliography which will serve as a guide for readers who require English translations of foreign works. It also provides a well-arranged compilation of reference books in English on authors, national literatures, and periods for those seeking more extensive information on a particular phase or section of the broad field surveyed in the first two volumes. We believe that this bibliography alone would justify these volumes, since no comparable bibliography for the needs of the general English-reading student is now in existence.

Although the hobgoblin of consistency has been perpetually tugging at our elbows, this grim spectre has been often deliberately warded off for the sake of holding to the criterion of inclusion of what will be most valuable to English-speaking readers. For example, Dante's religious epic is usually described as "The Divine Comedy" (not *La Divina Commedia*), but Dante's "Hell" is customarily referred to by its Italian title, *Inferno.* Because of such charming inconsistencies among English readers, the authors have listed both the original titles and their translated titles, but have given prior position to whichever version has become habitual in the English-speaking world. The same criterion, usefulness to English readers, has guided the authors in their selection of material, the placing of emphasis, and the kind and extent of treatment accorded individual authors and titles.

In a number of colleges, masterpieces of English literature are also included in the courses for which this work is intended. To supplement these pages on Continental literature, we call attention to Prof. Grebanier's *The Essentials of English Literature* issued by the same publishers in two volumes, to which our own volumes are companions in the series. If we may quote from the preface to that book, we too feel that "a history of literature can justify itself only to the extent that it succeeds in inviting its reader to study and enjoy the literature described." We too hope that the student "will find in this book much of the assistance required for sound reading, as well as enough pregnant suggestion to encourage the formation of individual judgment and opinion." . . . "With little sympathy with that company of 'scholars' which is familiar with literature by date and title only," the authors have provided summaries, commentaries, and background materials connected with major works to "smooth the road for the reader who goes directly to the work itself."

In the preparation of this comprehensive survey, the authors are keenly aware of their indebtedness to generations of scholars, translators, and literary historians. We are also indebted to the many instructors throughout the nation who in their enthusiasm for this book when projected have been extremely generous in supplying valuable information concerning European Literature courses given at their respective colleges, and, less obviously, we are indebted to the many students, past and present, whose questions and perceptions alike have indicated the kind of material which a book of this kind should contain. A special acknowledgment of gratitude is owed to Prof. Rod W. Horton of New York University for his contributions on several scholarly matters and to Miss Catherine Grace for her expert assistance in the preparation of large portions of the manuscript.

Vincent F. Hopper, New York University
Bernard D. N. Grebanier, Brooklyn College
June 15, 1952

CONTENTS

Part 1
THE EARLY MIDDLE AGES

Part 2
THE HEIGHT OF THE MIDDLE AGES

Part 3
THE RENAISSANCE

Part 4
NEOCLASSICISM

Part 5
NON-EUROPEAN LITERATURE

CHRONOLOGY OF HISTORICAL AND

HISTORICAL EVENTS

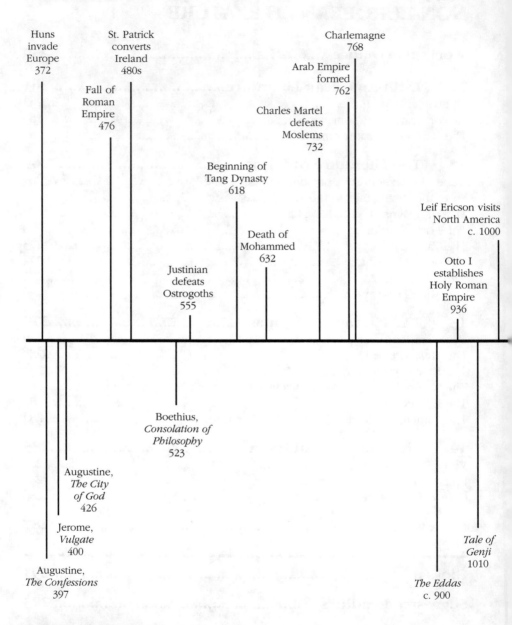

Huns invade Europe 372

St. Patrick converts Ireland 480s

Charlemagne 768

Arab Empire formed 762

Fall of Roman Empire 476

Charles Martel defeats Moslems 732

Beginning of Tang Dynasty 618

Leif Ericson visits North America c. 1000

Death of Mohammed 632

Justinian defeats Ostrogoths 555

Otto I establishes Holy Roman Empire 936

Boethius, *Consolation of Philosophy* 523

Augustine, *The City of God* 426

Jerome, *Vulgate* 400

Tale of Genji 1010

Augustine, *The Confessions* 397

The Eddas c. 900

LITERARY EVENTS

LITERARY EVENTS

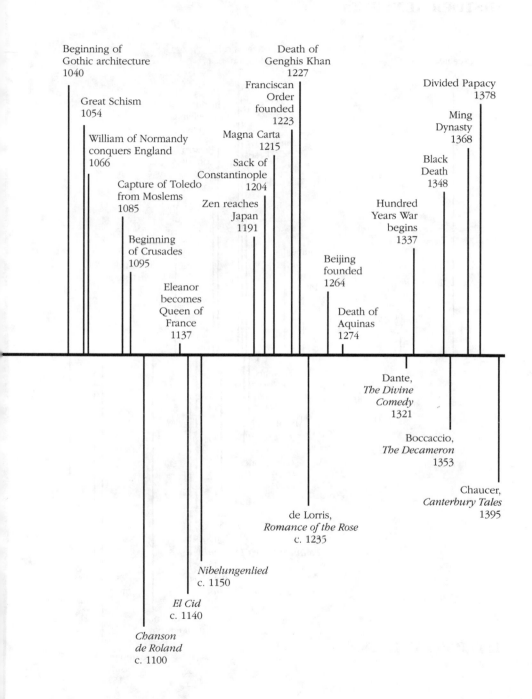

Beginning of
Gothic architecture
1040

Great Schism
1054

William of Normandy
conquers England
1066

Capture of Toledo
from Moslems
1085

Beginning
of Crusades
1095

Eleanor
becomes
Queen of
France
1137

Death of
Genghis Khan
1227

Franciscan
Order
founded
1223

Magna Carta
1215

Sack of
Constantinople
1204

Zen reaches
Japan
1191

Beijing
founded
1264

Death of
Aquinas
1274

Hundred
Years War
begins
1337

Black
Death
1348

Divided Papacy
1378

Ming
Dynasty
1368

Dante,
*The Divine
Comedy*
1321

Boccaccio,
The Decameron
1353

Chaucer,
Canterbury Tales
1395

de Lorris,
Romance of the Rose
c. 1235

Nibelungenlied
c. 1150

El Cid
c. 1140

*Chanson
de Roland*
c. 1100

CHRONOLOGY OF HISTORICAL AND

HISTORICAL EVENTS

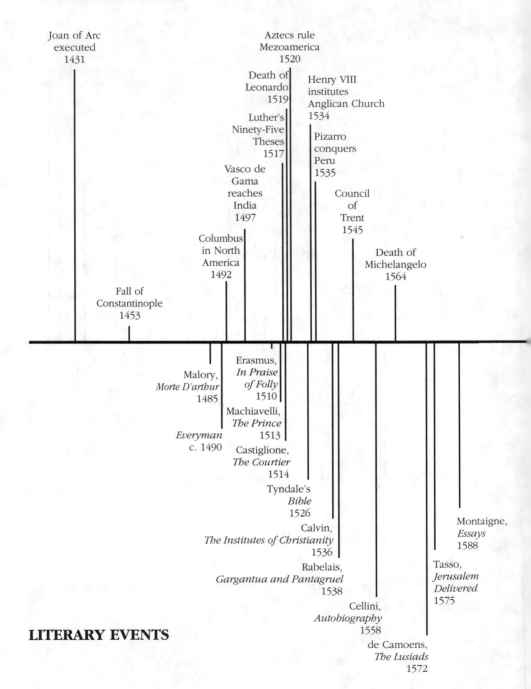

Joan of Arc
executed
1431

Aztecs rule
Mezoamerica
1520

Death of
Leonardo
1519

Henry VIII
institutes
Anglican Church
1534

Luther's
Ninety-Five
Theses
1517

Pizarro
conquers
Peru
1535

Vasco de
Gama
reaches
India
1497

Council
of
Trent
1545

Columbus
in North
America
1492

Death of
Michelangelo
1564

Fall of
Constantinople
1453

Malory,
Morte D'arthur
1485

Erasmus,
*In Praise
of Folly*
1510

Everyman
c. 1490

Machiavelli,
The Prince
1513

Castiglione,
The Courtier
1514

Tyndale's
Bible
1526

Calvin,
The Institutes of Christianity
1536

Montaigne,
Essays
1588

Rabelais,
Gargantua and Pantagruel
1538

Tasso,
*Jerusalem
Delivered*
1575

Cellini,
Autobiography
1558

LITERARY EVENTS

de Camoens,
The Lusiads
1572

LITERARY EVENTS

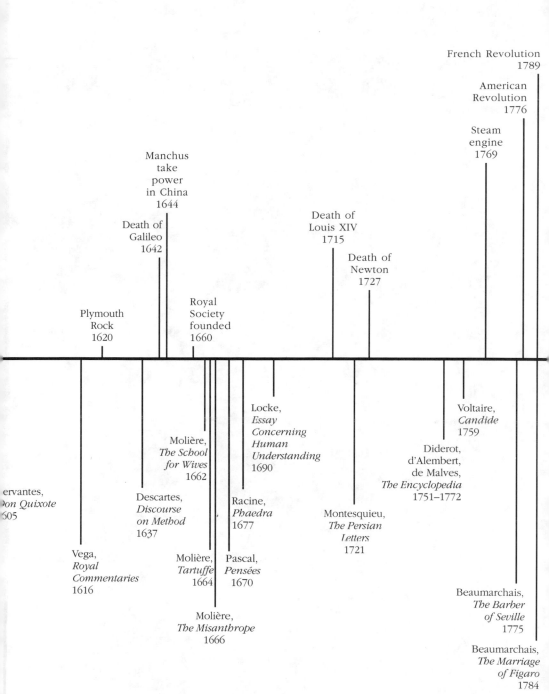

French Revolution
1789

American
Revolution
1776

Steam
engine
1769

Manchus
take
power
in China
1644

Death of
Louis XIV
1715

Death of
Galileo
1642

Death of
Newton
1727

Royal
Society
founded
1660

Plymouth
Rock
1620

Locke,
*Essay
Concerning
Human
Understanding*
1690

Voltaire,
Candide
1759

Molière,
*The School
for Wives*
1662

Diderot,
d'Alembert,
de Malves,
The Encyclopedia
1751–1772

ervantes,
on Quixote
605

Descartes,
*Discourse
on Method*
1637

Racine,
Phaedra
1677

Montesquieu,
*The Persian
Letters*
1721

Vega,
*Royal
Commentaries*
1616

Molière,
Tartuffe
1664

Pascal,
Pensées
1670

Beaumarchais,
*The Barber
of Seville*
1775

Molière,
The Misanthrope
1666

Beaumarchais,
*The Marriage
of Figaro*
1784

Part 1

THE EARLY MIDDLE AGES

The long span of years between the decline of the Roman Empire and the revival of that culture during the Renaissance is loosely known as the Middle Ages. Such a use of this term is convenient rather than accurate or universally acceptable. From the viewpoint of convenience it makes possible the common division of Western European history into three large periods: ancient, medieval, modern. It also prevents the embarrassment of being forced to isolate and date precisely any of the mingling cultural patterns that flowed and eddied from many diverse sources at indeterminate times toward the relatively static pool of medieval culture of the eleventh, twelfth, and thirteenth centuries. Those three centuries—Christian, feudal, organized, culturally productive—comprise a definite unit of history that may be accurately defined as medieval. The preceding centuries of flux, politically chaotic and groping toward integration, are often described as the Dark Ages, although this term has been denounced by many historians because of its implication of the total eclipse of thought. The period is dark only by comparison with the brilliance of the preceding and following eras, for much of the best of medieval achievement was but the flowering of vigorous plants that had achieved their full growth during the preceding centuries.

If one remains aware of the artificiality of isolating the specific elements of a highly complex and fluid age, it is possible to single out such major factors in the medieval equation as the decay of classical culture, the introduction of new traditions by the "barbarian" invaders, and the rise of Christianity.

WORKS AT A GLANCE

Origen

c. 240 A.D.   *De Principiis*

Ambrose

c. 390 A.D.   *Physiologus*   c. 395 A.D.   *Hexameron*

Jerome

382–402   *Vulgate*   c. 395   *Vitae Sanctorum*
393   *De Vivis Illustribus*

Augustine

c. 397*   *The Confessions*   413–426*   *The City of God*

Ancius Manlius Severinus Boethius

524*   *Consolation of Philosophy*

The *Eddas*

c. 800–1100*   *Elder (Poetic) Edda*   c. 1200–1240*   *Prose Edda*
                 composed   composed
c. 110–1250   *Elder (Poetic) Edda*
                 written down

The Sagas

c. 1100   *The Volsung Saga*   c. 1200   *The Nibelungenlied*

Chansons de Geste

c. 1100*   *The Song of Roland*

Spanish Songs of the Cid

c. 1140*   *Poem of the Cid (El Cid)*

---

*Date of composition

1
THE FALL OF ROME AND
THE RISE OF CHRISTIANITY

THE DECLINE OF CLASSICAL CULTURE

The power of the Roman Empire, which had given political stability to the Western World (the *Pax Romana*), had also insured a cultural unity for many centuries because of its adoption in essence of Greek religious, literary, and philosophical traditions. But from the high point of the Augustan or Golden Age (30 B.C.–14 A.D.), which had produced Virgil, Horace, Livy, and Ovid, and the somewhat dimmer glories of the Silver Age (14–117), whose literary lights were Seneca, Martial, Tacitus, Juvenal, and Epictetus, a slow decline of Roman preeminence took place. Roman bureaucracy became increasingly inefficient, and emperors who fancied themselves more and more in the roles of oriental despots were in the main unable to make headway against barbarian inroads at the borders of the empire and against social and economic unbalance within. Recognizing the growing power of Christianity and perhaps hoping that it would act as an integrating force, the Emperor Constantine gave up the Roman imperial pretensions to divinity, put the Christian monogram on the banners of his troops, and thus in the year 330 made Christianity the official Roman religion. He did indeed succeed in reuniting the Empire, which had been split into Eastern and Western segments in 284, but his placing the capital at Byzantium on the Bosphorus was in itself indicative of a waning power.

The final abandonment of the West by the Roman Empire in 476 left Europe in a chaotic state with a shifting population organized only in barbaric tribal units, in remnants of old Roman civic groups, or in the growing religious centers of Christianity. The common people sought, wherever possible, the protection of a local ruler, bishop, city official, or tribal chief. The resulting division of civilization into small units ruled by an overlord, together with the inevitable alliances made by the members of the ruling class, created the feudal system with its innate disposition to oppose any possible political unification into nationhood and its sharply drawn distinction between nobleman and serf.

From the sixth to the eighth century, organized scholarship, education, law, government, and the other accoutrements of civilization seemed to have disappeared, but there remained nevertheless a few individuals and groups who preserved and handed down the classical tradition of the past. Frowned upon by the Church, pagan books and pagan scholarship gradually disappeared,

5

and in such an uncertain world the impetus to original creation lapsed. But stories, such as the legends of Homer, remained alive in human memories to be written down later in medieval romances; and the dream of the restoration of the Roman Empire haunted the European mind until well past the Renaissance.

During this interval of turmoil, the Church was mainly responsible for the preservation of the formal learning of the past. Although repudiating pagan knowledge, Churchmen were forced to rely on the heritage of Greece and Rome as the only educational training available. Consequently, it was classical training that nurtured the organizing talent of the Church, and Christians whose natural bent was toward scholarship compiled encyclopedic works that were uncritical compendiums of pagan learning dressed in Christian clothes. When formal education reasserted itself, principally within the Church, the typical curriculum followed the guide of the Neoplatonist Capella in dividing the fields of knowledge into the *trivium* (grammar, rhetoric, dialectic) and the *quadrivium* (geometry, arithmetic, astronomy, music). In his *Marriage of Philology and Mercury*, Martianus Capella (5th C.) presented this material in the favorite medieval form of an allegory in which the seven liberal arts are figured as presents to the bride. For other textbooks, the early Middle Ages relied on Boethius (c. 480–520), who translated much of Aristotle and wrote commentaries on arithmetic, geometry, music, and logic. Cassiodorus (c. 490–c. 583) compiled Church history, commentaries on scripture, and theological treatises that owe much to the spirit of Aristotle's organizing talent. Around 530, Benedict of Nursia founded at Monte Cassino a library of both secular and religious works. Members of monastic orders laboriously copied such books and became the principal publishers of the Middle Ages.

Of the many classical works so preserved, only a few appear to have been generally known, but they remained safe until their rediscovery by the humanists of the early Renaissance. The most popular medieval encyclopedia was compiled by Isidore of Seville (d. 636), a Christian bishop who organized a voluminous mass of pagan and Christian learning, often from the least reliable sources, into a series of books, of which the *Etymologies* became the first essential of all libraries for centuries to come.

The survival of Platonism also played its part in the vigorous movement known as Neoplatonism. The essential idea of this half-philosophy, half-religion is best expressed in Plato's *Symposium:*

> And the true order of going, or being led by another, to the things of love, is to begin from the beauties of earth and mount upwards for the sake of that other beauty, using these as steps only, and from one going on to two, and from two to all fair forms, and from fair forms to fair practices, and from fair practices to fair notions, until from fair notions he arrives at the notion of absolute beauty, and at last knows what the essence of beauty is.

Plato held that ultimate reality resides in absolute ideals like truth and beauty, earthly truths and beauties being but transitory shadows from which a glimpse of the absolute may be caught. The chief distinction of Neoplatonism, as well as the many Gnostic creeds of the time, was the sense of mystic rapture to be experienced in climbing the ladder of love from earthly things to the vision of Essence, and in the elaborate mystical symbolic details with which the stages of approach into the heart of the mystery were decorated. The Pythagorean doctrine of numbers was also enlisted to illustrate the essential abstraction of the doctrine. The number *one*, represented geometrically by the point, is the essence of abstraction. *Two*, representing the line, possesses the earthly quality of length but, having no thickness, is still in the domain of the abstract. The number *three* symbolizes the triangle or first plane figure. *Four* is the elementary number of solids. As the numbers progress they image the multiple earthly reflections of the Divine Idea, which is unity. Neoplatonism became known in Christian Europe mainly through the Greek Porphyry (c. 233–c. 304) who was the devoted disciple of Plotinus, chief among the founders of Neoplatonism. Much of the Platonic spirit also survived in Christianity itself.

Later, another source of learning became available at the periphery of Christian Europe in the rise and expansion of Moslem power. Islam conquered most of what was left of the Roman Empire of the East, dominated the eastern Mediterranean for part of the seventh century, and had control of all Spain to the Pyrenees by the eighth century. Assimilating and retaining through Syrian translations much of the Hellenism that remained in the Eastern or Byzantine Empire, the Arabs revived and expanded the scientific and rational attitude of Greece, and added a great deal that was peculiarly their own, such as their attainments in mathematics and medicine. One of the greatest of Moslem schools at Cordova in Spain disseminated its influence throughout the Christian world through students who came there to study, and, particularly in the later Middle Ages, through Averroës (1126–1198) and Avicenna (980–1037) whose treatises made Aristotle the preeminent authority in European thought in the twelfth and thirteenth centuries.

Within Christian Europe, scholarship and the intellectual attitude were stimulated by Rhabanus Maurus (c. 776–856), whose *De Universo* enlarges on Isidore of Seville mainly through amplification of Christian learning; by Walafrid Strabo (806–849), who assembled past authorities to interpret the scriptures; by Alcuin (735–804), who was retained by Charlemagne to found his Palace School; by Gerbert of Aurillac (c. 950–1003), who became Pope Sylvester II and whose teachings include Latin writers and Arabic learning; by Fulbert of Chartres (c. 960–1028), who founded at Chartres a school of liberal learning that became the outstanding educational institution of the time; and by John Scotus Erigena (c. 810–875), who interpreted Christian theology in Neoplatonic terms. With the renewed intellectual vitality of the later Middle Ages, intense theological debates and the founding of scholasticism were to place Aristotelian thought and method in a dominant position.

Aristotle's Influence

Aristotle (384–322 B.C.), perhaps the greatest and certainly the most influential of the Greek philosophers, was looked upon as a final authority in many areas of thought, from logic to empirical science to ethics and poetics. Even today his writings continue to influence scholars of philosophy, literature, biology, and other disciplines. Thanks in part to his father, a physician with connections in the Macedonian court, Aristotle joined Plato's famed Academy in Athens in 367 B.C., first as a student and later as a teacher. After Plato's death, Aristotle worked in several royal courts, including that of Philip II, where he became the tutor to the young Alexander the Great. Aristotle returned to Athens in 335 B.C. to found the Lyceum, his own school, which pursued a much broader range of subjects than the Academy. He died in Chalcis in 322 B.C.

Although the establishment of an authentic *Corpus Aristotelicum* is in some ways impossible, much effort has been made to reconstruct the original form of Aristotle's writings. The body of his work is normally divided into three groups: logic, physics, and ethics. Two of Aristotle's most important texts (especially in connection with the humanities), the *Metaphysics* and the *Rhetoric and Poetics*, do not fit easily into any one of these groups.

The *Rhetoric* outlines, in a theoretical manner, some of the traditional methods used in the Greek schools of philosophy, as well as in the political arena. Aristotle insists on the importance of the creative element in an orator's formation of an argument. The *Poetics* is often called the first work of literary criticism/theory. Only a fragment of the complete text remains today, but in it one finds a wealth of insight into the nature of poetry. Contradicting Plato's criticism of poetry as imitative and mimetic, Aristotle sees the poetic creation as ultimately imaginative, presenting ideal truths that rival the records of history and the discoveries of science. Furthermore, poetry, in the Aristotelian conception, should not be judged by the morality of its subject. The much-disputed view that tragedy produces a catharsis or purging in the spectator is also presented in this text. Of course, it is unclear what influence this treatise may have exerted on medieval poets, but we know that much of the early structure of European institutions of higher learning was based on the teachings of Aristotle. Neoclassical writers, and especially dramatists such as Racine and Corneille, often consulted the work of Aristotle as a guide to their theoretical conceptions of drama and verse form. The *Poetics* continues to be at the base of many modern literary theories, including structuralism and the neo-Aristotelian critics.

Classical Ancestors of Literary Genres

It should be noted that most literary genres in Western literatures have their roots in classical predecessors and models. In drama, the tragedies of Aeschylus (525 B.C.–456 B.C.) such as *Prometheus Bound* and *Oresteia* and those of Sophocles (496 B.C.–406 B.C.), including *Antigone* and the *Oedipus* plays, established dramatic principles and themes that continue to influence playwrights and audiences to the present day. The comedies of Aristophanes

(450 B.C.–385 B.C.), such as *Clouds* and *Lysistrata*, led the way toward dramatic art as an entertaining form of social commentary and reform.

The epics of Homer, the *Iliad* and the *Odyssey* (composed perhaps as early as the tenth century B.C.), were vastly influential on Roman epics such as Virgil's *Aeneid* and the traditions of heroic narrative generally. In poetry, the lyric and ode owe their early development to such poets as Pindar (522 B.C.–443 B.C.) and Sappho (c. 600 B.C.). The elegy—a reflective poem typically treating such topics as the loss of youth, the death of a loved one, or a similarly serious contemplation—stems from such early Greek poets as Callinus (seventh century B.C.), Mimnermus (c. 630 B.C.), and Solon (c. 600 B.C.). Iambic and satiric verse, popular throughout virtually all periods of most Western literatures, took early form in the biting lampoons of Archilochus (c. 650 B.C.) and Hipponax (c. 550 B.C.) Greek historians established prose styles and, more generally, set forth rhetorical patterns with which to assert and support an argument. Herodotus (484 B.C.–424 B.C.) and Thucydides (460 B.C.–400 B.C.) wrote prose histories that, in their aesthetic design, rose to the stature of literature. In philosophy, the dialogues of Plato remain unsurpassed models for literary artistry. The treatises of Protagoras, Prodicus, and Hippias proved influential for the development of prose works in the fields of ethics and political science. Finally, in the area of oratory, the elaborate rhetorical systems evident in the speeches of Antiphon, Isocrates, and the great Demosthenes have provided models and a theoretical basis for the art of public speaking and rhetorical analysis up to the present.

The Barbarian Invaders

Although barbarian only in comparison with the high civilizations of Greece and Rome, the term "barbarian invaders" is commonly used to describe the tribes that swept over Europe during the fourth and fifth centuries, bringing with them traditions foreign to the Mediterranean world and constituting the nuclei from which the modern European nations were formed.

The largest of the national groups was referred to by Caesar and Tacitus as the Germans. Migrating from the west shore of the Baltic Sea, this vigorous tribal group had reached the shores of the Rhine at the time of Caesar and had occupied all of modern Germany and the low countries.

The most belligerent of the German tribes, the Goths, had pushed south as far as the southern Danube basin and the Black Sea by 200 A.D. Divided by the Dniester River into Ostrogoths (East Goths) and Visigoths (West Goths), they were actually two independent groups speaking a common language and possessing a common cultural heritage. Under pressure of the Huns, the Visigoths began a series of migrations that carried them through Greece, Italy (where they sacked Rome in 410), and finally into Spain, where they built up a strong kingdom and assimilated the Roman culture already established there. Their rule continued until the early parts of the eighth century, when they were defeated by the Moslems and became part of the mixed elements that make up the Iberian peninsula. The Ostrogoths, under similar pressure, settled in Italy (Theodoric the Ostrogoth became King of Italy in 493) until they were defeated by the Emperor Justinian and absorbed into the Byzantine Empire in 555.

The best integrated and least migratory of the Germans, the Franks, remained close to their homes in the western Rhineland, imitated the Romans in government and military organization, and gradually took over Gaul as the Roman occupation dwindled in strength. Their leader Clovis, who ruled from 481 to 511, drove the Romans out of northern France and then continued his aggression against the Ostrogoths until he controlled all the territory between the Rhine and the Pyrenees. After a period of internal conflict, Charles Martel, son of that Pepin who had reunited all the Franks, stopped the Moslem advance between Tours and Poitiers in 732. His son, also named Pepin, united Franco-Germany and handed down a consolidated empire to his son Charlemagne. Under the banner of Christianity, Charlemagne drove the Moslems from the Pyrenees as far as Barcelona and extended the boundaries of the Frankish Empire south into Italy and north into Brittany. Through him the tradition of the Roman Caesar was revived when, in keeping with the spirit of Augustine's *City of God*, he was crowned in 800 by the Pope as ruler of the Holy Roman Empire. Actually, the Empire did not outlast Charlemagne's son. In 987 the kingdom of France passed into the hands of Hugh Capet, who founded a new dynasty. But the legal line of Holy Roman Emperors passed to Otto I, King of Germany, and continued intermittently until 1804 as a symbol of an unrealized dream.

These various tribes brought with them their own legends and traditions. In contrast to the Greek love of light, beauty, and moderation, the Germans appear to have exalted such ideals as physical vigor, courage, and loyalty. Their religions, derived mainly from nature myths and an awareness of a world of deprivation and danger, were based upon the cold and joyless nature of both heaven and earth, and upon the endless struggle of good against overpowering evil. The Christian proffer of a Redeemer and the promise of a blissful immortality made ready converts of a people who must also have been impressed by the superior civilization of the Christian missionaries. In 341 Bishop Ulfilas came as a missionary to the Goths, translated parts of the Bible into Gothic, and won converts even before Christianity became the official religion of Rome. Other tribes were converted by later contact with Christian Romans. In this, as in many other ways, the Mediterranean and the northern civilizations commingled, so that, by 700 "Roman" meant the region around Rome; in Gaul the Franks were speaking Gallic-Latin or French; in Italy Lombards and Goths modified Latin into the various Italian dialects; and in Spain and Portugal Latin was becoming Spanish and Portuguese. Latin, which continued to be the language of the Church and the language of learning (almost synonymous phrases in the Middle Ages), became less rigorous, more fluid, and simpler in construction. Meanwhile, the very folklore of the various barbarian tribes became infused with morals and concepts obviously Christian in origin.

A Revised View of the Dark Ages

In some traditional treatments of world history, the period from the decline of the Roman Empire to the Crusades (c. 1200) is described as a cultural midnight of sorts—eight hundred years during which nothing of particular note happened in art, music, literature, religion, or politics. This view, however, misrepresents important cultural developments not only in the rest of the world but in Europe as well.

During the supposedly "dark" ages the Mayan Indians developed an advanced civilization in Central America and Mexico (beginning about 300). They perfected calendars, developed new mathematical and astronomical techniques, built architectural wonders, and forged new mythologies and religions. Not long after (320), India began its Golden Age under the Gupta dynasty. In the mid-500s, the Byzantine Empire reached its greatest extent and influence under Emperor Justinian I (a period of cultural history idealized by Yeats in his later poetry). Roman law was codified during this time, as was Judaic law in the compilation of the Talmud (c. 600). In 622 Mohammed fled from Mecca to Medina, his "Hegira," marking the beginning both of the Islamic calendar and the founding of a world-wide religion. From 700 to 1000, the first great black empire in Western Africa, the Ghana Empire, flourished as a trading state. Entire new civilizations emerged during this period, with Muslim Arabs in Africa conquering an immense empire extending as far as west-central France, where they were turned back by Charles Martel and the Franks in 732.

In Europe, Huns invaded the Baltic region about 400, driving Gothic tribes before them into the far western reaches of the continent and, eventually, to England. There, Patrick, Columba, and Columban were responsible in the fifth and sixth centuries for establishing a strong monastic tradition. Monasteries became repositories for both classical and Christian learning. Celtic mythology was recorded for the first time in these monastic centers, and a new decorative art style was developed, as evidenced in book illumination (such as the Lindisfarne Gospels and the Book of Kells, both eighth century). In contemporary France and Germany, the feudal system developed under the Merovingian kings. A mini-Renaissance occurred during the reign of Charlemagne and the intellectual influence of the Anglo-Latin scholar Alcuin (c. 732–804).

In the Arab Empire, a brilliant cosmopolitan civilization emerged with the founding of Baghdad in 762. Lyric poetry was reborn, and surviving libraries of Greek, Perisian, Syrian, and Sanskrit manuscripts were translated into Arabic. Baghdad, Cordova, and Cairo became important centers of science, medicine, and mathematics by the 900s.

In sum, therefore, the phrase "dark ages" should not be interpreted as a blanket judgment on all intellectual and cultural development during the first millennium A.D. In fact, the use of the phrase may stem more from ignorance of other cultures and traditions than from an actual lack of cultural activity during the period.

The Rise of Christianity

With the decline of the official and essentially lifeless Roman pagan religion, mystical and highly emotional religious cults from the East became increasingly popular in the Roman Empire. By the second century, Phrygia, Syria, Egypt, and Persia had all contributed ceremonials and rituals designed to cleanse the initiate of sin and prepare him for an eternal life of beatitude. Amid a welter of mystical beliefs and Neoplatonic creeds, the simple teachings of Jesus of Nazareth stand out in bold relief. It was not long, however, before the followers of Jesus, the architects of Christianity, had adopted the solid historical background of Hebraism, borrowed rituals from Greek mystery cults, allied themselves philosophically with Neoplatonism, and stressed the hope of immortality that was offered by the competing Persian religions of Mithraism and Manichaeism. From Persia, too, came the dominant Christian duality of light and darkness, heaven and hell, salvation and sin, together with the date chosen for Christmas and many rites and rituals. Combining the intellect of Greece, the organizing talent of Rome, the rich tradition of the Hebrews, the mysticism of the East, and the powerful personal appeal of its founder, Christianity quickly became a kind of all-inclusive religion that, in spite of official Roman attempts at suppression, was easily, by the third century, the most popular of religions.

Like its only serious rival, Mithraism, it provided ceremonies by which the initiate received the emotional experience of achieving salvation through mystical union with a risen redeemer. The Christian was also in possession of a body of doctrine or "mystery" that was understandable only to those who had been purified and were worthy to partake of the sacramental rites. Apparently satisfying the religious instinct more than any of the other mystery cults of the time, Christianity built a solid organization throughout the Roman Empire. In the third century each local capital was presided over by a bishop. Archbishops controlled the larger provinces, and at the head of the Church were the patriarchs in Rome, Constantinople, Jerusalem, and Alexandria. Under Constantine, Christianity was proclaimed the official state religion. In 451, Leo I, a Roman bishop, asserted that the Bishop of Rome was the successor of Peter, the founder of the church, and set up the Papacy at Rome as the supreme and undisputable head of the Church. Meanwhile, learned men within the Church had settled their many disagreements largely through the persuasion of the then still pagan Constantine, who presided over the Council of Nicaea in 375, and had built a solid body of doctrine. Wealthy converts provided a sound financial backing. The Church also possessed a document known as the "Donation of Constantine" (proved to be a forgery in 1440) by which the Emperor Constantine supposedly conferred upon Pope Sylvester I sovereignty over the western portion of the Roman Empire.

When Roman power declined in the West, the Church became its inevitable successor. As the heir to Greek and Roman culture, it possessed an intellectual superiority over the semicivilized tribes of Europe. Its organization was superior to that of any other power, ecclesiastical or temporal.

Taking advantage of the "Donation of Constantine," it held itself always exempt from civil control, and succeeded at intervals in actually ruling over various cities in Italy. By destroying or relegating to oblivion Greek and Roman books with their references to other deities and other religious and moral outlooks on life, it came close to establishing itself as the sole representative of God on earth. Simultaneously it established a near monopoly on education, so that learning became possible only through the channels of Christian education. Persecution of nonbelievers eliminated opposition, and the threat of excommunication (removal from Christian salvation), though seldom put into effect, acted as a cogent weapon to coerce individuals and governments. As the greatest single power in Europe, the Church often tended to become more concerned with earthly affairs than with spiritual salvation, and attracted to itself unscrupulous seekers of power whose personal lives were sometimes blatantly scandalous. It also educated many learned men. It was both the destroyer and preserver of classical culture, destroying books that would have continued a pagan tradition, but preserving many of the elements of Greek and Roman learning in a world that was being overwhelmed by the inroads of barbarians.

As opposed to the increasing worldliness of the official Church, many deeply religious men renounced entirely earthly pleasures to live in solitude and self-mortification. By the fourth century these individual hermits or anchorites also began to succumb to the organizing power of the Church and formed the monastic orders with well-defined rules of communal living. The most famous monastic regimen was the work of Benedict of Nursia (c. 480–550), who founded the monastery of Monte Cassino where a daily schedule of routines of prayer and work, together with explicit regulation of food and clothing, was put in force. The monasteries, scattered throughout Europe, not only acted as the most striking symbol of the Christian ideal of the saintly and contemplative life but also provided a refuge where learning and literature could survive. Each monastery had its *scriptorium,* where ancient books were stored and copied and where the great majority of Christian religious writings originated. Closely connected with the Benedictine monasteries were the schools that became, through the years, the medieval universities.

THE EARLY CHRISTIAN WRITERS

The official literature of Christianity begins with the records of Christ and his apostles set down by the early converts to the new religion. Four of the accounts of the life of Christ, known as the "gospels" or "glad tidings," together with the book describing the *Acts of the Apostles*, the inspirational and doctrinal letters written by St. Paul, and the visionary book of *Revelations*, were collected by a council into the Canon known as the *New Testament*. These "scriptures" together with all the riches of the *Old Testament* formed the basis for elaboration, commentary, and the creation of an intricate theology by a long line of learned Churchmen known as the Church Fathers. The earliest of these patristic writings were mainly defenses of the faith and attacks on rival religions, but soon turned to elaborations of matters of theology and doctrine. Following the lead of Philo, a devout Jew of the first century who found Neoplatonic doctrines concealed in the texts of Hebrew scriptures, various of the Fathers began to write figurative interpretations of passages from both the *Old* and the *New Testament*, and thereby not only made allegory a favorite medieval form but set the tone of the kind of thinking that was to dominate the period. From that time, speculation proceeded always on the basis of past authority, advances being made in compiling more and more interpretations of what was often originally intended as the literal story of the Hebrew patriarchs. Argument similarly proceeded mainly along the allegorical tradition of pointing out analogies. For example, a genealogical record of ten generations is explained as a veiled reference to the Ten Commandments.

Origen

Origen (c. 185–253) held that scripture contained a threefold meaning: corporeal (literal), psychic (applying to the soul), and pneumatic (a kind of ultimate spiritual meaning). He added that some passages do not contain a corporeal sense but are meaningful only when interpreted figuratively, illustrating by reference to the six waterpots, containing two or three firkins apiece, which figure in the story of the marriage in Cana (John 2:6):

> And perhaps on this account the water-vessels containing two or three firkins apiece are said to be for the purification of the Jews, as we read in the Gospel according to John: the expression darkly intimating, with respect to those who [are called] by the apostle the 'Jews' secretly, that they are purified by the word of the Scripture, receiving sometimes two firkins: i.e., so to speak, the 'psychical' and 'spiritual' sense; and sometimes three firkins since they have, in addition to those already mentioned, also the 'corporeal' sense, which is capable of [producing] edification. And six water-vessels are reasonably [appropriate] to those who are purified in the world, which was made in six days. (*De Principiis*, IV, 1.)

Ambrose

Ambrose (c. 340–397) found symbolic meanings everywhere and, by showing similitudes between Christian scriptures and both pagan practices and the world of nature, he did much to fuse pagan culture with Christian doctrine. His *Physiologus* is the earliest Christian bestiary that, allegorically, teaches moral and religious truths by illustrations from the animal kingdom, each beast symbolizing a moral or religious truth. His *Hexameron*, a series of sermons on the six days of Creation as the prototype of universal history, became one of the basic Christian authorities.

Jerome

Jerome (c. 340–420) was converted from devotion to classical culture by the appearance of a visionary figure saying, "You are a Ciceronian, not a Christian." A remarkable linguist, scholar, and imaginative creative writer, he produced many works, the most prominent being a translation of the *Old Testament* into easy Latin (the *Vulgate*), a series of brief biographies of prominent Christians (*De Viris Illustribus*), and the Lives of the Saints (*Vitae Sanctorum*). Composed for the purpose of providing popular literature of an edifying nature, these stories of the saints had numerous successors, which appealed strongly to the imaginations and emotions of all classes of people and culminated, in the thirteenth century, in the *Golden Legend* by Jacopo da Voragine.

AUGUSTINE (354–430)

IMPORTANCE

Towering above these earlier writers, synthesizing the doctrine of his predecessors, and creating a massive structure of dogma, Aurelius Augustinus remained the greatest Christian authority until the thirteenth century. His restless mind, packed with wide and varied knowledge, was brought to the service of a religion in which he passionately believed. The result was a series of extraordinary writings that combine the idealism of Plato, the organizing impulse (if not the talent) of Aristotle, the rhetorical eloquence of Cicero, and a depth of insight and feeling that was peculiarly his own. He also gave the final stamp of approval to allegory as a literary device and as a pathway to truth, explaining that by such investigation man may discover the mysteries of God which are set down in scripture, and simultaneously derive a keen esthetic satisfaction, for "the most hidden meanings are the sweetest." He also gave impetus to the increasing use of number symbolism among Christian thinkers. There being no better earthly medium of expressing abstraction (and hence the Divine Idea) than the relationships of numbers, the Divine Plan, as indicated by the Trinity, was understood to have been based on an archetypal numerical scheme whose physical expression was observable in the mundane world.

The Confessions

Of Numidian stock, Augustine was born in northern Africa of a pagan father and a Christian mother. This combination of circumstances gave him an unusual opportunity for intellectual and religious exploration, the extent of which is mirrored in his autobiography, *The Confessions (Confessiones)*, composed around 397, shortly after he became a bishop. His title is employed in the sense of the Christian confession of the glory of God. Intended for the comfort and salvation of all mankind, this volume is unusual for its period because of its highly personal and frank revelations of the author's inner life. It is also indicative of the important part played by Christianity in the inward turning of modern literature in contrast to the objectivity of classical literature. Ecstatic and devout in tone, interlarded with scriptural quotations, more concerned with spiritual struggles than literal external fact, the *Confessions* makes use of autobiography as inspiration for others to turn from evil and misguided ways to the True Life. It is also a highly dramatic narrative because of the long and bitter struggle it unveils between Augustine's propensity for paganism and sensuality, in which he was encouraged by his father, and his soul-searching spiritual and intellectual straining toward Christianity and chastity, the dream of his devout and somewhat overpowering mother.

His early years in the relatively small town of Thagaste are conveyed to the reader as the accumulation of the normal growing apperceptions of ordinary boyhood, to which was coupled a childish unthinking faith in God instilled in him by his devoted mother, Monica. His innate powerful masculinity which made him rebellious and recalcitrant in his studies he calls a sin against his spiritual Mother (the Church) and the mother of his flesh. His father Patricius, on the other hand, was apparently delighted with the indications of a potent sexual nature that he had observed in the growing boy. Baptism, almost administered on one occasion when he seemed mortally ill, was withheld possibly because of the parental conflict in the household. His father seems to have had ambitions for his son to become a professional rhetorician, to which end the boy was sent to the nearby city of Madaura for study.

The age of sixteen, although described in very vague terms in the autobiography, was clearly a critical period in Augustine's life. A tightening of family finances forced him to return home for a year of idleness during which he "wallowed" in licentiousness, possibly including homosexuality, and joined a group of "lewd young fellows" whose crimes he sought to emulate. One specific account is given, together with a searching and acute examination of his own motives, of the stealing of some pears, a minor theft that becomes in his account a symbol of the "attractiveness of beautiful bodies, in gold and silver, and all *things.*" He was probably alluding to this period when he refers in Book VIII to his youthful prayer, "Give me chastity and continency, only not yet!"

Meanwhile, he gave sufficient promise as a student for his father to send him to Carthage at the age of seventeen to continue his studies. During his first year he took a mistress or concubine who bore him a son the next year. The child was named Adeodatus, "the gift of God," and was baptised together with Patricius five years later. The irregular but at that time not uncommon family appears to have been a stabilizing factor in Augustine's high-strung and libidinous nature. He declares that he was entirely faithful to his unnamed concubine during the many years they lived together. He became a teacher at Carthage and found himself leaning toward the doctrines of Manichaeism which, based on a principle of two opposing forces of good and evil, seemed to correspond to the reality of his own nature. At one time he was sought out by a Christian bishop at the behest of his mother, whose prayers for her son's salvation were unceasing. The bishop very wisely determined to allow Augustine to find his own salvation, assuring Monica that her piety would ensure the ultimate good of her son. In time, Augustine became an active Manichean and remained in Carthage where, until the age of twenty-eight, he studied the esoteric doctrines, mainly astrological, of the East. In his twenty-ninth year he met the Manichean bishop Faustus whose far-famed skill in disputation proved such a disappointment to Augustine that he gradually lost faith and renounced the religion.

Becoming disgusted as well with the licentiousness of the students at Carthage, he traveled to Rome where he accepted an invitation to teach rhetoric at Milan. There his mother joined him and he listened eagerly to the famous Christian bishop Ambrose whose sermons stimulated in him a desire to attain the concept of a purer life. His approach to Christianity was further hastened by reading the Pauline Epistles in which Paul's own fear of the flesh clearly struck a sympathetic chord. Together with his friend Alypius he studied the writings of Paul and writhed in torment during a long struggle between flesh and spirit. At the same time a kind of practical wisdom caused his mother to arrange what must have been a financially and socially profitable marriage with a girl still two years too young for the ceremony. Augustine apparently concurred in the plans even though they forced him to send his concubine back to Africa after fourteen years; "torn from him," he says. She took the vow of celibacy; Augustine kept the child with him. He describes his anguish, and he also confesses that, soon after, he took another concubine.

At the age of thirty-one, he completely rejected Manichaeism but was unable to accept the Christian doctrine of the cause of evil until his reading of the Neoplatonists convinced him of the ultimate reality of the Divine Idea, of which the physical world is an imperfect copy. But the doctrine of the incarnation of Christ continued to perplex him until continued study of the Scriptures made him understand the role of the Son as the Mediator between Divine Reality and corporeal imperfection.

His personal struggle with fleshly desires continued into his thirty-second year, when he was strengthened by the story of St. Anthony and by the conversion of Victorinus, translator of the Neoplatonists Plotinus and Prophyry. At the height of an intense struggle, a childish voice from a nearby house repeated, "Take up and read." Interpreting this as a command of God, Augustine returned to Alypius, opened the volume of Paul at random, read the admonition in *Romans* XIII, 13–14, to put off the flesh and to put on the Lord Jesus Christ, and rushed in to his mother to tell her that her prayers had at last been answered. After his miraculous conversion, in the year 386, he gave up his profession and sought seclusion in the country to prepare himself for baptism. He was baptised at Easter in his thirty-third year and joined the Church together with his friend Alypius and his son Adeodatus.

Returning to Africa with his mother, he was with her at her death at Ostia in her fifty-sixth year, receiving her dying admonitions, burying her body, and finding himself secure in the knowledge that she was "not altogether dead." This extraordinary human and mystical drama is concluded in the tenth book by a confession of faith, an examination of the faculty of memory, and a discussion of the ways by which God is known to man. Here is to be found some of Augustine's most eloquent rhetoric, particularly in the magnificent paragraphs beginning, "But what do I love, when I love Thee?" and concluding, "I asked the earth and it answered me, 'I am not He' . . . and I replied unto all the things which encompass the door of my flesh, 'Ye have told me of my God, that ye are not He, tell me something of Him.' And they cried out with a loud voice, 'He made us.'" The three last books, XI–XIII, omitted in some editions, elaborate on one of Augustine's favorite subjects: the six days of Creation in which were allegorically disclosed the mystery of the Trinity (the factors of six being one, two, three) and the archetypal pattern of the Universe (whose history is composed of six ages). Thus the act of Creation gave substance and form to the Divine Idea.

The remaining years of Augustine's life began with the formation of a monastic community in his native city where he resided for three years. Then on a visit to Hippo he was persuaded by the Christians there to accept a vacant post as presbyter, from which he advanced to become Bishop. From then until his death in 430, he was entirely engaged in ecclesiastical duties, including the composition of voluminous works on Christian doctrine and in defense of Christianity against rival religions and heretical creeds, a career which brought him into a controversy with Faustus in which his own previous knowledge of Manichaeism served him in good stead.

The City of God

Augustine's greatest vindication of Christianity and his most brilliant theological work was a labor of thirteen years between 413 and 426. *The City of God (De Civitate Dei)*, as its title signifies, is the new Christian state that is to take the place of the decaying pagan Roman Empire. The work was composed in the shadow of the terrifying event of the sack of Rome in 410. At a time when Christianity was still contending with paganism, Gnosticism, Neoplatonism, and the many mystical faiths of Eastern origin, this invasion of the ancient and almost holy city seemed to many a clear sign of punishment by the gods for the official acceptance of Christianity.

Begun as an answer to such criticism, the first ten books are mainly concerned with citing the misfortunes of Rome under pagan gods. But in contrasting the temporal nature of Rome and the Christian promises of eternity, Augustine discovered a great theme in a reworking of his personal conflict between flesh and spirit. This same conflict that makes a drama of his *Confessions* is broadened in *The City of God* into the universal conflict between the City of Man and the City of God, a struggle that courses throughout all human and Divine history. He therefore devotes the last twelve books to a contrast between human and Divine history. His plan divides these latter books into three groups of four apiece. (The number twelve, Augustine explains elsewhere, is the symbol of the apostles preaching the Trinity through the four parts of the world.) The first four books describe the origin of the two cities in the nature of Adam, the second four relate their earthly history from Cain and Abel to the time of Christ, the third four predict their ultimate conclusions at the Last Judgment.

The book is fascinating in its insights into the spiritual, philosophical, and political turmoil of the period. It is esthetically magnificent in its grand design, and intellectually absorbing in its many intricate and ingenious arguments. It is penetratingly true in its analysis of the moral conflict in all human nature. It falls just short of ultimate greatness because of Augustine's fatal weakness for digression on topics which particularly excite his interest, most of which he treats at length in his other writings and which constantly interrupt the course of his main argument and the flow of his great human drama. From a purely historical viewpoint, *The City of God* is a wonderful first-hand commentary on the status of early Christianity at the time of a crumbling civil authority, clearly indicating the dependence of Christian doctrine on Platonism and the uphill struggle to create a solid core of doctrine amidst innumerable conflicting religions and philosophies.

ANCIUS MANLIUS SEVERINUS BOETHIUS (c. 475–525)

Actually more a survivor of Graeco-Roman learning than a member of the group of Church writers, Ancius Manlius Severinus Boethius was easily the outstanding purveyor of pagan knowledge to the medieval Christian world. The last of the pagan philosophers, he was canonized by the Church with the result that his writings became an effective bridge between the two worlds. As Cassiodorus put it, with more eloquence than strict precision:

> Through your translations the music of Pythagoras and the astronomy of Ptolemaeus are read by the Italians; the arithmetic of Nicomachus and the geometry of Euclid are heard by the Westerns; the theology of Plato and the logic of Aristotle dispute in the language of Quirinus; the mechanical Archimedes also you have restored in Latin dress to the Sicilians; and whatever discipline or arts fertile Greece has produced through the efforts of individual men, Rome has received in her own language through your single instrumentality.

Boethius was born in Rome around the year 475 under the last of the Roman emperors. He grew up under King Odoacer as an unusually studious lad, possibly guided by his father who became consul in 487. After his father's death, he was cared for by men of noble families, married the daughter of a senator, and had two sons. When Theodoric the Ostrogoth succeeded Odoacer, the talents and ability of Boethius made him a favorite of the monarch. He became consul in 510 and his two sons were made consuls in 522, an event that the father describes as the height of his felicity. There is no reason for not accepting his own statement that his passion for justice was the cause of the misfortunes which soon followed. Towards the end of the reign of Theodoric he was accused of conspiring against the king in attempting to maintain the integrity of the senate and restore liberty to Rome. He was condemned, sent to prison where he wrote his famous *Consolation of Philosophy* (524), and was executed in 525. Although there is no real evidence that Boethius was a practicing Christian, succeeding centuries came to regard him as a martyr who had been persecuted because of his opposition to the Arian heresy held by Theodoric. He was canonized as Saint Severinus, his prison became a shrine, and in 996 his bones were moved to a beautiful marble tomb in the Church of Saint Augustine.

It was the ambition of Boethius to translate all of Aristotle and Plato in an attempted reconciliation of the two philosophies. He did translate some of Aristotle, wrote commentaries on works of Aristotle, Porphyry, and Cicero, and was the author of several books on logic and school books on the *quadrivium* (arithmetic, music, geometry, and astronomy), which remained basic texts throughout the Middle Ages.

The Consolation of Philosophy

IMPORTANCE

Boethius's best known and most original literary composition, *The Consolation of Philosophy (Philosophiae Consolationis),* comes nearest to his desire to harmonize the philosophies of the past, combining Aristotle, Plato, Stoicism, and even a faint trace of the impact of the Christian attitude. Quiet and gentle in tone, unpretentious in content and simple in exposition, the *Consolation* remains a great humanistic document, examining into truth with humility and upholding the highest moral ideals with conviction. The work, divided into five books, is an allegory, written alternately in prose and verse, and imitating the form of Capella's *Marriage of Philology and Mercury.*

Book I begins with a verse lament for his many sorrows. As if in answer to his complaint, a woman whom he comes to recognize as his guardian, Philosophy, comes to comfort him. From his answers to her questions, she discovers that Boethius knows that the world is ruled by God but that he has forgotten his destiny as a man, and that this lack of self-knowledge is the cause of his distress.

In Book II, Philosophy introduces Fortune who describes to him the many blessings he has enjoyed and explains the transitory and uncertain nature of Fortune's gifts.

In Book III, Philosophy promises to lead him to true happiness which is in God, since God, the highest good, and true happiness are synonymous. It follows that real evil cannot exist since it is not the wish of the omnipotent Deity.

In Book IV, Boethius asks the reason for the existence of evil and for the apparent fact that the evil are often rewarded and the virtuous punished. Philosophy explains that this is true only in appearance, that actually vice is always punished and virtue rewarded, and the Divine Providence is always good.

Book V examines the problem of the apparent logical conflict between human free will and Divine foreknowledge. It is concluded that the knowledge of an event is not the cause of an event, and that for God time does not exist; therefore God sees past, present, and future at once as an eternal present in which evil is punished and goodness is rewarded. "Wherefore fly vice, embrace virtues, possess your minds with worthy hopes, offer up humble prayers to your highest Prince. There is, if you will not dissemble, a great necessity of doing well imposed upon you, since you live in the sight of your Judge, who beholdeth all things."

THE MEDIEVAL BIBLE

During the Middle Ages, the *Vulgate* was the Bible used in churches, though rarely owned or read by common folk. This translation of the Bible into "easy" or common Latin was prepared by Jerome about the year 400. Jerome's version separated the generally accepted books of the Bible (such as *Genesis, Exodus, Leviticus,* and so forth) from the "Apocryphal" books (including *Tobit, Baruch, Judith, I and II Maccabees,* and others), which Jerome regarded as proper for spiritual growth but not for use as authoritative Scripture. In 1516, Erasmus completed his Greek *New Testament,* with Latin annotations. This erudite approach to translation inspired other Biblical scholars to undertake English translations of the Bible. In 1526, William Tyndale moved to Germany to accomplish the two-volume English translation of the Bible forbidden by English religious authorities (and thereafter banned by the Bishop of London). Tyndale as well as those involved in the printing of his Bible were savagely persecuted, with eventual imprisonment and execution for Tyndale himself.

Simultaneously in England, King Henry VIII had befriended Biblical translators, and the Coverdale Bible appeared in 1535 with an extended dedication to the King. A later version of this Bible, printed in Paris, showed in a prefacing plate the King handing the Word of God to his adoring people. In 1611, the King James Bible was the result of a conference of religious scholars called by King James in 1604. He appointed fifty-four scholars, working in six groups, to prepare the "authorized" version for use in the Church of England. That version remains a primary scripture of the Protestant churches to the present.

The Influence of Biblical Materials on Literature

For both educated and uneducated people through the Middle Ages and into the Renaissance, the plots, characters, and themes of the *Old* and *New Testament* were better known than any competing literature. Although few readers had direct access to scripture (in the form of the *Vulgate*) prior to the Reformation, the stories of the Bible were told and retold in religious services and, graphically, in the brilliant religious imagery appearing in stained glass windows and sculpture within cathedrals. Any list of the traditional "matters" of literature—the Matter of Britain, the Matter of France, and the Matter of Spain—must include, as an underlying foundation, the Matter of Scripture. It is not unfair to assert, in fact, that most of the literature of the Middle Ages and much Renaissance literature would have been inconceivable apart from the availability of Biblical materials for the writer's use. Dante's *Divine Comedy*, for example, relies not only on Biblical themes and characters but, just as important, on the reader's familiarity with the implication of Biblical symbols and allegories. Even non-Biblical narratives, such as Tasso's *Jerusalem Delivered*, make frequent use of Biblical allusions and symbols, as do autobiographies such as Augustine's *Confessions*.

For a modern-day secular audience, it may be difficult to conceive of a set of stories so pervasive and respected in their cultural influence that relatively trivial details can be used by authors to engage rich associations on the reader's part. The phrase "water into wine," for example, from one of Jesus's miracles, would likely recall for a medieval audience not only the entire New Testament story but also the allegorical significance attached to that story by the Church—for example, the use of wine in communion as the blood of Christ. Biblical materials, in short, were used as a shorthand of sorts by which both secular and religious writers drew into play a shared world, or language, of spiritual meaning.

2
THE NATIONAL EPICS

While the official Church writings continued the Graeco-Roman tradition both in language (Latin) and partially in substance, the invading semibarbarian tribes brought with them their own myths and legendary heroes. These traditions, mingled with Christian learning and culture when finally written down in the vernacular languages of Europe as they were in the process of formation, constitute the epics of the Scandinavians, Germans, and Franks. Many of these works were not committed to writing in their present form until the height of the Middle Ages, but the legends and folklore which they commemorate were gradually accumulated through the many centuries of living and storytelling by these peoples.

THE EDDAS AND SAGAS

IMPORTANCE

Northernmost of the Germanic peoples, the Scandinavians consisted of the Norwegians, Danes, Swedes, and Icelanders, closely related by language and ancestry. Their legends and traditions were commemorated by minstrels or "skalds" who composed, orally at first, narratives based on a rich background of fact and fable. In Iceland, settled mainly by Norwegians (874–930), there flourished a most vigorous and imaginative literary movement which produced the Eddas and the Sagas. Robust and fast moving, these tales are brilliantly imaginative, many of them magnificent in their sharp awareness of the heroic spirit of mankind contending against a fate-decreed doom in a world of cold and darkness.

The Eddas

The best of the Eddic literature is to be found in two volumes, written in the Old Norse or Icelandic language, known as the *Elder* or *Poetic Edda* and the *Younger* or *Prose Edda*.

The *Elder* or *Poetic Edda* is a magnificent collection of poems in alliterative verse composed between 800 and 1100, put into writing between 1100 and 1250, and organized by an unknown compiler in the thirteenth century.

In all world literature there is little to compare with these writings in their striking images so tensely, almost laconically, phrased, as if the bitter climate had sharpened and intensified the imaginations of their composers. The *Elder Edda* includes the *Voluspa,* in which a sibyl reveals to gods and men the Norse version of the beginning of the world and its fated end; a group of proverbial sayings called the *Havamal* or "Sayings of the Exalted One"; the *Thrymskvida,* which narrates how Thor regained his stolen hammer; and a series of poems that present an early version of the *Nibelungenlied,* later used by Richard Wagner in the composition of his *Ring of the Nibelungs.*

The *Prose Edda* was written by Snorri Sturluson (1171–1241), a prominent historian who also wrote the biographies or *Sagas of the Norwegian Kings.* Made up of several parts, the *Prose Edda* opens with a brief preface that traces the history of the world from the Garden of Eden in keeping with Christian tradition, followed by an invaluable summary of Norse mythology and religion. The second and largest part of the book, in dialogue form, is a technical discussion of the art of poetry illustrated by many examples from the outstanding poems of Iceland. The work concludes with a commentary on three of Snorri's own poems in honor of Hákon, King of Norway.

Scandanavian Mythology: From these two sources is derived, in the main, our knowledge of Scandinavian mythology with its gloomy views of both heaven and earth and of the bitter endless struggle of good against evil. According to the Eddas, the world originally consisted of a great chasm bounded by the two realms of Niflheim to the north and Muspelheim to the south. From a fountain in Niflheim twelve icy rivers flowed into the chasm and froze into an immense glacial deposit. But warm winds blowing from Muspelheim created a mist over the ice from which cloud formations gradually appeared. Emerging as drops of water from the clouds, there came into being the frost maidens, Ymir the frost giant, and the cow Audhumbla, who supplied food for this newly created race.

Audhumbla, in turn, had no source of nourishment except the ice. One day, while licking the hoarfrost and salt from a block of ice, she began to turn it into a human shape. On that day hair was formed, on the second day a head, on the third a complete body. This was the first god, to whom a frost maiden bore the three brothers, Odin (Woden, Wotan), Vili, and Ve. When the three brothers grew up, they attacked the frost giant, Ymir, and destroyed his power by pinning him under Yggdrasil, the great ash-tree that supported the universe.

The brothers then turned to the task of creation. They made earth from the body of Ymir, seas from his blood, mountains from his bones, the sky from his skull, and clouds from his brain. They used his eyebrows to fashion a massive wall to encircle Midgard (mid-earth), which was to become the dwelling place of man. Sparks from Muspelheim became the sun, moon, and stars, under whose benign warmth vegetation was coaxed from the earth.

Supporting the universe was the tree Yggdrasil whose three roots reached to Asgard, the home of the gods, Jötenheim, the land of the giants, and Niflheim, the region of cold and darkness. The root leading to Asgard was cared for by the three Norns, Urda, Verdandi, and Skuld, who sat beside the Well of Fate and ruled respectively the past, present, and future; the Jötenheim root was nourished by the Well of Wisdom, but the Niflheim root was constantly gnawed by the adder Neidhogge, or darkness. Four harts, symbolic of the four winds, nibbled the buds of the tree, and what was left of the giant Ymir sometimes struggled beneath the roots of Yggdrasil, thus causing earthquakes. Because of these destructive forces the universe was not regarded as eternal or even very secure.

After the creation of the physical world, the gods made the first man, Aski, out of an ash tree, and used an elder to form the first woman, Embla. They also created the Dwarfs, master craftsmen who lived under the earth, and the Elves and Sprites, who watched over the flowers and streams. Odin endowed man with life and soul; Vili gave him reason and power of motion; Ve bestowed upon him the five senses and power of speech.

The gloomy Eddic conception of an insecure universe is based, as has been seen, on the awareness of an eternal conflict between the constructive powers of light, warmth, and wisdom and the destructive agencies of darkness, cold, and brute force. The forces of light triumphed in the creation of the world, but the victory was believed to be only a temporary one. Darkness and cold would eventually resume their sway, and the giants of Jötenheim would hurl the gods to destruction, an inevitable *Götterdämmerung* ("Twilight of the Gods"). Since the gods were aware of this eventuality, they sat in their domain at Asgard stoically awaiting Ragnarok, or the Day of Doom.

The event which had particularly aroused the enmity of the giants occurred during the construction of Valhalla, which was planned by Odin to be a fortress for the gods and a heaven for warriors slain in battle. There also lived the Valkyries, his warrior daughters, who visited the battlefields and brought back the heroic slain to live among the gods. This paradise had been built by the giants upon promise of their being given Freyr, goddess of love and beauty, as payment. When the task was completed, Odin refused to give her up. In the ensuing argument, Thor, the thunder god, killed one of the giants with his hammer. From that time onward, the giants remained implacable enemies of the gods.

Other outstanding inhabitants of Asgard were Frigga or Fricka, wife of Odin; her sister Freyr; and Thor's brothers Frey, god of fertility, and Tyr, god of war. The most beloved of the gods was Baldur the good. He was supposedly invulnerable, and the gods used to amuse themselves by throwing deadly missiles at him and watching them bounce like pebbles from his body. Only the fire-god, Loki, the mischief-maker, knew that the beloved Baldur was vulnerable to the mistletoe, and one day he induced one of the gods to pelt Baldur with a twig of this plant. Baldur was instantly pierced to the heart, and, despite all the efforts of the gods to save him, went to Hela, the realm of the dead.

The Sagas

The Sagas, made up of historical, legendary, and biographical materials, often revolving about real or legendary families, were written between the twelfth and fifteenth centuries, and were also usually based on oral tradition. These prose narratives are remarkable examples of story telling, particularly so in view of the discursive character of most medieval narration. Rapid in movement, vigorous, clear, objective, with only occasional moralizing and almost no intrusion of the author's personality, they record the Norse virtues of physical strength, loyalty, and hardihood needed to combat the supernatural as well as natural forces of a forbidding universe. The best known of these, such as the *Njals*, *Egils*, *Laxdaela*, and *Grettis Sagas* are adventure stories of achievement, combat, and revenge, little concerned with love. The women involved are generally conceived on a heroic scale similar to Greek heroines rather than conforming to the sweet, delicate models of the more southerly medieval romances. Essentially realistic in portrayal of incidents, these stories are particularly notable for their sharp and solid characterizations and rapid, lively dialogue.

The Volsung Saga

Some of the sagas are almost completely mythical in nature. The most famous of these, the *Volsung Saga* (c. 1100), supplements the Eddic or earliest known version of the *Nibelungenlied* (c. 1200). Made up of a vexing combination of history and myth, the historical events described presumably occurred during the period of the great migrations of the fifth and sixth centuries, but the mythical elements hark back to prehistoric times.

The story of the Volsungs begins with the account of three gods, Odin, Honir, and Loki, who, in their journeying together, come to a waterfall where they kill and skin an otter. That evening they spend the night with Hreidmar who recognizes the skin as that of his son who had adopted the otter's form. Aided by his sons Fafnir and Regin, Hreidmar seizes the gods and spares their lives only after exacting the promise that they will fill the skin and also cover its surface with gold. Loki procures the gold from a dwarf Andvari whom he has caught at the waterfall in the shape of a fish. When Loki thwarts Andvari's attempt to retain a ring from the gold hoard, the dwarf invokes a curse upon the gold and its future possessors. When the gold, together with its curse, is relinquished to Hreidmar, a family quarrel over it concludes with the slaughter of Hreidmar, the seizure of the gold by Fafnir who adopts the shape of a dragon to guard it, and the promise of revenge against Fafnir on the part of Regin.

The story now turns to King Volsung, a descendant from Odin, and his family of ten sons and one daughter, the oldest being Sigmund and his twin sister Signy. When Signy is being married to Siggeir, king of Gautland, an old one-eyed man enters the hall, thrusts a sword into a huge oak tree in the midst of the hall, and departs with the explanation that the sword shall belong to anyone strong enough to extract it from the tree. When Sigmund alone is able to accomplish the feat, Siggeir offers to buy the sword but is refused. Several years later, Siggeir invites the Volsungs to Gautland where, in spite of Signy's warnings, King Volsung is killed and his sons bound in the forest to be devoured on successive nights by a wolf, said to be Siggeir's mother. Of the Volsungs, only Sigmund, aided by his sister, escapes to a hiding place in the woods.

Signy then sends her two sons to Sigmund to determine if either is mighty enough to aid in getting revenge. When neither proves worthy, she comes to Sigmund in disguise and makes love to her own brother in order to bear a child of Volsung stock. The child Sinfiotli, when ten years old, is sent to Sigmund who, believing him to be Siggeir's son, trains him and returns with him to Siggeir's castle. There Sinfiotli kills the king's two sons and sets fire to the hall. Signy then reveals to Sigmund the truth about Sinfiotli's parentage and returns to perish in the fire with Siggeir.

Sigmund returns home to rule as king. His first wife, Borghild, poisons Sinfiotli. His second wife, Hjordis, is the cause of an invasion by her former suitor Lyngvi, son of King Hunding. Because of the interposition of the old one-eyed man who breaks Sigmund's sword in two, Sigmund is badly wounded. He refuses to be healed by his wife, and instructs her to preserve the pieces of the broken sword for her unborn son. The child Sigurd is tutored by Regin who repairs the sword with which the child avenges his father's death by killing the sons of Hunding. Still instructed by Regin, he then kills the dragon Fafnir, and gains possession of the gold. Regin tells him to roast Fafnir's heart. While doing so, he burns his finger in the blood and, upon putting it in his mouth to cool, he finds himself suddenly able to understand the language of the birds. The birds warn him to beware of Regin, whom he immediately kills. The birds then tell him of the beautiful valkyrie Brynhild who is being punished by Odin for disobedience by having been placed in an enchanted sleep on the top of a fire-encircled mountain, to be rescued only by a hero who knows no fear. Sigurd passes through the wall of fire, cuts the armor from the sleeping Brynhild, and makes with her a pledge of mutual love. For three nights he stays with her, but always with the sword between them.

Leaving Brynhild, Sigurd then sojourns with King Gjuki and Queen Grimhild and their sons Gunnar and Hogni. Grimhild gives him a potion of forgetfulness to cause him to marry her daughter Gudrun. Gunnar, desirous of Brynhild, persuades Sigurd to exchange his appearance with him, ride through the flames on his horse Grani, and bring back the valkyrie. Only after exchanging shapes again, and after Gunnar has married Brynhild, does Sigurd remember his own pledge of eternal love. During a subsequent quarrel between the two wives, Gudrun reveals to Brynhild the secret of her wooing, proving her story by showing the ring which Sigurd had taken from Brynhild's finger. Enraged by the deception, Brynhild incites the two men against each other. Gunnar procures his stepbrother Gutthorm, who has not sworn blood-fellowship with Sigurd, to kill Sigurd in his sleep. Awakened by the wound, the dying Sigurd hurls his sword after the fleeing murderer and cuts him in two, tells Gudrun that Brynhild was the instigator of the crime, and dies. Brynhild commits suicide and, by her own request, is burned on the funeral pyre beside Sigurd, the sword between them as on his first wooing.

The long narrative concludes with Gudrun's marriage to Atli (Atilla), King of the Huns, who then invites Gunnar for a visit in order to steal the gold-hoard from him. Gunnar, warned by Gudrun, sinks the gold in the Rhine before making his visit. The expected treachery occurs, Gunnar's men are slaughtered, Gunnar and Hogni are bound and commanded to reveal the hiding place of the gold. Gunnar offers to tell the secret if Hogni's heart is brought before him. When Atli carries out this strange demand, Gunnar exults that now only the Rhine knows where the treasure is hidden, and is thrown into a den of serpents. Gudrun, pretending to be reconciled to Atli, secretly kills his two sons, feeds him their blood and hearts at a banquet, and that night plunges a sword into his heart and sets fire to the castle, destroying all his men. So the curse of the gold is finally ended, the gold itself having been returned to the earth whence it had come.

The Nibelungenlied

The *Nibelungenlied*, or *Song of the Nibelungs*, is the German version of the *Volsung Saga*, independently composed from the same basic traditional material described above. The earliest extant version, seemingly based on an earlier rendering which used the traditionally alliterative verse of the Germanic peoples, was written by an Austrian court poet of the twelfth century in four line stanzas of essentially iambic lines with assonant endings (the concluding vowel sounds rhyme but the consonants do not). In later versions, rhyme was generally substituted for assonance. Using only parts of the complex legend of the Volsungs, the *Nibelungenlied* tells a more unified story, but it also sacrifices much of the imaginative power of the Icelandic version by ignoring the supernatural elements and by transforming the tale into a much more realistic account; the heroes of the fifth century Germanic tribe of Nibelungs are made into contemporary knights and the mystical element is converted into medieval magic. Divided into thirty-nine *Adventures* or episodes, the poem presents something of the effect of a play with many scenes. The essentially dramatic intent of the work is aided by ominously prophetic passages spaced throughout its length, but the German Homer all too frequently nods and many of the episodes are long-winded and uninspired. As in the *Volsung Saga*, the theme of the poem revolves about the certain catastrophe which results from greed and deception, though far more emphasis is placed on deception than on the greed for gold.

I: Setting the ominous tone of the epic, the first *Adventure* describes the prophetic dream of the beautiful princess Kriemhild (Gudrun), who is the sister of three noble Burgundian princes, King Gunther (Gunnar), Gernot, and Giselher, whose palace is at Worms. In Kriemhild's dream two eagles destroy her pet falcon. Her mother Uta interprets the falcon to mean her husband; the author adds that the eagles are her brothers.

II: *Adventure* II turns abruptly to the nurture and knighting of Siegfried (Sigurd), son of King Siegmund and Queen Sieglind whose court is at Xanten.

III: Siegfried, hearing of Kriemhild's beauty, is determined to woo her, despite his parents' fears of harm that may befall him. He cannot be dissuaded, and consents to be accompanied by his father's knights, though limiting the number to eleven. The ladies at Xanten work day and night to outfit them with fine garments. When Siegfried and his men arrive at Worms, Gunther's uncle Hagen (Hogni) guesses who the handsome stranger is as he sees him from a window. Hagen tells his nephews how the brothers Shilbung and Nibelung unreasonably quarreled with Siegfried and attacked the hero, who in self-defense slew them with his magic sword Balmung, and made himself master of the Nibelung treasure. After a fight with the dwarf Albric (Andvari), Hagen relates, Siegfried swore Albric to allegiance and made him keeper of the Nibelung hoard. Siegfried also slew a dragon (Fafnir), bathed in its blood, and so made himself invulnerable. Gunther decides to greet Siegfried with honor. Siegfried, courteously received, to everyone's chagrin offers to fight them for their lands. At first Gunther's men are angered, but Gernot makes peace among them and offers Siegfried their friendship and the service of all the men. They all make merry, and Siegfried wins at all their games. The women at the court ask about the stranger. Kriemhild watches him from a window. Meanwhile Siegfried pines for a sight of her. He doesn't see her for a year.

IV: Messengers arrive to tell Gunther that the Saxon King Ludeger and the Danish King Ludegast are marching with an army against the Burgundians. Gunther confides his worries to Siegfried, who offers to fight for him. One thousand men will suffice for him to tackle thirty times the number. At the head of his small army, Siegfried encounters forty thousand men. Siegfried overcomes Ludegast, who offers his lands in exchange for his life. Ludeger's men are routed too. Ludeger, fighting Siegfried, recognizes him and will fight no more. He sues for peace. He is also taken prisoner. At Worms, messengers arrive with the good news. Kriemhild questions one of them about Siegfried's great deeds. Siegfried, on his return, suggests returning to his own land, but Gunther will not hear of it. The hero agrees to remain because he still hopes to see Kriemhild.

V: On Whitsunday a feast is held at Worms. The ladies are invited because Gunther thinks it time that Siegfried meet his sister. The two meet and fall in love. The Danish captives depart for home, and Siegfried is persuaded to remain at Gunther's court.

VI: Beyond the Rhine lives fiery beautiful Brunhild, a queen whose suitors are required to compete in three sports against her. If they lose once, they forfeit their heads. Gunther desires her as a wife. But Hagen urges him to have Siegfried act for him. Siegfried undertakes to win Brunhild for Gunther if he can have as a reward Kriemhild for his own wife. Gunther gladly agrees to the bargain. Siegfried, taking with him the cloud-cloak won from the dwarf Albric, which renders the wearer invisible, sets out with Gunther,

Hagen, and Dankwart. On their departure they are furnished with the costli-
est of raiment, worked by Kriemhild's ladies. Siegfried promises to take care
of Gunther. Siegfried acts as pilot, and they come to Brunhild's castle at Isenstein. The hero suggests that they all agree to say that he is only a man in
Gunther's service. He tells them that he is doing this only for Kriemhild's
sake.

VII: At Isenstein one of Brunhild's maidens recognizes Siegfried by his
bearing. He approaches Brunhild, who at first thinks he has come to woo
her. But he assures her that he is only Gunther's vassal and that his master is
her suitor. She warns him that they all will perish if Gunther fails in the test.
Her suitor must cast a stone beyond hers, then leap farther than she, and
sustain the thrust of a javelin better than she can. Siegfried assures Gunther
that he can manage by his arts to outdistance Brunhild. He retires to the boat
and puts on the cloak of invisibility. Brunhild hurls a powerful javelin at
Gunther's shield, but Siegfried is behind it (invisible) and takes the mighty
stroke. He removes the weapon from the shield, courteously turns it with its
point towards himself, and hurls it at Brunhild. She staggers beneath its
impact. Next she casts a mighty stone a great distance and leaps farther after
it. Hagen thinks all is over with them, but the invisible Siegfried casts the
stone in Gunther's hand even farther, and carries him through the air to a
greater distance than Brunhild has leapt. She angrily admits her defeat but
insists on delaying her departure until she has taken leave of her people, for
whom she sends far and near. Suspecting foul play, Gunther's party expects
the worst. But Siegfried assures them he will help them. To this end, he takes
leave of them for a while, promising to be back with reinforcements in time.

VIII: Siegfried sails to the Nibelung's country and there overcomes a giant
porter and Albric before he is recognized. He summons together a large
army and they go back to Isenstein. When Brunhild sees them, she greets
them, and bids Gunther's men distribute gifts among the newcomers. But she
is disturbed at the open-handed generosity with which her wealth is given
away. Leaving her uncle in charge of her domains, Brunhild departs with
Gunther's company together with an escort of her own men.

IX: Siegfried journeys ahead to Worms to tell the good news to Gunther's
family. Kriemhild is very happy, and all the court prepares for the wedding
feast.

X: Brunhild is kindly greeted by Gunther's family. Siegfried reminds Gunther of his promise, and Kriemhild proves willing; and so Siegfried and she
are married. When Brunhild beholds her sister-in-law married to what she
believes to be her husband's vassal, she weeps for shame. Gunther tries to
silence her and informs her that Siegfried is a king in his own right. When
she persists in complaining, he promises to explain to her some other time
why this marriage had to take place. In their wedding chamber, Brunhild
refuses to yield herself to her husband until he tells her the story. When he
refuses, she takes her girdle, binds him with it, and hangs him up on the
wall, where he is forced to remain all night. Siegfried's night has been one of

pure joy. When his brother-in-law tells him privately of his own mishap, Siegfried promises to subdue Brunhild for him that night by using his cloak of invisibility. At the feast that night Siegfried suddenly disappears. In Gunther's bedchamber he engages in a furious battle with Brunhild and nearly loses his life. But he finally subjugates her, and she, thinking her victor in the dark has been her husband, agrees to behave herself. Gunther takes his place and consummates his marriage. But Siegfried has slipped a ring from off her finger and has taken her girdle. Both of these he gives as presents to his own wife. For the rest of the feast Gunther is happy once more.

XI: Siegfried takes his bride home to Xanten, where they are joyfully met. After ten years Kriemhild bears him a son whom they name Gunther. The same year Brunhild bears a son whom his parents name Siegfried. Sieglind dies that year, and Kriemhild takes her place as mistress of the land.

XII: Brunhild, still rankling with suspicion of Siegfried's marriage, gives Gunther no peace until he send Gary as a messenger to urge his sister and Siegfried to visit them at Worms. The invitation is accepted, and Siegmund agrees to accompany his son too.

XIII: Siegfried, Kriemhild, and Siegmund arrive at Worms and are royally entertained. Brunhild resolves that Kriemhild shall explain to her why Siegfried, a vassal of Gunther, should live in such splendor and be treated as an equal.

XIV: Kriemhild boasts to Brunhild about her husband's prowess, and Brunhild rejoins with the taunt that he is only a vassal. Kriemhild counters with the retort that she will prove that Siegfried is Gunther's superior. She has her maidens dress her in her finest array, and goes to church. But Brunhild bids her, as a vassal's wife, to enter after Gunther's Queen. In fury, Kriemhild insults Brunhild with the accusation that she was subdued by Siegfried and that she yielded up her virginity not to Gunther but to Siegfried. With that she sweeps ahead into the church. After services, Brunhild demands that Kriemhild prove her charges. The latter then shows the ring and the girdle which Siegfried had taken from Brunhild. When Brunhild weepingly complains to Gunther, the King upbraids Siegfried. He is astonished at his wife's folly, explains that she is lying, and promises to punish her. Hagen now decides, however, that Siegfried must die for this insult to the Queen. Gunther objects, but some of the knights agree with Hagen. Weak Gunther is made to agree, but leaves the planning to Hagen.

XV: On Hagen's advice, it is pretended that Ludeger and Ludegast intend again to war against Gunther. Siegfried is ready once more to fight for Gunther. Kriemhild, having been beaten by Siegfried for her indiscretion, hopes that her dear lord will be safe. Hagen, craftily pretending that he wishes to shield Siegfried from danger, wins from Kriemhild the secret that there is one spot on Siegfried's body that is not immune from hurt. When he was bathing in the dragon's blood, a linden leaf fell on his shoulder, and in that spot he is vulnerable. Hagen bids her sew a tiny cross covering the spot on Siegfried's garment, so that he may know where to protect him. This new folly she commits. Then Hagen has Gunther announce that there is no danger of war after all. A hunting party is proposed, which Siegfried joyfully joins. Gernot and Giselher do not join the hunt, though they fail to warn Siegfried.

XVI: During the hunt, Siegfried proves the mightiest hunter of them all. By Hagen's direction there develops an absence of wine, and the hunters become thirsty. He challenges Siegfried to race him to the brook. Siegfried reaches the brook first and lays down his armor by its side. As he kneels to drink, Hagen thrusts him through the shoulder with a spear. In surprise and anguish, the dying Siegfried hurls his shield at Hagen, and curses his line. He bids Gunther take care of Kriemhild, and dies. He is carried back on his shield.

XVII: Kriemhild and Siegmund bitterly bewail Siegfried's death. She manages to prevail on Siegmund not to attempt to fight the Burgundians: his men are overwhelmingly outnumbered. She asks him to bide his time until revenge may be had. As Siegfried lies on his bier, his wounds bleed afresh as his murderer Hagen approaches, an incontestable proof of the latter's guilt.

XVIII: Gernot and Giselher persuade Kriemhild not to go back to Xanten with Siegmund. Her mother Uta also begs her to remain. She finally consents, and Siegmund departs without her.

XIX: Out of policy she at last pretends to make peace with her brother Gunther. She asks that he send an envoy to bring from Albric the Nibelung treasure which is now rightfully hers, so that she may distribute gifts to Siegfried's men. Gernot and Giselher bring the fabulous hoard back. But Hagen disapproves of her generosity in giving gifts, fearing that she will win too many to be loyal to her. In her brother's absence, Hagen seizes the treasure, and hides it in the Rhine. She cannot procure justice for this either against Hagen. For thirteen years she broods over her wrongs.

XX: King Etzel (Attila, the Hun), now a widower, desires to wed Kriemhild, of whose beauty he has heard much. He sends his kingly vassal Rudeger as emissary to Gunther's court. Gunther is only too willing that his sister marry Etzel, but Hagen warns that the marriage may mean danger for them—that it may give Kriemhild her chance for revenge. Her brothers refuse to listen to him and approve the match. At first Kriemhild objects. Besides, Etzel is a pagan. She is assured he will become a Christian again for her sake. It is only when Rudeger promises her that he will make amends for all past ills, that she sees a chance to avenge herself on her foes. So she consents, and departs with Rudeger in the company of Siegfried's trusted men.

XXI: They stop off at Rudeger's castle where the margrave's wife Gotelind entertains them royally. They arrive in Hungary.

XXII: The Huns are delighted with their new queen, and agree that she exceeds their last in beauty. Etzel holds revelry and tournament in her honor.

XXIII: After seven years as Etzel's queen, Kriemhild bears him a son, Ortlieb. But she still broods on revenge against her kinsmen. She tells Etzel she is lonely for her family, and he willingly sends an invitation to them to visit him through his minstrels Swemmenline and Werbel.

XXIV: Gunther is delighted to hear that his sister is happy. He takes counsel on the invitation brought by the minstrels. Hagen is against the visit, fearing that Kriemhild plans revenge against the old evil done her. The younger brothers are angry at Hagen for suggesting such a thing; they stingingly bid him remain at home if he is afraid to accompany them. Hagen, feeling honor is at stake, announces he will go, against his better judgment, as a protector of the crown, even though he has not been invited. Brunhild refuses to see the minstrels. Kriemhild, learning that Gunther, Hagen, and her two brothers are coming, is delighted.

XXV: Uta has a dream that causes her to bid her children stay at home. But the die is cast, and Hagen mocks at such fears. At the Danube, Hagen, wandering off by himself for a sign of a crossing, comes upon three mermaids who warn him that only the King's chaplain will come back to Burgundy alive. They also direct him to a ferryman upstream. This ferryman proves rancorous, and Hagen kills him and pilots the ferry himself back to where his company awaits him. To test the veracity of the mermaids, Hagen throws the priest overboard and tries to keep him under. But by good luck, the priest reaches shore again. Thus Hagen knows the prophecy will come true.

XXVI: The ruler of the country, Gelfrat, is angered at the murder of his ferryman. The knight Dankwart slays him during combat. Tired and hungry, the army comes upon Rudeger's land. He greets them and makes them comfortable.

XXVII: Rudeger extends every hospitality to his guests. Gernot seems smitten with Rudeger's beautiful daughter and a match is arranged. Gotelind gives a valued shield to Hagen as a present. Many gifts are distributed. A courier is sent ahead to announce the arrival of the Burgundians at Etzel's court.

XXVIII: On their arrival they are warned by Sir Dietrich to beware of Kriemhild. By Kriemhild's direction the Burgundians are dispersed over widely separated quarters. Kriemhild comes to welcome the chiefs. She kisses only Giselher and asks the rest what gifts they have brought that she should welcome them. Then she asks after the Nibelung treasure. Hagen answers that it is at the bottom of the Rhine. She asks them to give up their armor while they are her guests, but Hagen will not let them do so. Etzel is delighted to hear that Hagen is also his guest.

XXIX: The brave minstrel Folker and Hagen become inseparable companions-in-arms for the rest of their lives. They both deliberately insult Kriemhild on her appearance in the hall by refusing to rise before her. Hagen does not hesitate to admit before Kriemhild's men that he was Siegfried's slayer. Her Huns decide not to fight for her sake against such opponents. In the hall Etzel welcomes Gunther and his followers.

XXX: Hagen and Folker decide to keep watch at night so Gunther and the rest may safely sleep. A band of Huns, under Kriemhild's direction, approaches their lodgings, but seeing the two doughty knights, turns back.

XXXI: Taking no chances, Hagen has the Burgundians go to church next morning in full armor, much to Etzel's honest surprise. A tournament is held.

Kriemhild knows that if anyone is hurt, then the game will become earnest. Nothing disturbing happens, however, until a wealthy Hun enters the lists, and Sir Folker, to show them that Burgundians know no fear, kills him. The Huns are now ready to fight in anger, but Etzel will not permit it. Etzel admits it is annoying to have his guests in full armor at his feast, but warns his men that he will kill anyone who does injury to the Burgundians. Kriemhild tries to enlist the help of Sir Hildebrand against Hagen, but he is not interested. Sir Dietrich also urges her to forget vengeance. But she finally engages the help of Etzel's brother, Sir Bloedel, with the promise of wealth and a beautiful damsel. Little Ortlieb is brought to the banquet, but to Etzel's anger Hagen prophesies a brief life for the child.

XXXII: Bloedel and his men approach Dankwart in the hall where he feasts his yeomen, and challenges them to fight. Dankwart protests, then in self-defense kills Bloedel. A fight ensues, five hundred Huns are killed, and the rest escape. Two thousand more Huns arm themselves without informing Etzel, and march against Dankwart. Almost single-handed he keeps them off, slaying many of them.

XXXIII: Dankwart bursts into the feasting-hall to tell Hagen what has happened. Hagen, in anger, strikes off young Ortlieb's head with his sword. A general butchery begins in the hall. Folker and Hagen do terrible slaughter all around them. Dankwart prevents any others from coming to the Huns' aid by guarding the stairway. Dietrich, Hildebrand, Etzel, and Kriemhild are allowed safe passage out of the hall. The Burgundians slay all the Huns that remain.

XXXIV: They throw the corpses of the slain Huns out of the building.

XXXV: Only Iring of all the Huns seems willing now to go against the fierce Burgundians. After dealing much carnage in the hall, he escapes outside. He girds himself for battle again, and goes in once more only to be killed.

XXXVI: The battle continues until night. The brothers appeal to Kriemhild and Etzel for a chance to fight in the open, but are refused. She bids her men set the building on fire. Hagen counsels the men trapped inside to relieve themselves of thirst by drinking the blood of the newly dead. They do this and are refreshed. At dawn Kriemhild is enraged to find her brothers and Hagen still alive. Every kind of missile is thrown into the building. Many try to force entry into the hall but are kept back. The Huns continue to be slaughtered by the thousands.

XXXVII–XXXVIII: Rudeger is charged on his allegiance to Etzel to go into the hall and engage in the combat. He would rather die, having been the host and guide of the Burgundians—and having married his daughter to one of them—but he cannot evade his duty. Full of sorrow, he approaches the hall, and even gives his shield to Hagen. He explains to the Burgundians that he fights against his will. He enters the hall with his men. Gernot and Rudeger give each other a death-blow. Dietrich now feels obliged to ask Hagen for Rudeger's corpse. He sends Hildebrand who is refused, and Dietrich's men begin a struggle. Hildebrand kills Folker, and escapes to tell the news of the new slaughter to Dietrich. Dankwart has been slain by Helfrich, and Giselher by Wolfhart. Only Hagen and Gunther are left of the leaders.

XXXIX: Dietrich goes into the hall and with his own arms overcomes the weary Hagen and Gunther, one at a time, binds them, and hands them over as prisoners to Kriemhild, bidding her to be generous to them. She sends them to prison. She kills Gunther and bears his head to Hagen's cell. Hagen refuses to tell her where the Nibelung treasure may be found. With Siegfried's sword she kills him. Etzel is horrified at the deed. And the aged Hildebrand, revolted too, kills her with his sword.

IMPORTANCE

Perhaps the most peculiar elements in this redaction of the traditional story are the few mentions of the gold-hoard, which is retained as part of the plot without much of its motivating power, and the complete disappearance of Brunhild from the story as it approaches its conclusion. Lacking the mysticism of the Volsung epic and the urgent sense of the working of a superhuman law, the *Nibelungenlied* nevertheless remains highly dramatic in feeling by emphasizing conflicting loyalties such as that of Rudeger, caught between his liege lord Etzel and the Burgundians whom he had entertained and to one of whom he had married his daughter. Its chief dramatic quality, however, comes from the sense of the frailty of armed strength or the highest skills of chivalry against the smoldering hatred of a wronged woman.

THE FRENCH *CHANSONS DE GESTE*

IMPORTANCE

The *Chanson de Roland* or *Song of Roland* is the best of the French epics. Although not set down in its present form until the end of the twelfth century, it represents an epic tradition that had been continued by the Franks from the time of their early migration. For centuries, oral poetic narratives of heroic deeds had apparently been part of their national heritage. These songs differed from the northern epics in that they were more apt to deal with heroes than gods, and were more self-consciously national and historical than mystical, moral, or philosophical. Women play an even smaller part than in the *Nibelungenlied*, the favorite subject being the valorous exploits of mighty men. Whole cycles of such poetic narratives, well named *chansons de geste* ("songs about deeds"), revolved about heroes, their followers, and even their fathers and sons.

Whatever epics there were about the early traditions of the Franks appear to have been overshadowed by the hero-worship accorded Charlemagne, so that the Frankish king, Charles the Great, who ruled what is now France from 768 to 814, became the central figure of a series of legends ranging from the relatively reasonable to the most fantastic flights of imagination, as in the story of the *Pélérinage de Charlemagne*, which describes a riotous journey of Charles and his peers to Jerusalem and Constantinople. As in the case of the King Arthur legends, which the Charlemagne stories somewhat resemble, many versions of the same incident often exist, all of them usually far removed from actual historical happenings. To make matters more complicated, storytellers seem at times to have confused the rule of Charlemagne with that of his grandfather, Charles Martel, who as Mayor of the Palace was actual, if not nominal, king of France from 714 to 741.

Most of the Charlemagne legends hinge upon that noble warrior's championship of Christianity against the powerful attacks of the Saracens across the Pyrenees. After the death of Mohammed in 632, the Moslems had spread rapidly from Arabia through Asia Minor, Egypt, and North Africa. In 711 they entered Spain and began to cross the Pyrenees for murderous raids on the Franks, remaining a primary danger to Frankish security for nearly a century thereafter. In 732 they captured Bordeaux and spread so menacingly over southern France that drastic action to check their advance became immediately necessary. In October of that year, Charles Martel, aided strategically by King Eude of Aquitaine, overwhelmed the Saracens at Tours and checked their advance for all time. In 759, at the battle of Narbonne, Charles's son Pepin destroyed Islamic power in France completely. Thus, when Pepin's son, Charlemagne, came to the throne in 768 there were no longer any Moslem forces north of the Pyrenees, nor did Charlemagne ever fight Saracens on French soil, though he did campaign against them incidentally in Spain. The battle of Roncesvalles, where in 778 Charlemagne's rear guard under the legend-magnified Roland was wiped out to the last man, was fought not against the Mohammedans as the *Song of Roland* has it, but against Gascons as Christian as the great king himself. Incidentally, the poem presents Charlemagne as having attained the impressive age of 200 at the time of this battle; actually he was about 35.

The source of most of the Carolingian legends is therefore not unvarnished history. Rather it is a Latin chronicle, *De Vita et Gestis Caroli Magni*, formerly attributed to the Archbishop Turpin, a contemporary of Charlemagne. According to legend, Turpin died heroically in the battle of Roncesvalles; he really died of natural causes about the year 800. Actually the work has little to do with history and nothing to do with the Archbishop, but much to do with the great wealth of folk and literary epics of Charlemagne that appeared in great profusion from the eleventh century onward. The *Vita et Gestis* makes Charlemagne a white-bearded patriarch of supernatural powers, served by noble knights conceived in the best traditions of medieval chivalry. Outstanding among his followers are the twelve Peers, or Paladins, who, as noble companions of the king and dauntless champions of the right, greatly resemble the knights of Arthur's Round Table. The most famous of the Paladins is Charlemagne's nephew Roland (or Orlando, as he is called in Italian), who is the central figure of many medieval *chansons de geste* as well as the anonymous *Song of Roland* and the Italian versions, Pulci's *Morgante Maggiore*, Boiardo's *Orlando Inammorato*, and Ariosto's *Orlando Furioso*. Other well-known Paladins are Roland's cousin Rinaldo, Florismart (who is Roland's close friend), Ogier the Dane, Ganelon the Treacherous, Oliver the Wise, and the brave Archbishop Turpin.

The Song of Roland

The *Chanson de Roland* (c. 1100), oldest and best of the existing songs, is divided into *laisses* of decasyllabic lines, each *laisse* concluding with the lyric refrain *Aoi*. (A *laisse* is a stanza of indeterminate length in which the lines are held together by a single assonance or vowel-rhyme that does not necessitate identity in the consonants.) An unusually rapid, simple, and straightforward narrative, it concerns the heroism of Roland, the wisdom of Oliver, the piety of Turpin, the worthiness of Charlemagne, the treachery of Ganelon, and the final justice accorded him.

After having fought in Spain for seven years, Charlemagne has conquered the entire country except the city of Saragossa. King Marsilla at Saragossa ruefully admits to his council that he is no match for Charlemagne and accepts the advice to attempt to save the situation by trickery. Accordingly, envoys of peace are sent to Charlemagne, who bids them stay the night before he gives his decision. When Charlemagne asks the advice of his Peers, Roland opposes any peace that depends on trusting the word of King Marsilla. Ganelon, his stepfather, accuses him of being more desirous of glory than of peace. Duke Naimes suggests a compromise which entails sending a return emissary to King Marsilla. When Roland suggests Ganelon for the mission, Ganelon becomes violently incensed against his stepson and vows revenge. Nevertheless, Charlemagne entrusts Ganelon with the mission, and Ganelon accepts from the hand of Charlemagne the royal credentials but drops the sovereign's glove, a mishap which is regarded as a bad omen.

On his way to Saragossa, Ganelon talks with the Saracen emissaries who openly wonder that the two-hundred-year-old Charlemagne should be interested in further conquest. When Ganelon explains that Charlemagne is being spurred on by the vainglorious Roland, the Saracens suggest a plot whereby Roland will be ambushed and destroyed in the valley of Roncesvaux (Roncesvalles), a pass in the Pyrenees. Ganelon reaches Saragossa and delivers the terms of his mission, offering Charlemagne's proposal to divide Spain between Roland and the Saracen king. When he adds that Charlemagne pledges his complete destruction unless the offer is accepted, Marsilla becomes so enraged that he orders Ganelon's execution. But the Saracen emissaries interpose with a recital of the scheme for Roland's death which is eagerly seized upon by Marsilla, and Ganelon is sent safely home laden with gifts.

Upon his return, Ganelon tells Charlemagne that King Marsilla has capitulated and that a hundred thousand of his men have sailed to the East, refusing to live in a Christian country. Assured that the war is over, Charlemagne makes ready to return to France through the narrow passes of the Pyrenees. Warned by nightmare dreams of attack, he divides his army, entrusting the rear guard to Roland at Ganelon's suggestion. Roland is boastful of his ability and prowess, but Charlemagne sheds tears as his advance unit nears France because of an ominous dread concerning Roland's safety.

In conformity with the plan, the rear guard is attacked by the Saracens. Roland's friend Oliver thrice begs Roland to sound his horn Oliphant as a signal to Charlemagne. Foolhardy in his warrior's pride, Roland refuses. The Archbishop Turpin inspires the army with a promise of paradise, wherefore, in spite of the superior numbers of the enemy, the Saracens are put to flight but are succeeded by the appearance of another Saracen army. With only sixty of the French left alive, Roland blows Oliphant twice. Each time Charlemagne is dissuaded by Ganelon from turning back. The third time, too late, he turns back to give assistance. Meanwhile, Roland has killed twenty-four of the best Saracen warriors and has cut off the right hand of King Marsilla himself. The King and most of his followers flee, but numbers of the Moors remain to destroy the handful of remaining Frenchmen. Roland's small remaining forces are cut to pieces until only four are left; then only the mighty Archbishop Turpin and Roland remain alive, but by this time the Saracens have been completely routed. The wounded Roland brings the dead bodies of the Peers to the Archbishop Turpin for a final blessing. When Roland faints from his labors, Turpin tries to fetch water for him but falls and dies on his way to the stream. Roland recovers from his swoon and attempts to climb a hill in order to die facing Spain, his enemy. At the summit he encounters a Saracen who has been pretending to be dead to escape slaughter. When the Saracen seizes his sword Durendal, Roland crushes his skull with his horn. To prevent the sword from falling into enemy hands after his death, Roland attempts to break it but only splits the rocks, so that he lies down upon it and dies praying. Charlemagne arrives to find his body and returns to Spain to take vengeance upon the Saracens, aided by a miracle that prevents the sun from setting until the enemy is destroyed.

Meanwhile, the wounded Marsilla has returned to Saragossa where his wife bids him place his last remaining hope in the Emir who has just arrived in Spain. Charlemagne arranges for the burial of the dead and then sets out to destroy the Emir, engaging in a personal duel in which he is aided by angelic encouragement. Entering Saragossa in triumph, he discovers that

Marsilla has died of his wound and directs that his widow be sent to France to be converted to Christianity through the power of love. The remaining Saracens are all baptized and accept Charlemagne's rule.

Upon his return to France, Charlemagne must break the news to Oliver's sister Alda that her fiancé Roland is dead. Although he promises his own son in exchange, she dies of grief. Ganelon is subjected to trial by combat and is punished by being torn apart by horses. Charlemagne is left at the end bearing his overwhelming burden of grief which is intensified by a visit from the angel Gabriel enjoining him to continue his warfare against the pagans.

THE SPANISH SONGS OF THE CID

Both the Charlemagne and the Roland of Spain in the sense that he became the outstanding national hero and was similarly glorified by a cycle of extravagant legends, Rodrigo Diaz de Bivar actually lived during the eleventh century. By virtue of the historical fact that he was a great leader and a valiant warrior in a battle-torn era of civil war and conflicts between Christians and Moslems, he was known to the Arabs as the Cid (the lord) and won the idolatry of his fellow Castilians (Spanish Goths) in a single combat with a picked champion of the enemy, after which the added title of Campeador (champion) became part of his designation. Although born of a noble family of Bivar, employed by the king in high state affairs, and married to the granddaughter of Alphonso V, the Cid later aroused the king's enmity and became a freebooter on a heroic scale, collecting hordes of personal followers and fighting on any side of any quarrel which seemed opportune. His greatest exploit was the taking of Valencia in 1094. He died there in 1099, leaving his wife to hold the city successfully for three more years.

IMPORTANCE

This picaresque hero, given to cruelty, plunder, and self-aggrandizement, was exalted in the popular imagination to the status of a saint, devotedly invoked as "my Cid," prayed to and known to be a worker of miracles even after his death. Ballads, chronicles, and epics about him began to multiply along with legends of incredible exploits and impossible glories. The *Poem of the Cid*, a fragment in crude Alexandrine (six feet) assonanced lines, was composed in the second half of the twelfth century. Although this record of achievements is nearly as remote from historical accuracy as possible, it is a true epic in its simple, forceful representation of the age, the people, and the fervid devotion to the Cid which has made him the favorite and most often delineated character in all Spanish literature.

Ballads on the Cid

Fragmentary ballads describe the early part of the Cid's career, which begins by his killing of Don Gomez in revenge for an insult to his father. He is thereby named head of the family. Next, he defeats five Moorish kings who attack Castile and thereby earns the epithet of "Cid." Then, when Donna Ximena demands satisfaction for her father's death from King Ferrando of Castile and consents to waive her claims if Rodrigo will be her husband, she is married to the Cid and placed under the care of his mother until he has won sufficient fame to be worthy of her. In a dispute over the possession of Calahorra, King Ferrando chooses the Cid as his champion to fight in single combat to decide the issue. On his way to the lists, the Cid pauses to raise a leper from a bog, takes him to an inn, insists on sharing his own bed with him, and awakes to discover St. Lazarus beside him, who assures him of his future success. Needless to say, he triumphs in the succeeding duel.

High in the royal favor, the Cid arouses the jealousy of the other courtiers who plot with the Moors against him. When their treachery is revealed, the king banishes them, but the wife of one of them, Don Garcia, persuades the Cid to commend her lord to one of the conquered Moorish kings. Don Garcia is accordingly given the city of Cabra, proves untrustworthy, and is expelled by the Cid. In retaliation for a Moorish invasion, the Cid conquers the city of Coimbra and is made a knight with the added title of "Campeador" and awarded the rule of Coimbra and Zamorra. When the Pope sends an army to enforce King Ferrando's homage, the Cid ensures the independence of Spain by winning a total victory.

On the verge of death, Ferrando divides his realm among his children. The oldest, Don Sancho, attempts to reconquer the entire country, falls prisoner to one of his brothers, and regains his own and the brother's portion through the Cid's prowess. A third son, Alfonso, is also defeated by the aid of the Cid and seeks refuge in the Moslem city of Toledo. Don Sancho now attempts to enlist the Cid's help in the conquest of Zamorra which had been allotted to his sister. The Cid refuses. Don Sancho attempts to fight without assistance, is tricked into an ambush, and is killed. The Cid immediately takes vengeance and reluctantly makes Alfonso king in spite of the fact that Alfonso has made a solemn treaty with the Moors. Under the new king, the Cid wins three castles from the King of Navarre by single combat, rises from a sickbed to save Alfonso from a sudden reprisal, and becomes more famous than ever before. Jealous of his glory, Alfonso banishes him.

The Poem of the Cid

The extant *Poem of the Cid (El Cid)* begins at this point. The Cid determines to live henceforth by warring on the Moors. Joined by many devoted knights he sets out, raising six hundred marks from two Jews in Burgos by giving as security two heavy locked chests that are actually filled with sand. Leaving his wife and two daughters in the care of a prior, he proceeds against the Moors with three hundred followers and takes the city of Alcocer by an ingenious stratagem. He beats off a Moorish attempt to reclaim the city, sends gifts to Alfonso and his wife, and attracts many more Castilian knights to his side. When asked by Alfonso for assistance, the Cid agrees only at the price of the Monarch's reform of certain unjust laws. His terms are accepted, he conquers several more Moslem castles, and is welcomed back to Castile in triumph. After the death of the King of Toledo with whom Alfonso had made a compact, the Cid wins the city, makes it Christian, and becomes its governor.

Jealousy among the courtiers again alienates the Cid from Alfonso, but the Cid's prowess forces a truce and the King's assurance that he will never disturb him again. A plan by the Moslem Abeniaf to deliver Valencia into Moorish hands leads to the Cid's great nine-month siege of Valencia. When the city falls, the Cid generously attempts to allow the Moors to govern their own city, but is finally forced to end the constant conflicts between Moslems and Christians within the walls by expelling the Moors and taking personal charge of the city. Having vowed never to cut his beard until completely restored to the royal favor, the Cid is now as distinguished for his prodigious beard as for his wealth and prowess. He sends a sumptuous gift to Alfonso and asks to be permitted to bring his wife and daughters to Valencia. He also repays his loan to the Jews and asks their forgiveness for having deceived them with the chests of sand. In spite of further jealousies at the court, Alfonso grants his request, and the Cid is reunited with his family at Valencia.

Three months later, fifty thousand Moors who attempt to invade the city are repulsed by four thousand warriors of the Cid. From the booty won in this engagement the Cid sends rich gifts to King Alfonso, who replies by asking the hands of the Cid's daughters in marriages to the Infantes of Carrion. Agreeing to the royal request, the Cid goes forth to meet the Infantes and escorts them back to Valencia where the double wedding takes place. Shortly thereafter, a lion escapes from its cage and is captured single-handed by the Cid, but not before the cowardice of the Infantes has been revealed. Scorned by the people, the Infantes are granted their request to return home with their wives. When the Infantes have journeyed two days from Valencia, they take revenge by tearing the clothes off their wives and beating them cruelly.

Word of these monstrous deeds reaches King Alfonso, who summons the Cortes and bids the Infantes and the Cid to appear before it in judgment. The Cid is clearly in the right, and a duel between the Cid's champions and the Infantes results in public humiliation of the erstwhile bridegrooms. A second marriage of his daughters to the princes of Aragon and Navarre, together with honors showered upon him by far-distant monarchs, salvages the Cid's pride. Told by St. Peter that death is near, the Cid dies just as another Moorish army besieges Valencia. In obedience to his dying words, the Cid's followers place his body upon a horse and, by the mere sight of his heroic frame and stupendous beard, are enabled to ensure the safe conduct of the Christians through the Moslem ranks. For ten years after his death, the body of the Cid sat enthroned in a monastery performing miracles and striking awe into all beholders. His wife died four years later, leaving grandchildren to be kings of Aragon and Navarre.

REVIEW QUESTIONS

THE EARLY MIDDLE AGES

Multiple Choice

1. _____The period between the sixth and eighth century is notable for
   a. organized scholarship
   b. law
   c. stable governments
   d. lack of original creation

2. _____Boethius contributed to the knowledge of the Middle Ages by
   a. translating Aristotle
   b. writing commentaries about arithmetic
   c. writing commentaries about music and logic
   d. all of the above

3. _____Plato believed that truth lies in
   a. absolute ideals of truth and beauty
   b. cultural ideas of truth and beauty
   c. faith in a higher power
   d. knowledge of oneself

4. _____Origen believed that the meaning of scripture was
   a. corporeal
   b. psychic
   c. pneumatic
   d. all of the above

5. _____To prove his theological theories St. Augustine used
   a. pagan rituals
   b. numerology
   c. arguments against Aristotle
   d. the Pythagorean theorem

6. _____Augustine's *Confessions* were intended to be
   a. a guide for moral conduct
   b. a comfort and guide to salvation for mankind
   c. an objective analysis of Christianity
   d. all of the above

7. _____The French *Song of Roland* includes
   a. romantic tales about unrequited love
   b. strong female characters
   c. hero-worship of Charlemagne
   d. anecdotes about pagan gods

8. _____The Cid
   a. was admired by Castilians
   b. captured the city of Valencia
   c. was mythologized in Spanish ballads
   d. all of the above

9. _____The Scandinavian *Eddas*
   a. are accounts of historical events
   b. are accounts of mythological events
   c. include the Voluspa
   d. all of the above

10. _____The body of the Cid
    a. was burned by the Moors
    b. sat on a throne and performed miracles for ten years
    c. was enshrined in a French cathedral
    d. was buried in Chartres

True or False

11. _____The term "Dark Ages" is accurate and universally acceptable.

12. _____The Church was largely responsible for preserving the formal learning of the classical era.

13. _____During the early Middle Ages scholars compiled encyclopedias of pagan knowledge disguised as Christianity.

14. _____Members of monastic orders were the principle publishers of the Middle Ages.

15. _____Early patristic writings were attacks on other religions and defenses of Christianity.

16. _____Theological advancement during the early Middle Ages relied mostly on compiling new interpretations of what was originally intended as a literal story of the Hebrew patriarchs.

17. _____Augustine disapproved of the use of allegory as a literary device or pathway to truth.

18. _____The *Eddas* are poems of alliterative verse.

19. _____Attila the Hun is a character in *The Nibelungenlied.*

20. _____The French *Chansons de Geste* are mostly mythologized historical events.

Fill-in

21. The common division of Western European history is into three large periods called _____, _____, and _____.

22. Since the Church repudiated _____ knowledge, it was forced to rely on classical works for educational training.

23. Martianus Capella presented the Neoplatonic divisions of fields of knowledge in the form of an _____ in which seven fields are presents for a bride.

24. The essential idea of Plato's _____ is that the true order of knowing will begin with the beauties of earth and end with knowledge of the essence of beauty.

25. In trying to achieve Christian purity, Augustine struggled against his _____ nature.

26. Boethius' work _____ is notable for its harmonizing of the philosophies of the classics and Christianity.

27. A distinctive quality of the _____ is their emphasis on the heroic spirit of man contending with a fate-decreed doom.

28. The German version of the *Volsung Saga* is called _____.

29. Charlemagne is the hero of most French _____.

30. Odin, Honir, and Loki are characters in the _____.

Matching

31. _____ trivium   a. last pagan philosopher

32. _____ Augustine   b. *Symposium*

33. _____ Boethius   c. The ash tree that supports the universe

34. _____ skalds   d. Palace School

35. _____ Yggdrasil   e. *The Confessions*

36. _____ the Cid   f. "Sayings of the exalted one"

37. _____ Havamal   g. Platonic study of grammar, rhetoric, and dialectics

38. _____ Jerome   h. Scandinavian minstrels

39. _____ Alcuin   i. "You are a Ciceronian"

40. _____ Plato   j. Spanish Hero

Answers

1.	d	13. t	23.	allegory	32. e
2.	d	14. t	24.	*Symposium*	33. a
3.	a	15. t	25.	sensual	34. h
4.	d	16. t	26.	*Consolation*	35. c
5.	b	17. f		*of Philosophy*	36. j
6.	b	18. t	27.	*Eddas*	37. f
7.	c	19. t	28.	*The Nibelun-*	38. i
8.	d	20. t		*genlied*	39. d
9.	d	21. ancient,	29.	*Chansons*	40. b
10.	b	medieval,		*de Geste*	
11.	f	and modern	30.	*Volsung Saga*	
12.	t	22. pagan	31.	g	

Part 2

THE HEIGHT OF THE MIDDLE AGES

The mixture of cultural forces, which appeared in Europe after the collapse of the Roman Empire, eventually crystallized and solidified into relatively definite patterns by the beginning of the eleventh century. The barbarian invaders had become civilized mainly through the influence of the Church; shifting populations had settled down in a tight feudal system; and the remnants of Graeco-Latin culture had been thoroughly assimilated by Christianity.

The new kind of world was, at least in theory, an unusually regimented one. Veneration for authority, together with a love of rules and regulations, produced the complicated codes of chivalry and the elaborate classifications of feudal society. The great power of the Church had welded Europe into a single cultural pattern where national boundaries were not as important as class distinctions. The medieval knight, who swore fealty to God, his lord, and his lady, knew himself to be a different kind of being from the peasant, and felt a closer bond to any distant member of the nobility than to the peasant in his own neighborhood. The only real political units were relatively small areas under the control of a duke or baron; kings existed in the main only on the sufferance of these titled aristocrats. In this universal rather than international society nearly everyone was bound to a higher personal authority; yet codes of conduct were generally observed relating to everything from the order of the mass to the number of days of labor owed by the serf to his overlord.

Such was the ideal of the Middle Ages. In point of fact, a society made up of priests, half-literate professional warriors, idlers, impoverished and ignorant peasants, subject to plagues, addicted to superstition, made for an age of license and abuse in which the rigidly constructed framework often seemed to have little relationship to what it enclosed. Churchmen were often more politicians than religious men. Struggles for power, in which the Church had a part, made for incessant local wars. Knights neglected their duties. Ladies forgot their chastity. Monks ignored their vows. Even heresy flourished. Yet, in comparison with preceding centuries, the period must have seemed peaceful and stable, for there appeared a revival of spiritual and intellectual vitality that was evidenced in many ways. The Crusades (1071–1270), undertaken to free the Holy Land from the infidels, provided an outlet for the energies of the idle feudal barons but also held forth the inspirational promise of a direct pathway to heaven. The common man, meanwhile, found a way to express his devotion by the worship of Mary, mother of Jesus. As a mortal woman and a mother, Mary seemed less remote and more accessible than the now highly formalized Trinity of official Christianity, and it was felt that she would better understand human problems and act as an intercessor with her Son. The story of Our Lady's Tumbler *reproduces the spirit of this simple devotion as well as the common belief in the graciousness of Mary. Mariolatry also brought with it the theory, especially espoused in Italy, that earthly women, as sisters of Mary, were deserving of particular veneration (a part of the code of chivalry), and that earthly love was an imperfect mirror, in the Platonic sense, of the love of God. Thus Dante's love for the earthly Beatrice led him to a vision of "the love that moves the sun and other stars."*

The great European cathedrals were constructed during this period as monuments to the power of the Church and to the revived inspiration that resulted from this renewed personalization of Deity. It was largely devotion to Mary that accounted for the triumphs of architecture, the intricate carvings in statuary and decoration, and the rich color and design of the stained glass windows. The same urgency to express spiritual devotion, as well as a desire to return to the simple humble way of life of the original disciples, led to the establishment of the orders of friars or "brothers." The Franciscans, Dominicans, Carmelites, and Augustinians abjured worldliness to devote their lives to simple pastoral work and teaching, begging their bread and living in poverty. Others retired from the secular world to join the already established monastic orders like that of St. Benedict, whose strict rules and austerities of living became proverbial.

Resurgence of intellectual vitality within the limits of Christian dogma gave renewed vigor to the search for hidden meanings in the scriptures. Believing that every word in both the Old and the New Testament was directly inspired by God, Christian scholars continued to deduce figurative meanings from otherwise flat statements of fact or tradition. The resulting belief in hidden meanings and symbolic writings led to the widespread medieval love of allegory, where the hidden meaning was more important than the veneer of story which was presented in an entirely symbolic spirit. Allegory was more than a literary device. It was a way of thinking which paid tribute to the general understanding that all things were related to each other, and that physical and spiritual things were all part of a divine plan as systematically conceived as the feudal system, which was, in a sense, its earthly representation. The elaborately conceived orders of the angels were clearly related in spirit to the orders of knights and clergy.

Christian scholarship was simultaneously stimulated by the discovery of hitherto unknown works of Aristotle through the commentaries of the Moslem scholars Avicenna (980–1037) and Averroës (1126–1198). The tradition of relying on logic rather than entirely on faith and authority, which began with John Scotus Erigena (c. 810–875), culminated in the great movement known as scholasticism. Peter Abelard (1074–1142) in his famous treatise Yea and Nay made a brilliant attack on the appeal to authority by citing contradictions among Christian writers, and formulated the methodology of scholasticism by posing forty-eight questions which he held fundamental in Christian theology. Thereafter, his followers multiplied the questions, *following each question with logical arguments pro and con (citing previously held views by learned Churchmen) and terminating with the logical conclusion. The growing universities of the time based their courses heavily on Aristotle and aided in the production of the great scholastics Peter Lombard (c. 1100–1164), Albertus Magnus (1206–1280), and Thomas Aquinas (1225–1274). The* Summa Theologiae *of Aquinas is a monumental compendium of Christian tenets proved by Aristotelian logic. Although much of the voluminous work of these philosopher-theologians seems to the modern mind to be made up of intricate quibbles about trivialities, they enlarged and solidified the structure of Augustine's* City of God *and created a solid theology and a vast body of doctrine, besides inducing new respect for intellectual achievement.*

Aristotle was known as "the philosopher" throughout the Middle Ages; but the spirit of Plato, continued by Neoplatonism, was the energizing force behind prominent mystics like Hugh of St. Victor (c. 1097–1141), Bernard of Clairvaux (c. 1150), and Hildegard of Bingen (c. 1170), who held that all earthly things, macrocosm (the physical universe) and microcosm (man) were imperfect mirrors of the Essence of Godhead. The great Dominican Thomas Aquinas, the "angelic doctor," was rivalled by the Franciscan Bonaventura (1221–1274), the "seraphic doctor," who rejected the authority of Aristotle and propounded the doctrine that knowledge is obtainable only through illumination attained by prayer, meditation, and the exercise of the virtues. In the contemplation of God, Bonaventura taught, the mind rises by three steps or stages: by sense experience, through which the outward imperfect manifestations of the Divine Idea are known; by reason, which examines the inner soul which is an image of the Divine; and finally by pure intelligence, which through intense devoted love consummates unity with the Essence of Godhead. The Divine Ideas are evidenced in universals from which all individual variations are shaped, matter being pure potentiality subject to molding by ideas.

WORKS AT A GLANCE

Medieval French Poetry

c. 1300	*Aucassin and Nicolette*	c. 1200–1300*	*The Romance of the Rose*
c. 1300	*Our Lady's Tumbler*		

François Villon

1456	*Petit (Little) Testament*	1461	Grand Testament

Marie de France

c. 1180	*Lanval*	c. 1185	*Frene*

Dante Alighieri

1292–1294*	*La Vita Nuova (The New Life)*	c. 1312–1315*	*De Monarchia (On Monarchy)*
c. 1303–1304*	*De Vulgari Eloquentia (On Eloquence in the Vernacular)*	1321	*The Divine Comedy (La Divina Commedia)*
c. 1304–1307	*Il convivio (The Banquet)*		

*Date of composition

3
MEDIEVAL FRENCH LITERATURE

The most prolific source of medieval secular and non-Latin literature was twelfth century France, where professional minstrels and courtly troubadours composed and sang lyrics, fables, and narratives in Old French, the variation of Latin spoken by the common people.

NARRATIVES AND LYRICS

The Three "Matters"

Breathing the spirit of romance, adventure, chivalric love and chivalric honor, the many romances then current were divided into three groups or cycles: the "matter (subject matter) of France," the "matter of Britain," and the "matter of Rome." The "matter of France" centered about the knightly prowess of Charlemagne and the twelve peers of France, already mentioned in connection with the *Song of Roland.* The "matter of Britain" included the Arthurian legends and the interwoven Celtic romance of Tristan and Iseult. Of the known authors of these romances, Chrétien de Troyes was the most outstanding as well as the most prolific. Emphasizing romantic love (not connected with and often antithetical to marriage), he describes the noble spirit of his Launcelots and the inspiring beauty of the Guineveres who worshipped at the altar of love. The idealized legend of the quest for the Holy Grail, medieval symbol of ultimate purity and perfection, is given its basic form in his *Percéval* where the hero, simple and ignorant, learns knowledge of the world and sees the mysterious Grail at the castle of the Fisher King. The poem was left unfinished, but many other authors attempted to complete the story, making the Grail the cup in which Joseph of Arimathea caught the blood of Christ.

The matter of Rome was made up of stories that survived from the classical world. Virgil and Ovid were the two most prominent authentic sources of these legends, but the actual narrative material was based on a sixth century forgery known as *The Fall of Troy,* supposedly translated from the Greek of Dares the Phrygian, said to have been an eyewitness of the Trojan War. There also existed a similar though less popular history of the Trojan War supposedly composed by another eyewitness, "Dictys the Cretan." The most popular of medieval writers who used Dares as a source was the twelfth century Benoit de Sainte-Maure, who, true to his age, turned Greek warriors into knights, and the Trojan War into a tale of chivalry in which the love story of Troilus and Cressida became more interesting than the central conflict.

Aucassin and Nicolette

Apart from these broad and compendious cycles, there were also written many isolated romances, secular and religious. Of secular romances none is more exquisite than the delicate and hauntingly beautiful *Aucassin and Nicolette*. A *chante-fable*, written in prose interspersed with verse, this wandering narrative tells of the forbidden love of Aucassin for the almost mystically beautiful Nicolette, of their struggles to be united, which include a grotesque adventure, and of their final union. In fluid prose and fragile verse this little masterpiece conveys a sense of the beauty of youthful idealism and innocence that has hardly been equalled elsewhere in literature.

Our Lady's Tumbler

Of the religious romances, the story of the *Tombeur de Notre-Dame* (*Our Lady's Tumbler* or *Our Lady's Juggler*, as it has been variously translated) is an outstanding example of the medieval belief in the power of simple uneducated devotion. Much more unified than most medieval narratives, this simple story describes the professional acrobat who enters a monastery where his stupidity makes him an object of scorn. Out of whole-hearted devotion he performs his tumbling feats for the sole benefit of the Virgin, who rewards him by granting him a personal visitation.

Le Roman de la Rose

Fables and lyric poetry also flourished in great profusion (the Provençal lyric instituting a school of writing that culminated in the sonnets of the Renaissance), along with allegorical and didactic literature, whose best-known representative is the *Roman de la Rose* (*Romance of the Rose*). Begun early in the thirteenth century by Guillaume de Lorris, the allegory represents a lover in search of a rose (his lady) but hindered by allegorical figures representing various difficulties of courtship. Broken off at the end of some four thousand lines, the work was concluded toward the end of the century by Jean de Meun, who added approximately eighteen thousand lines which changed the entire tone of the poem and turned it into a satire and commentary on his age, being particularly vicious to women and the clergy. Although brilliant and effective at moments, this curiously inharmonious poem strikes the modern reader as being generally dull and long winded; yet few medieval works were as well known or as often imitated during the ensuing two centuries.

The Provençal Lyrics

Although lyric poetry was by no means unknown in northern France where the *langue d'oïl* was spoken, the flowering of the French lyric genius in the Middle Ages centered in the south, especially in Provence, where the *langue d'oc* was the medium for the love songs of the troubadours. In the highly formalized feudal society of Provence every castle had its troubadour, a composer of verse as distinguished from the *jongleur,* who was essentially a performer. Deriving much of its inspiration from the Moors of nearby Spain, a flourishing school of love poetry developed, closely regulated in form and highly conventional in theme. This was the poetry of courtly love in which the lover lies swooning at the feet of his ineffable, and rather vaguely described, mistress. The lover has been stricken by the eyes of his goddess; he trembles in her presence, suffers chills and fever, sleepless nights, indescribable anguish. He begs to be her slave. He weeps and blames her for her coldness. He will certainly die unless she takes pity and grants him mercy, "mercy" being a euphemism for complete fulfillment of his desires. The monotony of the subject and repetition of even the same figures of speech make the Provençal lyric more of a regional form of poetry than the work of a few gifted composers. Flourishing from around 1100 to 1300, it produced so many troubadours that the names of over four hundred are still known. A few distinguished themselves by unusual felicity in versification or by occasional freshness, sincerity, or originality of expression. Of these the best known are Guillaume de Poitiers, Guiraut de Borneil, Arnaut Daniel, and Bertran de Born. The traditional aspects of the Provençal lyric were too limiting to ensure its continued vitality, and its decline was hastened by the thirteenth century Albigensian Crusade, which destroyed the independent society and culture of southern France.

Eleanor of Aquitaine and the Courtly Tradition

Often referred to as the most powerful woman in twelfth century Europe, Eleanor of Aquitaine (1122–1204) exercised her influence in the literary as well as the political arena. After inheriting the Duchy of Aquitaine (a region of southern France) in 1137, she married in that same year the heir to the French throne, Louis VII, thus becoming queen of France at the age of fifteen. Eleanor's marriage to Louis lasted through the Second Crusade (1147–1149) but they were estranged by their return to France, and the marriage was annulled in 1152. Eleanor regained possession of Aquitaine and promptly married Henry II, with whom she had five sons and three daughters.

Near the end of the twelfth century, the court of Poitiers, to the south of Paris in Northern France, became a center for the poetry and song of the troubadours, and a model of the tradition of courtly love that this mainly oral form of literature represented. As patron of this poetic movement, which included the historical *Matter of Britain,* Eleanor had an undeniable influence on the literary world. Through her long and politically active life Eleanor continued her support for the arts and established herself as one of the most singularly important figures of the Middle Ages.

FRANÇOIS VILLON (1431–c. 1463)

The medieval lyric found its greatest genius in France after the great age of Romance and at a time when Italy was already witnessing the flowering of the Renaissance. François de Montcorbier, called François Villon, was born in 1431, and attended the University of Paris, where he mingled with nobility (including the future king of France), but where he also consorted with the lowest scoundrels in the city. His vagabond disposition apparently made him prefer the company of the latter to such a degree that he became a thief, was condemned to death at one time, and was pardoned only by the personal intercession of the king. He disappears from recorded history around the age of thirty, but he left an extraordinary collection (mainly *ballades* with a repeated refrain) of highly personal lyrics that describe his lusty satisfaction with his adventurous and sensual life, along with anguished prayers for the ultimate salvation of his sinful soul.

His principal poems were collected in two volumes known as the *Petit (Little) Testament* and the *Grand Testament*, modelled on a medieval fancy of bequeathing poetic legacies to friends and enemies. Remembered widely by virtue of their unforgettable refrains, his "Ballad of Dead Ladies" is known to all by its repeated "But where are the snows of yester-year?", his rueful "Ballad of Things Known and Unknown" by its pungent "I know all save myself alone," his glorification of "The Women of Paris" by "There's no good girl's lip out of Paris." His "Ballad of the Gibbet" owes its power to the circumstance of its having been composed in the shadow of death, as well as to the sharply focussed pictures of suspended bodies scorched by the sun, blown by wind, pecked at by birds, but washed clean by the rains from heaven. Anticipating much of the Byronic attitude, Villon was the inspired genius whose affinity for the diabolical must have tortured him in the moments of self-realization which occasionally broke up the mad course of his adventures into crime and sensuality.

MARIE DE FRANCE (LATE TWELFTH CENTURY)

Like King Arthur, Marie de France is from our distance an amalgam of historical fact, intriguing speculation, and unsubstantiated legend. What is known is that she wrote a number of lays, about love and adventure set in lands populated with fairies and filled with magic. Among the best of these are *Lanval* and *Frene,* dedicated to a "noble king," perhaps Henry II. She also wrote a collection of fables and, in French, a version of the Purgatory of St. Patrick. More speculative is the matter of her birth, which most medieval scholars place in France even though most of her life and work took place in England. Even more speculative is the possibility that she was a half-sister to Henry II, as the natural daughter of Geoffrey Plantagenet. To Marie de France we owe some of the earliest versions of the patient Griselda story, the Tristram and Iseult tale, Aesop's fables in English, and a few Arthurian stories.

4
MEDIEVAL ITALIAN LITERATURE

The beginning of Italian literature was almost coincident with the shaping of vulgar Latin into the Italian language. At the Sicilian court of Palermo, early in the thirteenth century, Frederick II, Holy Roman Emperor of Germany and King of Sicily, was surrounded by poets, players, and intellectuals from Italy and France. There the impress of learning and imagination made the Sicilian dialect, existing side by side with Latin, superior to all the other dialects spoken by the common people in Italy. The natural attraction to this court of the troubadours of Provence was intensified by a Papal crusade against the Albigensian heretics, so that many of the troubadours fled from Church-dominated areas to the safe and tolerant country of Frederick. They brought with them the stereotyped love poetry of France. In this conventionalized poetry the lady was pictured as coldly indifferent and the poet offered feudal homage while expressing the extremes of his anguished devotion. Some of the narrative, political, and satirical tradition of France was copied by Italian poets, notably by Sordello, but it was French love poetry that was easily the most admired model for the poets of the Sicilian School. These poets, Enzio, Pier delle Vigne, Inghilfredi, Guido and Odo delle Colonne, Jacopo d'Aquino, Rugieri Pugliese, Giacomo da Lentino, and Arrigo Testa, seem to have been perhaps too much awed by their French models or too conscious of their new language, because the artificiality of the French lyric became even more artificial in their hands.

Nevertheless, the short-lived glory of Frederick's court was an inspiration for technical perfection to the poets of central Italy where, in the latter half of the thirteenth century, a much more able Tuscan school of poetry was sired by Guido Guinicelli of Bologna (d. 1276). Guido was a philosopher, a scientist, and a professor, a man of high and varied education, at one time Mayor of Castelfranco. For a long time he was a disciple of Guido delle Colonne, head of the Sicilian school, in writing conventional love lyrics. Then he apparently came in contact with the very vigorous philosophical and poetical activity of Arabic Spain, where the creed of Platonism defined the true gentleman as a gentle man, regardless of his birth, whose innate virtue made him the lover not of the physical charms of his lady but of her spirituality. "Love and the gentle heart are one same thing" is the celebrated line of Guido, and it indicates the principal subject of his later poetry, which piles up figures from his own storehouse of natural and scientific knowledge. His poetry is sincere, often fresh and vivid, but its overall effect bespeaks the philosopher and scholar rather than the poet.

Following his lead, the other outstanding lyric poets of the time were further inspired by the contemporary religious piety of the Dominicans and Franciscans, best seen in the inspired devotional lyrics of Jacaponi da Todi. Worshipping the Virgin Mary, they combined the formalities of the Provençal lyric with the Platonic conception that the beauty of earthly woman, inaccessible like Mary, was an inspiration and a stepping stone to an understanding of Heavenly Beauty. By devotion to the inaccessible earthly woman, the lover's abasement before Mary is symbolized.

The curious phenomenon of poet-scholar, as in the case of Guido, reappeared in Brunetto Latini whose *Tesoro* (*Treasure*) and *Tesoretto* (*Little Treasure)* were versified encyclopedias. However dull they may appear to the modern eye, they must have satisfied a contemporary thirst for knowledge because three of his students at Bologna, Guido Cavalcanti, Cino da Pistoia, and Dante formed a circle of poets who revered him, and who drew the theme and manner of Guido Guinicelli through intricate allegorical labyrinths in which woman becomes the deified symbol of perfection. All learned men, they wrote to and for each other in cultivation of what Dante calls *il dolce stil nuovo* ("the sweet new style"). Cino wrote an ode to Dante at the time of Beatrice's death in which he notes that the name of Beatrice signifies Beatitude. Guido Cavalcanti, to whom Dante dedicated his *New Life,* became prominent socially, philosophically, and politically. He was a genuine poet, though, in contrast to Dante, cynical, pessimistic, skeptical, and essentially a poet of despair. He grieves that love, a dark ray from Mars, creates only tumult in the lover who aspires to the peace of the beloved lady.

DANTE ALIGHIERI (1265–1321)

Summing up the Middle Ages but also foreshadowing the Renaissance by his broad interests in humanity and human achievements and by his defense of Italian as a literary language, the author of *The Divine Comedy* is one of the five or six greatest writers of all time. Like other literary giants, Dante Alighieri possessed a many-sided nature. He was a man of thought and a man of feeling; he had studied the science of his time and as much as he had available of the classic learning of the past; he was early known as a master of scholastic theology and he was something of a practical politician; he combined intensity of poetic insight with a disciplined ability to project and complete so massive an architectural design as *The Divine Comedy.*

In a sense, there are two lives of Dante. One is the objective biography of the man against his physical historical background. The other is the inner life that is revealed by his writings. The two lives are, of course, closely interrelated, but partly because so little is known of names and dates and so much is revealed by his writings, it sometimes seems as if two men were involved: the married man who never refers to his wife in his writings and the poet in love with a Beatrice who may actually have figured very little in his public life. It will be in the interest of clarity, therefore, to summarize briefly the story of Dante the man and then to examine the career of Dante the poet and thinker as it is revealed in his works.

Life

Born in 1265 in the city of Florence, Dante, "a Florentine by birth," came into the world at a time when Italy was divided into a group of city states, which maintained a precarious balance of power among themselves but which were all zealous to expand at the expense of each other. The Roman Catholic Church, by virtue of its broadly dispersed power, had a finger and sometimes a thumb in all of the political moves, and was always alert to seize or control indirectly the affairs of any of the states. In an Italy made up of separate sovereign states, Florence had become a prominent commercial center with a thriving middle class and intense local pride, but the chaotic nature of the times prevented it from being for very long at a time a peaceful community.

Throughout all of Italy two factions, the Guelfs and the Ghibellines, had determined the lines of political conflicts since the middle of the twelfth century. The origin of the conflict dates back to the establishment of the Holy Roman Empire under Charlemagne. Some years after this empire fell apart, the imperial title was revived by Otto I, King of Germany, who was invited to Rome for the coronation in 962. The ensuing struggle for temporal power between Emperor and Pope makes up a large part of the confused political history of the Middle Ages. In Italy, the Guelfs, opposed to the authority of the German Holy Roman Emperor, preferred the independence of the Italian cities even though it meant reliance on the temporal power of the Pope who, in turn, depended on French support. Hence the Guelfs, though not noted for religious piety, were known as the party of the Church. The Ghibellines were equally as much opposed to papal domination and looked forward to the conquest and control of Italy by the Emperor.

These were the basic ideologies involved. In point of fact, the parties acted mainly along lines of local political expediency with little regard for principle. At the time of the Lombard League in 1167, each town and city belonged to one of the factions; then changing of sides began, and soon the quarrel became an internal argument in many of the cities. Thus Florence was predominantly Guelf. Dante's teacher Bruno Latini was a Guelf, but Dante's "first friend," Guido Cavalcanti, was a Ghibelline. Dante was born in a Guelf family but clearly adhered to the Ghibelline side in his political arguments.

A more momentarily vital quarrel arose shortly after Dante's birth among rival factions of Florentine Guelfs, the Blacks and the Whites. The Blacks, led by the Donati family, were essentially aristocratic and closely allied to the Pope. Under the leadership of the Cerchi family, the Whites were composed of the new rising mercantile class, relatively wealthy, lacking in ancient traditions, and independent in spirit. Again, Dante's friendships involved members of both parties although his opposition to the temporal claims of the Pope placed him mainly on the side of the Whites. But these political affiliations concern his later life.

Dante was born into a noble but not over-powerful Guelf family, enjoyed an aristocratic upbringing, and was early pledged to his future wife, Gemma Donati. He was obviously unusually well educated for his time, imbibing the fundamentals both of Dominican Aristotelian scholasticism and Franciscan Platonic mysticism. His first friendships were formed through his own enthusiasm for poetry and included a circle of versifiers made up of Guido Cavalcanti, Brunetto Latini, Lapo Gianni, and Cino da Pistoia. Through his connection with the Donati, he also became friendly with Forese Donati, the brother of the leader of the Blacks. The youthful Dante engaged in at least two military campaigns, mixed in politics, and in 1300 became briefly a member of the Council of Six which governed Florence.

In that momentous year, date of the otherworldly journey described in the *Divine Comedy*, Dante joined in an objection to claims on the city made by Pope Boniface VIII and, probably late in the next year, undertook a mission to Rome to effect an agreement with the Pope. During his absence, the Pope turned the city over to Charles of Valois, brother of the King of France, who set up a Black Government, which in 1302 condemned the absent Dante to exile and confiscated his property. Gemma, whom he had married in 1297, remained in Florence with their two sons and (probably) two daughters. Dante appears to have attempted a revolution together with others who were exiled with him, but succeeded only in being sentenced to death by fire if he should ever be apprehended. Upon this sentence, he set out on his life-long exile as "a party by himself." A wanderer and a man without a country, he found refuge in various of the courts of Italy. In 1310 his personal hopes as well as his dream of a restoration of the Roman Empire were revived by the attempted invasion of Henry VII of Luxembourg who had been made Emperor in 1309. From four letters still extant it is obvious that Dante did what he could to pave the way for the new champion. But the sudden death of Henry in 1313 ended his campaign. Dante appears to have turned to Can Grande della Scala in Verona, chief of the Ghibellines who was also Henry's Italian representative, as the only remaining powerful champion of Empire; Dante probably lived in Verona for a time. His last refuge was Ravenna where his final years until his death in 1321 appear to have been spent in honor, acclaim, and outward peace.

While the outward man was being thus buffeted about by circumstances, the supernal mystic-poet-scholar was slowly being formed within him. As a member of the group of youthful poets who were concerned with techniques of versification and the cultivation of the "sweet new style," Dante selected one Beatrice Portinari as his life-long symbol of the beatitude that is induced in the gentle heart by platonic adoration of a perfect woman. "To the gentle heart repaireth ever love," Guido Guinicelli had written. The earthly Beatrice was probably little aware of Dante's devotion. She married one Simone dei Bardi, and died in 1290. Dante may have been her ardent admirer, but it is fairly clear that his intensity of feeling was the rapture of the mystic in contemplation of absolute perfection, and that Dante's real Beatrice was an image self-created within him. He wrote a number of songs and sonnets in celebration of love and of his friendship with the other poets, Guido Cavalcanti, Cino da Pistoia, and Lapo Gianni. There are also poems celebrating an unknown Violetta and a Fisetta, implying that Dante's early adoration was apt to be devoted to beautiful women in general. But from his early poetic experimentation there crystallized his first extended work, probably written around the age of thirty.

La Vita Nuova

La Vita Nuova (The New Life) (1292–1294) is a kind of spiritual autobiography in prose, interspersed with songs *(canzoni)* and sonnets. Possibly inspired by Augustine's *Confessions* and by Horace's idea that a young man should have a mentor until the age of thirty-five, the title may be interpreted in the sense of "the young life" or in the sense of a renewed life made possible by the inspiration of Beatrice. Probably having both concepts in mind, Dante tells his own idealized story of the part played by Beatrice in raising him to a plane of noble love and in inspiring him in the composition of verses (whose technical forms he analyzes at the end of each poem). Combining prose and verse, inspiration and analysis, the very medievalism of this work is extraordinarily appealing in its revelation of the tenderness of the visionary poet in love with love, in love with mystic idealism and with the cultivation of a new Italian language and literature.

Telling the story of his love for Beatrice, Dante records from "the book of his memory" his first meeting, which occurred at the end of his and "almost" from the beginning of her ninth year. She was actually eight years old, but for Dante the number nine is significant, being a celestial number, number of the revolving heavenly spheres and of the orders of the angels. Overwhelmed by her angelic presence, he recognized her instantly as his "beatitude," a daughter of God, and knew himself to be mastered by noble love. Many times thereafter he sought her out until on a special occasion, precisely nine years after his first meeting and at the ninth hour, in company with two older ladies (the trio reminiscent of Trinity), she saluted him so ineffably that he experienced the height of beatitude. This rapture was followed by a mystic vision of Beatrice in the arms of the lord of love who forced her to eat Dante's heart and then bore her heavenward. The vision occurred in the first of the last nine hours of the night and inspired the composition of the sonnet, "To Every Captive Soul and Gentle Heart," repeating the vision in the form of verse.

Continuing the narrative in the same vein, Dante describes his devotion to another lady whom he used as a "screen" to shield his love of Beatrice from the public. When this lady left Florence, Dante selected a second "screen" to whom he became so devoted as to make himself the subject of scandalous rumor, wherefore Beatrice denied him her salutation. A ballad to Beatrice begs her forgiveness; other poems describe his despair and praise her perfect virtue. The death of her father was the occasion for two further sonnets of sympathy and produced in Dante an intolerable physical pain which resulted on the ninth day in his realization that she too would some day die. From this was induced a vision of her death, mingled with a vision of multitudes of angels. Shortly thereafter, he saw Beatrice coming toward him preceded by a lady named Giovanna and often called Primavera. He perceived that the name "Primavera" (Spring) signified that she would come first *(prima verra)* and that "Giovanna" (Joan) was derived from John, the forerunner of the True Light. This was his last sight of Beatrice who died in the ninth day of the month and, "according to the Syrian style," in the ninth month of the year, and in the Christian Era in that year wherein the perfect number (ten) was completed nine times in her century (1290). Dante's explanation of the relationship of Beatrice to the number nine is that the Trinity is the sole factor of miracles and that Beatrice was a nine, a miracle whose root was the Trinity alone.

After her death, Dante aroused the sympathy of a compassionate lady, who first gazed at him from a window, who tempted him to love, but from whose appeal he was saved by a vision of Beatrice. The *Vita Nuova* concludes with mention of a final wondrous vision that determined Dante to write no more of Beatrice until he should "write of her what hath never been written of any woman."

Il Convivio

After the death of Beatrice, Dante appears to have plunged deeply into the study of philosophy which, at that time, meant all branches of human and divine knowledge. As a result, the mystic poet of *La Vita Nuova* became a man of learning after the scholastic pattern, a man who intended to present an intellectual feast in his never-completed encyclopedic work entitled *Il Convivio (The Banquet)* (1304–1307). Explaining that his inconstancy to Beatrice as described in his earlier work might lead to misunderstanding, he here proposes to explain the allegorical meaning of his *canzoni* and parts of the *Vita Nuova*. Intending to write fifteen treatises, he planned the first as a general introduction and the others as elaborate line-by-line allegorical commentaries on fourteen of his *canzoni*, in which the interpretations would serve as springboards for disquisitions on theology, philosophy, and science. He actually completed only four of the proposed books. Apart from the explanation that the "lady of the window" is to be interpreted allegorically as Philosophy, denoting his turning to scholarship after the death of Beatrice, the chief interest in this work lies in Dante's eloquent defense of his use of the vernacular instead of Latin and in his fine-spun extraction of allegorical meanings from his own earlier poems. The first chapter of Book II explains the four meanings to be derived from a text: literal, allegorical, moral, and anagogical. The allegorical is any hidden meaning, the moral applies to human behavior, the anagogical is the spiritual or eternal sense applying to the universe. Because of an early editorial mistake, the *Convivio* is sometimes called the *Convito*.

De Vulgari Eloquentia

Dante's great interest in Italian as a literary medium, an interest which appeared in the first treatise of *Il Convivio*, half as apology and half as a defense, found its most complete expression in another unfinished work, *De Vulgari Eloquentia (On Eloquence in the Vernacular)* (1303–1304), written in Latin as was customary for all learned treatises. Probably composed either simultaneously or shortly after *Il Convivio*, this work illuminates two of Dante's major enthusiasms: his devotion to Italian and his interest in prosody. The first book reviews the many dialects of the vulgar tongue, finds none worthy to be chosen as a standard language, and proposes the creation from these vernaculars of an Italian language which shall be illustrious (exalted), cardinal (basic), courtly (worthy of use at court), and curial (balanced by reason). Book II begins as an elaborate analysis of metrics and forms of poetry but breaks off abruptly in the midst of an examination of stanza structure.

De Monarchia

Dante's other Latin work, the *De Monarchia (On Monarchy)* (1312–1315) is important for its clear statement of his political beliefs. Typically medieval in its arguments based on authority and allegory, it calls for a dual authority of one World Empire to rule over temporal affairs and one Universal Church to be concerned exclusively with spiritual matters. The first book demonstrates the divinely ordained rightness of monarchy, one emperor being the earthly counterpart of one God. The second book argues that the Roman Empire, descended from Aeneas and reaching its perfection in the Augustine Age, was intended by God to have universal jurisdiction over the world. In the third book the argument is concluded by the contention that both Church and State derive their powers directly from God and that each authority is independent of the other, only God himself being ruler of both spiritual and temporal things.

From the foregoing, it is clear that Dante's aim was not the establishment of a new social or political order but a return to the Divine Plan as it had existed in the days of Augustus when the Roman Empire had ensured universal peace and when Christ had descended to found His Church. Since that golden age, humanity had strayed from its predestined course, and Dante's faith first in Henry VII and then in Can Grande was faith in a savior who would rebuild the Divine Order from the chaos into which the world had fallen.

The Divine Comedy

The greatness of *The Divine Comedy (La Divina Commedia)* (1321) proceeds in part from the fact that Dante poured into this, his final work, all the sincerity and passion for the various causes and ideals to which his life had been devoted. Written in grim earnest, it is simultaneously the autobiography of Dante and the drama of humanity's search for perfection. Its original title was simply *The Comedy of Dante Alighieri*, using the term *Comedy* in its usual medieval sense of a work which begins in misery and ends in happiness. The adjective "Divine" was added to it in the sixteenth century possibly because of Dante's own internal reference to it as a "sacred" poem, or by way of expressing the universal admiration felt for this masterpiece.

IMPORTANCE

The widespread appeal of this medieval poem can be attributed in part to veneration for the wonderful intricacy of its vast design, in part to the compulsion of its imaginative power, somewhat to delight in the many brilliant passages that succeed each other throughout its course, and somewhat to the fact that the *Comedy* is so many things at once. It is an encyclopedia which includes nearly all the phases of the Middle Ages: political, social, cultural, scientific, and religious. Even in its theology, Dante is all-inclusive, basing his work on the scholasticism of the Dominican Aquinas, but arriving at his ultimate vision through the guidance of the Franciscan mystic, St. Bernard. It is a glorification of love, the love of Beatrice leading Dante to the vision of "the love that moves the sun and other stars." It is fiercely human in its revelation of Dante's intense hatred of evil and of his enemies. It is a great spiritual poem, certainly the greatest of all religious poems. Its length includes a multitude of dramatic incidents, scenes of horror and visions of bliss, interposed brief stories, and a succession of wonderfully varied poetic images and colorful phrases. His most telling effects are achieved in the highest dramatic moments by an abrupt precision of language which leaves it to the reader's imagination to fill out the extent of the implication. Famous passages of this sort include the inscription over the gates of Hell, "Abandon hope all ye who enter here"; the description of the human ineffectuals as "hateful to God and to the enemies of God"; the summation of the plight of the damned who "have not the hope to die"; the infinite disgust of Dante for a traitor implied in the line, "To be rude to him was courtesy."

The intellectual attraction of the *Comedy* lies in the challenge it poses to ferret out the multiple meanings of its elaborate allegory. In his letter to Can Grande which accompanied the first canto when it was sent to him, Dante explains that his poem is polysemous, of many senses. In its literal sense it concerns "the state of souls after death." More completely it describes in its three canticles the journey of Dante through Hell, Purgatory, and Heaven. In its moral allegory it is concerned with an understanding of sin (Hell), the process of moral redemption (Purgatory), and ultimate spiritual salvation (Heaven). As a political allegory it supplements the *De Monarchia* in predicting the establishment of world peace through an independent universal

Church and a universal Empire. In its anagogical sense, it presents a mystic vision of the Divine Plan, temporarily unrealized because of the sinful nature of man. According to St. Bernard, the pattern of Trinity was to be repeated in the three ages of humanity, Before Christ, Under Christ, and With Christ. Bonaventura spoke of these ages as the Days of Wrath, Grace, and Glory— terms that are almost precise epithets for the three canticles of the *Divine Comedy*. In Hell Dante learns the Power of the Father and meets the virtuous pagans who lived before Christ. In Purgatory, he learns the way to salvation through Christ and arrives at Purgatory's summit, the Earthly Paradise, where a pageant reveals the world as it should be under Christ if it were not still held back by the corruption he has seen punished in Hell. In Paradise, he is permitted to view the ultimate destiny of the redeemed. The entire purpose of the work, Dante declares, "is to remove those living in this life from the state of misery and lead them to the state of felicity." "In this life," such a desirable aim would be accomplished by rooting out corruption in State and Church, by the realization of a co-equal Empire and Church both subservient to God, by a rejuvenation of the moral nature of man, and by giving to mortal man a glimpse of the spiritual joy of submission to the will of God. In the same sense that Dante, inspired by Virgil (representing human reason and Roman Empire) and Beatrice (representing Divine Revelation and Church), is the hero of the Comedy, so the contemporary corrupt Church (figured as she-wolf, whore of Babylon, thief) is the principal villain, depraved by earthly greed and ignoring its ordained spiritual function. The *Inferno*, filled with images of ruin and examples of sin, is the present state of man and of Italy, where the imperfect nature of matter prevents the full achievement of the Divine Plan. The *Purgatorio* represents man's pathway to repentance, guided by reason, inspired by revelation, and culminating with the vision of earthly paradise. The *Paradiso* gives the revelation of the mystery of ultimate redemption and Divine Love.

The form and structure of the *Divine Comedy* depend on the use of number symbolism to shadow forth the ultimate abstraction of the Divine Plan. Conforming to traditional medieval usage, the number one, the point in geometry, is the expression of the unity and abstraction of Godhead. Like emanations from God, the decimals, ten and one hundred, reproduce this unity in a form more humanly comprehensible. The number two is indicative of the dual nature of all things, appearing in flesh and spirit, the active and contemplative lives, the *Old* and the *New Testament*, Church and State, and sanctified by the dual nature of Christ. When added to unity it produces the mystery of the Trinity as described in Dante's vision of Godhead in Paradise, three circles of which the third is "breathed" equally from the first and second. The number three therefore manifests the unity of God as expressed in three Persons and attributes. Power is the attribute of the Father; Wisdom, of the Son; Love, of the Holy Spirit. The three theological virtues, Faith, Hope, and Love, the three ladies who instigate Dante's journey, the many triads, Trinities and anti-Trinities of the *Divine Comedy* all testify to the archetypal nature of the

Three-in-One. The addition of the number four (number of earth with its four seasons, four directions, four cardinal virtues) creates the universal number, seven, as seen in the seven days of creation, seven ages of the world, seven virtues and seven vices. But three multiplied by itself produces the angelic and miraculous number nine, as witnessed by the three hierarchies of angels, each made up of three orders. Finally, the addition of one to nine, adding unity to a type of unity, produces another image of unity in the number ten.

The *Divine Comedy* is therefore divided into three canticles, the *Inferno*, the *Purgatorio*, and the *Paradiso*. The verse form is *terza rima*, in which each rhyme appears three times; thus, *aba bab cbc,* etc. The entire poem is made up of one hundred cantos, divided into 34 *(Inferno)*, 33 *(Purgatorio)*, and 33 *(Paradiso)*, numbers reminiscent of the life of Christ who died in His thirty-fourth year at the age of thirty-three. Like the ages of the world, Dante's journey is completed in seven days. In Hell there are nine circles to which the addition of the first category, the "Trimmers," makes a total of ten. In Purgatory the seven ledges correspond to the seven sins, two categories of sinners in the Ante-Purgatory raise the total to nine, and the addition of the earthly paradise at the summit completes the ten. In the *Paradiso*, the nine revolving heavens comprise the seven planets, the heaven of the fixed stars, and the primum mobile. The Empyrean, out of time and out of space, again brings the total to ten.

Keeping this general plan in mind, the following commentary will attempt to add to the reader's understanding of the intent of the individual cantos and their connection with the grand design.

Inferno:

CANTO I: In the middle of his life, at the age of thirty-five, Dante's story begins. The opening line, together with subsequent references, fixes the date of the beginning of Dante's actual journey at Good Friday, 1300. The trip through Hell follows Christ's descent to Hell on Good Friday evening and His rising on Easter Sunday morning. On the preceding Thursday evening, Dante refinds himself, comes to himself, in a dark forest, signifying worldliness and also suggesting politically the White or "Rustic" Party. On Good Friday morning, led by the sun (Godhead, the light of Wisdom), he essays to climb a mountain, symbolically Purgatory, but is prevented by the appearance of three beasts. The leopard and the lion represent Florence and France in the political allegory. The she-wolf, ensign of Rome, stands for the Roman Church or, more specifically, the corrupt papacy of Dante's time, and is therefore in a sense the villain of the Comedy.

In the moral allegory the beasts symbolize sins that prevent man from reaching salvation. One interpretation sees these beasts as representing the three divisions of Hell: Fraud, Violence, and Incontinence. From internal evidence it seems more likely that the she-wolf is understood by Dante to represent Avarice rather than Incontinence, since Dante inveighs repeatedly against the avarice of the Church, refers directly to Avarice as a she-wolf in *Purgatorio XX*, and makes a similar implication in *Inferno VII* in the circle of the Avaricious. The lion is likewise apparently symbolic of Pride rather than Violence, to judge by Dante's description of Sordello in *Purgatorio VI.* The leopard may then represent Luxury or Lust as many commentators believe, or it may stand for Envy in view of the accusation in *Inferno VI* that "Pride, Envy, and Avarice are the three sparks which have set the hearts of all on fire." In *Inferno XV,* the Florentines are also described as "avaricious, envious, and proud."

Dante's progress is somewhat checked by the leopard and the lion, but the she-wolf destroys his hope of continuing the ascent until Virgil (human Reason, the wisdom of antiquity, prophet of Empire, Dante's literary master and authority) appears to lead him by another road (through Hell), implying that knowledge of evil is necessary to Salvation. Virgil predicts that a Greyhound (possibly Can Grande, whose name is literally "Big Dog") will destroy the wolf.

CANTO II: It is evening. Dante inquires of Virgil the reason for the journey. Only Aeneas (Empire) and Paul (Church) had previously been permitted to descend to Hell while yet alive. Virgil explains that Mary (the originating Power) had commissioned Lucia (the light of Wisdom) to send Beatrice (Revelation of active Love, whose place in Heaven is beside Rachel, type of contemplative Love) to rescue Dante. Beatrice has appointed Virgil as Dante's guide; whereby it appears evident that Dante, prophet of independent Church and Empire, guided by Beatrice and Virgil, is divinely ordained to harmonize the achievements of Aeneas and Paul.

CANTO III: The Gate of Hell again reflects the Trinity of Power, Wisdom, and Love. Before the gate are those "who never were alive," the Trimmers who never took sides, who never exerted themselves for either good or evil, and who are so contemptible in Dante's eyes that he describes them as rejected alike by Hell and Heaven. Reaching the encircling river Acheron, Dante pays tribute to his master Virgil by paraphrasing the lines of the *Aeneid* in which Charon is described together with the souls longing to cross the river. Dante and Virgil cross, in spite of Charon's obstinacy, by the will of God.

CANTO IV: The first circle of Hell, Limbo, is the pagan paradise where the greatest of Greeks and Romans live in the afterworld in which they believed. To Limbo had also descended the Jewish patriarchs until Christ had taken them with Him to Heaven. Here Dante is made sixth of a company of poets including Homer, Virgil, Horace, Ovid, and Lucan. As sixth among the singers of the Empire, Dante probably conceives of himself as the representative of the sixth age of earthly perfection, the age in which God assumed human form and lived among men.

CANTO V: The first of the sins of Incontinence, Carnal Love, is punished in the second circle of Hell. Here Dante meets Paolo and Francesca, and listens to one of the world's greatest and briefest short stories, as Francesca, speaking for both, whirled about as they still are by the gusts of passion, tells of the treachery of her marriage to the deformed Giancotto and of her giving herself to his younger brother Paolo, to whom she had believed herself married when he had wooed her as his brother's proxy. Dante is very gentle with these lovers but assigns to the bottom of Hell the legal husband who surprised and murdered them.

CANTO VI: The third circle of Hell is reserved for the Gluttons, who exist amidst the smell of putrid earth and rain, hail, and snow, clawed at by Cerberus, the triple-headed dog of Hell. Representative of the group is Ciacco, who predicts that "the party of the woods," the Whites, will triumph until "the one who now keeps tacking," Boniface VIII, the contemporary pope, will prevail.

CANTO VII: Still another form of Incontinence, in the double guise of Avarice and Prodigality, is punished in the fourth circle where the practicers of the two Aristotelian extremes roll huge stones in semicircles until they meet, and then repeat the process in the opposite direction. To Dante's active mind, the ultimate in punishment lies in the eternal monotony of fruitless endeavor. Among the Avaricious are found popes, cardinals, and priests. The guardian of this circle, Plutus, is addressed by Virgil as a greedy wolf. Implicit is the connection of the corrupt Church with greed and with Satan. The defection of Satan is here described as an adultery, conveying at least a hint that the Church, described elsewhere as a harlot and a thief, has been corrupted by Satan in its flirtations with temporal powers.

CANTO VIII: Preceded by a description of a still unexplained signaling of lights across the marshy Styx, which flows through the fifth circle of the Wrathful, the narrative describes the dramatic encounter with the proud Filippo Argenti, a Florentine especially hated by Dante. Approaching the City of Dis where the graver sins of Malice and Bestiality are punished, as distinct from the preceding sins of Incontinence, Dante loses faith momentarily in Virgil or Reason. Entrance to this world below the level of reason is accomplished only by Divine Assistance in the form of an Angel.

CANTO IX: The furies and Medusa, Bad Conscience and Obstinacy, symbolize the impossibility of regeneration for the inhabitants of Dis and the fallen angels who hover above it. Against these reason cannot prevail. Heaven's Messenger clears the way for the poets but returns quickly to his more important functions. In the sixth circle, buried in flaming tombs, are the Heretics, guilty of unreason in the sense of their failure to perceive the True Faith.

CANTO X: Departing momentarily from allegory for the sake of dramatic realism, Dante describes among the heretics the Ghibbeline Farinata and the Guelf Cavalcante Cavalcanti, respectively father-in-law and father of Dante's friend Guido. Cavalcante's query concerning Dante's appearance without Guido beside him is an eloquent testimony to their friendship and also a decided hint that Dante, in his pursuit of "Philosophy," had dabbled with Guido in one or more of the esoteric varieties of diabolical science that Cavalcante thinks might have made Dante's visit to Hell possible.

CANTO XI: After a brief encounter with the heretical Pope Anastasius, Virgil describes the plan of Hell. Dividing sins into three categories, Incontinence,

Malice, and Bestiality, he explains that the sins of Incontinence, which are punished in the second, third, fourth, and fifth circles, are less offensive to God than those in the lower circles. Omitting to mention Limbo (unbelief) and the Circle of the Heretics (disbelief), he proceeds to expound the plan of the circles to come. The seventh circle of the Violent is divided into three subsections representing Violence to neighbor, to self, and to God. The eighth circle is made up of ten varieties of simple Fraud. The ninth circle is reserved for Treacherous Fraud. In this scheme, Violence is apparently considered the same as Bestiality, and Fraud the same as Malice.

CANTO XII: Symbol of unreasoning Brutishness, Bestiality, or Violence, the Minotaur rages while the poets make their way along the boiling river of blood in which are immersed the Tyrants, violent to their neighbors, who inhabit the first round of the seventh circle.

CANTO XIII: The Violent against themselves, the Suicides, metamorphosed into gnarled trees, appear in the second round of the seventh circle. Here Dante meets Pier delle Vigne, master of the Sicilian school of poets from which Dante's circle was derived, and Jacomo of Padua, who rushes past in the dramatic semblance of his roistering earthly life.

CANTO XIV: The third round of the seventh circle, containing the Violent against God (the Violent against nature and art being indirect revilers of Divinity), presents the unforgettable picture of a sandy desert rained on by slowly falling flakes of fire to torture the blasphemers, usurers, and sodomites. Here Virgil describes the Old Man of Crete, symbol of Rome, with head of gold (the golden age of Saturn), breast of silver, stomach of brass, and legs of iron. The cleft which forms the legs signifies the division of power between State and Church instituted by the coming of Christ, and the right foot (Church) on which he now mainly rests is described as being made of clay. The present disunity of the world is represented by a crack which appears in every part except the ideal golden head. From this fissure tears descend to form the rivers of Hell and create a kind of Noah's flood, referred to in *Purgatorio XX* as a Flood of Avarice, to indicate the grievous degeneration of the contemporary world.

CANTO XV: Still among the Violent against nature, Dante meets Brunetto Latini, the poet-scholar whom he had revered in his early life.

CANTO XVI: In the same circle, Dante's conversation with three more of his countrymen gives him occasion for continuing the rebuke of the Florentines which Latini had begun in the preceding canto. After this encounter, Dante takes a cord, with which he had hoped to catch the leopard, from about his waist, throws it into the abyss below, and thereby attracts the monstrous figure of Geryon, symbol of the Fraudulent. The symbolism involved in this episode is the most teasing mystery of the *Divine Comedy*. Its solution would provide an explanation of the cord and the ultimate significance of the leopard and Geryon.

CANTO XVII: Dante and Virgil on the back of Geryon descend to the eighth circle called Malebolge or "Evil Pouches," made of stone and divided into ten valleys representing variations of Simple Fraud.

CANTO XVIII: In the first valley, the Fraudulent in Love include Jason, perpetually scourged for his deception of Hypsipyle and Medea. In the second valley, dipped in human excrement, are the flatterers like Thais who, as harlot, is indirectly associated with Dante's conception of the contemporary Church.

CANTO XIX: One of the climaxes of the entire poem, this canto, which describes the third valley, is an attack on the Simoniacal Clergy, selling the Divine Office for money and thus representing Avarice, the she-wolf. Here, inverted in a flaming tomb, Pope Nicholas III is included in the anti-Trinity of the popes of Dante's time, the others being Boniface VIII and Clement V. Boniface is accused of the rape of the Church, and all three are described as committing fornication with the kings like the whore of *Revelations*. The donation of Constantine, giving temporal power to the Church, is blamed as the source of ecclesiastical greed for earthly dominion.

CANTO XX: In the fourth valley, soothsayers and similar peddlers of Diabolic and Fraudulent Knowledge are suitably punished by distortion of their bodies.

CANTO XXI: The fifth valley of Malebolge contains the Grafters, corresponding in political life to the religious fraudulent of Canto XIX. The fierceness of Dante's previous attack on the Simoniacal Clergy here gives way to a disgusting grotesquerie of black demons presiding over the sinners enmired in boiling pitch, reminiscent of the Blacks of Florence. Probably symbolizing his own expulsion from Florence on the false charge of barratry or grafting, Dante exhibits great fear as he and Virgil are assigned ten demons to escort them from the valley. One of them tells the poets that the sixth arch was broken by the coming of Christ, a reference that incidentally gives the date of Dante's journey.

CANTO XXII: A continuation of the preceding scene adds to the picture of the vicious treachery of the politically corrupt.

CANTO XXIII: The Hypocrites in the sixth chasm, painfully moving under monastic cloaks and hoods of lead, brilliantly gilded on the surface, present one of Dante's most striking pictures in which the punishment especially suits the crime. The solemnity of this scene, in which Dante and Virgil also proceed like friars, offers a striking contrast to the obscene nonsense of the preceding valley. In this chasm are jolly friars and the transfixed figure of Caiaphas, the high priest who refused to defend Christ.

CANTO XXIV: A very beautiful series of opening lines prefaces a brief pause for rest for both reader and the two travelers amidst these ruins and horrors. Then they plunge into the seventh valley where the Thieves, naked, are horribly tormented by fire and serpents. One Vanni Fucci, described as a beast, had robbed a sacristy. In *Purgatorio XXIII*, Beatrice describes the corrupt papacy as a thief. Dante's feeling is clearly violent towards major and minor robbers of the Holy Office.

CANTO XXV: Continuing the description of the metamorphoses of thieves and reptiles, the entire canto is a self-confessed *tour de force* in emulation of Ovid and Lucan.

CANTO XXVI: Beginning with bitter sarcasm at the expense of Florence for having produced as noblemen the five thieves of the preceding canto, the continuity of Dante's overall allegory is hinted at in Florence's aristocratic connections with Rome and the conception of the papacy as a thief in Dante's mind. Dante and Virgil reach the flame-lit eighth valley of the Fraudulent Counsellors. Here Ulysses, although punished as a false counsellor, becomes another symbol, like Virgil, of the quest for wisdom of the ancients as well as a premonition of the man of the Renaissance. Just as Virgil later guides Dante up Mount Purgatory, so Ulysses, symbol of the questing spirit, had come in sight of Purgatory. Then his ship had whirled around three times and sunk at the will of "Another." Dante, aspiring to ascend the mountain, had met three beasts but then was saved by "Another." Throughout the *Comedy* it is implied that the great minds among the ancients had lacked *only* Divine Revelation.

CANTO XXVII: A meeting in the same chasm with the Ghibbeline Guido de Montefeltro allows Dante to describe the tyrannies which have befallen his countrymen and to permit Guido, in turn, to describe his evil counsel to the "Prince of the new Pharisees, Pope Boniface VIII."

CANTO XXVIII: In the ninth valley, Mahomet and lesser Sowers of Schism are horribly, yet suitably, punished by having their entrails hang down from their bodies, which are split down the middle.

CANTO XXIX: The tenth and last valley of Malebolge contains the Falsifiers whose moral illness is punished by physical diseases endured in a malignant atmosphere. The alchemists are symbolic of the Falsifiers of Things.

CANTO XXX: Falsifiers in Deeds and in Words complete another anti-Trinity. Two Falsifiers in Deeds lie together: Potiphar's wife who falsely accused Joseph, prototype of the betrayer of Church; and Sinon who brought about the destruction of Troy, seed-bed of the Roman Empire.

CANTO XXXI: Approaching the ninth and smallest circle of Hell, the poets perceive three huge giants, each distinguished by the number five, number of the five senses, as if in premonition of an overgrown animalism without a trace of human morality or Divine Revelation. Nimrod of Babel shouts five unintelligible words, Ephialtes is five times surrounded by a chain, Antaeus rears up five ells from the cavern and lifts the travelers down to the bottom of the universe.

CANTO XXXII: The dark pit of the ninth circle is divided into four concentric rings. Caina, named after Cain, holds in ice those who were Traitors to Kindred. Antenora, named after Antenor, a betrayer of Troy, contains the Traitors to their Country.

CANTO XXXIII: Count Ugolino, encountered at the termination of the previous canto, tells his story of horrible suffering at the hands of Archbishop Ruggieri. The narrative is one of the sharpest, most intense and terse dramatic moments contained in the *Inferno.* Dante and Virgil proceed to Ptolomaea, the third ring, devoted to those who Betrayed their own Guests, and probably named after that Ptolemy who, as captain of Jericho, invited Simon and two of his sons into his castle where he slew them. Dante's hatred of such unspeakable treachery is manifested by his conception that the souls of such sinners often go immediately to Hell, leaving their living bodies to be tenanted by demons, and by his own rudeness which, he says, is courtesy to such as they.

CANTO XXXIV: The concluding canto of the *Inferno* is filled with suggestions of the exact opposition of the center of Hell to the perfection of Heaven. Greeted by a parody of a Christian hymn, the poets reach Judecca, named after Judas, Betrayer of Christ, where those who betrayed their masters are locked beneath the ice. A cold wind of Hate from the batlike wings of Satan contrasts to the soothing breeze of Love which comes from the wings of the Seraphim. Satan is also an anti-Trinity whose three faces are in opposition to the attributes of Trinity: the red face of Hate in front opposes the Love of the Holy Spirit; the right face, pale yellow, is Impotence in opposition to the Power of the Father; the left face, the Black of Ignorance, opposes the Wisdom of the Son. The Tortured Traitors hang from the mouths: Judas who betrayed from hate, Brutus who was ignorant, and Cassius who led Brutus to the betrayal of Caesar but who was impotent to act without him. Dante's conception of an earthly paradise calls for an independent but all-powerful Church and State. Two of the traitors betrayed Caesar; Judas betrayed the Founder of the Church. In the descriptions of Satan and Judas are implications that Dante also had in mind the three simoniacal popes of Canto XIX, especially Boniface VIII, who was indirectly responsible for Dante's exile. Satan is first described as a windmill, suggesting Dante's views on the vacillating policies of Boniface. The description of Judas plying his legs is precisely reminiscent of the posture assigned to the simoniacal popes of Canto XIX. Finally, when Dante looks back after climbing over Satan, he sees him, legs upward, in the same position. Proceeding by a tunnel through the earth, the poets move upward from the base of evil toward the mount of Purgatory, from darkness to light, rising like Christ on the morning of the third day, and emerging to see the "stars," the word which concludes each of the three canticles of the *Comedy*.

Purgatorio:

CANTO I: The mountain of Purgatory rises from an island at the antipodes of Jerusalem in the midst of the ocean which was believed to cover all the world except for the continents of Europe, Africa, and Asia. Whereas Hell was a place of eternal punishment for nonbelievers, Purgatory is a mountain above ground where Christians endure cheerfully their purgations in their ascent to Heaven. Dante and Virgil arrive on the first day of Spring, Easter Sunday morning, to meet Cato, guardian of the entire mountain below the Earthly Paradise. His face is illuminated by the four stars of the cardinal or earthly virtues, the virtues of human reason. Cato is the symbol of the free will granted by God, whereby man chooses between good and evil or between temporal and eternal good, the choice of temporal or earthly good being cleansed away in Purgatory. At the end of the canto, "as one who returns to a lost road," Dante is back at the starting point of his journey but no longer hindered by the three beasts.

CANTO II: An angelic boatman conveys a group of souls to the island chanting a hymn which Dante's letter to Can Grande explains as signifying the release of the blessed souls from earthly corruption to the freedom of eternal glory. One of the passengers is Dante's friend Casella, a musician who sings a song of Dante's composition in praise of wisdom. Just as the Power of the Father was most obvious in Hell, so Purgatory, established after the coming of Christ, is a monument to the Wisdom of the Son.

CANTOS III–V: At the foot of the mountain are the excommunicates whom Dante, here at variance with the usual Church doctrine (possibly because Can Grande was excommunicated), represents as being penalized only by having to wait thirty times the length of their earthly contumacy. Here is Manfred, a Ghibbeline chief, natural son of that Frederick II whom Dante held to be the last real Holy Roman Emperor. A second group in the Ante-Purgatory are the Late-Repentant who must wait the same length of time as their earthly delay. Concluding a series of terse short stories of individuals in these classes, the story of La Pia is told in four lines with a brevity and pathos reminiscent of the tale of Paolo and Francesca.

CANTO VI: Comparable to the violent outburst against the papacy in Canto XIX of the *Inferno*, this canto uses Sordello, an early Italian poet dear to Dante because of his denunciation of princes, as a vehicle for a bitter tirade against the current political state of Italy, described as a ship without a pilot, a brothel, a vicious beast with an empty saddle. The haughty Sordello, sitting apart, also represents a type of pride which Dante obviously admires, sinful though such admiration may be.

CANTOS VII–VIII: Still in the valley of Negligent Rulers whose presence here continues with less violence the theme of Canto VI, Dante sees the four stars of the Cardinal Virtues replaced by the three stars of the Theological Virtues, indicating that the true function of Purgatory is soon to be revealed. He also witnesses the strange appearance of the serpent Satan, who is routed by two angels clad in green. Green is the color of Hope, the dominant attribute of Purgatory, just as Love is to be predominant in Heaven. As in the image of the four stars of the active life and the three stars of the contemplative life, Action and Contemplation may be represented by the two angels, their blunted swords probably implying the lack of any need in Purgatory for the punitive power that created Hell.

CANTO IX: In contrast to the gloom of Hell, Dante travels only in daylight in Purgatory. On the first of the three nights spent on the mountain, he experiences the first of three allegorical dreams. Fancying himself being carried up to the sky just as Ganymede was snatched by an eagle to be the cupbearer of the gods, he experiences symbolically his spiritual ascent. Upon awakening, he is borne upward by Lucia, representing the Light of Wisdom or Illuminating Grace. Reaching the gate of Purgatory, Dante ascends three steps representing the history of man until the coming of Christ. The first of white marble is the state of innocence, corresponding to the golden head of the Old Man of Crete in *Inferno* XIV. The second, dark and cracked like the body of the Old Man, represents the fall into sin. The third, blood-red, clearly indicates the redemption of man through the blood of Christ. Whereas the symbolism of the Old Man was keyed to political history (Augustine's "City of Man"), the reference here is to the spiritual history of man *(The City of God)*. On the top step Dante falls prostrate before the guardian angel of Church Authority who holds the two keys given to Peter, the gold key of power to unlock Heaven and the silver key of discernment or judgment of sin. The angel places seven Ps, standing for *Peccata* or the seven sins, on Dante's forehead, and opens the gate.

CANTOS X–XII: When the gate closes behind the poets, they find themselves within Purgatory itself. In sharp contrast to the images of ruin and the gothic irregularity of Hell, the plan of Purgatory is orderly and symmetrical. As Virgil explains in *Purgatorio* XVII, Love is the basis of all human action, which is rightly directed toward God or, in moderation, toward temporal things. But Love may err through being directed toward evil or by excessive or defective exercise of its function. Purgatory is therefore built on a trinity of Perverted Love (Pride, Envy, Wrath), Defective Love (Sloth), and Excessive Love (Avarice, Gluttony, Lust, the three sins of the flesh). These seven deadly sins are purged on the seven successively rising ledges or terraces that encircle the mountain. The soul progresses upward from the Ledge of Pride, where all must suffer since all sins spring originally from Pride, and pauses for an appropriate period of purgation on whichever of the ledges cleansing is necessary, until the summit is reached. On each successive terrace are "checks" or deterrents from sin. These consist of representations of sinners chosen from religious and pagan history. "Goads" or "spurs" to virtue are represented by similar historical examples of the opposite virtue, these examples always beginning with an event in the life of the Virgin Mary. On each ledge one of the seven Ps is erased from Dante's forehead, and one of the beatitudes is chanted. On the first ledge of Pride, Mary, David, and Trajan are pictured as examples of humility. The sinners accept cheerfully, as everywhere in Purgatory, the self-imposed burdens that they carry on their backs. They are brilliantly described as grubs who will slowly change into angelic butterflies. Dante confesses his own great pride in his poetic achievements; converses, as in Hell, with several of the penitents; sees the sculptured figures of those historically notorious for pride (describing the sculptures in an architecturally constructed series of verses); hears the first beatitude, "Blessed are the poor in spirit"; and discovers that his ascent is easier because one of the Ps has been removed from his forehead. On each successive ledge this general pattern of admonition, description of the penitents, and incitement to good is repeated in varying forms.

CANTOS XIII–XIV: A stairway leads to the Ledge of Envy where the sinners sit in haircloth with their eyelids stitched together with iron wire. Dante confesses that his own sins of envy are far lighter than his sins of pride, and uses two of the spirits as spokesmen for a highly dramatic diatribe against the vices of Italy.

CANTOS XV–XVI: After the angel of Fraternal Love has removed the second P from Dante's forehead, the climb to the third ledge provides the opportunity for an inspiring discourse from the lips of Virgil on the unique quality of heavenly as opposed to earthly goods, the heavenly goods increasing by giving and sharing. The Ledge of the Wrathful reveals the penitents blinded by a dense rolling smoke. One of them, Marco Lombardo, becomes Dante's spokesman, explaining that free will is God's gift to man and that the world goes astray because man refuses to exercise this gift with discretion, deliberately choosing evil leadership and allowing the papacy to assume temporal rule in default of man's failure to accept an emperor.

CANTOS XVII–XVIII: The experiences of the third ledge are followed by the second night in Purgatory. Reaching a halfway point, the journey halts temporarily as it had done in the *Inferno* for an explanation of the plan of Purgatory. In this connection, Virgil explains the distinction between man and nature. Nature is inspired by Instinctive Love that seeks God as its source. Man knows instinctive love but is also given free will through the exercise of Rational or Elective Love, which may sin by being directed toward evil or by being immoderate in its following of the good. Since no creature can hate itself or God (according to Aquinas), direction toward evil may be Self-love at the expense of one's neighbor (Pride, Envy, Wrath), Defective Love (Sloth), or Excessive Love of Temporal Things (Avarice, Gluttony, Lust). The danger inherent in free will is balanced by God's other gift of reason, which makes it possible for man to make right decisions. Virgil breaks off his discourse by promising that Beatrice will answer further questions, and Dante is startled from a drowsiness befitting his approach to the Ledge of the Slothful by the onrush of a throng of now zealous penitents. Described as rapidly as their passing, they leave Dante in a daze from which he sinks into sleep and experiences his second dream.

CANTOS XIX–XX: Dante's dream of the Siren who tempted Ulysses is symbolic of the temptations of fleshly desires that are purged in the ensuing three ledges of Purgatory. Just as Virgil is to guide Dante to an understanding of these sins, so in the dream a lady (Reason) reveals to Dante the foul woman who was hidden beneath the Siren's beguiling appearance. At the approach of morning, the poets proceed to the fifth ledge where the Avaricious and the Prodigal, representing contrary extremes of Aristotle's golden mean, lie face downward in the dust, bound hand and foot. As might be expected, Dante's emphasis is on Avarice, the she-wolf. Here Adrian V, pope slightly longer than a month, explains that he had been wholly avaricious until, upon attaining the papacy, he perceived the emptiness of earthly glory, and repented. Seeing the world filled with a flood of Avarice, Dante has Hugh Capet describe his founding of a royal line of France, which was to harass Italy and culminate its viciousness in the seizure (in 1303) of Boniface VIII, who, much as he was hated personally by Dante, was still the Vicar of Christ. Accordingly, Dante sees Philip the Fair as a second Pilate repeating the crucifixion of Christ. At the conclusion of Canto XX an unexplained earthquake is followed by the chant, "Glory to God in the Highest."

CANTOS XXI–XXII: The earthquake of the preceding canto is explained by the encounter of Statius, the first century author of the *Thebaid*, a Latin epic poem that Dante much admired. The complete cleansing of the soul of Statius from the sin of Avarice caused the earthquake, as such cleansing always does in Purgatory when the conditioned will of any penitent becomes pure. According to Aquinas, the soul ascends whenever free will shakes off its predilection for sin and directs itself wholly toward God. Statius is made a Christian by Dante either through his own invention or by following a legend of the time. Statius ascribes his conversion to the well-known passage of Virgil's *Fourth Eclogue*, which was believed to have been an inspired prediction of the coming of Christ. Dante and Statius are therefore both disciples of Virgil. Statius, by addition of Christian faith to the reason of Virgil, becomes the symbol of Purgatory itself.

CANTOS XXIII–XXIV: On the sixth ledge of Purgatory, the Gluttons, introduced in the preceding canto, suffer from hunger and thirst. Dante meets his friend Forese Donati, who berates the licentiousness of Florentine women. Forese introduces Dante to Bonagiunta of Lucca, a predecessor of the "sweet new style" of Dante and his circle, who now perceives the difference between his own work and these new followers of Virgil. A gracious compliment to an unknown woman who befriended Dante in his exile is put into Bonagiunta's mouth in the form of a prophecy of Dante's future meeting of Gentucca. Forese adds a more sinister prophecy concerning the death of his brother Corso, leader of the Blacks, who is made chiefly to blame for the downfall of Florence.

CANTO XXV: The afternoon of the third day in Purgatory is the occasion for another philosophical discussion on the distinction between man and nature. Nature, which is the result of the operations of the angels, gives man a vegetative soul like the plants as well as an animal soul. These spirits are developed in plants and animals to the limit of their capabilities. Man is distinguished from nature in that he possesses also an intellectual soul given directly by God at birth.

CANTO XXVI–XXVII: The seventh ledge, containing the Lustful who are purged by fire, was reached at the conclusion of the preceding canto. Here Dante meets Guido Guinizelli, the poet of love who had been a major inspiration to Dante, and Arnaut Daniel, an earlier Provençal poet to whom Dante owed his command of metrics. After an indication that Dante himself must endure the torments of this ledge, Dante, Statius, and Virgil pass through the flames together as a prelude to evening and to Dante's third dream of Leah and Rachel, wives of Jacob, representing respectively the active and contemplative life. The vision of these lives is a symbolic preamble to Dante's entrance first to the Earthly and then to the Heavenly Paradise. He is also to see in the Earthly Paradise two women: Matilda who, gathering flowers like Leah, represents the perfection of earthly or active love; and Beatrice who descends from Heaven as symbol, in this section of the poem, of divine or contemplative love. Upon his awakening, he is told by Virgil that he is now a free agent, "crowned and mitred" over himself. Having symbolically passed through Purgatory, Dante knows his will to be directed only toward God.

CANTO XXVIII: Without a guide, containing within himself the dual authority of State and Church ("crowned and mitred"), Dante enters the Earthly Paradise on the top of Mount Purgatory at sunrise. Here is the Garden of Eden, below Heaven but above earthly sin. Passing through a fragrant forest, he reaches Lethe, the river of forgetfulness, where he sees on the other side the image of original purity in Matilda. Unlike all the other symbolic characters, Matilda has no known earthly counterpart, but Dante's graceful picture of her, singing as she gathers flowers, must have been inspired by some real Matilda of his personal acquaintance. Matilda explains that the breeze in the Earthly Paradise proceeds directly from the movement of the heavens and that water from a fountain springing from the Will of God flows into the two streams of Lethe (forgetfulness of sin) and Eunoe (memory of good deeds).

CANTOS XXIX–XXXI: The pageant that occurs in the Earthly Paradise is Dante's way of describing the history of Church Militant, or the Church on Earth. Led by seven flaming pennants representing the gifts of the Holy Spirit as named by Isaiah, the twenty-four elders, symbolizing the books of the *Old Testament,* indicate the spirit of God on earth during the time before Christ. The advent of Christianity is then figured by four beasts, the Evangelists, surrounding the car of the Church with its two wheels, Action and Contemplation, Dominican and Franciscan, drawn by the Griffin, a beast of two natures symbolic of Christ who was both human and divine. The three Theological Virtues dance beside the right wheel of Contemplation. The four Cardinal Virtues are at the left. Then follow representatives of the books of the *New Testament.* A thunderclap halts the procession, marking by a signal from Heaven the appearance of Beatrice whose essential hue is the red of love but who wears also the white and green of the other Theological Virtues. Symbol of the perfect Church, of divine grace, she is for Dante what Christ is for the world. When Dante turns to the left, the temporal side, to seek comfort in Virgil only to discover that he is gone (since he is not permitted to enter a Christian Eden), Beatrice stands on the left side of the car to rebuke him for his personal defection from her as described in *La Vita Nuova* and *Il Convivio.* Dante is saved from overwhelming remorse by being plunged into Lethe by Matilda, after which he sees the four Cardinal Virtues as handmaids of Beatrice. Led by these Earthly Virtues to Beatrice, he sees the reflection of Christ in her eyes and perceives the dance of the three Theological Virtues, thus repeating in miniature the story of his virtuous love for Beatrice and of his being led by her to Ultimate Beatitude.

CANTO XXXII: The personal sense of the allegory in the Earthly Paradise is followed by Dante's broader meaning when the pageant wheels about and proceeds toward the sun, or backward in time, until it reaches the Tree of Adam, or Original Innocence. Finding it bare of leaves, significant of the original sin which stripped it of its beauty, the Griffin joins the pole (the cross) of the car of the Church to the Tree which in its sudden blooming signifies the redemption through Christ. Its purple color means that this redemption occurred under the rule of Empire. A transition is marked by Dante's falling asleep. When he awakes, he sees Beatrice sitting on the root of the tree and guarding the car, possibly symbolic of the coming of the Holy Spirit (Love) after the resurrection of Christ, and certainly indicating Beatrice (Revelation) as the rightful guardian of the Church. Bidding Dante to transcribe for the benefit of the world what he is now to see, she presents in allegorical form the history of the defections of the Church. The swooping of an eagle betokens early persecution by the State. A fox leaping into the car signifies heresy. The return of the eagle to leave its feathers in the chariot is Dante's way of describing the damage done to the Church's spirituality by the well-meant Donation of Constantine. Next, a dragon wrenches part of the chariot away in a graphic portrayal of the Great Schism between Eastern and Western Churches. The part that remains, the Church of Rome, then becomes hidden by temporal plumes springing from Constantine's gift, and sprouts three two-horned heads (Pride, Envy, Wrath, affecting both self and neighbor) and four one-horned heads (Sloth, Avarice, Gluttony, Lust, which damage the sinner alone), which complete the seven deadly sins now nurtured by the corrupt Church. Last, a harlot, the Papacy, and a giant, France, ride on the chariot as lovers. For turning her covetous eyes on Dante, now possibly symbolic of Florence or Italy, the giant scourges the harlot, and then drags the chariot through a forest (worldliness), allegorically representing the removal of the papacy to Avignon.

CANTO XXXIII: Beatrice, in the red color of Love, attribute of the Holy Spirit (which the mystic Joachim of Flora had foretold would be the symbol of a third age of earthly perfection, following the ages of Adam and Christ), predicts the coming of an avenger of the giant and harlot, darkly named as a "five hundred, ten, and five." Of the many proposed solutions for this enigma, the translation into Roman numerals, DVX or *Dux* (leader) seems the most satisfactory, hinting at a Holy Roman Emperor or at such a chief as Can Grande della Scala who might be instrumental in restoring the Empire in Italy. Promising that henceforth she will speak no more in enigmas, Beatrice leads Dante and Statius at high noon through the stream of Eunoe, knowledge of good, and prepares them to mount to the stars.

Paradiso:

CANTO I: Although the Heavenly Paradise is actually the Empyrean, the abode of God, out of time and space, Dante adheres to his general scheme of steps or stages in the third canticle of the *Comedy* by representing different natures among the Blessed as tenanting for his instruction the nine revolving spheres of Heaven. These nine revolving Heavens of the seven planets, the Heaven of the fixed stars, and the *primum mobile* (which as "prime mover" transmits motion to the others) are governed by the nine orders of the angels. These represent the operations of Nature, and are reflected astrologically on earth by the diversified qualities assigned them.

Opening with a majestic statement of the Divine Glory, the first canto finds Dante with Beatrice at high noon overwhelmed by the absolute order and harmony of the celestial spheres. Throughout the *Paradiso*, Dante makes inspired use of patterns of light, motion, and sound to describe the splendor of Heaven.

CANTOS II–V: After a technical discussion concerning the shadows on the moon and a theological explanation of the workings of Divinity through the agencies of the stars, Dante meets in the first Heaven of the Moon, symbol of inconstancy, blessed spirits of nuns who were inconstant in their vows. One of them, Piccarda, resolves Dante's wonder at their happiness in the lowest of spheres by the simple response, "In His will is our peace." Denying Plato's fancy that souls inhabit the stars, Beatrice explains that all souls actually live in the Empyrean but that there are degrees among the Blessed in relationship to the absoluteness of their visions of Divinity. The nuns who broke their vows under pressure were perfect in intention but faulty in performance. The breaking of vows is regarded by Heaven in connection with the spirit of the vow rather than by the completeness of literal fulfillment.

CANTOS VI–VII: Having ascended in the preceding canto to Mercury, devoted to those who sought Earthly Fame, Dante meets Justinian, who made the great compilation of Roman law, and hears from him the history of Rome. Following this history of Empire is Beatrice's explanation of the redemption of man by Christ, reminding the reader again of the dual functions of State and Church.

CANTOS VIII–IX: The third Heaven of Venus, of Earthly Lovers, constrains Dante to describe Venus as his point of origin, referring probably to his earliest poetry of love or possibly to Venus as the star of his nativity. Among the inhabitants of this sphere is Charles Martel who comments on Dante's poem, "Ye who by understanding move the third heaven," and explains the power of the stars (the preordained operations of Nature) in giving diversified endowments to mortals that cannot be altered. This encounter leads to another attack on the ruin of the contemporary world where priests govern and military men rule the Church. The appearance of three others whose love was wrongly directed is concluded with an attack on Florence and another prophecy of the delivery of the Church from the papal adultery (described in the Earthly Paradise).

CANTOS X–XIV: The entrance into the fourth Heaven of the Sun is the occasion for a reminder that the physical sun is a sense-perceived reflection of God and that the order of the universe is a witness to the perfect creation by God of the objects of sense. The image of the Father, contemplating Himself in the Son, both persons breathing forth Love (the Holy Spirit) as the source of all creation, is a precursor to Dante's ultimate vision of Godhead in Canto XXXIII. Among the circling dance of sun-like flames, the souls of the Prudent, Thomas Aquinas, the greatest of the scholastics, introduces Dante to Albertus Magnus who had preceded him and been his master. Renewing one of Dante's favorite themes, Aquinas tells him that the Dominican and Franciscan orders were founded to support the Church but that both had become degenerate. After Aquinas has extolled St. Francis, a second circle made up of the Franciscans appears to relate through the voice of the great mystic, Bonaventura, the praise of St. Dominic. In this circle are the mystics who preferred the contemplative to the active life. After the two flaming circles have joined in singing the mystery of the Trinity and the dual nature of Christ, Aquinas explains earthly imperfection by alluding to the Platonic theory that the Divine Idea, begotten by the Source (the Father), the Light (the Son), and Love (the Holy Spirit) is reflected in the world of nature only insofar as the grossness of material substance is capable of receiving it. Dante is then reassured that the resurrected body at the Last Judgment will be a perfect body free of earthly defects and capable of enjoying the highest delight. Just before leaving the Heaven of the Sun, Dante perceives the first of four great symbolic spectacles, as the two circles of lights, Dominican and Franciscan, or Action and Contemplation, emanate a third circle in imitation of the breathing forth of Love by the Father and Son. This image is succeeded immediately by a second spectacle of star-rays forming a cross, whereby Dante comes to know that he has risen into the Heaven of Mars.

CANTOS XV–XVII: The fifth Heaven of Mars contains the Courageous or those who fought for the Faith. Dante meets his ancestor Cacciaguida, who recalls the peaceful and virtuous days of Florence in the past. After rehearsing the names of the great families of that time, Cacciaguida predicts the forthcoming exile of Dante, in one of the few highly personal sections of the entire poem.

CANTOS XVIII–XX: In the sixth Heaven of Jupiter, Justice is imaged in a third spectacular figure in which the heavenly lights form the opening words of the *Book of Wisdom*, "Love righteousness, ye that be judges of the earth"; they then remain fixed in the last letter, *M*, initial of Monarchy, which signifies earthly justice to Dante, and are finally transformed into the eagle of Empire. The vision of perfect justice inevitably causes Dante to cry out again against the contemporary corruption of spiritual and temporal rulers. Dante's question concerning the exclusion of virtuous pagans from salvation is partly answered in the Heaven of Justice by the appearance there of Trajan and the Trojan Ripheus, who were predestined to be saved since they followed Christ in spirit without knowing Him.

CANTOS XXI–XXII: Following the images of Trinity, Cross, and Eagle, the seventh Heaven of Saturn is marked by the Ladder of Contemplation. Meeting here such spirits as Peter Damiani and Benedict, who were notable for their insistence on rigorous monastic discipline, Dante is given hope of reformation of the evils of his time. Rising above Saturn, he gazes through the spheres of the seven planets, and smiles at the sorry spectacle of earth, secure in his new-won awareness of the pettiness of earthly things. Then he returns his gaze to the eyes of Beatrice.

CANTOS XXIII–XXVII: The eighth Heaven of the Fixed Stars, which wheel in a mass beyond the orbits of the planets, contains the souls of the Elect and is especially connected with the glory of Christ and His Church. Here Dante sees the Sun that is Christ, the Virgin Mary, the Apostles, and the multitudes of the Redeemed. Then is reenacted the Annunciation by Gabriel, the Ascension of Christ, and the Assumption of Mary. Three apostles catechize Dante: Peter on Faith, James on Hope, and John on Love. Adam then joins the group to answer Dante's unspoken questions concerning the origins of life on earth, after which Peter, founder of the papacy, denounces the popes and clergy of Dante's time. The ascent to the ninth Heaven is accompanied by another outburst against the degeneracy of earth together with a prophecy of a reformation soon to come.

CANTOS XXVIII–XXIX: The *Primum Mobile* or "Prime Mover" imparts motion to the lower Heavens, the speed of revolution diminishing in proportion to the distance from the ninth Heaven, or remoteness from that unity that is God. Here are visioned the Angelic Choirs, who are assigned to the various Heavens from the first through the ninth in the order of Angels, Archangels, Principalities, Powers, Virtues, Dominations, Thrones, Cherubim, and Seraphim. The highest order of Seraphim have the function of Love and are therefore particularly connected with the motion of the spheres caused by the ninth Heaven. Beatrice explains how the entire universe came into existence as a reflection of the Eternal Love of God which manifests itself in three ways: pure spirituality (the angels), matter (physical substance), and the combination of spirit and matter (man).

CANTOS XXX–XXXIII: Attaining the tenth Heaven, the Empyrean, out of time and space, the abode of God and the Blessed, Dante makes his last temporal allusion, referring to the uncompleted victory of Henry VII and the damnation of Popes Clement and Boniface. The Redeemed appear to him sitting rank on rank in the form of a vibrant rose of the white color of Faith, joined to Godhead by swarming angels of gold and living flame. Turning to question Beatrice, Dante finds the contemplative St. Bernard beside him, who points out Beatrice sitting beside Rachel in the third rank of the Rose. Directing Dante's eager gaze, Bernard indicates many of those who make up the Celestial Rose. On one side of the topmost row of petals is Mary with Peter and John on her right and Adam and Moses on her left. Beneath her, row by row, are other sainted women from Old Testament history: in order, Eve, Rachel (with Beatrice on her right), Sarah, Rebecca, Judith, and Ruth. Directly opposite Mary is John the Baptist, who filled a corresponding role in being the spiritual precursor of Christ. St. Anna and St. Lucia are at his right and left respectively. In opposition to the women before Christ who sit directly below Mary is a line of Christian men below John, of whom St. Francis, St. Benedict, and St. Augustine are named in order of their positions below John. The petals between the right side of the men and the left side of the women are made up of pre-Christian Hebrews. The opposite side, with many places still empty, is composed of Christian souls. The lower part of the entire Rose holds the souls of children who died in innocence and were saved by the faith of their parents. Dante has been prepared by degrees for his final vision of Godhead. After the vision of the order and glory of the

Rose, his eyes seek out Mary whose glory he can tolerate by having gazed so long into the eyes of Beatrice. Now he sees the flaming love for Mary of the angel Gabriel, who was intermediary between God and Mary, and is thus prepared for his ultimate vision, which he describes in such halting symbols as language is capable of conveying. He sees God as three circles of equal size and of three colors (doubtless the white, green, and red of the Theological Virtues—Faith, Hope, and Love). One of the circles (the Son—Wisdom) is reflected by another (the Father—Power), and the third (the Holy Spirit—Love) is breathed forth equally by the other two. The mystery of the eternity of matter or flesh as well as spirit is suggested by the mystic appearance of the human form as a part of the trinal circles. Able to perceive, but unable to comprehend this essential unity of spirit and matter, Dante speeds to the magnificent conclusion of the *Divine Comedy,* knowing his desire and will fulfilled as perfectly as the ordered revolution of the trinal circles by "the Love that moves the sun and other stars."

REVIEW QUESTIONS

THE HEIGHT OF THE MIDDLE AGES

Multiple Choice

1. _____The major civilizing force upon the barbarian invaders was
   a. agriculture
   b. the printing press
   c. the Church
   d. Aristotle

2. _____In the social structure of the feudal society
   a. women were equal to men
   b. each person was bound to a higher authority
   c. national identity was the primary unifying factor between people
   d. there was no standardized form of conduct

3. Allegory
   a. was a way of thinking in the Middle Ages
   b. is a literary device
   c. uses symbolic meanings
   d. all of the above

4. _____Chrétien de Troyes wrote
   a. the "matter of Britain"
   b. about romantic love
   c. *Percéval*
   d. all of the above

5. _____Italian lyric poets believed that love of an inaccessible earthly woman
   a. honored the Virgin Mary
   b. expressed the innate gentleness of the poet's heart
   c. reflects divine perfection
   d. all of the above

6. _____The Platonic adoration of a woman was considered
   a. frustrating for a poet to express
   b. an expression of a poet's sensitivity
   c. crude and unpoetical
   d. degrading to women

7. In the Middle Ages a comedy was best defined as
   a. any work that was not a tragedy
   b. a humorous work
   c. a work that begins in misery and ends in happiness
   d. a short farcical play

8. _____In Dante's *Purgatorio,* purgatory is where
   a. Christians are cleansed of their sins
   b. sinners suffer for never choosing between good or evil
   c. nonbelievers suffer eternal punishment
   d. those reside who lack free will

9. _____The tale of Paolo and Francesca in the *Inferno* is about
   a. the punishments for gluttons
   b. carnal love
   c. bad conscience
   d. limbo

10. _____Dante portrays the papacy as a
    a. mountain
    b. jackal
    c. thief
    d. glutton

True or False

11. _____National boundaries were more important than class distinctions in the height of the Middle Ages.

12. _____Scholars from the Middle Ages felt that symbolic meanings in a text were less important than literal meanings.

13. _____*Le Tombeur de Notre-Dame* is an example of the medieval belief in the power of simple, uneducated devotion.

14. _____Italian lyrical poems are more artificial than their French contemporaries.

15. _____French poets were still producing medieval lyric poems while the Renaissance was beginning in Italy.

16. _____Platonic philosophy states that only a man born of noble lineage can be a gentleman.

17. _____*The Divine Comedy* is an autobiographical work by Dante.

18. _____*The Divine Comedy* is about man's search for perfection.

19. _____In *The Divine Comedy* Dante satirized the use of number symbolism.

20. _____In Dante's *Paradiso,* heaven has seven revolving spheres.

Fill-in

21. Many of the artistic accomplishments of the Middle Ages were due to people who gave devotion to _____.

22. Renewed interest in _____ was inspired by references to his unknown works in texts by Moslem scholars Avicenna and Averroes.

23. Scholars like Hildegard of Bingen who believed that the world imperfectly mirrored the Essence of Godhead was inspired by _____.

24. Dante Alighieri brought about acceptance of _____ as a literary language in works like *De Vulgari Eloquentia*.

25. Politics, morality, and numerology are three of the many levels of _____ in *The Divine Comedy* by Dante.

26. "Where are the snows of yesteryear?" is a passage from _____'s poem *Ballad of Dead Ladies*.

27. In Dante's *Purgatorio* the seven ledges represent the seven _____.

28. In *The Divine Comedy* human reason and the wisdom of the ancients are represented by _____.

29. In *The Divine Comedy* the revelation of active love is represented by _____.

30. In Dante's *Paradiso*, God lives in the _____.

Matching

31. _____ Scholasticism
32. _____ Allegory
33. _____ Matter of Britain
34. _____ Provençal lyrics
35. _____ François Villon

36. _____ Dante

37. _____ Beatrice
38. _____ Frederick II
39. _____ a secular romance
40. _____ Empyrean

a. Arthurian legends
b. object of Dante's Platonic love
c. *Aucassin and Nicolette*
d. logic before faith
e. King of Sicily whose court popularized the Sicilian dialect
f. system of belief in the interrelation of surface and deep meaning
g. precursor to Renaissance sonnets
h. the tenth heaven
i. French medieval poet
j. *The Divine Comedy*

Answers

1. c	15. t	28. Virgil
2. b	16. f	29. Beatrice
3. d	17. t	30. tenth heaven
4. d	18. t	or Empyrean
5. d	19. f	31. d
6. b	20. f	32. f
7. c	21. Mary, mother	33. a
8. a	of Jesus	34. g
9. b	22. Aristotle	35. i
10. c	23. Plato	36. j
11. f	24. Italian	37. b
12. f	25. allegory	38. e
13. t	26. François Villon	39. c
14. t	27. sins	40. h

Part 3

THE RENAISSANCE

The vitality that was expressed in the spiritual and intellectual revivals of the height of the Middle Ages gradually shifted its emphasis from spiritual to earthly things to create that period in history known as the Renaissance. Although called a "rebirth," this beginning of modern as opposed to medieval attitudes was distinctive mainly in a growing secularism—a frank appreciation of what Augustine condemned as "the city of man." It was not as strikingly original as is popularly believed, nor did it break completely from the medieval dependence on authority in blazing new trails. Rather, it substituted the authority of the classics for the authority of the Church, and, thus stimulated, produced a new composite culture that was part Christian and part pagan, part traditional and part original. The cultural vitality of the Renaissance began in Italy in the thirteenth century, continued through the early fifteenth century, and produced the masterpieces that inspired the cultural revivals of France, Spain, Portugal, and England in the sixteenth century. The most obvious manifestations of the new spirit are readily discernible in the declining prestige of the Church, the disintegration of the feudal system, the rise of patriotic nationalism, the revival of interest in the classics, the greater diffusion of knowledge, and the urge for exploration.

Although all of these gradual changes made for a new period in history, the most definite clue to the new direction of men's minds is to be found in the failure of the autocracy of the Church. Ample doubt concerning its fitness as a temporal or even spiritual guide is expressed in Dante's Divine Comedy, *which is sometimes held to be the first literary monument of this new period. The venality of the clergy in general and the increasing worldliness of the Dominican and Franciscan orders, which were founded originally to inject new spirituality into the fabric of Christianity, were symptomatic of a growing lack of faith. The control of the papacy by politicians and by politically minded churchmen could no longer be ignored when Philip the Fair of France ensured the election of Clement IV as pope and removed the Papal See to Avignon in 1305, where it remained until 1377. In 1378 the Christian world was treated to the unedifying spectacle of two popes, Urban VI in Rome and Clement VII at Avignon, each claiming to be God's sole representative on earth. Seeds of the complete revolt from papal authority, which was to culminate in the Reformation, began to appear in various more or less underground movements like that of John Wycliffe (c. 1320–1384), who denounced the authority of the pope and translated the Bible into English. John Huss, who preached Wycliffe's doctrines, was excommunicated in 1412. Pope Martin V proclaimed a crusade against the Wycliffites and Hussites in 1420.*

In the centuries before Luther and Calvin, the Roman Catholic Church had involved itself increasingly in secular politics and financial dealings. As directed by their bishops, local priests often found themselves charging money for spiritual privileges, such as absolution through the sale of so-called "indulgences," and for access to religious relics. Such manipulations of the pious and often simple faithful bred confusion and anger toward an established church that was seen as increasingly bankrupt in its spiritual authority. Within the medieval church, early reformers such as Peter Waldo, John Huss, and John Wycliffe decried spiritual abuses by the clergy and papacy. These brushfires swept together to a conflagration on October 31, 1517, when Martin Luther nailed his Ninety-Five Theses (propositions for discussion) on the door of All Saints Church in Wittenberg, Germany.

Luther went beyond previous reformers in attacking not only the corruption within the Church but its theological doctrines as well. Specifically, Luther felt that the Roman Catholic Church (in which he served as a monk) had betrayed the gospel of free and undeserved forgiveness of sins in favor of a manipulative emphasis upon good works (as prescribed by the Church) as the key to salvation. In 1521 at the Diet of Worms, Luther was tried and eventually excommunicated. Freed from his commitment to the Church, Luther married and went on to lead a religious and political rebellion. Simultaneously, Zwingli in Switzerland and the Anabaptists (the "left wing" of the Reformation) broke with the Church over the issues of the Eucharist and baptism. John Calvin, a lawyer who fled France after his conversion to Protestantism, published his Institutes of the Christian Religion *in 1536 and, in Geneva, applied his doctrines to the unification of church and state.*

By the mid-1500s, Lutheranism was the predominant faith in northern Europe. In 1534 Henry VIII, angry over the Pope's refusal to grant him a divorce, set himself up as head of the Anglican Church. At the same time, John Knox founded Presbyterianism in Scotland, a movement that proved influential in the eventual union of England and Scotland.

With this weakening of the authority that had been humanity's official guide for so many years, an era of individualism was almost inevitable. The very symbols of authority like the Roman Catholic Church or the Holy Roman Empire had now only a shadowy reality. When Constantinople was taken by the Turks in 1453, even the Eastern branch of the Roman Empire ceased to exist. Deprived of dependable world authorities, states assumed more sovereignty, and individuals began to think of themselves as members of nations rather than of classes in a world commonwealth. In 1430 the English were driven from France through the inspired leadership of Joan of Arc, the peasant girl who fought for France rather than for bishops or nobles. Coinciding with the emergence of individual nations from the international society of feudalism, this new feeling of self-sufficiency led to the quest for earthly fame gained through human achievement. Whereas Dante's symbol for perfection is Beatrice, heavenly beatitude, Petrarch a generation later chants the praises of Laura, symbol of the laurel of earthly glory. Spurred by desire for preeminence and by a new appreciation for earthly things, the men of the Renaissance set out to explore the secular world. In one direction, physical exploration in search of new routes to the Indies broadened the compass of the physical world. In another direction, scholars made persistent efforts to exhume and compile the treasures of ancient Greece and Rome. In contrast to the scholastics of the Middle Ages, who based their reasoning on Holy Scripture, the humanists of the Renaissance came to revere the fertile minds and imaginations of the Greeks and Romans.

A new feeling that life was to be enjoyed rather than endured began to assert itself. "Let us enjoy the papacy since God has given it to us," a statement made by Pope Leo X, describes a state of mind that is illustrated in its extremes by the notorious excesses of the Borgias. Yet from this exuberant love of the physical world sprang the magnificent achievements of Renaissance art and architecture, headed by the great trio—Leonardo da Vinci, Michelangelo, and Raphael. The reexamination of nature, which was the beginning of modern science, resulted in the astronomical investigations of Copernicus. The exertions of individual ingenuity created such inventions as printing for the wider dissemination of knowledge. In 1446 the first books were printed in Haarlem by Coster, and after 1500 numerous editions of the classics and contemporary works were available.

The Renaissance is rightly called the beginning of the modern world and the modern state of mind. It should be remembered, however, that it was only a beginning. Many medieval attitudes still lingered, and the authority of the classics was often blindly substituted for the authority of the Church. At its best, the period produced many-sided geniuses such as Leonardo da Vinci (naturalist, anatomist, engineer, and artist)—lovers and explorers of a universe still sufficiently uncharted to preclude the necessity of devoting a lifetime to a narrow field of specialization.

WORKS AT A GLANCE

Francesco Petrarch

1337–1342	*Africa*	c. 1347	*Letters*
1337	*Concerning Illustrious*	1366	*Songs*
	Men	c. 1370	*The Triumphs*

Giovanni Boccaccio

c. 1336	*The Labors of Love*	c. 1343	*La Fiametta, The*
c. 1338	*The Man Conquered*		*Vision of Love*
	by Love	c. 1346	*The Fiesolan Pastoral*
c. 1340–41	*The Thesiad*	1353	*The Decameron*
c. 1341–42*	*Pastoral of Ameto*	c. 1354–55*	*The Whip*

Lorenzo Valla

1471	*Elegances of the Latin Language*

Lorenzo de' Medici

c. 1474	*Nencia of Barberina*	c. 1480	*Forest of Love*

Poliziano

1475	*Stanzas*	c. 1480	*Orfeo*

Luigi Pulci

1482	*The Greater Morgante*

Count Matteo Maria Boiardo

1495	*Orlando in Love*

Jacopo Sannazaro

1495	*Arcadia*	1526	*Eclogae Piscatoriae*

Niccolò Machiavelli

1509	*Annals of Italy*	1513	*The Prince, The*
1518	*Discourses on the First*		*Mandrake*
	Decade of Titus Livy	1520–1524*	*History of Florence*

*Date of composition

Baldassare Castiglione

| 1528 | *The Courtier* |

Vittoria Colonna

| 1544 | *Canzoniere* |

Lodovico Ariosto

| 1504–1516 | *Orlando Furioso* | c. 1530 | *The Students* |
| 1509 | *The Substitutes* | | |

Benvenuto Cellini

| 1558* | *Autobiography* |

Teofilo Folengo

| 1517 | *Baldus* |

Giangiorgio Trissino

| 1547 | *Italy Liberated from the Goths* |

Torquato Tasso

| 1573 | *Aminta* | 1575* | *Jerusalem Delivered* |

Giovanni Battista Guarini

| 1585 | *The Faithful Shepherd* |

Giambattista Marino

| c. 1620 | *Kisses* | 1623 | *Adonis* |

Clement Marot

| 1532 | *Clement's Adolescence* | 1534 | *Successor to the Adolescence* |

Marguerite of Navarre

| 1558 | *Seven Days of Stories* |

*Date of composition

François Rabelais

1532	The Horrible and Dreadful Feats and Prowesses of the Most Renowned Pantagruel	1538, 1546	Gargantua and Pantagruel
1533	Pantagrueline Prognostications		

John Calvin

1536	The Institutes of Christianity

Pierre de Ronsard

1552	Les Amours	1578	Sonnets for Helen
1572	La Franciad	c. 1580	Last Amours

Joachim du Bellay

1549	L'Olive, Défense et Illustration	1553–1557	The Antiquities of Rome, The Regrets

Guillaume Saluste, Seigneur du Bartas

1572	Judith	1578	The Week
1573	Urania or the Heavenly Muse	1584	The Second Week

Theodore-Agrippa d'Aubigné

1615	Histoire Universelle	c. 1620	Hécatombe a Diane
1616	Les Tragiques	1630	Adventure du Baron de Faeneste
c. 1618	Circé		

Michel de Montaigne

1580, 1588	Essays	1774	Travel Journal

Honoré d'Urfé

1607	Astrée

Miguel de Cervantes Saavedra

1585	Galatea	1613	Exemplary Stories
1605, 1615	Don Quixote		

Lope Felix de Vega Carpio

| 1609 | *New Art of Composing Comedies* | c. 1610 | *Punishment Without Vengeance* |

Juan Ruiz de Alarcón Mendoza

| c. 1622 | *Walls Have Ears* | 1628 | *Truth Suspected* |
| c. 1625 | *The Examination of Husbands* | | |

Pedro Calderón de la Barca

| c. 1630 | *The Physician of His Own Honor, The Painter of His Own Dishonor* | 1635 | *La Vida es Sueno* |
| | | 1637 | *El Magico Prodigeoso* |

Luiz de Camoens

| 1572 | *The Lusiads* |

Desiderius Erasmus

| 1509 | *In Praise of Folly* | 1519 | *Colloquies* |

5
THE RENAISSANCE IN ITALY

The fact that Renaissance Italy took away from France the leadership in literature, as it became also supreme in Europe in painting, sculpture, music, architecture, and the arts and refinements of living, was the result of the continued belief on the part of the Italians that they were the direct heirs of Rome, whose crumbling monuments were still to be seen everywhere. Believing that a rebirth of the Roman Empire was possible, Petrarch appealed to the Roman citizens as "by right" the rulers of the world; and Lorenzo Valla studiously attempted to revive classical Latin on the theory that "wherever is spoken the Roman tongue, there is the Roman Empire." This was, to be sure, the purest romanticism, for while national units were being formed elsewhere in Europe, there was actually no political semblance of a Roman Empire or even a united Italy. The peninsula was cut up into numerous city-states like those of ancient Greece, and those who lived in them were not "Italians" but citizens of Rome, Naples, Venice, Ferrara, Perugia, and other lesser "nations." Florence and Venice were the only nominally "republican" states, and they were usually controlled by influential families or patrician groups. The others were outright despotisms, the court of Ferrara being almost oriental in its ceremonials and homage to the reigning duke. All of these small political units were constantly subject to French, Spanish, and German interference.

But with a kind of sublime indifference to the parlous political situation, each state developed its own court and courtly society. Wealthy and often talented rulers rivaled each other in an attempt to reproduce the grandeur as well as the accomplishments of the golden age of the Roman Empire. Like the Emperor Augustus, they became patrons of poets, scholars, artists, musicians, and men possessed of any talents that might add to their fame. Enjoyment of earthly elegance became the mode even among Churchmen. Pope Pius II wrote an improper novel and wished to be known primarily for his *eloquentia* or skill in Latin. Popes Pius II, Nicholas V, and Sextus were all zealous patrons of secular learning. The Borgias, Alexander and his son Cesare, were capable and brilliant, but also sensual, perverted, and avaricious worldlings who openly sold Church appointments and had their critics assassinated.

The ebullient zest for living, which encouraged the lawlessness of a Benvenuto Cellini as well as that of the Borgias, was coupled, as in these two instances, with an intense passion for beauty. Plato succeeded Aristotle as the guiding philosopher, and at the *Academe*, founded at Florence by Cosimo de' Medici, the new gospel of beauty was formalized. By the sanction of Platonic idealism, sensuous beauty could be worshipped as a shadow of intellectual or ideal beauty. By realization of earthly beauty, it was held that man might catch a glimpse of the eternal. Cardinal Pietro Bembo, accordingly, called woman "the illumination of God." The scholar Lorenzo Valla commented, "What nature has shaped and formed cannot be other than sacred." "Our instincts demand happiness," he added.

These two comments, the one idealistic and the other practical, give the tone of the Italian courts of the period. The reawakened love of beauty ("Who does not praise beauty?" asked Valla), the renewed interest in nature, and lust for knowledge and experience found sanction in the authority of Plato whose birthday was solemnly honored. The Renaissance princes lived in magnificent palaces, surrounded by sumptuous tapestries, paintings, and furnishings. Highly cultivated men and women made up the courts, and professional painters, poets, and musicians were well paid to entertain them. In Florence a prominent banker, Cosimo de' Medici (1434–1492), became the popular head of the government. Both cruel and generous, but with a great zest for learning and elegance, he attracted grammarians, manuscript hunters, connoisseurs, translators, scholars, and authors to encourage the study of Italian, Greek, Latin, Arabic, and Hebrew. His grandson, Lorenzo the Magnificent, was a many-sided genius who was not only a great patron of the arts and learning but practiced them himself. Boccaccio attained an ambassadorship at Florence because of his literary ability rather than his knowledge of practical affairs. Artists were signally honored by celebrations tendered to them, and poets were invited by bishops, Roman senators, and university rectors to be crowned with laurel wreaths in recognition of extraordinary achievement.

Every attempt was made by these courtly societies to reproduce what they believed to be the elegance of Rome. Roman monuments were restored, and some important Greek and Roman statuary was unearthed. In imitation of the triumphal processions of Roman emperors and victorious generals, "triumphs" were instituted in which symbolic figures on foot or in chariots or floats represented current events, ecclesiastical doctrines, or gods and goddesses of ancient mythology. Hawking parties, running, leaping, swimming, wrestling, riding, and boat racing were the sports of the elite. Castiglione, author of a book called *The Courtier*, set the fashion for polite behavior throughout all Europe. Costumes were colorful, elaborate, and weighted down with heavy and intricate jewelry. Cosmetics and perfumes were used by both sexes to accentuate the magnificence of the human figure; at festivals even mules were treated with scents and ointments.

In consequence, while serious scholars, the humanists, were transferring the concerns of scholarship from the next world to this, poets, novelists, playwrights, artists, and musicians were mainly concerned with offering elegant entertainment. Tragedies and comedies were written on Latin models, to be played in sumptuously decorated settings with solid elaborate scenery painted by the best artists of the day and accompanied by choral dances and music. Poets aspired to walk in the footsteps of Virgil, prose writers to recapture the elegant periods of Cicero. Both attempted to entertain an immediate sophisticated audience by public readings of their works. Under these circumstances, scholars like Petrarch turned occasionally to elegant versification, and poets like Boccaccio to fashionable *novella* writing. Poets like Ariosto and Tasso were retained solely to entertain and add literary distinction to Italian courts. In most cases, the high seriousness of Dante was replaced by the desire to give delight, both by the subject matter and the form and style of the compositions.

For convenience, the Renaissance in Italy is usually divided into three periods or phases. The *trecento,* or fourteenth century marked the brilliant beginnings of the period. In the *quattrocento,* or fifteenth century, creative genius was superseded in the main by vigorous scholarly activity and interest in classical Latin. The *cinquecento,* actually including the last third of the fifteenth and the first half of the sixteenth century, saw a revival of Italian as a literary language but also considerable imitation and criticism rather than the original creations of genius. This was the end of Italy's great age of literary achievement.

FRANCESCO PETRARCH (1304–1374)

IMPORTANCE

Described by such epithets as "the father of the Renaissance" or "the first modern man," Petrarch is remembered today chiefly in connection with the sonnet, one form of which still bears his name. In his own time his significance was far greater as the first humanist, originator of a new method of scholarship that attempted to seek out earthly reality by studying it at first hand rather than finding it in Divine revelation. Humanism regarded the ancient Greeks and Romans as better guides than the allegorists of the Middle Ages. This new spirit imposed no limitations on the proper areas for research as Christian authority had done in the past. The term *humanism* calls attention to human values in contrast to the medieval preoccupation with eternity, and is broadly definable by reference to the line of Terence, "I am a man and nothing human is alien to me."

Francesco Petrarca was born in 1304 at Arezzo, where his family had taken refuge after their expulsion from Florence along with Dante. After a period of wandering, during which the growing boy acquired the Tuscan dialect that he was to use in his Italian poetry, the family took up residence in 1313 at Avignon, the new seat of the papacy. After four years of study of the humanities at Carpentras, he was sent by his father in 1319 to Montpellier to study law. Here his acquaintance with Cicero appears to have been the beginning of his determined enthusiasm for the classics as well as his aspiration to become another Cicero, skilled in oratory and the writing of elegant Latin. In spite of four years at Montpellier and another three years at Bologna spent in legal training, Petrarch had obviously no inclination in that direction and soon turned from it to the pursuit of literature. When, in 1326, his father's death left him entirely free to follow his own inclinations, he returned to Avignon, took minor orders in the Church, and entered into the fashionable life of the city with obvious pleasure.

It was in April of the next year, by his own account, that he was smitten by the beauty of the unknown young lady who bears the name of Laura in his sonnets. Seeing her in church, he knew himself to be enslaved by her love. His personal relations with her may have been more intimate than those of Dante with Beatrice, but the pattern of his devotion is so close to Dante's that it is possible that she was selected by Petrarch to be the object of his amorous verse in more or less deliberate imitation. Petrarch also found wealthy patrons in the powerful Colonna family, and was rapidly becoming famous for his oratory and for his literary achievements. During these years at Avignon he undertook the first of many journeys that were to send him all over Italy and into France, Flanders, and Germany, where he made the acquaintance of learned men and hunted for classical manuscripts to read and copy.

In 1337, a desire for solitude and a very real love of nature moved him to retire to the beautiful countryside of Vaucluse. Abandoning society for solitary scholarship, he simultaneously substituted domesticity for the life of the fashionable gallant, forming an attachment that resulted in the birth of a son Giovanni and a daughter Francesca, both of whom were legitimized by papal decree. In 1341 he experienced what must have been the supreme moment of his life when he was crowned laureate by the Roman Senate, after having rejected a simultaneous invitation to receive the coveted laurel from the University of Paris. For the remainder of his life he was sought after by the most brilliant courts of Europe where he was honored, entertained, and handsomely remunerated for his compositions in Latin (still the recognized literary and diplomatic language) and often for his mere presence, which was regarded as a distinguished ornament to any noble house.

Meanwhile, Laura's death in 1348, followed by the deaths of several of his friends, plunged him into a period of gloom and religious devotion. In 1350 he became the close friend of Boccaccio, whom he had known casually before. In 1351 he refused an invitation to become rector of the University of Florence, and returned to Vaucluse. Finally, after a series of diplomatic missions and other services performed for Milan and Padua, he retired to another country retreat at Arquà, where his daughter cared for him until his death in 1374.

The conflict between Petrarch's ardent love of fame and desire for retirement was the external evidence of a much deeper conflict within his personality and was symptomatic of his age. Orthodox and religious by nature, he was nevertheless drawn to his beloved Latin writings as dependable guides of life. Caught between the here and the hereafter, he attempted to compromise by insisting that there are two glories. The glory of Heaven is certainly the greater and the more eternal blessing. Yet, since man possesses also a mortal life, he is justified in seeking earthly fame while he lives. The very urgency of his protestations makes it obvious that Petrarch did not quite believe his own theory and that he lived in a kind of inner purgatory of self-condemnation for his irresistible worldly proclivities. Yet in the very fact that he felt the conflict so deeply is the evidence that his was a new attitude toward the classics, that he was reading them not for allegorical meanings nor merely for instruction in style, but for subject matter and for the broader view of life which they inspired.

The Latin Works

Although Petrarch was continually engaged in affairs of state and although he wrote patriotic poetry and gave his support to the impossible attempt of the tribune Cola di Rienzi to restore the Roman nation in Italy, his real devotion was to the cultivation of the elegant Latin of Cicero and Virgil. He composed with the greatest of care and scarcely any inspiration a now-forgotten epic poem, *Africa* (1337–1342), which celebrates Scipio Africanus in the conquest of Carthage, a victory that defeated Rome's last powerful enemy. His Latin prose is by no means as stilted or artificial. With long practice he made the diction of Cicero into an individualized language of his own, less elegant but more real than the polished Ciceronianisms of the following century, writing *Letters* (c. 1347) to the living, to ancient Romans, and even to posterity, composing many philosophical treatises, and helping to bring to life the world of Rome by a series of biographies of Romans, *De Viris Illustribus* (*Concerning Illustrious Men*) (1337).

The Sonnets

It was part of Petrarch's character to scorn imitation of any except the ancients, and he explained in a letter to Boccaccio that he avoided reading Dante for fear of imitating him unconsciously. Yet he came very close to following Dante's pattern in his Italian poetry. The *Canzoniere* or *Songs* (1366) is made up principally of sonnets, interspersed with other forms such as the ode and sestina, most of them relating the progress of his love for Laura. Unlike the *Vita Nuova*, where poetry alternates with prose, the poems speak for themselves and thereby inaugurated that universally popular form of love poetry known as the sonnet-sequence. The record of Petrarch's love is amazingly akin to Dante's in its broad outlines, describing his first meeting with Laura, his love for her, her coolness, her death, her compassion in heaven for his "exile" from her, the bitterness of his grief, and his imagined joining her in heaven. But Laura is clearly more than a symbol of either fame or beatitude. Following the notion of the ladder of love whereby man's contemplation of earthly beauty in woman leads him to the vision of heavenly beauty, Petrarch is obviously quite content with Laura's physical charms, which he catalogues and describes in a manner utterly at variance with Dante's mystical vision of Beatrice. Laura, for her part, is on earth a very human coquette and, in heaven, a very warm and very real woman.

Some of the sonnets are very moving in their devoted sincerity and devout worship of the loved one. Many of them are ingenious elaborations of trivial moods and moments, seeming more clever than sincere, and engaging chiefly because of the fancies which the lover's alert mind suggests. Paraphrasing Shelley's cruel criticism of them, they sometimes begin with a sob and end with a simile. But in expressing his love and his torment in an essentially intellectual manner, he set the pattern for love sonnets throughout Europe for the next two centuries, with their now familiar conceits and images. Love pierces his heart like an arrow, the eyes are the way to the heart, the loved one's birthplace is a sacred shrine, her name is made into an anagram, she is his "sweetest foe." The lover is caught in the meshes of love, is like a ship in a tempest, endures sleepless nights weeping copious tears, lives in a state of freezing fire and burning snow, fears his imminent death, but is caught like a fish on a baited hook. Much of this is derived from a language of love as old as the Provençal lyrics of the Middle Ages, but a great deal is original with Petrarch, and, in any case, the expression is always deft, neat, and highly polished. Although missing the sense of real sincerity behind the "neat wit and refined elegance" of these poems, Gabriel Harvey came closest to describing their nature when he wrote, "Petrarch was a delicate man, and with an elegant judgment graciously confined love within the term of civility." Harvey praised them for being "the grace of art, a precious tablet of rare conceits, and a curious frame of exquisite workmanship."

The Triumphs

A second work devoted to Laura, written in *terza rima* like the *Divine Comedy*, was given the name *Trionfi* (c. 1370), suggesting the triumphs or processions accorded a victorious general in ancient Rome. Written with epic seriousness, the book begins with *The Triumph of Love,* in which the poet sees in a dream Cupid in a great procession of all who loved and thereby suffered torments. Naming the great lovers of the past, secular, Biblical, and mythological, he speaks to various ones like Dante, who is there with Beatrice, and hears their stories. Only Laura refuses to be made captive. Then, in like manner, he records *The Triumph of Chastity*, in which Laura is preeminent, and *The Triumph of Death,* wherein Laura suffers physical death and thereby sets Petrarch free, coming to comfort him with visions of immortal life. He is momentarily obsessed by *The Triumph of Fame,* which can also overcome death, but *The Triumph of Time* makes it clear that earthly glory is, after all, a fleeting shadow. The sixth and final book describes *The Triumph of Eternity,* in which Laura, lovelier than ever, is envisioned in heaven. The scheme of the work is logical and well-planned but quite obviously owes its inspiration to Dante and is stiff and cumbersome in comparison to the fluid progress, the innate naturalness, and the inevitability of Dante's journey to Paradise.

In one sense, Petrarch's Italian poetry turned the clock backwards to the artificiality and labored conceits of the Provençal troubadours, as if Dante's glowing sincerity had never been. In another sense, Petrarch modernized and secularized Dante's expression of love, exchanging the mystical sublimation of Mariolatry for human desire and stressing the mixed and high-strung emotions that accompany passion rather than dehumanizing it for the sake of philosophy or theology.

The Development of the Sonnet

As noted in the discussion of Petrarch, the sonnet was of Italian origin. As a general rule, the form restricted itself to fourteen lines (although Milton wrote a sonnet using twenty lines) and, in England, iambic pentameter (again, with many exceptions). From their earliest use of Petrarch, Castiglione, and others, sonnets commonly appeared in cycles or sequences. These were collections of sonnets, sometimes more than one hundred, linked by a common theme, such as the progress of a love relation or the changing seasons. In extended sonnet sequences (including Shakespeare's sonnets), the unifying theme can at times be difficult to perceive.

Typically, the Italian sonnet is composed of an octave (the first eight lines, usually rhyming *abba abba*) and a sestet (the concluding six lines, usually rhyming *cde cde*). The octave develops a problem or tension of some kind that is then resolved or relieved in the sestet. A lover's complaint, for example, would be stated in the octave and answered in some way in the sestet. The Italian or Petrarchan sonnet form was used by Sidney in the *Astrophel and Stella* sonnet cycle and, in modified form, by Spenser in the *Amoretti* sequence. Most English sonnets, however, have since been written in the so-called Shakespearean form, rhyming *ababcdcdefefgg* (or a variant). As a non-inflected language, English is less able than French or Italian to find the repeated and rhymes required by the *abba abba* format. (In an inflected language, the recurring grammatical endings such as *-i* or *-ae* or *-am* make recurring rhymes more natural.)

GIOVANNI BOCCACCIO (1313–1375)

In much the same way as Petrarch's voluminous and serious writings became so outmoded as to make his enduring reputation depend on his Italian sonnets, Boccaccio's fame among English readers now rests mainly on a single book that he later regretted having written. With the *Decameron* a cycle of human interest had swung from Dante's religious devotion through

Petrarch's intellectual quest for fame to a worldly and sophisticated delight in a good story told for its own sake. If love is used as a touchstone, three diverse attitudes are similarly revealed. Dante's immaculate adoration was for Beatrice or Beatitude. Petrarch's Laura was assaulted with verse in much the same manner as her lover laid siege to the laurel of earthly fame. Boccaccio found love a stimulating pastime and named his fickle mistress Fiametta or "Little Flame." Unlike Petrarch, he wrote mainly in Italian, his prose and poetry owing most of its inspiration to this affair.

Giovanni Boccaccio was born in 1313, probably in Paris, the illegitimate son of an Italian merchant and an unknown French woman of a good (and possibly noble) family. After an elementary education at Florence, he was apprenticed to a merchant in keeping with his father's plan to have his son follow in his footsteps. Apart from the advantages of travel gained thereby, Boccaccio found little pleasure in these six years of apprenticeship, having already developed a passion for literature and an intense aversion for the transactions of business. In deference to this dislike but still with the aim of providing him with a practical means of livelihood, his father made provisions for him to undertake the study of law. When another six years proved the futility of engaging Boccaccio's interests in anything except an "invincible" love of poetry, his legal training was also abandoned.

The strained circumstances of Boccaccio's preparations for a profession were added to by the unnaturalness of his home environment. The very obvious devotion of his father to his natural son undoubtedly increased the sense of hostility that the merchant's wife must have felt toward this child of passion. A kind of practical arrangement seems to have been worked out, whereby the young Boccaccio was allowed to pursue his own life away from home and was left pretty much to his own devices, provided he would devote some attention to business, either his father's or that of one of his father's associates. By some such arrangement Boccaccio took up residence in Naples around 1333. Here at the court of King Robert of Anjou he found himself very much at home, his attentions being divided equally between the wit and talents of the learned men and the exciting challenge of the game of courtly love with which Neapolitan society was saturated. The one attraction led him to a dramatic vow at the grave of Virgil to devote his life to poetry. The other resulted in his passionate love for Fiametta, Maria d'Aquino, young wife of a nobleman and reputed illegitimate daughter of King Robert himself. By his own account she returned his love for a time but then jilted him for another lover. In spite of the fact that Fiametta and the circumstances of the brief affair seem hardly weighty enough to have inspired a lifetime devotion, Boccaccio seems never to have become very deeply attached to any other woman and, possibly because of her early death in the same plague that destroyed Petrarch's lover, he kept her memory warm and alive in his heart.

In 1340 or 1341, as a result of financial reverses in the family, Boccaccio was required to return to Florence, where he found consolation in an extensive literary productivity that gradually made his name known throughout

Italy. By 1346 his prestige was sufficiently great to win him a Florentine ambassadorship, the first of many such missions to adorn his later life. On one of these occasions, in 1351, he was the proud bearer of an offer of a professorship at the University of Florence to Petrarch, then residing at Padua. Although Petrarch did not accept, Boccaccio's mission probably deepened an already-formed friendship and a reverence on Boccaccio's part that turned him gradually away from creative writing to the then-considered more enduring concerns of humanistic scholarship. Although he never lost his admiration for Dante, on whom he lectured at Florence and whose biography he wrote, he followed Petrarch at a distance in searching out and copying manuscripts, in being instrumental in establishing the first professorship of Greek at the University of Florence, and in compiling Latin treatises on the ancient world.

With a reputation as a poet and scholar and widespread popularity as the author of the *Decameron*, published in 1353, he continued to live in Florence until 1360 when he retired to his father's native town of Certaldo. In 1361 he received a strange visit from a Carthusian monk who prophesied an early death for him if he did not repudiate his godlessness. Boccaccio was sufficiently impressed by this message to determine to sell his library, give up literature, and devote the remainder of his life to piety. Communicating his intentions to Petrarch, he received in reply a very sensible letter, which is still extant, in which the older poet advises him to reform his morals if he pleases but to continue his scholarship. Boccaccio did indeed enter the Church in 1362, but his interest in scholarship remained alive until his death in 1375, in spite of the poverty and illness that attended his last years.

Il Filocolo

Boccaccio's first published work (c. 1336) was written at the request of Fiametta and is dedicated to her. Borrowing its plot from the medieval story of *Flore and Blanchefleur*, it bears the title *Il Filocolo* or *The Labors of Love*, and in seven books of Italian prose it transfers the medieval adventures of these lovers to the artificial background of Neapolitan courtly society and simultaneously refers to his own love affair. After meeting Fiametta in church, he arranges a rendezvous in a convent parlor, and there, in order to declare his love in a veiled manner, he tells her the love story, after which she asks him to make a book of it in the vulgar tongue. Tedious and stilted in the main, its popularity continued principally because of Book Five (which was separately translated into English in 1567) in which a group of Neapolitan ladies and gentlemen discuss thirteen questions of love, a game of which the Renaissance apparently never wearied.

Il Filostrato

Turning from prose to poetry, Boccaccio continued to celebrate love in a series of narrative poems. Dedicated to Fiametta, *Il Filostrato* (*The Man Conquered by Love*) (c. 1338) is the story of Troilus and Cressida, which Boccaccio compares to his own love story. Again using medieval sources, such as Benoit de Saint-More's *Roman de Troie*, Boccaccio supplies the atmosphere of the society of his own time. Written in eight-line stanzas, the tale describes the Trojan Troilo who scorns love and disapproves of women until he happens to see the widowed Griseida. For love of her he becomes a hero in the Trojan War. One day Pandaro, Troilo's young friend and Griseida's cousin, discovers his love. Demanding the utmost secrecy of Troilo, he sets out to win Griseida's love by praising the valor and discretion of Troilo, pointing out that many other women take lovers, and suggesting that youth and the opportunity for youthful love do not long endure. A subsequent love letter written by Troilo produces the desired union. Shortly thereafter through an exchange of prisoners, Griseida is returned to her father, who has gone over to the enemy. There she gives herself to Diomede, who uses the same arguments to win her. Troilo learns of her new affair and rushes to his death in battle. The story is known to English readers chiefly from Chaucer's less ironic, warmer, and more subtle and delicate handling of the theme in his *Troilus and Criseyde*; the verse, *ottava rima* (*abababcc*) is the form used by Byron in *Don Juan*.

Il Teseida

In a second "epic" in *ottava rima, Il Teseide* (*The Theseid*) (c. 1340–1341), Boccaccio uses Virgil as his model, composing exactly the same number of lines as the *Aeneid* and similarly dividing it into twelve books. An account of war and love, describing the battle of Theseus against Thebes and the strange love of the captured brothers-in-arms for the enchanting Emilia, it remains a pompous and decorative exercise in versification from which Chaucer took the ingenious situation and "question of love" of the triangle plot and turned it into his *Knight's Tale* of Palamon and Arcite.

La Fiametta

Boccaccio's *La Fiametta* (c. 1343), was written as an attempt to revenge himself for his scorned love. In the form of a novel in which Fiametta tells her own story, she describes her love for Pamfilo (Boccaccio), and his necessary departure to Florence. Although he has promised to return in four months, he does not reappear. She is plunged into a passion of grief, and discovers finally that he has married. Alarmed at her condition, her husband attempts to divert her by a change of scene but to no avail. At the point of suicide, she hears that Pamfilo is about to return. She dresses herself with the greatest of art for the occasion, and, when Pamfilo fails to come back, she despairingly seeks consolation by recalling how many other wives are forced to bear similar anguish. Typical of the attitude toward marriage that accompanied the code of courtly love, this tale is held by some to be the first psychological novel in its attempted analysis of a woman's feelings. From the standpoint of a modern reader, it is extremely tedious and artificial, particularly in the classical allusions that flow most learnedly from the lips of the heartbroken lady.

Minor Italian Works

Another strange attempt to do what his talents made him unfit for was an imitation of Dante, the *Ninfale d'Ameto* or the *Pastoral of Ameto* (1341–1342). In prose interspersed with verse, the story of the innocent Ameto who meets a group of nymphs who tell of their rather racy experiences in love, suddenly turns into an allegory when the Three-in-One descends on Easter, with the bizarre result that the nymphs are revealed as the seven virtues, whose stories were allegorically intended, their lovers having been vices! A similar inept imitation, *L'Amorosa Visione* (*The Vision of Love*) (c. 1343), describes in *terza rima* a dream in which Boccaccio is guided by a lady to a vision of past heroes and lovers, after which he meets Fiametta who is to be led with him to Paradise by the lady guide now revealed as Virtue. A most extraordinary peculiarity of this long and dull composition was not discovered until the nineteenth century when it was pointed out that the initial letters of the tercets spell out three long dedicatory poems to Fiametta, and that the initial letters of the first, third, fifth, seventh, and ninth lines of the first dedicatory poem spell *Maria*. What was Dante's subtlety compared to that!

An imitation of Ovid, the *Ninfale Fiesolano* (*The Fiesolan Pastoral*) (c. 1346), is more in the tradition of late Greek pastoral romance, which was also revived during the Renaissance. Taking the names of two rivers that flow into each other from the slopes of Fiesole, Boccaccio tells of the love affair of the shepherd Affrico and the nymph Mensola, who were changed into streams because of Affrico's presumption in daring to love an immortal. Amidst much that is artificial are snatches of peasant conversation and folk song reproduced with fine feeling for local color.

Latin Works

Along with this prolific output of the years between 1338 and 1346, Boccaccio composed nearly all of his sixteen Latin eclogues modeled on Virgil and Petrarch. One of them, the seventh, is of autobiographical interest in its apparent confession of an affair with a nun and of a daughter born of the union. Between 1363 and his death, Boccaccio compiled a series of encyclopedic Latin works on ancient history and geography and an elaborate *Genealogy of the Gods* (*De Genealogia Deorum*). He also wrote *Of Illustrious Women* (*De Claris Mulieribus*), a sequel to Petrarch's *Illustrious Men,* and a work on *The Downfalls of the Great* (*De Casibus Virorum et Feminarum Illustrium*), in which the ghosts of the dead visit him in his study to tell their stories.

Il Corbaccio

The kind of literary revenge taken in *La Fiametta* was repeated in 1354 or 1355 when his advances toward an unknown widow had apparently been rejected. *Il Corbaccio* or *The Whip* describes Boccaccio's rescue from a forest of love by the spirit of the widow's dead husband, who tells him that he has come from Purgatory where he is expiating the sin of having been excessively patient with his wife. He then expiates at length on the faults of women in general, and concludes by leading the author to a mountain top from which he can see that "the labyrinth of love" (the subtitle of the book) leads to Hell. Here Boccaccio is in his native element, writing with realism, irony, humor, and an obvious gusto which sharpens alike his perception of earthly reality and his expression of it. Only the length and monotony of harping on a single subject, together with the inclusion of the inevitable illustrations from the ancients, get in the way of Boccaccio's natural genius for seeing life on its lower and less presentable levels.

The Decameron

This aptitude for portraying the human beast, rather than the demigod man often fancies himself to be, found its fullest expression in the collection of one hundred prose stories, which were composed over a period of several years and were organized into the unifying framework of a long narrative. The book was published in 1353 as *The Decameron* (*Il Decamerone*), a Greek title meaning "Ten Days." In the preface he explains that when he had suffered because of the cruelty of his beloved, he found comfort in the pleasing conversations of friends. Time gradually healed his sorrow, but the memory of the consolation offered him moves him to a desire to repay his debt by offering similar consolation to others who find themselves afflicted in the same way. Since women are more emotional and more delicate than men, and since they have fewer ways of finding distraction from melancholy, this book is offered particularly to them. In it they will find many examples of the whimsicality of fortune and many stories of joy and grief in love which will serve both as solace for the past and advice for use in the future. The tone of the preface gives no indication of whether Boccaccio is being serious or playful—it might well be a combination of both—and is typical of the impersonal objectivity of the entire book.

The Decameron then opens with a vivid and detailed description of the plague of 1348, a serious, sober, and factual account in which the effect of horror is piled up by the accumulation of details of suffering, terror, sudden death, and mass burials. The imminence of death sent one part of the population into a roistering career of guzzling, stealing, and frantic pleasure-seeking. Others shut themselves up in their homes and hoped to escape the infection by isolation and temperate living. Still others sought safety by fleeing to the country.

Using these conditions as a natural and logical reason for throwing ten storytellers together for an extended period of time, Boccaccio then narrows the scene to a church where, on a Tuesday morning, seven young society ladies, ranging in age from eighteen to twenty-eight, are discussing the horrors of the plague. Finding themselves to be bereft of relatives and responsible only to themselves, they eagerly agree to the suggestion of Pampinea, the oldest, that they take refuge in one of the country villas they have inherited. The plan suffers a momentary setback when their timidity and inexperience makes it seem foolhardy to attempt the trip alone, but the lucky appearance of three young men of their acquaintance saves the day and completes the total of ten storytellers. The names of the members of the group are symbolic of dominant traits of character which are only faintly apparent throughout the book. Unlike Chaucer's *Canterbury Tales*, the stories are not fitted to the characters, and these ten young people serve little other purpose than to be mouthpieces for the author and to provide transitions between the stories. It is mentioned, moreover, that the men are suitors of (presumably) three of the girls, but nothing at all is made of this circumstance, which might have provided amusing by-play between narratives. Of special interest among the ten are Pampinea whose twenty-eight years give her a natural position of leadership; Fiametta, who is described with a trifle more warmth than is expended on the other girls; Pamfilo, Boccaccio's name for himself in *Il Filocolo* and *La Fiametta*; and Dioneo, who is distinctly individualized by his boldness in telling racy stories.

On the next day, a two-mile journey takes them to a beautiful country estate, where Dioneo suggests that they make plans to enjoy themselves during their sojourn. Pampinea gives practical effect to this suggestion by proposing that each in turn shall be master of ceremonies, king or queen, for each of the succeeding days. The following days are accordingly occupied with music, singing, dancing, exploration of the estate, and banqueting; and it is decided that the afternoons, during the heat of the day, will be devoted to story telling, a favorite form of amusement of the period.

THE FIRST DAY of storytelling begins immediately with Pamfilo's very amusing story at the expense of the Church, in which an incredible scoundrel so imposes himself upon a gullible friar that he is buried with the highest reverence and held to be a saint. Pamfilo concludes with the solemn observation that the scoundrel may possibly have been received in Heaven and that the mysteries of God are beyond understanding.

Neifile, one of the young ladies, follows with one of the cleverest and most ironic stories in the book, concerning an earnest attempt to convert a Jew to Christianity. When words fail to convince him, he determines to go to Rome to see for himself the holiness of the Papal See. His would-be missionary is in despair, knowing that Rome will present a degrading spectacle of luxury and vice, and is the more amazed when the Jew returns ready to embrace Christianity on the grounds that a religion that can flourish on such a rotten foundation must indeed be inspired by God. In Boccaccio's organization of this collection of stories, the effect of naturalness is finely maintained by the device of having the theme of one story remind the succeeding narrator of a similar tale.

After another anecdote that revolves about religion and is given point by a very ingenious story within a story whereby a Jew saves his life, Dioneo is called on to tell the fourth story. Unlike the previous narratives, this turns out to be a very clever and very cleverly told account of the lechery of a monk and his abbot. The method by which the monk, discovered in his cell in the act of love-making, escapes punishment by luring the abbot into the identical sin, is ingenious enough, but the story is made hilarious by the added twist of the monk's method of informing the abbot that he has witnessed the abbot's love-making. And here the point depends on a *double entendre* that refers to the different methods of copulation used by the two men. When the story is completed, the girls react in much the way that might be expected of the Neapolitan society women of Boccaccio's acquaintance or, in fact, any group of moderately sophisticated women of almost any age. They blush, look covertly at one another, and then are overcome by the humor that is sufficient excuse for the impropriety of the story. They do indeed rebuke Dioneo "gently," but their unconfessed complete approval is signified later when they permit him the special privilege of telling always the last story of the day and on any subject he pleases.

The clever turning of the tables upon the abbot by the monk reminds Fiametta of an incident in which a virtuous lady subtly rebukes the amorous advances of a royal suitor. This brings similar incidents to the minds of the remaining storytellers, and the day concludes quite naturally with five more anecdotes of the same nature. It is then decided that hereafter a subject for the stories of the ensuing days shall be assigned in advance by the ruler of the day, but that Dioneo's privilege shall be reserved, thus giving Boccaccio an opportunity for some slight variety. By way of ending the ceremonies, the company dances to the accompaniment of a *ballatella,* or little dancing song, a graceful conclusion with which each ensuing day ends.

THE SECOND DAY is provided with nine discourses on what the Middle Ages and Renaissance held to be comedy, a happy ending to a calamitous situation. These are in the main pointless to the modern reader in their use of improbable coincidences and chance occurrences. But Boccaccio's contemporaries were still fascinated by the operations of chance or Fortune, that strange power that directed human destinies. The seventh story, "The Sultan's Daughter," although it relies on the ancient lost heir plot, has more point than the others and also a "moral" in the best Boccaccio tradition, "Lips for the kissing forfeit no favor; nay, they renew as the moon doth ever." The ninth story, which touches upon another favorite subject of the time, the patient endurance of a wronged wife, begins with a husband's wager on his wife's virtue, turns to a shoddy scheme whereby the wager is won by the taker by means of trumped-up evidence of the wife's unfaithfulness, and concludes with the husband's attempt to put her to death and her triumphant vindication by her solution of the deception and unmasking of the deceiver. This is the plot used by Shakespeare in *Cymbeline.* Dioneo concludes the day with a humorous tale that makes a point of the necessity for husbands to satisfy the sexual requirements of their wives.

An interlude is provided by the decision to refrain from this form of amusement in honor of the sanctity of Friday and to give the ladies an opportunity to wash their hair on Saturday. On Sunday the company moves to a more magnificent villa, the description of whose rooms and grounds offers a sample of Renaissance elegance.

THE THIRD DAY of story telling resumes with the subject of the Attainment or Recovery of Some Much-Desired Thing, a theme that provokes some of the most ingenious stories in the book. The first story is an entertaining account of a clever man's method of becoming the lover of all the nuns of a convent and of his subsequent protestations about the fatigue that results. The second is of an ingenious ruse whereby a commoner escapes punishment for deceiving a queen into taking him into her bed, believing him to be the king. The third story describes the elaborate device of a lady for gulling an innocent friar into acting as a pander to procure her a lover. The fourth story is a distasteful account of a ruse whereby a monk enjoys the favors of the wife of a pious man without arousing his suspicion. Story Five relates the outwitting of an ardent lover by a jealous husband and the subsequent lover's outwitting of the outwitter. The sixth narrative also concerns the conquest by a lover of a wife who is victimized by the lover's taking advantage of her jealousy of her husband. The seventh story relies on coincidence more than guile to restore a lover to his lady's favor as well as gaining the good will of her husband. Story Eight describes a highly improbable device by which a monk enjoys in safety the wife of a simple-minded husband, in a manner similar to that of Story Four. The ninth story returns to the theme of the patient wife in detailing how she regained her husband's love by substituting herself in the dark for his mistress. The day concludes with Dioneo's absurd but undeniably amusing account of how a hermit taught an innocent girl to put the devil in hell.

THE FOURTH DAY is given over to pathetic tales of tragic love affairs, the first of which, "Tancred and Ghismonda," was a favorite of the time and was made into an English play by Robert Wilmot around 1567. Dioneo's concluding tale is of amorous intrigue.

THE FIFTH DAY provides relief from the gloom of these woeful tales by reversing the subject to that of Happy Conclusions of Unlucky Love Affairs. Most of these are unimaginative records of events which terminate agreeably to all concerned, the stuff of medieval and modern romance. The fourth story emerges from the doldrums as a pleasant, realistic, and rather touching account of adolescent love, made amusing by the indulgent father's realistic interpretation of his daughter's romantic language. The eighth story conjures up a vision of terror in a vein usually foreign to Boccaccio but highly complimentary to his ability in this genre. Next is the well-known poignant tale of "Federigo's Falcon," and the day concludes with Dioneo's bringing an anecdote involving homosexuality to a highly skilled and pointed conclusion.

THE SIXTH DAY is given over to the retailing of accounts of Clever Retorts to Insults, a subject that results in a series of unusually brief and singularly unimpressive anecdotes that, like the anecdotes of any age, often find their reason for existence in being attached to well-known personages. On this day even Dioneo follows the prescribed pattern with a lively satire on the impositions put upon the simple-minded populace by professional exhibitors of holy relics like Chaucer's Pardoner.

THE SEVENTH DAY has Dioneo as the king and he lives up to his reputation by proposing as subject the Deceptions Practiced by Wives upon their Husbands. The theme provides ample material both for descriptions of illicit love and accounts of the ingenuity born of love. One wife convinces her husband that her lover is a phantom, another that he has come to the house to buy a vat, a third that he is a conjurer. In the fourth story an errant wife who is locked out by her husband very neatly turns the tables on him. A jealous husband, thinking to outsmart his wife by giving her confession in the guise of a priest, is judiciously outsmarted by her in the fifth story. In the sixth, seventh, and eighth stories suspicious husbands are outrageously beguiled by their wives. The ninth tale is a bizarre account of the method used by the wife of an ageing nobleman to convince a servant that she sincerely desires him, together with an equally bizarre sequel of their devising a scheme for making love in plain sight of the beguiled husband. Chaucer's version of this story, the *Merchant's Tale* of "January and May," omits the first part and gives probability to the second part by making the husband blind. Dioneo's final story is a singularly pointless narrative of the return of a soul from Purgatory to assure his friend that it is no more grievous a sin for a godfather to make love to the child's mother than to indulge in any other kind of illicit love.

THE EIGHTH DAY of story telling is devoted to Tricks Played by Men or Women on Each Other. The first story, the plot used by Chaucer in the "Shipman's Tale," is the cleverest of the group, relying on a device whereby a woman who wishes to charge for her favors is effectively maneuvered into a position of having to give them away. The second story is an inferior variation of the same plot. The third and sixth, and the third and fifth stories present the character of an archsimpleton, Calandrino, and the tricks played upon him. In a kind of sequence, the first results in a beating administered to his innocent wife, and the others award her a well-justified revenge. Story Four turns again to the carnal desires of the clergy wherein a rector is fooled by the indifferent lady he desires and is disgraced before the bishop. The fifth story describes an unimaginative method of embarrassing a judge. The seventh trick, far more vicious than the others, describes the revenge of a mistreated wooer. Having been forced by his lady to spend a frigid night in the snow, he retaliates by luring her into a situation whereby her naked body is horribly burned during a day of isolation on the top of a tower. The eighth story, involving an exchange of wives, terminates in the unusual social arrangement of the sharing of husbands and wives by the two married couples. The ninth story turns on another favorite theme of magic and the impositions by would-be magicians upon a credulous neophyte. Dioneo's story keeps to the theme in describing the fitting revenge taken by a merchant upon a lady who, in return for her favors, had cheated him out of all his money.

THE NINTH DAY, on which no theme is set, is devoted to a variety of tales. First, a lady ingeniously rids herself of two troublesome wooers. Then, in a variation of the fourth story of the first day, an abbess who accuses one of the nuns of having a lover is discovered by the nun to be equally guilty. In the fourth tale, a servant plays a scurvy trick upon his master. The sixth story, an elaborate variation on the theme of the traveling salesman and the farmer's daughter, was also told by Chaucer in the "Reeve's Tale." The seventh tale reverts to the then engrossing subject of premonitions in dreams. The eighth story concerns another revenge upon a cheat, and the ninth interprets the veiled advice given by Solomon for the disciplining of an unruly wife. Dioneo concludes with a bawdy but ludicrous description of a priest's cavortings with a wife in the presence and with the approval of her husband.

THE TENTH DAY includes some of the best pure stories in the entire book. Hinging on the theme of Generous Behavior, they are "comedies" and typical medieval romances as on the second day, but with the difference that most of these stories turn on some amazing event or extraordinary point of character, or else involve a moral lesson. The effectiveness of nearly all of them depends on some variety of recognition, surprise, or sudden reversal. Story One, returning to the popular theme of Fortune, relates the method by which a Spanish king convinced a Florentine knight that ill luck was his appointed destiny. Story Two proves that even a churchman can be taught to be magnanimous. Story Three is a kind of parable which revolves about a contest in generosity, the attempt of the loser to kill the winner, and the most remarkable extremes of generosity whereby the winner completely converts the loser from his envy. Story Four makes the most of a kind of Enoch Arden situation and the saintly behavior of a lover who returns his beloved to her husband. Story Five, very similar to Chaucer's "Franklin's Tale," is a variation on the same theme, whereby the lover gains the consent of his lady and her husband by decidedly underhand means, and is subsequently shamed by the husband's nobility into attempting to emulate his generosity. Story Six indicates that even a king can learn to control his shameful desires. The seventh story, also concerned with regal generosity, makes as little sense as its predecessor to readers who have lost their awe of kings. The generosities described in the eighth story likewise depend on a contemporary state of mind concerning the superiority of male friendship over love of a mere woman. Story Nine uses the very popular plot of the generous entertainment of a celebrity traveling incognito and the unexpected and fabulous reward of the host. The concluding story of *The Decameron*, told as usual by Dioneo (of all people), is the last word on the contemporaneously popular subject of patient wives. "Patient Griselda" endures and endures and endures, and earns the dubious eventual reward of not having to endure any longer. Petrarch, who did not approve of *The Decameron*, was so touched by this pathetic tale that he translated it into Latin to give it an enduring form, and Chaucer admired it sufficiently to include it in his *Canterbury Tales* as the "Clerk's Tale." When the story is ended, Pamfilo points out that the morrow will complete fifteen days since they have been together and that more stories might prove an irresistible incentive to lecherous behavior among themselves. He therefore suggests that they return to Florence (plague or no plague!) and after a final song by Fiametta, *The Decameron* concludes with the return of the party to the church where their original meeting had taken place.

Here is a collection of the current stories of the time, picked up here, there, and everywhere by Boccaccio, and retold for no nobler purpose than sheer amusement. Like the anecdotes of any age, these stories told for the story's sake, are not necessarily probable or even believable. An oddity of the entire book is the author's insistence on the fact of the entirely proper behavior of the company in spite of the large proportion of improper stories told, stories that often conclude with a pious prayer on the part of the narrator that the assembled group may continue to enjoy their loves in an equally lusty manner. There is no pat solution to this strange and very obvious discrepancy between speech and behavior; yet it reflects in a way the code of the age by which illicit love was the order of the day provided that absolute discretion and the appearance of decorum were preserved.

Many of the stories are, as has been indicated, the popular romantic narratives of the period, especially the "tragedies" and "comedies." The continuous vein of satire on the clergy and the many descriptions of lecherous churchmen are equally in keeping with the spirit and attitude of the age. Much more individual is Boccaccio's accent on cleverness, whereby a great many of the stories are neither moral nor immoral in intent but find their excuse for being told in pointed witticisms or in neat and dextrous turns of speech or behavior. It is, in fact, indicated by the author that the society women of his time might profitably enhance the attraction of their physical charms by the added adornment of wit. In the accounts of illicit love, success is nearly always the reward of cleverness rather than virtue or nobility. The simpleton, like Calandrino, is the inevitable and apparently deserving victim and laughingstock of the astute.

Distinctive also is Boccaccio's treatment of the science of love. Looking back to his own youthful adventures in Naples, he finds evident relish in detailing the many love encounters that have given *The Decameron* its popular reputation. Some of these stories are bawdy and very witty. Others are bawdy but irresistibly comic in their delineation of utterly ludicrous, however improbable, situations. A rare few are merely bawdy. In most of them much of the humor derives from the multiplicity of elaborate innuendoes whereby copulation or the sexual organs are described. Here, at any rate, is love reduced to its lowest common denominator. The male animal desires possession of the female's body and suffers agonies from frustrated or delayed attainment of his desire. The female, being weaker and having a larger natural capacity for love, suffers even more from being denied complete satisfaction of her sexual urgencies. Whereas Dante turns his back upon a carnal world to experience the complete spiritualization of his Beatrice, one of Boccaccio's ladies terminates the seventh story of the fourth day with the ecstatic comment that Heaven would indeed be heaven if lovers were there permitted as much enjoyment as they had experienced on earth. The only unforgivable sin is the commercialization of sex.

There are probably very few who will subscribe to such a completely physical evaluation and glorification of love; yet Boccaccio, like Rabelais, provides an excellent antidote to the vaporizings of the sentimentally romantic. In his presentation of the human comedy, he also strikes at the very heart of the comic spirit. The elementary situation of the silk-hatted alderman and the banana peel is funny because human pretentiousness is suddenly collapsed. Similar pretentiousness and the conspiracy of silence on the subject of physical love-making is thoroughly deflated by Boccaccio. Somewhere between *The Divine Comedy* and *The Decameron* lies the truth about human love. It does no harm to have both sides of the picture presented even in extreme form. Perhaps the most telling argument that can be urged against Boccaccio in this respect is that instead of a healthy straightforward coarseness, he usually resorts to implication and innuendo. To Boccaccio this suavity was probably his greatest pride, and the comic effect of the undermining of human delicacy is immeasurably enhanced by the unromantic metaphors by which sexual intercourse is variously described.

IMPORTANCE

Boccaccio's claim to fame is his reputation as a storyteller and as the father of Italian prose. In this department, there is no question of his ability. He is indeed occasionally careless and often unnecessarily involved in sentence structure. This latter fault is a fairly obvious result of his devotion to the intricate periods of Cicero. Such involvements are ordinarily at the beginnings of the stories where he accumulates a kind of circumstantial evidence for the veracity of the anecdote by elaborating on the setting and personages of the plot. But when these preliminaries are over, the stories proceed with sure and rapid strokes to their conclusions. The irrelevant or the digression dear to the Middle Ages almost never intrudes, and highly involved situations are exactly and vividly presented with a remarkable economy of language. His very great ability to describe scenes that are seldom static, his rapid narration of events, his natural and vigorous dialogue all flow together without apparent effort. Except for the delineation of extreme types like Calandrino or Griselda, he is not at all concerned with character, but he excels in conveying to the reader the states of mind of the people involved. When all of these qualities are added to an innate capacity for the clever turn of phrase, a great relish for the incongruous, and an ironic detached attitude toward human frailties, the fluid narratives that result constitute the evidence that Boccaccio is one of the greatest masters of the short story of all time.

THE HUMANISTS OF THE FIFTEENTH CENTURY

After the diversified and original writings of the three giants, Dante, Petrarch, and Boccaccio, Italian literature came to a temporary standstill, apparently in deference to Petrarch's repeated pronouncements to the effect that Latin was the only worthy and enduring language. Spurning the vulgar tongue and spurning as well medieval Latin which was still a living language, the humanists who dominated the fifteenth century assiduously cultivated ancient Latin, with Cicero as their model and guide. It is clear that they sincerely believed that classical Latin was to become the universal and eternal language of educated men. They held that a sound education had its foundation in the study of the Church Fathers and the Latin authors, and that the ultimate distinction in scholarship was the ability to write elegant Latin. Although they continued to venerate Christian writers, the heart of the movement lay in the emphasis placed on Greek philosophies and secular learning in general. With a new objectivity they began to study the Greeks and Romans for their own sake, and to emulate the most polished style produced by the ancients. Deriving therefrom a much more exact historical perspective than that of Petrarch and Boccaccio, they mark the beginning in the modern world of the scholarly examination of the classics. One of the humanists, Lorenzo Valla, was able to prove that the *Donation of Constantine* was a forgery by demonstrating that the Latin in which it was written was impossible in Constantine's time.

These men held posts at the various universities and were often subsidized by princes who considered their presence an addition to the prestige of their courts. Under such patronage the discovery of manuscripts, the building of libraries, and the constant broadening of the scope of knowledge continued rapidly. In 1396 Chrysolaras of Constantinople accepted the chair of Greek at Florence. His pupil Battista Guarino, who taught at Bologna and Ferrara, edited the first Greek manual and aided in establishing the first humanist school in Venice. Barzizza, greatest Latin scholar of the time, occupied the chair of Rhetoric at Milan. Poggio, attached to the papal court, was an assiduous collector of manuscripts and composer of moral essays. Petrus Paulus Vergerius, who taught at Florence and Padua, composed a treatise on education, *De Ingenuis Moribus* (*On Liberal Manners*), which was used everywhere. Other outstanding works on education were written by Lionardo Bruni, Chancellor of the Republic of Florence, and Aeneas Silvius who later became Pope Pius II.

Vittorino da Feltre (1378–1446)

One of the most remarkable educators of the time was Vittorino da Feltre. Born in 1378, he was educated at the University of Padua where he remained for nearly twenty years as a teacher of grammar. Having already received the highest degree, having become widely known for his ability as a teacher, and having earned universal popularity because of his personal humility, he undertook privately the teaching of mathematics, for which no chair existed. In 1415 he joined Guarino in establishing a school at Venice, and returned to Padua in 1420 where he took rich and poor alike into his own home to supervise personally their progress in Latin, Greek, and mathematics. A man of high moral character who attempted to combine ancient learning with the highest Christian principles, he became discouraged by the drinking and wild behavior of the students, and left Padua to conduct a private school at Venice. In 1423 he was invited to Mantua where he perfected the first great school of the Renaissance. Beginning by accepting students, rich and poor, for private tutoring, he was given a palace by Gianfrancesco Gonzaga, Lord of Mantua, which he renamed *La Giocosa*, "The House of Delight," and supervised the teaching of some sixty students at a time with the help of able assistants in the cultivation of "a sound mind in a healthy body." Believing always in leading rather than driving, he set a new standard for teaching, and completed a useful and satisfying life in 1446.

Lorenzo Valla (c. 1406–1457)

Of quite a different stamp was the egotistical and sharp-tongued Lorenzo Valla. Born at Rome around 1406 and educated there by Leonardo D'Arezzo in Latin and Giovanni Aurispa in Greek, he became a renowned professor of rhetoric, accepting brief engagements at one university after another until his talents procured him the post of apostolic secretary at the Vatican and gave him the opportunity to found his own school at Rome. His most widely used work, the *Elegantiae linguae latinae* (1471) in which the *Elegances of the Latin Language* are set forth and copiously illustrated, became a kind of a standard phrase book for aspirants to fine Latinity. His greatest originality, however, was displayed in a series of essays in which the principles of nature are championed against the tenets of religion. Preaching a philosophy of hedonism, he insisted long before Rousseau that the natural was the good and that right living was to be found in the instinctive search for happiness. He criticized celibacy, virginity, and even the sacrament of marriage. He praised beauty as a primary source of delight, and especially the beauty of women. While thus completely overturning the medieval ideal, he was so much in harmony with the spirit of the time that he was rewarded by Pope Nicholas V, in spite of torrents of abuse which he had directed against the Church. At the same time he was unbearably arrogant, made innumerable enemies of other scholars who were very nearly as jealous of their own abilities as he, and, in the midst of endless vitriolic controversies, he died at Naples in 1457.

The Platonic Academy

In 1438 representatives of the Eastern and Western divisions of the Catholic Church met at Florence to attempt a reconciliation. With the Eastern delegates came two philosophers of the Neoplatonic school, Gemistho

Pletho and Bessarion, who stimulated an already reviving interest in the works of Plato, particularly the *Symposium*. Valla's enthusiasm for feminine beauty, together with the enthronement of woman by Dante and Petrarch, prepared the ground for a ready acceptance of the new philosophy. Augustine had said that the Platonists were "almost Christian," and it was by no means difficult to transmute Jacob's ladder into the ladder of love (*Scala d'Amore*) by which the initiate mounts by successive steps from earthly to heavenly beauty. Under the patronage of Cosimo de' Medici, a Platonic Academy was founded at Florence to enlarge the knowledge of Plato and to reconcile Neoplatonism with Christianity. The most notable of the priests of this new cult was Marsilio Ficino who translated the works of Plato and of the Neoplatonist Plotinus, and who, with more enthusiasm than acumen, insisted that all philosophies were essentially alike and that Christianity was the revelation of the identical truth which philosophers had arrived at by reason.

One of his pupils, Girolamo Benivieni, became a poet after the new mode, elaborating the specific rungs of the ladder of love whereby the lover rises from the attraction of a beautiful face to the concept of beauty itself and from that to a yearning for that Ultimate Divine Beauty which will be revealed only beyond the grave. In England Edmund Spenser was later to attempt this same kind of reconciliation of Christianity and Platonism in his *Fowre Hymnes*.

THE REVIVAL OF THE VERNACULAR

Although the period of the humanists did nothing to further Italian literature at the time, it had undeniable effects on the revival of composition in the vulgar tongue which followed. The setting of standards in scholarship and literature led to a series of books like *The Courtier,* which attempted to set similar standards for human conduct. The analytical methods of the humanists resulted in more painstaking evaluations of history and realistic analyses of government such as Machiavelli's *Prince*. The cult of Platonism, linked with the devotion to beauty in women, found many variations of expression both in prose and verse. Even the studied artificiality which resulted from the cultivation of elegant Latin was carried over into an attempt to make Italian a highly formal and distinguished language.

Lorenzo de' Medici (1448–1492)

The return to Italian as a literary language was principally owed to Lorenzo de' Medici, celebrated member of a remarkable Florentine family of businessmen. His great-grandfather, Giovanni, had acquired wealth and esteem and was honored by being granted various offices in the Republic of Florence until his death in 1428. One of Giovanni's sons, Cosimo, carried on his honorable reputation and added to it the patronage of science and learning signalized by the founding of the Platonic Academy. A grandson of Cosimo and son of Piero, who was also a patron of letters, Lorenzo de' Medici was instructed by Ficino and became a devoted adherent of the Platonic Academy and the current attempts to emulate the ancient Roman court of Augustus. He won the first prize in a revival of the tournament, studied the ancients assiduously, wrote love sonnets, and became the devoted platonic lover of an unknown mistress. In 1469 he was invited to take charge of the government of the city, and as "Lorenzo the Magnificent" he ruled Florence as a benevolent dictator, a tyrant with the consent of the governed. At a time of extraordinary peril he maintained the integrity of Florence in the face of almost constant conspiracies on the part of the pope and rival secular powers by rare diplomatic skill and astute political maneuvering. His "magnificence" asserted itself in the public celebrations held in honor of Plato, the "Triumphs" or pageants of allegorical floats accompanied by music and poetry, much of which he composed for the occasions, the holding of games and races in which he himself participated, the high level of behavior and conversation at the court, the retention of scholars and poets of whom he made personal friends, and the generally sumptuous and exquisite conduct of what amounted to an unofficial royal household.

In 1488 he invited the reformer Savonarola of Ferrara to Florence, allowing him complete liberty in his attack on luxuriousness and even upon himself. After attempting to instruct his son Piero in the art of government, he died in 1492, his death occasioning widespread grief and deeply felt public mourning. It was after his death that Savonarola whipped the Florentines into the frenzy that established him briefly as the head of a theocratic government during which Piero (who also wrote poetry) was exiled. The Medici were later restored to power in Florence and continued to distinguish themselves both in government and in patronage of the arts and scholarship. One of Lorenzo's sons became the renowned Pope Leo X in 1513, a great executive, churchman, and patron of letters. In 1532 Giulano de' Medici assumed the papacy as Clement VII. Another Lorenzo, son of Piero, also governed Florence, and his daughter Catherine de' Medici became queen of Henry II of France and the mother of three other kings.

Lorenzo's poetic career and defense of Italian began as early as 1465, when he sent some samples of his work to Frederick of Naples by way of defending the use of the vernacular. In 1476 he completed a sonnet sequence of Platonic love poetry together with a prose commentary, in the vein of Dante's *Vita Nuova*, and an extended defense of the Tuscan language. This was followed by the *Selve d'Amore* (*Forest of Love*) (1480), in which he celebrates his meeting with the unknown Lucrezia and his rise from carnal desire through the stages of Platonic love to the contemplation of pure beauty. The theme of the work is Ficino's, but the tone of gaiety and the natural, if not over-inspired, descriptions of the commonplaces of youthful ardor are his own. His principal originality lies in the insertion of backgrounds of natural scenery. His love of nature, particularly flowers, is a new note and an obviously sincere one. Some of his later poetry is deliberate imitation of the Roman poet Ovid, involving metamorphosis and eroticism. For the sake of his mother he also wrote hymns and a religious play.

His best work, *La Nencia da Barberina* (*Nencia of Barberina*) (1474), in *ottava rima*, leaves the classic world far behind to talk of the honest love of the peasant Vallera for the country girl Nencia. Vallera has clearly been to the city, and in a series of eight-line poems he attempts to imitate the style, manner and substance of the sophisticated sonnet sequences. The result is a ludicrous combination of borrowed artificial phrases and down-to-earth realistic rustic similies. It is an original idea and the kind of parody that makes it hard to say whether the courtier or the peasant is being the more ridiculed. Best of all is the breath of fresh air amidst so much artificial versification and the clear enthusiasm for rustic feelings, frank statements, and images drawn from observation rather than study. It is fortunate that the reputation of Lorenzo the Magnificent does not have to depend on his literary productions; yet they are interesting testimonials to the breadth of his character and were important in their time as incentives to the restoration of literature written in Italian.

Poliziano (Angelo Ambrogino) (1454–1494)

Angelo Ambrogino, called Poliziano from his birthplace Montepulciano, was one of the writers who was closely associated with Lorenzo. Brought to Florence when he was ten years old, he studied at the Academy, aroused a great deal of attention by his talents, and was taken into Lorenzo's household at the age of nineteen. Remaining a close friend of his patron until Lorenzo's death, he became one of the finest scholars and teachers of his time, writing distinguished prose and poetry in both Latin and Greek.

As a distinct side issue, probably in deference to Lorenzo's championship of the vernacular, he wrote a few pieces in Italian. The first, written in two days when he was only seventeen years old, was a play designed to provide momentary entertainment for a special occasion. As in England, the only theatrical performances had been mystery plays depicting in simple terms Biblical narratives and events from the lives of the saints. Poliziano accomplished at one stroke the transition from religious to secular drama by adapting a classical story to the form of the *sacra reppresentazione* (religious play). Using the story of Orpheus and Eurydice, he created in his *Orfeo* (1480) a graceful, beautifully finished idyll which, in its combination of poetic dialogue and song, is also a precursor to the opera. (The first Italian opera used the same subject.)

After a brief outline of the plot delivered by Mercury, Scene One reveals the rustic Mopsus in search of his calf. Pausing to talk with the shepherds Aristaeus and Thyrsis, he hears of the passion of Aristaeus for a beautiful woman (Eurydice) he had seen the day before. After the interlude of an enchanting love song describing her flight from love ("Tell her, lute, that beauty fades"), Thyrsis, who has gone off to tend his flock, returns with news of having seen the maiden. Aristaeus exits to find her. A brief second scene describing the pursuit by Aristaeus is followed by a chorus of dryads in Scene Three lamenting the death of Eurydice who was stung by a serpent during the pursuit. One dryad tells her husband Orpheus. Scene Four is devoted mainly to a long and eloquent speech whereby Orpheus in Hades convinces Pluto to relinquish Eurydice in memory of his own love. In the fifth scene Orpheus loses Eurydice, and in the last scene he renounces love and women, railing at their lightness and inconstancy. A chorus of maenads drag him off and kill him in fury. A highly rhythmic paean to Bacchus by the chorus ("Each one, Bacchus, worships thee; Bacchus, Bacchus, eù, oè!") closes the play. Not dramatic in the sense of being tragedy or comedy, failing to dignify the catastrophe of the fifth and sixth scenes, this play nevertheless instituted a new form of drama known as the pastoral, which substitutes pleasantness for dramatic conflict and finds its excellence in light, delicate, and fluid entertainment. Written with a facile grace of style, it represents a special kind of talent for the tapestry-like movement of scene and event which distinguished the late Italian Renaissance and found its most effective form in Italian opera.

Poliziano's other outstanding Italian work is the unfinished *Stanze (Stanzas)* (1475) celebrating a tournament held by Giuliano de' Medici in 1475 in honor of Simonetta Cattaneo. What there is of this elaborate poem merely describes the role of Cupid in causing Giuliano's heart to be smitten by the beauty of Simonetta and prepares the way for a description of the tournament by having Cupid extol the glories of Lorenzo and invite Giuliano to emulate him by glory in arms. All in the same tone of sweetness and delicacy, the monotony of long drawn out descriptions kills what little life the subject might have inspired. But as decoration, the creation of this series of minutely detailed word pictures provided the specifications for Botticelli's *Primavera* and *Birth of Venus*. As seen in the plethora of great paintings of this period, the special genius of the Italian Renaissance seems to have been primarily pictorial and decorative. Poliziano also wrote a series of songs both in the Petrarchan manner and in the new more realistic rustic mode of Lorenzo, but he was always more concerned with polish than with feeling.

Luigi Pulci (1432–1484)

The other contribution to Italian literature which resulted from the patronage of Lorenzo de' Medici was the first of a series of romantic epics composed by the somewhat frivolous rhymer Luigi Pulci. For many years professional minstrels had entertained audiences with tales derived from the "three matters." Since these were lengthy narratives, they were usually prolonged through several performances. Consequently it became a tradition for the minstrel to break off his narrative at a critical point in order to assure himself of a good audience when the story was later resumed. This method, adopted by Pulci and his followers, resulted in the custom of breaking off cantos in the midst of action. Of the many stories current all over Europe, those dealing with Charlemagne and his peers found particular favor in Italy.

Pulci was retained by Lorenzo apparently for the purpose of providing light random entertainment, and when Lorenzo's mother asked for a Carolingian story in rhyme he could hardly refuse to oblige her. The result was a romance in *ottava rima* of twenty-three cantos composed over a period of ten years, and an additional five cantos appended twelve years later. Because of this later addition the entire poem came to be known as *The Greater Morgante* (*Il Morgante Maggiore*) (1482). He uses the common Italian version of the French material in which Orlando (Roland) and Rinaldo (Regnault) are the principal heroes. Through the agency of the traitor Gano (Ganelon) one or the other is repeatedly betrayed but overcomes the villainy by incredible exploits. On the framework of such a rudimentary situation, minstrels had created endless variations and a type of literature known as the romantic epic. It is epic in its dealing with folklore and tradition; romantic in the irresponsible addition of every variety of decorative episode invented on the spur of the moment with no faintest regard for either historicity or probability.

Pulci's version is a wild hodgepodge of ridiculous events in doggerel verse that debases whatever of the heroic there was in the basic story by describing both characters and events in a vein of irreverence and low comedy. Intending to produce a humorous effect possibly by way of parodying the stories which were the delight of the common people, Pulci now and again creates a genuinely ludicrous scene or produces amusement by a sudden descent into bathos or by a preposterous side comment on a scene. But the joke wears thin very rapidly, and the task of satirizing what is absurd to begin with is clearly beyond his powers. Perhaps wearying of his own forced jesting, he became much more serious in the last five cantos and apparently took considerable interest in the sheer process of stringing events together. Byron, who described him as the "sire of the half-serious rhyme," translated the first canto of the epic and confessed that he owed the manner of *Don Juan* to Pulci's inspiration.

Count Matteo Maria Boiardo (1434–1494)

The first Italian poet to make serious use of the material which Pulci had parodied was Count Matteo Maria Boiardo. He was born in 1434 at Scandiano on one of the family estates, and acquired the highest degrees in philosophy and law after an education at the University of Ferrara. He became attached to the most aristocratic and most completely feudal court in Italy, the court of Ferrara, ruled over by the long-established Este family. From the two successive dukes under whom he served, he received many government appointments, the highest of which made him governor of the town of Reggio where he died in 1494. His writing was done in intermittent periods of seclusion on his estates, and many of the names of the characters in his epic appear to have been derived from the local peasants he met there. His literary productivity was small, but it includes a Petrarchan sonnet sequence addressed to Antonio Caprara, in which a very sincere and honest love is expressed with a minimum of the conventional conceits common to love lyrics of this type.

For the amusement of the Duke and his court, he began the composition of the elaborate romantic epic *Orlando Innamorato* (*Orlando in Love*) (1495). The very title suggests the inclusion of a new note in the use of the Charlemagne material. The "matter of France" dealt almost exclusively with tales of mighty adventure and heroic deeds. The "matter of Britain," comprising the Arthurian legends, was centered much more on the subject of love. It was the ingenious and entirely deliberate idea of Boiardo to combine the two appeals. In the second canto he explains that the court of Arthur preceded that of Charlemagne, that the Frankish court had ignored the power of love, and that he proposes to remedy this defect since love is the primary inspiration for all noble deeds. On this basis, Boiardo weaves the usual intricate pattern of battle, magic, pursuit, and fantasy, occasionally revealing a faint glimmer of amusement but principally concerned with weaving a colorful tapestry of brilliant events.

The basic plot that serves as a framework for the varied episodes gets under way on the occasion of a great feast held by Charlemagne at which Angelica of Cathay, the bewitching Saracen, puts in her appearance together with her brother Argalio. All of the paladins, including Charlemagne, are stricken by her beauty, but especially Orlando who loses all sense of everything except his sudden overwhelming passion. During a subsequent tournament in which Argalio fights all potential suitors of his sister and is defeated by Ferrau, Angelica disappears, and three of the paladins, Ferrau, Orlando, and Rinaldo, set out in search of her. During the pursuit, Rinaldo drinks water from a magic spring of hate, which causes him to abstain from the quest and go to sleep. Angelica drinks of a neighboring spring of love, and, seeing the sleeping Rinaldo, becomes infatuated with him. Thereupon, Angelica pursues the fleeing Rinaldo and is in turn pursued by the passionate Orlando.

Exhausted by the pursuit, Angelica falls asleep. Orlando espies her and is gazing spellbound at her beauty when Ferrau appears to claim her. Ferrau and Orlando engage in combat until Angelica is awakened and takes refuge in invisibility through the aid of a magic ring. A messenger summons Ferrau to Spain to engage in a war that has broken out, and Orlando sets out in search of Angelica. Angelica meanwhile persuades the magician Malgigi to conduct Rinaldo to an island that she rules. Rinaldo escapes, but is about to be devoured by a monster when Angelica rescues him. Still spurning her, he continues on his way. At the same time, Orlando meets a sorceress who gives him a potion of forgetfulness and holds him captive on another island.

The other knights who have fallen in love with Angelica set out on an invasion of her father's city. Apprised of this, Angelica rescues Orlando and enlists his aid on her father's behalf. After an indecisive battle with Rinaldo en route, Orlando goes to the salvation of Cathay and returns to France with Angelica, who pretends that she has become a Christian. On the way back through the forest, they encounter the same two fountains of love and hate. Angelica drinks of the fountain of hate and is freed from her love of Rinaldo. Rinaldo coincidentally drinks from the opposite fountain and now is frantic with desire of Angelica. Orlando's jealousy is so aroused that Charlemagne intervenes, declaring that Angelica shall be the prize for whoever fights most valiantly in the war that has been brought about by the monarch Gradasso's determination to possess Orlando's sword Durinda and Rinaldo's horse Bayardo. During the varied adventures of the war, Orlando and Rinaldo are accompanied by the Amazonian Bradamante, Rinaldo's sister. Their mightiest opponents are Ruggiero and the pagan Rodomonte, whose continual boasting has added the word *rodomontade* to the English language.

Both of these major themes of love and war are constantly interrupted by the introduction of all manner of subsidiary incidents and stories taken from all three "matters," and possibly occasionally invented by the author himself. Written in *ottava rima*, the now-traditional form of the romantic epic, the poem represents a sincere attempt to tell a complicated and entertaining traditional story with vigor and skill, stressing action and creating multiple suspense by turning from a crucial moment in one episode to continue or begin another.

In the midst of the third book, with a little more than sixty-nine cantos completed, the poem is suddenly broken off with a reminder of Italy's parlous political position in the midst of this entertaining unreality: "I see France arming against Italy and the horizon bright with flames. Hereafter, I will piece out the tale which I leave unfinished, if it be permitted me." That was in 1494 when Charles VIII invaded Italy. Boiardo did not live to complete his work, but an inferior writer, Niccolo degli Agostini, later added three more books to it. Years later, in 1541, a revision of Boiardo's poem called the *Refacimento* (*Recasting*) was published and became much more popular than the original. The author, Francesco Berni (1490–1536), was a popular comic or burlesque poet who added comments, satire, and moral reflections to the opening of each canto and revised the entire poem, line by line, substituting polish and refinement for its original earthy vigor.

Jacopo Sannazaro (1458–1530)

The revival of Italian in Florence and Ferrara was echoed in Naples by the writings of Jacopo Sannazaro. A student of Pontano, who was a Neapolitan humanist and one of the most original Latin verse and prose writers of the time, Sannazaro became attached to the court and also wrote a great deal in Latin, including a religious epic. In a lighter vein he composed a considerable amount of Italian verse and a kind of pastoral for the local fishermen called the *Eclogae Piscatoriae* (1526), which was imitated by the English Phineas Fletcher in his *Piscatory Eclogues*.

His principal Italian work is the *Arcadia* (1495), a pastoral romance of twelve chapters in prose and verse. Rejecting the Neapolitan dialect as uncouth, he deliberately chose the literary Italian of Petrarch and Boccaccio to present an urbane and debonair account of the joys and loves of shepherds, where everything is beautiful and the only hindrance to pure delight is that the beloved does not always return the affection of the lover. What plot there is concerns the unhappy lover Sincero who has come to Arcadia to find peace for his aching heart. He takes pleasure in the peasants' songs and ceremonies, and hears their stories. Sincero tells them his own story of unrequited love and eventually returns home to find his lady dead. One of the peasant stories is devoted to the grief of the shepherd Ergastus who fails to respond to the beauties of nature or to the songs of his friend Selvaggius. Besought to reveal the reason for his melancholy, he describes how he swooned at sight of the loveliness of a maiden whom he chanced to spy singing and washing her clothes in a stream. Although she ran to help him, she remained cold to his protestations of love. Now he roams about calling her name and inscribing it on trees.

Sannazaro's devotion to the ancients appears in the deliberate and elaborate compliment of building up the scenes of his book by phrases taken from Longus, Theocritus, Bion, Moschus, Virgil, Ovid, Catullus, and many other Greek and Latin writers. The subject, the idea of escaping from urban cares to sylvan simplicity, and the mannered treatment of nature and nature's children had many imitators, the best known being the Portuguese *Diana* by Montemayor and the English *Arcadia* by Sidney. In a less obvious way the same basic idea is reflected in Shakespeare's *As You Like It,* where the royal court turns rustic in the Forest of Arden.

The Novella

Meanwhile, unaffected by the quarrel between the defenders of Latin and the writers of Italian, the popularity of the novella or short story, as indicated by the reception accorded *The Decameron*, continued to insure the production of short narratives that have little literary merit but provided plots for many later writers and contain many glimpses of the people and manners of the time. The stories, as already seen in *The Decameron*, tend to fall into four categories: the anecdote told for its point alone, the practical joke at the expense of a simpleton, satire directed principally against the clergy, and romance mainly involving pathetic accounts of tragic love among aristocratic characters. One of the most ambitious collections was made by Franco Sacchetti, a Florentine who composed three hundred novellas between 1388 and 1395. Most of the two hundred and twenty which have survived are anecdotes and practical jokes, generally brief and often told of well-known figures like Dante and Giotto.

In the fifteenth century the outstanding collection was published in Naples in 1476 by Masuccio of Salerno and entitled *Il Novellino.* Violently attacking monks and priests, audaciously telling libelous tales about living people, indulging an obvious appetite for the obscene, he arranges his fifty stories in moral categories and concludes each with the hypocrisy of a lecture against the vice just described. An apparently really moral writer, Giambattista Giraldi Cinzio (or Cinthio), published in 1565 a hundred and twelve stories designed to prove the superiority of virtue over vice under the title *Ecatommithi (The Hundred Tales).* Another prominent sixteenth century collection is Antonfrancesco Grazzini's *Cene* or *Banquets*, modelled on Boccaccio in having the stories told by a group of young men and women before and after dinner on successive occasions. He also follows Boccaccio in his fondness for the amusing anecdote, and he considerably outdoes his master in lasciviousness and brutality, or so it would seem from the twenty-two of the stories which have survived. The *Tredici Notte Piacevoli* or *Thirteen Nights of Entertainment* by Gianfrancesco Straparola, which also uses the scheme of *The Decameron*, differs from the others chiefly in its use of the supernatural and in the telling of folktales like *Puss-in-Boots,* which have become universally known.

The most talented successor to Boccaccio was Matteo Bandello (c. 1480–1561). A Dominican monk later made a bishop, he was obviously more interested in secular than in religious life. He wrote a considerable amount of poetry and was a conscientious workman who composed with great care the two hundred and fourteen tales which make up his *Novelle.* In spite of his position, a great many of the tales sharply satirize the Church, and several stories of actual fact are included. Although not possessed of innate literary ability, Bandello tells a story directly and vigorously with the effect of spontaneity and the inclusion of many lively touches. He is at his best in the vein of romance, providing many plots like that of *Romeo and Juliet* for later dramatists. Some of the narratives indulge the contemporary appetite for horror; others deal lightly and amusingly with the theme of love; some are obscene. But like Boccaccio, Bandello was a man of the world who wrote only to entertain. Human beings do indulge in gross behavior and they are not condemned by Bandello who says, in connection with the customary berating of women, "I am not minded to blame either men or women, for my mother was a woman, and I was born a man."

NICCOLÒ MACHIAVELLI (1469–1527)

IMPORTANCE

"Machiavellian politics" and "Machiavellian intrigue" are common terms that bring to mind the unscrupulous, the expedient, the slick. This reputation that has accrued to Machiavelli is entirely justified on the basis of his most famous political treatise; but *The Prince* is also the product of a particular political situation, a monument to the new objective method of scholarship developed by the humanists, and a foretaste of the attempt to establish universal principles of behavior.

Niccolò Machiavelli was born in Florence in 1469 of a family whose ancestors boasted of noble blood. After having been apparently well educated, he entered public life in the Florentine Republic in 1494 by holding a minor office, from which he was elevated to posts of considerable importance. This was during the period of Savonarola's brief dictatorship and the later restoration of the republican form of government. The wealthy city was hard put to it to maintain its independence, and Machiavelli, who was made secretary to the Republic in 1498, was engaged in many diplomatic missions abroad, through which he undoubtedly learned the necessity of shrewdness in the game of politics. In 1502 he married Marietta Corsini, who bore him several children and with whom he apparently lived amicably in spite of his own infidelities. During the same year he was sent to treat with and observe Cesare Borgia, who was then successfully engaged in the great design of creating a firm temporal state for the Church. Observing the astuteness of Cesare's moves and the practical success that attended them, Machiavelli was later able to use him as a model of effective statecraft.

On his return to Florence in 1503 he instituted a project to create a national militia, which he pushed through in spite of the many objections that were raised, such as fear of rebellion or military dictatorship. After the collapse of the Borgias, Machiavelli attended the new pope, Julius II, in a military campaign against his rebellious provinces, traveled through Switzerland and into Germany to visit the Emperor Maximilian, and somehow found time to write his poetic *Decennali* (*Annals of Italy*) (1509) and a play that has been lost. Returning from Germany in 1508 he was largely instrumental in carrying out a successful campaign against Pisa, which fell in 1509. In 1512 Cardinal Giovanni de' Medici completed a march into Tuscany with the aid of Spanish troops and was accepted as governor of Florence.

At the termination of the Republic, Machiavelli seems to have hoped to retain his position under a new master for whom he had no apparent dislike. Instead, he was exiled for a year and, upon the outbreak of a minor conspiracy, he was tortured and briefly imprisoned although he was not actually implicated in the attempted revolution. In 1513 he retired to a farm near San Casciano, where his active mind found exercise in the composition of what remain his major works. Gradually, in part as a result of his political writings, he was restored to favor if not to eminence. In 1527 the Medici were again expelled and the Republic reinstituted. Machiavelli's final disappointment came when he found that he was not acceptable as a member of the new government, and he died a few weeks after its formation.

Machiavelli's special talents were those of a political analyst and military commentator. From his own practical understanding of the affairs of state he wrote his *Discorsi sul Primo Libro delle Deche di Tito Livio* (*Discourses on the First Decade of Titus Livy*) (1518) on Livy's *History of Rome*, examining the origin, maintenance, and decline of states, and attempting to deduce from history effective principles for the formation and organization of successful government. He concludes that the republic is the ideal form of government but that a constitutional monarchy is much more secure at the contemporary stage of political development since it checks alike the emotional extremes of both ruler and people. His uncompleted *Istorie Fiorentine* (*History of*

Florence) (1520-1524) is a modern kind of history, which examines causes as well as events, and is provided with a similar commentary or interpretation of history.

The Prince

The best known of Machiavelli's political analyses, sometimes described as a "handbook for dictators," is the relatively short work entitled *Il Principe* or *The Prince* (1513). He planned originally to dedicate it to Giuliano de' Medici who, being installed in Florence by his brother Giovanni, now Pope Leo X, was in a position to consummate at least part of Machiavelli's dream of a united Italy. When Giuliano died in 1516, however, Machiavelli could find no better candidate than another member of the Medici family, and accordingly inscribed the book to Lorenzo, the lesser Lorenzo who was Giuliano's nephew and was the last of the Medici to govern Florence.

To gain something like perspective on the much vilified author of *The Prince*, one should read the dedication and the last chapter (XXVI) first. In the dedication is to be found the forthright statement of Machiavelli's desire to be restored to political activity. But along with this fawning request to be allowed to engage again in the kind of life that was his passion is the concluding flaming exhortation to the prince to lead Italy in a united drive to throw off foreign domination. His analysis of the factors that brought Italy to its current dilemma is exact and just; his dream of unification was inspired by the models of France, Spain, and England. For Machiavelli was an Italian as well as a Florentine, and with the abandonment of Dante's cherished scheme of Roman Empire, the practical road to peace lay clearly in the establishment of an Italian nation. Because of this underlying state of mind, the advice given in *The Prince* is intended for a rising leader rather than for an established ruler. And there must have been many Italians besides Machiavelli who would then have echoed the words of Cardinal Bellarmine, "It is better to have an evil prince than no prince at all."

Whatever the ultimate incentive that caused Machiavelli to write the book, its subject provided free scope for an objective analysis of political man. Using the new methods of scholarship, Machiavelli coldly examines the problems of conquest and government. Drawing illustrations from the facts of history, he demonstrates the rules of the game, and is no more concerned with what ought to be or who ought to win than an expert writing a manual on bridge. In his fifteenth chapter he strikes the keynote of practical realism, explaining that "it has seemed wiser to me to follow the real truth of the matter than what we imagine it to be." One might be tempted to say that Machiavelli's resulting estimate of man as a political animal is an accurate picture only of his own age, which was unused to democratic procedures and was too poorly educated for representative government. One would be so tempted were it not for the dictators of recent years, some of whom might have lasted longer had they adhered even more than they did to Machiavelli's precepts.

The principles of establishing and maintaining government, many of which apply equally well to leadership in a democracy, are founded on Machiavelli's estimate of human nature. Men, he says, are generally simple-minded, gullible, forgetful, fickle, greedy, and wicked. They are easily taken in by display and dramatic behavior. The would-be governor must therefore preserve always the appearance of generosity, piety, justice, and, above all, firmness and dramatic decisiveness in action. He may then, to gain his practical ends, indulge in treachery, cruelty, or oppression, provided that he acts circumspectly or attacks only minorities or behaves so only at infrequent intervals. Possibly feeling that something is lacking in the formula, Machiavelli is forced to admit that such procedures are not always successful and that a great deal depends on fortune. The ablest leader in the world cannot create favorable circumstances, but the successful ruler is he who is able to recognize the propitious moment when it comes and to apply these principles with an unwavering hand.

The first two chapters of *The Prince* are devoted to a rapid definition of the field of politics to be examined. Dividing monarchies into the classes of hereditary and acquired, he notes that the sheer effect of custom on human behavior is so strong that the hereditary type offers no problem and may be eliminated from the discussion. Turning then to new monarchies, he launches into a series of observations of all sorts and in no particular order on methods of governing newly acquired states. Occasionally he reduces his observations to such maxims as these: Men must be flattered or crushed. Force is the best persuader. A prince must shrewdly estimate current forces and play the majority against the minority. Evil is permissible if necessary. A prince must present as perfect a character as possible outwardly; his private life may be as licentious as he pleases. A prince should be spectacular and heroic. A prince need not keep his word if it is not expedient to do so. Some of Machiavelli's own theories, such as the superiority of a native militia over mercenaries, are, of course, included, together with many bits of shrewd advice. In international politics, for example, he advises the defense of weak neighboring states and a policy of diplomacy aimed at dividing and weakening the strong. He is aware that a feudal state with its many noblemen is less manageable than an absolute monarchy, and consequently urges a strong central government. He advises the greatest care in the selection of subordinates and advisers, since a head of government is inevitably at their mercy. After law and order have been established, innovations should be avoided unless absolutely necessary.

The readability of this textbook is the result of Machiavelli's informal and chatty style, which is at the same time rapid and clear, and his own love of the dramatic which fills the book with startling generalities and spectacular illustrations.

La Mandragola

Another side of Machiavelli's genius was displayed in the writing of a series of comedies on the Latin model but depicting scenes of Florentine middle class life. The best of these, *La Mandragola* (*The Mandrake*), was written after 1512 in his retirement, and illustrates again his essential realism and cynicism but also a lively vein of humor. Based on the supposed magical effects of the mandrake root in producing virility, the plot revolves about the love of the clever Callimaco for Lucrezia, who is saddled with a wealthy simpleton for a husband. Nincia, the husband who desires children, falls prey to the wiles of Callimaco, who masquerades as a doctor, and, through a series of extravagant wiles, finally persuades Nincia to put Lucrezia in bed with the doctor. The best comedy of Renaissance Italy, this unmoral piece of foolishness, reminiscent of Boccaccio and foreshadowing English Restoration drama, is filled with clever sallies and boisterously comic situations. The characterizations present a wonderfully varied gallery of types: the simple-minded husband, the plastic wife, the adventurous lover, the hypocritical priest, the profligate parasite, and the worldly mother. Here too reappears Machiavelli's apparently basic theory that "virtue" is boldness or strength of character, which inevitably succeeds in a world populated by hypocrites, charlatans, and fools.

BALDASSARE CASTIGLIONE (1478–1529)

Machiavelli's analysis of political man was destined to be generally reviled by the world and frequently consulted by politicians. More in keeping with the tone of an age that preferred charm and elegance to overmuch pondering on the tragic political condition of Italy was Castiglione's standardization of the ideal gentleman of society. His handbook of manners, *The Courtier*, was destined to be a universal guide for elegant deportment, and had much to do with the establishment all over Europe of the salons of the seventeenth century.

Baldassare Castiglione was born in 1478 at Casatico in Mantuan territory. Of a noble family, his mother being a bosom friend of Isabella d'Este, he was well schooled at Milan and entered the service of Lodovico Sforza, Duke of Milan, in 1496. When Sforza was taken to France as prisoner in 1500, he transferred his services to the Mantuan Francesco Gonzaga, and became attached in 1504 to the court of Guidobaldo Maletesta, Duke of Urbino. While holding high offices and being engaged in diplomatic missions, he was also a model courtier in society, idolizing the Duchess of Urbino and finding time to write an eclogue in the tradition of the time. When Guidobaldo died without issue in 1508 and the pope gave Urbino to Francesco Maria della Rovere, Castiglione was retained as envoy for the pope. On a papal mission to Spain in 1524 he was greatly honored and made Bishop of Avila. Although distinguished for fidelity and gentlemanly behavior, he was accused of treachery when the marauding army of Spanish and German troops, supposedly acting for French imperialism, captured the pope in 1527, and he died shortly thereafter—it was said of grief and shame—in 1529. *The Courtier* (*Il Cortegiano*) was written in 1514. It was published in 1528 just before Castiglione's death, became immediately popular, and was translated into English by Sir Thomas Hoby as early as 1561.

The Courtier

The four books of *The Courtier* are written in the form of a dialogue purporting to record a conversation held at the court of Urbino, through which the ideals of the courtier are specified and at the same time exemplified in the intelligence, taste, and graciousness of the speakers who are real personages rather than fictitious spokesmen. Book I tells something of the history and the glory of the court, and then turns to a typical after-dinner gathering held by the Duchess Elizabeth. In a most natural and charming manner, a random conversation leads to a proposal to play the game of "Questions." Several possible topics are proposed, during which an urbane, sophisticated group touch on questions of language, painting, and personal topics which are enlivened by anecdotes, jests, and witty repartee. It is finally decided to discuss the perfect courtier. In the same lively and genial manner the figure of the perfect gentleman is gradually built up. He must be versed in all the arts of war and skill. He must have knowledge of literature and the fine arts. He must always act with ease, effortlessness, grace, *savoir faire*.

On the following evening the participants gather again, and Book II begins with fuller elaborations of gentlemanly sports, clothes, and relationships with others and with one's prince. A long interpolated discourse on jests results in the telling of many stories, a division of jests into types, and a warning against unseemly talk concerning the honor of women. At this, three of the gentlemen belittle women and are descended upon by all the women in a body. The chief result of this altercation is the conclusion that love must be more than physical and that forced love or treacherous love is like making love to a corpse. This quarrel about women—beasts or angels?—was echoed by many other authors who took sides in what came to be known as the *"Querelle des Femmes."* At the end of the evening it is decided to devote the next meeting to a discussion of the perfect court lady.

Book III reveals the perfect lady as corresponding in most respects to the perfect gentleman. Her chief virtue is in inspiring men to do great deeds. Another attack by the misogynists leads to the recounting of stories of famous women showing them equal to or better than men. Then follows a discussion on the broad subject of chastity in women and on the delicate question of how, to whom, and when to make love, during which women are rather debased on grounds of cruelty and inconstancy, but from which proceeds the concept that woman, employing a kind of golden mean of reserve, encouraging the bashful and checking the impudent, should be the intelligent and beautiful inspiration of the gentleman, administering to the worthy the benison of love. It is finally decided to return, on the following evening, to the subject of the courtier, since so much remains to be said.

The concluding book concerns the more serious side of the courtier. He is to be considerably more than an ornament, and his intelligence and poise are to be used in services to the state. Reverting finally to the subject of love, the book specifies the refinements of gentlemanly courtship, and the work ends with a discourse, from the lips of Cardinal Bembo, on Platonic love.

Young men may love sensually, but the mature love spiritually. Kisses are permissible since the soul comes to the lips. Contemplation of earthly beauty raises the soul to the heavenly. The Cardinal is so carried away by his own eloquence that he stands in a trance, from which he is roused by the caution that his soul may forsake his body unless he returns to earth. His response is, "Madam, it would not be the first miracle that love has wrought in me." After mention that women are also capable of this perfect love, the assembled company decides to put off further talk until the morrow, whereupon they discover that it is already dawn and that only one star, Venus, remains in the sky.

IMPORTANCE

The Courtier, mingling sense and fancifulness, emphasizing intellectual acumen, spiritual grace, genteel behavior, and moral stability, is a kind of ultimate symbol of the contribution made by the Italian Renaissance to the arts and refinements of living. With scarcely any changes, the principles set forth became the standards of good behavior in all succeeding societies, including our own. The normal manners of polite society, implied in the group of storytellers of the *Decameron*, are here specified, enlarged upon, and as much dignified by seriousness of purpose as made attractive by the gracious, pleasant tone of the dialogue itself.

Other books on manners were Giovanni della Casa's *Galateo* on upright and elegant behavior, published in 1558, and Agnolo Firenzuola's Platonic discourse *On the Beauty of Women* (*Dialogo delle Bellezze delle Donne*) published in 1548.

MINOR POETS

Vittoria Colonna (1490–1547) and
Michelangelo Buonarotti (1475–1564)

A natural result of the revival of Platonism as seen in the above dialogues was the return to popularity of the Petrarchan sonnet. Simultaneously, Castiglione's ideal lady came to life in the Marchioness of Pescara, Vittoria Colonna. After a marriage of real love in 1509, her husband's absence at war, which included a protracted imprisonment, left her free to create her own highly cultivated court over which she presided with great charm and brilliance. Left a widow at the age of thirty-six, she retired for a time to a nunnery and, upon her return to secular life, began her career as a poet of sincere religious feeling.

Colonna's *Canzoniere* (1544) is a collection of lyric poems, mostly sonnets but also several in the *canzoni* and *capitoli* forms. The first segment of this collection focuses on various memories associated with Colonna's departed husband. The poems then broaden in scope for the latter half of the work to more general moral and religious themes. Colonna's poems exemplify the classic Petrarchan style, as amplified by the poetic precepts of Pietro Bembo.

This extraordinary woman aroused the admiration and adoration of outstanding writers and artists such as Michelangelo Buonarroti, who met her when he was sixty-three, became her great friend, and was apparently inspired by her to the composition of verse. Michelangelo's sonnets, not published until after his death, are casual and private. He is an idealist and a Platonist but very serious and very real in his feelings. Inevitably borrowing images from sculpture, he creates a kind of rough-hewn, sturdy, carefully molded verse in which a powerful creative genius breaks through the many conventionalities of the Petrarchan mode. Of greatest interest in his verses are fellow-feeling for the austere grandeur of Dante, his descriptions of his own agonizings in the creation of sculpture and fresco, and his burning idealism which finds a glimpse of eternity in the earthly beauty of Vittoria Colonna, a glimpse which leads him to bewail his own incompetence as an artist.

LODOVICO ARIOSTO (1474–1533)

The creator of the supreme example of the romantic epic, Lodovico Ariosto was so much the child of his age that his *Orlanado Furioso* (1504–1516), in spite of a completely foreign subject, is almost a real epic of sixteenth century Italy. While Machiavelli was beseeching Italians to unite and expel the invader, there was in Italy so little impetus or power to achieve such a united front that the politics of the city-states came to be much more the concerns of the rival powers of France, Spain, and the papacy than of the citizens themselves. After having been for so many years endangered by France, the Italian duchies were turned over to Spain and the papacy by the Treaty of Cambray in 1529. The now tributary courts had little opportunity for exercising independent judgment of any kind, and salvaged what pride they might by their social leadership and artistic prestige. In such a society Ariosto was universally acclaimed as a supreme genius.

Lodovico Ariosto was born at Reggio in 1474, son of the commander of the citadel. His own early devotion to literature was thwarted, as in the case of Boccaccio, by a father who caused him to study law until five "wasted" years were convincing proof of its futility. Showing the independent spirit which marked all the rest of his life, he won the victory for his own inclinations and turned to a study of the classics. His composition of prose comedies and short poems attracted the attention of Cardinal Ippolito d'Este and secured him a position as one of the gentlemen of his house. Ariosto complained of the Cardinal's failure to appreciate his abilities and the meagre stipend which he received. When, therefore, his company was required on a journey to Hungary in 1518, he begged to be excused, and transferred his allegiance to the Cardinal's brother, Alphonso, Duke of Ferrara. Under both patrons Ariosto was employed on strenuous missions, which partially destroyed his health, and under Alphonso he served for three years as governor of a bandit-infested province in the Apennines. Other offers of embassies, which might have led to worldly advancement, were refused by the poet, who stubbornly lived out the rest of his life in Ferrara, writing comedies, supervising the building of a theater, and endlessly engaged in the reworking and polishing of his epic masterpiece, which was completely published, only a year before his death. Partly because of his love of freedom and partly because of a self-confessed changeable disposition, he did not marry until near the end of his life. He died of tuberculosis in 1533, universally mourned, and leaving two illegitimate children by different mothers.

Orlando Furioso

Attached to the same court and family for which Boiardo had composed his *Orlando Innamorato*, Ariosto naturally seized upon the idea of completing the unfinished work. It was also natural that he should have viewed the entire fable of knightly exploits with a kind of quiet ironic detachment, since there was no glory in the skirmishings of his own time and since he had become by experience politely cynical about the glories of princes. He therefore completes the poem of Boiardo with no sense of ultimate significance, no particular concern with design, but with an artist's devotion to each line of jewelled verse which will do exact justice to the event, the scene, or the person being described.

Using the same stanza form, *ottava rima*, he continues the story from exactly where Boiardo had left off, with Angelica in flight from the enamored Rinaldo while the siege of Paris continues. In forty-five cantos of fifty thousand lines, narrating an unending succession of events, the *Orlando Furioso* weaves untiring variations around real and mythological figures, human passions and magical illusions, pursuits of love, and a trip to the moon. The siege of Paris remains the background throughout, but is given as little attention as Boiardo gave it. The title, *Mad Orlando*, is apparently also in deference to Boiardo's presentation of the bafflement of Orlando in his love for Angelica. Orlando's consequent insanity is the occasion for Astolfo's trip to the moon to bring back his senses. What basic plot there is revolves about the love story of the pagan Ruggiero and the woman-warrior Bradimante, the many obstacles they encounter (including the temporary wanderings of Ruggiero's affection to other women), and their final marriage, to become ancestors of the House of Este.

Singing "of loves and ladies, kings and arms" at the time when the Moors under King Agramante of Africa and Marsilio of Spain ravished France, Orlando begins his epic by recalling the situation of the *Orlando Innamorato,* in which both Orlando and Rinaldo are in love with Angelica, who hates Rinaldo. Charlemagne tries to take advantage of the situation by holding Angelica as a prize for whoever slays the most pagans. But when she escapes, Charlemagne's best paladins desert him for a more interesting adventure. Rinaldo finds her but is distracted by a combat with Ferrau, who had established a claim to her by combat in the previous epic, and she flees again. Ferrau returns to the scene of their battle to look for his helmet. There the phantom Argalio (Angelica's brother, who had been defeated by Ferrau) tells him to get Orlando's or Rinaldo's helmet. While Rinaldo is again distracted by pursuing his horse Baiardo, Sacripant, King of Circassia, meets and carries off Angelica. Angelica catches Baiardo and is met again by Rinaldo who fights Sacripant, and Angelica flees again to take refuge with a hermit, who tells the knights that Orlando has carried Angelica off to Paris.

Rinaldo's warrior sister Bradamante meets a knight who recounts that the magician Atlante, possessing a winged horse, has emprisoned the pagan Ruggiero, with whom Bradamante has fallen in love. Trapped by him into falling into Merlin's cave, she hears of Angelica's magic ring, which is in the possession of the pagan Brunello. She cleverly obtains the ring, breaks the magic of Atlante, and frees Ruggiero, who attempts to ride the winged horse, and who is carried off on its back first to a magic island of an enchantress and then to the island of Ebuda, where Angelica is about to be sacrificed to a monstrous Orc.

Meanwhile, in a digression, Rinaldo fights to save Ginevra from being burned at the stake for adultery; for why should woman be more blameworthy than man? Ruggiero is now discovered being entertained by the beautiful fairy Alcina, who conducts a castle of love but changes her lovers into trees. He is saved from her charms by Melissa, who reveals Alcina as an ugly hag and releases all her other victims, including the English knight Astolfo.

Orlando now undertakes the rescue of Angelica who, he hears, is chained to a rock and being snapped at by the vicious Orc. Ruggiero has already freed her, only to see a giant conquer Bradamante and carry her away. Orlando kills the Orc with an anchor and is then entrapped in Atlante's castle along with Ruggiero, Ferrau, and Sacripant. Angelica comes there looking for a knight. Ferrau and Orlando fight for Orlando's helmet. Angelica steals it and gives it to Ferrau. Bradimante also arrives at the enchanted castle.

Charlemagne, continuing the battle at Paris, prays to God for help, sends Discord to the enemy camps, and commissions Silence to round up the paladins. Agramante sets fire to Paris, and Rodomonte wreaks havoc within its walls. A miraculous rain extinguishes the fire, and Rinaldo arrives in the nick of time to rout the pagans. Angelica, meanwhile, falls in love with the country man Medoro whose wounds she has tended. After carving their names on trees, they are respectably married. Astolfo, who has captured the giant who carried off Angelica, routs a bizarre city of women and breaks up Atlante's magic castle by sounding his horn. Ruggiero and Bradamante are reunited, plan to be married as soon as Ruggiero is baptized, and are separated again. Bradamante is returned to her own home by Astolfo to remain until Ruggiero comes to claim her.

Orlando, continuing minor fights and adventures, happens to see the trees where Angelica and Medoro have carved their names, and goes mad. An allegorical interlude concerning the fox of avarice and an interpolated tale by a landlord in search of a faithful woman are followed by more of Orlando's madness and berating of women. Astolfo routs with his horn the harpies that have feasted on Italy, chases them to the entrance to hell, and then takes a trip on the hippogriff via heaven to the moon, where he finds Orlando's wits stored in a vial. It is explained that his wits have gone astray because of his demented love for a Saracen.

Meanwhile, Ruggiero rejoins the Saracens, where Discord has set Rodomonte and Madricar in opposition for the love of a lady. They are about to engage in combat when the umpire suggests that the lady state her own preference. She selects Madricar, and Rodomonte rages into the war to be defeated finally by the French. Hearing that Ruggiero has been wounded in the same combat and is being nursed by another woman, Bradamante again dons her armor and sets out to defeat him in combat. When she begins to fight him, he recognizes her, refuses to continue, and begs to be allowed to explain. But the woman who has nursed him now combats Bradamante and is very nearly killed by Ruggiero, when an enchanter's voice announces that she is his sister who was abducted in her infancy. The two women are thereby reconciled and agree to join Charlemagne until Ruggiero can be baptized and join the Christian forces.

A single combat is arranged between Rinaldo and Ruggiero to end the war, but the Saracens break the pact. Astolfo carries the war into Africa, where Orlando joins him and is freed from love. Agramante is put to flight and is later killed. Rinaldo, still in search of Angelica, is led by Disdain to drink the right fountain and is also cured of love. Ruggiero sets out to rejoin Bradamante but is shipwrecked on an island where a hermit converts him to Christianity. Rinaldo then gives his consent to the marriage of Ruggiero and Bradamante and goes with her to Charlemagne's court, only to learn that she has been promised by the monarch to the Greek Prince Leo, who is preferred by Bradamante's mother if the Prince is able to defeat Bradamante in combat. Ruggiero hears that the Prince is occupied with the siege of Belgrade, hastens to join him, and is captured by the enemy. The Prince rescues him but imposes upon him the obligation of impersonating him in the approaching combat with Bradamante. Ruggiero defeats Bradamante for the Prince and rides off to die of grief. But the Prince pursues him, discovers the true state of affairs, and relinquishes his claims to the fair warrior maiden. Ruggiero is invited to become King of the Bulgarians and receives Bradamante in a final reunion from the hands of Melissa. A concluding battle with Rodomonte, who has all but destroyed Paris while all this has been going on, ends the story with Rodomonte's death.

Infused into this melange of activity are all kinds of influences and states of mind. By turns, the story is purely romantic; laudatory to the House of Este, which is supposed to have sprung from the union of Ruggiero and

Bradamante; moral in preaching moderation and chastity; allegorical in the introduction of such figures as Discord, Care, Alcina, and Melissa; mystical in opposing the forces of God to the powers of evil; supernatural in the constant use of magic; grotesque and absurd in such nonsense as the uses of Astolfo's horn; mythical in the introduction of the Orc; contemporary in referring to such things as the use of gunpowder; serious in its admonitions to rout the modern Turk; prophetic like Dante in visualizing the coming of the golden fleece (Hippolytus of Este) "twenty years before the year marked by *M* and *D*"; traditionally epic in its catalogue of troops; and constantly moving through a gamut of moods from realistic humor to romantic fantasy.

IMPORTANCE

Whatever the scene or the mood, Ariosto apparently takes great pleasure in the sheer invention of episodes and in the introductory philosophical commentaries with which each canto begins. There are occasionally highly dramatic moments and touches of pathos. There are also moments of broad humor. But the almost intangible quality which makes this poem distinct from any other is the odd combination of exquisite versification, an essential sober seriousness which seems to grow as the poem progresses, and a simultaneous lack of concern and lack of veneration for any of the characters involved. Human feelings are given more amplification than scenery or setting, but no judgment of these feelings is implied. When Angelica ultimately refuses the prince and marries a country lad, the event is not presented as either a token of her commonness or as a triumph of love over convention. It is simply recorded with a shrug of the shoulders as a commentary on how things are apt to be. Speaking for its age, the *Orlando Furioso* says that the sensuous world is meant to give delight, that the world of human striving and passions is of engaging interest, and that the accidents of fate which befall human nature are inevitable and sometimes comic. The art of Ariosto was admired and imitated in France by the *Pléiade* and provided a principal model for Spenser's *Faerie Queene*.

I Suppositi

Ariosto's interest in the theater was the passion of a lifetime. Of his five comedies which conform to the rules of Latin play writing, the first, *I Suppositi* (*The Substitutes*) (1509), is best known to English readers because of Gascoigne's translation of it under the curious title *The Supposes*. Relying, like Machiavelli's *Madrigola*, on trickery and intrigue, the involved plot concerns Erostrato, who is sent with his servant Dulipo to Ferrara where he falls in love with Damon's daughter Polynesta. By changing places with his servant, Erostrato enters Damon's service in order to pay court to Polynesta in competition with the sixty-year-old Dr. Cleander. From this point the comedy of errors becomes increasingly tangled until a final series of revelations, including Dr. Cleander's discovery that Dulipo is his son, brings about the marriage of Erostrato and Polynesta. From the all but complete dependence of this play on Plautus and Terence, Ariosto gradually included more touches of contemporary life in succeeding works, but remained to his last play, *Las Scholastica* ("*The Students*") (c. 1530), dependent on Roman drama for both plots and technique. Although the plays contain considerable humor and satire, their chief importance is in their transference of the form and conventions of Latin comedy to the Renaissance, acting as models to later writers.

BENVENUTO CELLINI (1500–1571)

A nonliterary author of the late Italian Renaissance, unconcerned with stylistic graces or correct subject matter, wrote spontaneously the story of his life and thereby created one of the only realistic works of the period and one of the world's most celebrated autobiographies. Benvenuto Cellini was a goldsmith and sculptor by profession, valuable for his art to popes and princes. He needed to be, for, possessed of a fabulous instability of character, prey of violent passions, and apparently devoid of compunction of any kind, his tempestuous life was made up of a dime-thriller series of escapes and escapades.

Benvenuto Cellini was born of a landowning Florentine family in 1500. It was through his own desires that he became apprenticed to a goldsmith at the age of fifteen after having already given evidence of his irascible nature in a fracas for which he endured six months' banishment from Florence. Early in his career of making original designs in precious metals, he visited Rome, Bologna, and Pisa. On a third return to Florence he engaged in a brawl that compelled him to flee in disguise to Rome. There the production of a beautiful vase brought him to the attention of Pope Clement VII for whom he executed several works. He also became proficient in playing the flute and was appointed one of the pope's court musicians. He was at Rome during the French Imperial attack of 1527 and distinguished himself, according to his own account, by directing the defense of the castle of Saint Angelo. The reward for his exploits was the decision on the part of the Florentine magistrates to allow him to return to his native city.

After executing a series of medals there, he went to the court of the Duke of Mantua, then returned to Florence, and then to Rome. There he killed the murderer of his brother and in another quarrel wounded one Ser Benedetto. He fled to Naples for shelter and succeeded in obtaining a pardon. Notwithstanding another murder of a goldsmith, he was restored to honor by Paul III who succeeded Clement VII to the papal throne. This time the plots of the pope's illegitimate son Pier Luigi brought about a temporary disgrace, during which he lived at Florence and Venice; eventually he was again in favor. The pursuit of his profession then took him on a visit to the French court of Francis I; upon his return he was imprisoned, at the age of thirty-seven, on the apparently trumped-up charge of having stolen gems from the pontifical tiara. He made an incredible escape from the Castle Saint Angelo, was recaptured, and lived in daily expectation of death. Released again through the intercession of a powerful churchman, he returned to France where he mingled artistic productivity with constant quarrels and jealousies.

After five years he returned in disgust to Florence, where he continued to create works of intricate and beautiful design and also carried through the casting of his monumental bronze Perseus, which was placed in front of the old ducal palace of Florence. He was universally praised for his art but he was also accused of gross immorality, and fretted himself nearly to death by his rivalry with the sculptor Bandinelli. During the war with Siena, he was given charge of the defenses of the city, and won added admiration for his engineering sagacity. He died in Florence in 1571 and was buried with elaborate ceremony in the Church of the Annunciation.

IMPORTANCE

Cellini's *Autobiography* (1558), most of which he dictated at the age of sixty to a fourteen-year-old apprentice, is a classic of sheer spontaneity. With an almost complete absence of self-consciousness and with unbounded conceit, the aging artist recounts the remarkable exploits of that great man Cellini. Some exaggeration was inevitable, but the exaggeration is nearly always obvious and generally very amusing. Besides, it is difficult to exaggerate the events of such a life as his. With scarcely a trace of shame or modesty, he spreads out the record of plots, counterplots, loves, jealousies, street brawls, devoted artistic creation, defeats, and triumphs. "Revenge" is one of the most important words in his vocabulary, and no matter how fast he has to run he always comes off with "honor" from every engagement. With subject matter such as this and with Cellini's gusto and vivacity in delineating the rapidly moving events, the book well deserves its great popularity. There is also a considerable amount of space devoted to descriptions of his creative talent—the account of his casting of the Perseus is one of the most absorbing sections of the *Autobiography*. And from this constantly entertaining narrative of an extraordinary life, there is painted a marvellous picture of sixteenth century Italy with its passion for beauty, its love of pomp and ceremony, and its crudeness, lawlessness, dirt, and vulgarity. The strange combination of idealism and sensuousness, of fantasy and practicality that is the hallmark of this period finds full expression in the personality of Cellini, revealed often in a single sentence such as his observation in the midst of a fight with a rival over a woman, "There was a glorious heaven of stars which shed good light to see by."

MINOR CONTEMPORARIES

Teofilo Folengo (1491–1544)

Literary names once prominent but now all but forgotten, especially outside of Italy, deserve at least a passing mention. Teofilo Folengo found the possibilities of humor in the circumstance that Latin and Italian were still cultivated side by side by cultured Italians. In his *Baldus* (1517), the story of the superman hero who destroys the pirates, exterminates the fairies, discovers the mouths of the Nile, and goes to hell where the liars are found, he created a "macaronic" verse that satirized both schools and the quarrel between the defenders of Latin and the champions of Italian by mingling the two languages. Written mostly in correct Latin, there breaks in ever and again a provincial Italian word with a Latin case ending.

Giangiorgio Trissino (1478–1550)

At almost the opposite extreme of intense seriousness, Giangiorgio Trissino essayed the composition of a magnificent epic, *Italia Liberata dai Goti* (*Italy Liberated from the Goths*) (1547). Using Homer as his model and attempting to write a true classical epic concerning Justinian's restoration of Empire to Italy, he succeeded only in composing a long dull factual account in correct verse but without force or inspiration. Somewhat pathetic, too, is his choice of subject, implying as it does the hope that Italy may again be liberated from the "barbarians." It was noble in ambition but now seems as dead as the attempt of Luigi Alamanni (1495–1556) to use Arthurian characters in an imitation of the *Iliad* in his *Avarchide*, also written in Italian blank verse.

Pietro Aretino (1492–1557)

The ultimate scamp of the period was Pietro Aretino, who utilized his very considerable literary genius in blackmailing the wealthy and the powerful. Known as a deadly and libellous satirist, this "scourge of princes" levied tribute on those who could afford to pay him to suppress publication of even worse calumnies than those he celebrated in verse.

TORQUATO TASSO (1544–1595)

The growing artifice and artificiality of sixteenth century Italian literature was stimulated by the Catholic revival, the rigid censorship imposed by the Church after 1530, and the establishment of the inquisition in 1540. Free thought was no longer possible, and the impetus to originality was strangely lacking in any case. As a result, the only major figure of the second half of the sixteenth century is the self-tortured poet Torquato Tasso.

The son of the would-be epic poet Bernardo Tasso, whose *Amadigi*, based on the knightly exploits of Amadis, was so poorly received, Torquato was born at Sorrento in 1544. A precocious child of a father who had political connections, he was established at the court of Urbino in 1557 where he grew up amid the refined luxury and sophisticated literary criticism of that learned society. His father, obsessed by his own failure as a poet, sent him for a time to Padua to study law, but the young man devoted most of his attention there to philosophy and poetry, and produced by 1562 the romantic epic *Rinaldo* which attempted to give classic unity to the often used romantic material. Considered the most promising poet of the time, he accepted service with Cardinal Luigi d'Este at the court of Ferrara, where he spent five happy years between 1565 and 1570, made much of by the two princesses Lucrezia and Leonora, and becoming the idol of the entire court. In 1570 a disagreement with the Cardinal caused him to transfer his services to Duke Alfonso II of Ferrara. In 1573 he published his pastoral, the *Aminta*, and in 1575 he completed his epic, the *Gerusalemme Liberata,* which he dedicated to the Duke.

Apparently the same year was the beginning of his mental unbalance, which continued for the remainder of his life. His temperament became violent and melancholy by turns. He was obsessed by fears of damnation and felt himself persecuted by those around him. He submitted his epic to princes and churchmen for consideration and, upon being told that it was more romantic than epic and not really religious, he attempted to defend it by calling it a moral allegory. He finally reworded it entirely in his last years and renamed the patched-up result the *Gerusalemme Conquistata*. The original was saved through piratical editions; the revision has been rightly forgotten.

Meanwhile Tasso's mental condition proceeded from bad to worse. After several attempts to live elsewhere as if trying to run away from himself, he returned to the sympathetic atmosphere of Ferrara. Here his outbursts and violences were treated with extraordinary consideration until, in 1579, it was necessary to place him in confinement. During seven years of a very gentle kind of imprisonment, during which he enjoyed both physical luxuries and the company of friends, he continued to feel the terrors of persecution. His epic had been published without his consent. He feared the inquisition, poisoning, visits by spirits. In 1586 he was liberated and began long dismal wanderings from court to court. In 1592 he published his own revised version of the epic, was invited to Rome in 1594 to receive the coveted laurel wreath, but died in 1595 before the actual coronation took place.

Gerusalemme Liberata

IMPORTANCE

The *Jerusalem Delivered* (*Gerusalemme Liberata*) is the fruit of personal conflicts that were the conflicts of the age. Paying heed to the new power of Catholicism, the poem aspires to be a dignified and inspiring religious epic telling the story of the first crusade. Affected by the new critical tendency and insistence on obedience to classic rules, it attempts to achieve the unity of action that the Orlando poems had utterly disregarded in their multiplying of characters and episodes. But it was written by an Italian to whom the Charlemagne material and the romantic manner came as second nature, and at the court where Boiardo and Ariosto had done so much to develop this tradition. The result is an essentially romantic epic, much more straightforward and direct than preceding compositions in this genre and overlaid with religious feeling.

The essential plot concerns the military leadership of Godfrey of Boulogne in the campaign, the wrath and defection of Rinaldo caused by his love of the beautiful witch Armida who joins the crusade, and the love of Tancred for the pagan Amazon Clorinda complicated by her sister's love of Tancred. In twenty cantos of *ottava rima*, the complexities of this triple plot are untangled.

CANTO I: The Crusaders are assembled in the sight of God on the plain of Tortosa on their slow journey to the Holy Land. The angel Gabriel appears to Godfrey in his sleep to inspire him to rouse the host from its dilatory attitude. He calls a council, is elected Commander-in-Chief, and reviews his troops which include Tancred, who has lost his zest for battle since falling in love with the beautiful Clorinda, and the youthful Rinaldo. Meanwhile the opposing sultan, Prince Aladine, mercilessly taxes the Christians in his domain to carry on his defense.

II. Through the counsel of Ismeno, a sorcerer, Aladine steals the image of the Virgin Mary from the Christian temple and subjects it to magical incantations in his mosque. When the image vanishes, he decrees that all the Christians in the city shall be destroyed unless the thief discovers himself. Inspired by the noble spirit of self-sacrifice, Sophronia offers herself up as the perpetrator of the crime. But while she is being bound to the stake, her rescue is attempted by her rejected suitor Olindo, who confesses that he had stolen the image. Instead of effecting the desired result of setting Sophronia free, he is bound to the same stake. Both would have perished but for the proclamation of Clorinda that Allah himself had removed the Christian statue from his sacred shrine. The lovers are released and happily married.

Meanwhile, Alethes and Argantes come to Godfrey as ambassadors from Egypt to attempt to dissuade the Christians from their mission. Needless to say, they are sternly rebuffed.

III: The Crusaders reach Jerusalem and barefoot tread the consecrated way. In a sally made by the Turks led by Clorinda, Tancred's wondrous feats of arms excite the love of Clorinda's sister Erminia who views them from the city walls. Clorinda engages in single combat with Tancred who discovers the identity of his opponent, cannot strike back, and merely tells her of his adoration. They are separated by the tide of battle which rages bloodily until a truce is declared, during which the Christians decide that moving towers are necessary to besiege the city and send out woodsmen to cut down trees from a nearby forest.

IV: The scene now turns to a council held by Satan which results in the inspiration of Idraotes, wizard prince of Damascus, to send his niece Armida to the Christian camp. Her attempts to decoy them from their objectives in order to regain for her a lost crown are so effective that Rinaldo, who wants to accede to her wishes, leaves the camp with Godfrey's brother Eustace and several other valiant leaders.

V: On the fictitious expedition Armida decoys Rinaldo into a duel with Prince Gernando of Norway which results in the death of Gernando and the flight to Egypt of Rinaldo, who has broken a pledge of the Crusaders not to fight amongst themselves.

Back at the scene of battle, Godfrey is plunged into gloom by the defection of his leaders and by the news of the approach of an Egyptian army.

VI: The Egyptian army arrives, and when the Egyptian Argantes challenges the Christians to single combat, Tancred is chosen to oppose him. In the battle, Argantes is seconded by Clorinda whose presence causes Tancred to become impotent until Argantes defeats Tancred's second. Thereupon, Tancred attacks Argantes and fights with him all day, after which both are so sorely wounded that a six-day truce is arranged. Erminia applies her magic salves to Argantes' wounds and then puts on Clorinda's armor in an attempt to reach her beloved Tancred, but she is attacked by the Crusaders who believe her to be Clorinda.

VII: When Tancred hears the news, he arms and rushes forth, weak as he is, to protect his supposed Clorinda. Erminia flees for two days until she is taken in by shepherds. Tancred, attempting to follow her, becomes lost and is entrapped in the castle of the enchantress Armida.

Meanwhile, the aging Count Raymond takes Tancred's place in the duel with Argantes and is about to defeat him when an arrow is directed at him from the walls of Jerusalem. Incensed by such treachery, the Christians join in a general battle.

VIII: A storm arises and the Christians are beaten back. One of the wounded sends his sword to Rinaldo by messenger, and Godfrey is accused by the Italians of having ordered Rinaldo's death.

IX: Inspired by Satan, Solyman of Nicae joins Aladine and attacks the Christians at night, but the Crusaders are forewarned by the archangel Michael and beat them off, aided by the return of the leaders who had been decoyed by Armida. When a page of Solyman's is slain, the Sultan temporarily withdraws from battle for a period of mourning.

X: On his way back to Egypt, Solyman meets a wizard who magically returns him to Jerusalem to overhear proposals of peace being suggested. He quickly puts a stop to such cowardly counsels.

XI: Godfrey hears from the knights who had been lured away by Armida that she had enchanted them and attempted to force them to renounce Christianity, but that they have been rescued by Rinaldo. The Christians receive communion at the Mount of Olives and set out to lay siege to the walls of Jerusalem. In the opening assault Godfrey is wounded by one of Clorinda's arrows but is miraculously cured by an angel.

XII: Clorinda proposes to Argantes a daring plan to set out at night to burn the Christians' moving tower. In an attempt to dissuade her from this rash attempt, her slave reveals that she is of Christian birth. She nevertheless carries through her plan, is attacked by Tancred who is unaware of her identity, is mortally wounded, and is baptised by him in dying. His grief is such that he longs only to join her in death.

XIII: Argantes vows revenge on Tancred. The magician Ismeno enchants the forest to prevent the building of another tower. Tancred himself attempts to cut down a tree but is warned by the sight of blood flowing from his axe cut and by Clorinda's voice ordering him to desist.

XIV: Godfrey is warned by God to recall Rinaldo and sends Guelpho and Ubaldo in search of him.

XV: The two knights are led by magic to Armida's island and conquer all her sorceries.

XVI: They find Rinaldo and release him from the enchanted island of Armida, into whose power he has fallen as a result of having rescued his companions from her clutches. Having fallen in love with him, she begs him to remain with her but is rebuffed.

XVII: Seeking revenge, she falls in with the Egyptian host en route to battle and swears them all to Rinaldo's death.

XVIII: Rinaldo, with new armor prepared for him by Heaven, reaches the camp and frees the enchanted wood. With new towers the Crusaders capture the city.

XIX: Tancred slays Argantes in lonely single combat, falls in a swoon, and is discovered and nursed by Erminia.

XX: In a final battle the Egyptians are routed, remaining resistance is ended, and the Holy City is restored to the Cross. Armida tries to kill Rinaldo, fails, and attempts to kill herself, but is saved by Rinaldo who offers her marriage. She returns with him to his camp to be converted and married. The Crusaders all kneel before the Holy Sepulchre and offer prayers of thanks to God.

The great and lasting popularity of this poem is easily accounted for. Written with seriousness and skill, it tells a good story, which encompasses romantic appeals of every sort. Many of the scenes are very moving, whether dealing with religious fervor or romantic love. The characters are richly varied, some of them are exotic, and all are clearly delineated whether in terms of the fine dignity of Godfrey or the enchanting coquetry of Armida. The mass scenes of the army on the march, the army in prayer, or the army in battle are rapidly suggested with a keen feeling for the grandeur of the occasions. But with all this the poem shares the ultimate sense of unreality of its predecessors. It is descriptive rather than dramatic, beautiful rather than powerful. Tasso's own special contribution to the art of verse narrative is a lyric touch which softens and sentimentalizes the entire story and all its parts, and also provides much of the appeal of the poem. Carnage, battle, confusion, and even heroic boldness are somehow transformed, partly by the poet's tone and attitude, partly by the limpid verse which describes them, into idyllic glamour, and even the love stories are essentially touching and tender rather than impassioned.

Aminta

Tasso's predilection for the idyllic mood made him eminently suited to the composition of pastorals. His *Aminta* continues the tradition of pastoral play writing by the gentle recording of the crossed loves of shepherds and shepherdesses. The shepherdess Daphne and the shepherd Thirsis are companions; their friend Aminta has a hopeless love for the stony-hearted Silvia, who prefers the chase. Through Daphne's suggestion Thirsis leads Aminta to a place where Silvia bathes, but there they find her tied to a tree by a satyr attempting rape. Aminta looses her without thanks, and she flees again. Resolving to die, Aminta tries to force an arrow into his breast but is checked in time by Daphne. The news is brought that Silvia has been devoured by wolves, a bloody scarf being the token. Aminta throws himself off a precipice. Silvia reappears unhurt and, hearing of Aminta's fate, is moved to pity and then love. Intending to bury his body and kill herself, she finds him miraculously alive, and sends for her father to give consent to their love.

Following the classic rules to an extreme, Tasso allows no action to take place on stage. All events are related by messengers or by principals to confidantes; Aminta and Silvia do not even meet on stage! Cupid gives the prologue and a chorus of shepherds adds atmosphere. Most of the dialogue is devoted to light-hearted discussions of the nature of love, the behavior of lovers, and the effects of love. Stressing physical beauty and physical desire, the scarcely serious treatment of youthful ardor is encased in a bejeweled conversation piece as if to be preserved and cherished as a nostalgic memory for old age.

MINOR LATE RENAISSANCE AUTHORS

Giovanni Battista Guarini (1537–1612)

One of those who witnessed the performance of Tasso's *Aminta* was Giovanni Battista Guarini, who decided to emulate it. Abjuring the simplicity and rapidity of composition which distinguishes his model, Guarini spent nine years in the composition of the complicated plot of *Il Pastor Fido* (*The Faithful Shepherd*) (1585). Using both the lost heir plot and an elaborate chain of lovers, he labelled his play a tragicomedy and wrote an elaborate defense of this type of drama. The play was enormously popular and is the last outstanding example of Italy's creation of a kind of play which is neither tragic nor comic, which is more really "play" than earnest, and which relies for its appeal on charming pleasantries and tasteful production. In its use of elaborate

scenery and music it is another of the precursors to Italian opera. In its sophisticated tone and avoidance of either high seriousness or low comedy, it is a
predecessor of the social comedies of the seventeenth century.

Giambattista Marino (1569–1625)

The Italian Renaissance comes to a close with the idolized master of the
delicate. Giambattista Marino, whose name has become synonymous with
preciosity and sheer verbal display, was the deliberate creator of startling
images and far-fetched conceits. His verses on *Kisses* (*Baci*) (c. 1620) exhaust
the possibilities of the subject and the reader as well. His epic *Adone* (1623)
brings the story of Venus and Adonis to a moral conclusion whereby the
illicit love of Adonis is punished through the agency of the wronged husband Mars. But plot and moral alike are submerged beneath endless classical
scenes in which the sweetly sensuous vies with the extravagantly ingenious
to create the cloying effect of manner without either matter or art.

6
THE RENAISSANCE IN FRANCE

At the time of the beginnings of the Renaissance in Italy, France, which was more feudal and considerably more remote from the inspiration of classical civilization, was immersed in the Hundred Years War, which left little room for intellectual or artistic progress. During this still-medieval period Jean Froissart (c. 1337–1410) was collecting the combination of fact and gossip that he turned into his *Chronicles*, and poets like Guillaume de Machaut (c. 1300–1377) and Eustace Deschamps (c. 1346–1407) continued the graceful and skillful versification of the Provençal tradition. The fifteenth century produced Alain Chartier (c. 1385–1433), who wrote both courtly and allegorical poetry; Charles d'Orleans (1391–1465), who wrote a versified autobiography, *La Livre de la Prison* (*The Prisoner's Book*), while captive in England; and François Villon (1431–1480), who, though worldly and endowed with great lyrical genius, is still essentially medieval in character.

In writings like these there is a sense of an abortive movement toward Renaissance freedom, but the actual Renaissance in France did not begin until the sixteenth century, when it was inspired not by a rediscovery of the classics but by the discovery of Italian literature, a discovery that was hastened by France's political interest in her neighbor. Deriving from Italy all of the varied expressions and fashions of the Renaissance temperament, the productions of France were nevertheless apt to be more serious as befitted the land that produced Jean Calvin and which was also finding new liberty of thought in the Reformation. There was also a more vital sense of patriotism in a nation which had repelled the foreigner by virtue of the leadership of a peasant girl and had centralized and stabilized its government through the political sagacity of Louis XI and Louis XII.

The new spirit began to exhibit itself under the patronage of Francis I, who reigned from 1515 to 1547. The first Renaissance king, he established a cultured court center on the Italian model and patronized artists, scholars, and literary men. He selected Guillaume Budé (1467–1540), the outstanding French humanist, as his literary counsel and entrusted him with the building up of the royal library, germ of the *Bibliothèque Nationale*, and also followed his suggestion in establishing the first French Renaissance university.

EARLY WRITERS

Clement Marot (c. 1496–1544)

The most talented recipient of the king's patronage was Clement Marot. Born at Quercy around 1496 of a father Jean who also had some reputation as a poet, he received a good education in rhetoric and special training in law. At Paris he enjoyed the reckless student life that had so delighted Villon. A somewhat indifferent student, he was nevertheless an avid reader who came early in contact with French and Italian writers like Villon and Boccaccio. In 1513 he began his courtly career as a page, was made secretary three years later to the king's sister Marguerite of Navarre, and delighted his patroness by composing verses in her honor and in honor of Francis I. Upon the death of his father in 1526 he was transferred to the royal court, which remained his principal home until his death. In 1532 he published his collected poems under the title *L'Adolescence Clementine* (*Clement's Adolescence*) and followed this with another collection in 1534 entitled *Suite à l'Adolescence* (*Successor to the Adolescence*). Marot's liberalism finally placed him in danger from the fury of the Protestant movement, and he was forced to flee to Italy, where he died in 1544.

Writing eclogues, epigrams, epistles, religious verse, and love poetry, Marot excelled in light occasional verse, sparkling and debonair, and completely without depth or power. With supreme ability in combining delicacy with sureness of touch, he exhibits his highest skill in the clever and often unexpectedly turned phrase, the neat compliment, the happy thought. Seemingly effortless, graceful, and witty, gay and immediate in their effect, these brief compositions have set the standard for light verse the world over, and inspired an immediate school of imitators, *L'Ecole Marotique*, including Charles Fontaine (1515–1570), Mellin de Saint Gelais (1491–1558), and Bonaventure des Periers (c. 1500–1544). These disciples followed the master at a considerable distance but were among the first to introduce into French poetry traces of Neoplatonism, possibly through the influence of Marguerite of Navarre.

Marguerite of Navarre (1492–1549)

Marguerite d'Angoulême, Queen of Navarre, succeeded in really emulating the Florentine court of Lorenzo the Magnificent as her brother Francis I was attempting to do. Surrounding herself with poets, artists, and savants, she was herself deeply learned and highly talented. Being both ruler and woman, she was able to combine the atmosphere of the court and the salon. Possessed of a warm and rich character, of deep feeling and high intelligence, she was easily the most distinguished woman of her time and led a feminist movement in the direction of the Neoplatonic conception of woman as opposed to a medieval and still very active cult of defamers of the sex. She thus became a powerful leader in the current *Querelle des Femmes* already referred to in connection with Castiglione's *Courtier*. Borrowing Neoplatonism from Italian sources, she was also very sympathetic with the Protestant movement and succeeded in fusing the pagan and the Christian into a serious and essentially simple faith. "No man," she writes in the *Heptaméron*, "loves God who has not perfectly loved some one of God's creatures on earth." Although she had great respect for learning (having studied Latin, Italian, Spanish, German, Hebrew, and Greek), a sincere reverence for religion, and a delight in worldly pleasures, she believed in love as a kind of universal solvent, an activating principle for goodness, and a deterrent to fanaticism, superstition, and greed.

As a writer she produced a considerable quantity of thoughtful and highly personal poetry, which is usually prolix and technically sluggish. Her most enduring work is the collection of seventy-two prose tales published in 1558 as the *Heptaméron des Nouvelles* (*Seven Days of Stories*). Although modelled on *The Decameron* and including several licentious stories like those of Boccaccio, the tone and intent of the *Heptaméron* is actually much closer to Castiglione's *Courtier*. Most of the tales deal with high principles of morality and behavior, and some of them are particularly devoted to the idealization of women and the glorification of Platonic love. Between the stories are discussions, debates, and moralizations on the subjects that have been introduced. The company of ladies and gentlemen returning from the country and held up by a storm, which is the occasion for the storytelling, are intended to be members of her own circle led by Marguerite herself. The stories also purport to be based on fact. The total result is not a remarkable collection of stories, but the work offers a glimpse of Marguerite's court and indicates the interesting fusion of piety and worldliness, sincerity, and artifice that made up this remarkable woman.

FRANÇOIS RABELAIS (c. 1495–1553)

With little use for delicacy and no use for Neoplatonism, Rabelais bursts upon this somewhat idyllic scene of the early French Renaissance and overshadows it completely if only by virtue of his massive vitality. Boisterous, irreverent, realistic, humorous, vulgar, and deeply concerned with human progress, he has become an almost perfect symbol for the gusto and passion for knowledge of the Renaissance. For although he retains much of the superficialities of medievalism, he typifies the many-sided genius and the aggressive explorer of reality which the period produced. He completely transcends the period by his highly individual, genial, and yet powerful personality which makes a direct appeal to the reader of any age.

Of the early years of François Rabelais, very little is known. He appears to have been born at Chinon around 1495 as the son of a man who was an innkeeper or apothecary or both. He probably received his early education at the Benedictine school of Seully. Somewhere around the age of fifteen he went to the convent school of La Baumette where, traditionally, his later powerful friends Geoffrey d'Estissac and the du Bellay brothers were also enrolled. For no assignable reason he then entered the Franciscan monastery at Fontenoy-le-Comte, where he and a close friend, Pierre Amy, pursued a mutual quest for knowledge in defiance of a medieval order devoted to pious ignorance. Although ordained as a priest, Rabelais continued his devotion to the secular investigation of books, including some written in Greek; and through correspondence, he and Amy attracted the attention and encouragement of the learned Greek scholar Budé, who was secretary to Francis I. When this strange zest for worldly knowledge became sufficiently obvious to attract attention, Rabelais and Amy were placed in solitary confinement by way of punishment. Amy escaped to Switzerland, where he became a Lutheran. Rabelais succeeded in being transferred to the Benedictine order through the influence of d'Estissac, who was now a bishop and who made him his secretary.

Apparently unsatisfied by even this amount of liberty within the Church, Rabelais left the service of the Bishop in order to study medicine at the University of Montpelier. Receiving his medical degree within the incredible space of six weeks, he lectured on anatomy for a time at the University, and then, in 1532, began the practice of medicine at Lyons. At that cultural center where Francis I often held his court, Rabelais became vitally interested in the diffusion of knowledge through the editing of medical books. Simultaneously, the fun-loving side of his nature appeared in his editing of a rather obscure Arthurian romance entitled *Les Grands et Inestimables Chroniques du Grand et Énorme Géant Gargantua* (*The Great and Overwhelming Accounts of the Great and Enormous Giant Gargantua*), from which came the impetus for his own immortal work. The extraordinary popularity of this book was reason enough for Rabelais to issue a highly personalized imitation and sequel concerning *The Horrible and Dreadful Feats and Prowesses of the Most Renowned Pantagruel* (1532). This story of Gargantua's son proved equally popular and was followed by the *Pantagrueline Prognostications* (1533), both of these books being published under the name of Alcofribas Nasier, an anagram of his real name. Shortly thereafter, Rabelais joined Cardinal Jean du Bellay as his secretary and private physician.

The remainder of his life is very dimly outlined by occasional references to him. In 1535 he was removed from the medical faculty of Lyons. In 1538 appeared the first volume of his celebrated work entitled *Gargantua and Pantagruel*. The third book was published in 1546, his earlier *Pantagruel* having been incorporated as Book II. Probably because of the Protestant persecution which became intensified near the end of the reign of Francis I, Rabelais fled to Metz in 1546 where he continued the practice of medicine. In 1547 he joined du Bellay at Rome. Under the Cardinal's protection, he wrote the fourth and fifth books of his prolonged work, attacking many of the most controversial issues of his time. His fourth book, published in 1552, was censured by the Sorbonne which was the stronghold of Catholicism in France, and his last book was not fully published until 1567. Rabelais had meanwhile died obscurely in Paris in 1553.

Rabelais was keenly interested in knowledge and the enfranchisement of the human mind, but in no sense was he either fanatic or martyr. The statement attributed to him, "I will defend my opinions up to the fire exclusively," bespeaks the measure of a man who loved life and laughter, who enjoyed exploring the endless possibilities of living, but whose sense of balance in a troubled era gave him the vantage point of a complete outsider surveying the absurdities of human behavior.

Gargantua and Pantagruel

IMPORTANCE

With godlike disdain of literary conventionalities, Rabelais not so much wrote as poured forth the book of his own personality. The very circumstances of its publication indicate that no caherent, carefully planned design went into its making. Instead, with even less care than went into the construction of Goethe's *Faust*, its nearest analogue, it grew as the author grew, and became a repository of fancies, nonsense, and random ideas, held together by a unifying spirit of wholehearted acceptance of an endlessly interesting world. Unlike allegorical works, which can be separated into distinct layers of meaning, this book is all of a piece. Its nonsense, vulgarity, satire, constructive suggestions, philosophisings are all part of a wholesome all-encompassing optimistic survey and evaluation of the many strands that make up the fabric of living. As opposed to Goethe's similar lifetime attempt to evaluate man and his universe, the book of Rabelais proposes, following Aristotle, that laughter is a peculiarly human function. By virtue of this divine faculty, man can meet rebuff without bitterness and try again. With laughter anything can be surmounted, and Rabelais blazes the trail with the heartiest belly laugh ever heard in literature.

BOOK I: The first book opens with a mock genealogy and a parody on the kind of poem supposed to contain deep hidden meanings, and then turns to the birth of Gargantua, son of Grandgousier and Gargamelle who are both great gluttons and drinkers. After having carried him for eleven months, Gargamelle feels the birth pains as a result of having eaten sixteen hogsheads, two barrels, and six jugs of tripe, and then dancing on the green. Because of the congestion of her lower regions and the ineptitude of a midwife, the giant is finally born from her left ear, greeting the world like a true child of his parents by shouting, "Some drink, some drink, some drink!" After a prodigious childhood, Gargantua begins his education under the clergy until his father, becoming aware of the corrupting stupidity of such meaningless studies, transfers him to Ponocrates who represents the new humanistic methods. Riding on a terrific mare, he and Ponocrates go to Paris to find out what is being taught there. While studying, investigating, and amusing himself in a quite satisfactory fashion at Paris, he hears of the outbreak back home of a war (this episode is based on an actual occurrence) between the bakers and the shepherds. When the bakers are reinforced by their king Picrochole, Grandgousier sends to Gargantua for help. Gargantua returns, vanquishes the enemy with the aid of the mighty and liberal-minded Friar John, and rewards the Friar by building for him the Abbey of Thélème. He forgives his enemies but asks that the instigators of the war be turned over to him. While the subject matter of this first book is made up of all sorts of nonsense, the theme throughout concerns the battle of the new education against the old. Formal religion and pedantry are mercilessly satirized, and the Abbey of Thélème is founded on principles in complete revolt against monastic education. Here men and women are both to be admitted to delightful surroundings where force is never applied and where "rules" are unknown. The motto of the Abbey is "Do what thou wilt"; but bigots, liars, lawyers, and others possessed of littleness of mind and spirit are not allowed to enter, and natural instinct impels the selected scholars to honorable behavior.

BOOK II: Actually composed before the first book, the second concerns Pantagruel, the monstrous son of the now five hundred and twenty-four year old Gargantua and his wife Badebec, who dies in childbirth. Given a name which means "all-thirsty," he duplicates his father's ravenous appetite for experience, adventure, and sport, endures similar educational vicissitudes, and also goes to Paris. There he studies Latin, Greek, and Hebrew, and reads Cicero and Plato. There he also meets Panurge who is a great intellectual, a complete scoundrel, and a most amusing companion whose lively wit provides a great deal of the sparkle of the book. Pantagruel shows the new spirit when he settles a law case by throwing away the papers and getting at the facts. The second book, like the first, ends with a war. Hearing that the Dipsodes, or Thirsty People, are invading the land of Utopia and besieging the capital city of the Amaurots, Pantagruel goes to the rescue of the Utopians, overcomes the enemy, enters the land of the Dipsodes, and becomes king.

BOOK III: The third book begins with an account of the benevolent reign of Pantagruel over the Dipsodes, and then turns to the current *Querelle des Femmes* concerning the function and position of women (this book is dedicated to Marguerite of Navarre) by describing Panurge's desire to be married and his quest for counsel on the subject. His researches give Rabelais an opportunity to display his learning by bringing to bear on the subject conclusions obtained from science, philosophy, theology, law, magic, and the wisdom of the ancients. The total result implies a decidedly low opinion of both marriage and women.

BOOK IV: Pantagruel, Panurge, and Friar John set out on a long voyage to place the question before the Oracle of the Holy Bacbuc, or Holy Bottle. En route they visit several extraordinary lands, some of them purely fantastic, others containing symbolic representations of human depravity. Greed, underhanded dealings, fanaticism, and humbug are denounced. There is also an attack on the stupidity of secular authority and the materialism and hypocrisy of the Church.

BOOK V: The series of visits to outlandish places continues until the travellers arrive at Lantern Land (borrowed from Lucian) . Guided by an Illustrious Lantern, they reach the Island of the Holy Bottle, pass through a vineyard planted by Bacchus himself, descend into an underground temple, and come before the Holy Bottle. Following a ritual prescribed by the Priestess Bacbuc, Panurge hears the oracle speak the single and mysterious word "Trinc." The priestess explains that the word means "drink," and adds that it is the kindest and most favorable answer ever uttered by the oracle. Panurge remarks that man is a drinking rather than a laughing animal, that by drink man becomes divine, and that by drink the soul can be filled with all truth, learning, and philosophy. The outcome is not precisely stated, but Panurge appears to be inspired with a zestful desire to try anything, and one assumes that he will embark upon the experiment of marriage in spite of all that has been said against it.

The all-thirstiness of Pantagruel and the word of the holy oracle is the nearest Rabelais ever comes to specifying his philosophy of life. There is no doubt of the praise of literal drinking, but the jubilant remarks of Panurge that follow leave no doubt either that Rabelais means more than that, as indeed the whole tenor of his work makes clear. To drink is to imbibe all the experiences life has to offer, to live life rather than merely to read or hear about it. And nothing in the five books of Rabelais is as significant as the spirit that pervades them. Rabelais had a digestion strong enough to devour nearly everything in the world, including its crudest and most animalistic aspects. The only things he could not stomach were bigotry, crookedness, cruelty, and pompousness. He clearly preferred the animal in man to the pretence that he was some sort of minor god. An incurable optimist, he advocated complete freedom for man in his exploration of the world. "Abandon yourself to Nature's truths and let nothing in this world be unknown to you" is an aphorism that would sum up the essence of Rabelais if it were accompanied by his convivial earthy coarseness and by his broad generous spirit; for "wisdom cannot enter an unkind spirit, and knowledge without conscience is the ruin of the soul. We establish sovereign good not by taking and receiving, but by giving with both hands."

The style of Rabelais is a perfect expression of the exuberance of his nature. Possessed of a prodigious vocabulary, he pours forth torrents of synonyms and lists, seldom using one word where three will do, and tumbling word upon word for the sheer joy of doing it. Without concern for form or propriety, he shifts scene or point of view with startling abruptness whenever the mood strikes him. Always rhythmic and lively, his tumultuous sentences do as much as their subject matter in conveying the boisterous conviviality of one of the most natural and uninhibited authors the world has ever known.

JOHN CALVIN (1509–1564)

The opposite side of the picture is represented by one of the greatest leaders of the Reformation. John Calvin was born in Picardy and received a thorough education which included theology, law, and Greek in its later stages. Early converted to the Protestant viewpoint, he was forced to flee to Basle in 1534 where he wrote in Latin his most widely known work which he later, in 1541, translated into French under the title *L'Institution de la Religion Chretiénne* (*The Institutes of Christianity*) (1536). The twenty-eight years before his death in 1564 were centered at Geneva, which he made a stronghold of Protestantism.

Being essentially a technical theological work, *The Institutes* is not properly a concern for the study of literature, but it is important in the history of the period in specifying an attitude of self-abnegation and personal humility in contrast to the lust for experience and earthly fame that are hallmarks of the Renaissance. Furthermore, its clearcut, logical organization and its straightforward, lucid prose form a model of composition, which evades both the artificiality of Renaissance Latinity and the rambunctious looseness of Rabelais. From the point of view of subject matter, *The Institutes* became the basic work on which most Protestant theology was founded.

THE SCHOOL OF LYONS

Lyons, a wealthy intellectual and printing center remote from the religious supervision of the Sorbonne, maintained a close contact with Renaissance Italy and also with the court of Francis I. The introduction of Neoplatonism from Italy, encouraged by Marguerite of Navarre, here inspired a school of poets headed by Maurice Scève (c. 1510–1564). An early follower of Marot, he became an ardent Neoplatonist and a disciple of Petrarch after studying at Avignon, where he discovered what he believed was Laura's tomb. The result was the long and obscure Neoplatonic poem *Délie*, an anagram of *L'Idée* (*The Idea*). Made up of four hundred and forty-nine dizains (ten-line stanzas), it sings the poet's adoration of the image of pure intellectual beauty, which is mirrored in his cruel mistress whose beauty, grace, and virtue he praises, together with descriptions of the joys and sufferings induced by love. The number and grouping of the stanzas, together with the rhyme scheme, work out an intricate number symbolism which, to the initiate, signifies the union of the earthly with the divine. The other principal members of the School of Lyons were Antoine Heroët (c. 1492–1568) and two women, Pernette de Guillet (1520–1545) and Louise Labé (1526–1566). All of them were Neoplatonists and Petrarchists. The inclusion of two women in the circle indicates the increasing elevation of women in society, which was partly the result of the Neoplatonic revival.

LA PLÉIADE

The first organized attempt to establish a classical spirit in French writing, as had been done in Italy, was the work of a group of seven talented young poets led by Ronsard and named the *Pléiade* after the heavenly constellation. The movement began around 1547 among students at Paris. Its official handbook, written by one of them, Du Bellay, was the *Défense et Illustration de la Langue Française* (*Defense and Illumination of the French Language*). Analogous both in spirit and organization to Dante's defense of Italian in his *De Vulgari Eloquentia*, this basic manifesto of French Neoclassicism sought to ignore the Middle Ages and previous vernacular poets and to build a new distinguished French literature modelled on the writings of Greece and Rome. The new literature was to be created on the basis of classic themes written in classic forms; of more recent writings only the Italian sonnet was admitted. The language was to be deliberately formed, as Dante had also proposed, by a selection of French words that must avoid the extremes of both pedantry and colloquialism. By such conscious selectivity and combination of a new language with classic modes, an official distinguished diction and style would be created to vie with the literary language of Rome.

Pierre de Ronsard (1524–1585)

The leader of the group, Pierre de Ronsard, was born of a distinguished family at the Château de la Possonière near Vendôme. After a brief education at the College of Navarre, he entered upon what might have been a brilliant career at court as a page to the Duke of Orléans. In the service of the Duke and other members of the nobility he travelled to Scotland, England, and Germany, acquired skill in languages and a great deal of worldy experience, and at seventeen was well on the way to eminence in courtly society when he was suddenly stricken by deafness. Returning to education, he became an accomplished Greek and Latin scholar under the tutelage of Daurat, head of the Collège de Coqueret. Completing his studies in 1550, Ronsard devoted the remainder of his life to reviving the classical manner. He was honored by being named the official court poet until 1574 when he retired from active life, but he continued to compose until his death in 1585.

His many works cover nearly every form of poetry except dramatic. Beginning with the composition of love sonnets in the Petrarchan vein, occasional light verse, odes, and hymns, he provides the best example of his early manner in the one hundred and eight-one sonnets of *Les Amours* (1552), which are more carefully imitative than original or sincere. During his following period as court poet, he continued to write occasional pieces but aspired to become another Virgil in the creation of the epic *La Franciad* (1572), which was never completed and was poorly received even in its own day because of the remoteness of its subject, unfortunate choice of the decasyllabic line, and the introduction of artificial pagan gods. Assuming the role of counsellor, he also wrote advisory works on the government and well-being of France.

After 1574 when he retired from public life, he returned to his original mood of personal lyric expression. In the *Sonnets pour Hélène* (*Sonnets for Helen*) (1578) and the *Dernières Amours* (*Last Amours*) (c. 1580), he looks back pensively and philosophically upon his youth, and strikes a new and highly engaging note in a series of genial, delicate, half-serious and half-humorous poems. Always at his best in the elegiac mood, he plays on the themes of the beauty and permanence of nature, the sublimity of love, and the certainty of death. As an experimenter in verse forms, he achieved remarkable harmonies and an exquisiteness of form that was to be a model for succeeding poets.

Joachim du Bellay (1525–1560)

Less of a poet than Ronsard, Joachim du Bellay was his most gifted disciple and the major theorist of the group. Born at Lire in Anjou, son of the governor of Brest, he lost his parents at the age of seven and endured an unhappy youth under the careless supervision of an older brother. In 1545 he went to Poitiers to study law, and became interested in poetry through the enthusiasm of a newfound friend, Jacques Peletier du Mans. Through a chance meeting with Ronsard at a wayside inn, he joined the Collège de Coqueret and took part in the formation of the *Pléiade*. In 1549 he published *L'Olive* and the *Défense et Illustration*. He also suffered a severe illness, which left him as deaf as Ronsard. In 1533 he traveled to Rome as secretary to his uncle Cardinal du Bellay, who had employed Rabelais as his physician, and his four years in Rome became the inspiration for his succeeding poems. He died suddenly of apoplexy in 1560.

In spite of his short life, Du Bellay is known for three books of poetry besides the *Défense*. The first, a sequence of one hundred and fifty sonnets, is entitled *L'Olive*, the olive being symbolic of Pallas Athena, and the name being also an anagram of his Platonic mistress Viole. In pseudo-personal poetry of the Petrarchan type, he hymns the beauty of his goddess, immortalizes her hair, eyes, hands, and records his hopes and fears. Skillful but imitative in composition, these sonnets are distinguished principally for their ability in suggesting the varying moods of the lover. The two later poems, *Les Antiquités de Rome* (1553–1557) and *Les Regrets,* which were inspired by his Roman visit, become increasingly personal and sincere. *The Antiquities of Rome*, translated by Spenser as *The Ruins of Rome*, makes much of the grandeur that was Rome, narrates the history of its decline, and enlarges on the romance of decay in a melancholy vein. *The Regrets* is a much more personal and direct expression of the poet's own bitter sense of unhappiness. Decrying the degradation and immorality of Rome, grieving over his wasted life, he laments the unhappy hour he left his own little French village with its smoking chimneys. Here the artificialities of borrowed forms and semi-borrowed feelings are absent. In their place is the affecting yearning and homesickness of a suffering man. Even in his earlier poems the nostalgic note in Du Bellay's writing gives him his chief distinction as a poet of melancholy, predecessor of Gray and the "graveyard school" of English poets.

The Lesser Stars

The other members of the *Pléiade* were less distinguished. Remi Belleau (1528–1577) is remembered for his *Journée de la Bergerie* (*Daily Life of the Shepherd*), which intersperses prose links between light, lovely, and dainty verses in praise of country life. Antoine de Baif (1532–1589) wrote classic plays and poetry with scholarly seriousness and little inspiration. His *Amours de Francine*, cast in the form of a dream, is his most genuine work. Étienne Jodelle (1532–1572) was concerned with classical comedy and tragedy, scrupulously observing all the rules, and subordinating action to poetic dialogue. The group was completed by the undistinguished Ponthus de Tyard and Jacques Peletier du Mans. Although the *Pléiade* attempted to write in classical form and vein, its lasting merit is in the personal lyricism of the less ambitious works. It may be that much of the individual talents of its members was warped by being misdirected in attempted imitation of a literature and a world that was not their own.

A second generation of the *Pléiade* appeared after the accession of Henry III in 1573. Of these imitators, Philippe Desportes (1545–1606) was the outstanding courtly poet who made flattery into a fine art in his precious imitations of Italian models.

Guillaume Saluste, Seigneur du Bartas (1544–1590)

The effectiveness of the Reformation in France is seen in the second half of the sixteenth century when the Huguenots carried away the literary honors in what is sometimes described as the third generation of the *Pléiade*. A then world-famous poet was Guillaume Saluste, Seigneur du Bartas, who combined the Renaissance ideals of classicism and universality with piety and religious devotion. Beginning as a disciple of the *Pléiade* with a great admiration for Ronsard, he was turned away by Huguenot affiliations from worldly frivolities to the heavenly muse Urania. He began his "praises of God" in 1573 with *L'Uranie où Muse Celeste* (*Urania or the Heavenly Muse*), in which the Muse commands him to sing the honor of the Almighty. This was followed by the *Judith* (1572), treating a Biblical theme in the manner of Virgil. His masterpiece was the work of many years. *La Semaine* appeared in 1578 and the first part of the never-completed *Seconde Semaine* was published in 1584, its completion being interrupted by the poet's death.

In this epic work, *The Week*, Du Bartas takes the favorite medieval theme of the seven days of creation, filling in the text of Genesis with vast symbolic interpretations. *The Second Week* then becomes a universal history of the seven ages of the world from the Christian point of view. The chief appeal of this elephantine work is the sincerity and descriptive power of its author. Its most obvious defects are overelaboration, exaggeration, and extravagant language. In imitation of Homer he overdoes the device, already employed by the *Pléiade* of using compound epithets; and in search of technical elegance he conceives of an onomatopoetic effect achieved by duplicating syllables; "*battre*" (to beat) becomes "*babattre*." In spite of this absurdity he aroused universal admiration. He had a host of English imitators, and even Goethe admired him.

Theodore-Agrippa d'Aubigné (1550–1630)

A somewhat more colorful figure, Theodore-Agrippa d'Aubigné, was by turns a fighter, poet, playwright, governor, and novelist. Careless and impulsive by nature, he created works which show many flashes of inspiration but which are lacking in finish and a sense of form. Author of one hundred sonnets to Diana, *Hécatombe à Diane* (c. 1620) a tragedy, *Circé* (c. 1618) which includes satire of the contemporary court; and a picaresque novel, *Aventure du Baron de Faeneste* (1630) his masterpiece, entitled *Les Tragiques* (*The Violences*) (1616), essays to give epic treatment to the current religious wars. Considerably more sober and of more lasting value is his *Histoire Universelle* (1615), which "universal history" gives a lively account of events in France from 1550 to 1601.

MICHEL DE MONTAIGNE (1533–1592)

The sixteenth century in France concludes as it began with the appearance of a gigantic literary figure who is as broad and as realistic as Rabelais but who substitutes quiet reflection for the boisterous nonsense of his predecessor. Father of the discursive familiar essay, which to many is the only kind of essay worthy of being dignified as an art form, creator of the personal, easy, conversational tone in writing, Montaigne was not so much a lover of the world as a lover of mankind. He took delight in human absurdities and was forever engrossed in exploring the ideas and modes of behavior which had emanated from human minds.

Michel Eyquem, Seigneur de Montaigne, was the third son of a notable father who had filled public office, engaged in war under Francis I, married a Jewish woman, and was extraordinarily humane and advanced in his ideas of raising a family. Michel was born in Perigord near Bordeaux in 1533, was given peasant godparents, and was put out to nurse with a peasant woman. When he returned home, his father, who forbade corporal punishment and believed in persuasion rather than threats, saw to it that his son learned Latin by the ingenious method of forcing everyone in the household, including servants, to learn and speak Latin exclusively when in the child's presence. This extraordinary parent also devised an unsuccessful method of teaching Greek, and arranged that the children should be awakened in the morning only by the sound of music. When Montaigne was six years old he was sent to the Collège de Guienne at Bordeaux, then at the height of its reputation. At the age of thirteen he went to Toulouse to study law, where he remained in law practice and met Etienne de la Boëttie, who remained his close and revered friend until the early death of the latter six years later. During the following years Montaigne led a somewhat dissipated life, according to his own account, and was apparently variously engaged in diplomatic missions and in legal offices.

In 1566 he married Françoise de la Chassaigne, a very capable woman to whom he was very glad to turn over his burdensome practical affairs. When his father died in 1569, Montaigne fell heir to the estate because of the earlier deaths of his two older brothers, and in 1571 at the age of thirty-eight, "weary of the servitude of law courts and public offices," he retired from active life to seek comfort and diversion from the thousand books in his tower library. Here he began to set down in essay form the random observations that came to him from reading, from his hospitable entertainment of everyone and anyone, and from analysis of himself. After publishing his first two volumes of *Essais* (1580), he undertook a journey for his health through Switzerland, Germany, and Italy, and kept a journal of the trip. This account was discovered and published in 1774. He had already begun to suffer severely from the stone and gravel (calculus formation in the kidney), a condition which made his later years exceedingly painful. He returned home to become Mayor of Bordeaux by the King's desire, but after instituting a number of reforms, he abandoned the city during the plague of 1587, and was relieved of his office. The publication of a third volume of essays in 1588 indicates that officialdom had not been allowed to interfere too much with his writing. His only other interest was his devotion to Marie de Gournay, who became his protégé and bosom companion during his final years. He died in 1592 after a long ordeal of suffering from the stone.

The *Essays*

In the one hundred and six essays that fill the three volumes, Montaigne follows a simple and amiable method. Proposing as a topic almost anything that suggests itself, he examines the opinions of former authors, quotes from their books, makes his own comments, and sometimes, not always, reaches a conclusion on the subject. Often, when faced with two diametrically opposed points of view, he shows characteristic good sense by choosing a middle course. As he continues to write, the essays become longer, less reliant on the ideas of others, and more highly personalized. A motto for all the essays is his "Know thyself as thou wouldst know all men," and the guiding spirit of his inquiries is "What do I know?"

VOLUME I: The first volume, influenced by Plutarch and Seneca, is made up principally of discussions of the emotions. Essay I notes that pity can be overdone as can sorrow—the idea advanced in Essay II. It is important to know oneself to prevent being ruled by imaginings (III). Intention is more to be judged than action (VII). Idleness destroys both will and mind (VIII). Essays IX and X attack respectively lying and superstition. Essays XII and XIX preach stoicism. The power of sympathy is examined in Essay XX; one coughs and so do others in the company. In Essay XXII he notes that custom is the basis of authority. In Essay XXIV he inveighs against pedantry, and follows this attack by presenting an excellent plan of education in Essay XXV. Essay XXVII praises friendship as the highest and noblest affection, with tender reference to La Boëtie. Essay XXIX is in praise of moderation. Essay XXX on the cannibals praises the natural simplicity of the savage, in anticipation of Rousseau. In Essay XXXV Montaigne returns to the fascinating subject of custom, noting that the wearing of clothes is purely a habit; the face is bare all the time. Essay XXXVI preaches toleration of others. Solitude and self-dependence, the subject of Essay XXXVII, are considered more admirable than the servilities and shams of public life. In Essay XXXIX on Cicero and Pliny, the pungent observation is made that good writing must have something to say. In Essay L, comparing Democritus, who laughed at life, with Heraclitus, who wept, he prefers the first attitude as being above life. Essay LVI, "Of Prayers and Orisons," is marked by reverence and simplicity, pointing out that only the pure in heart can pray.

VOLUME II: The essays of Volume II were influenced by Montaigne's acquaintance with the Greek skeptic Sextus Empiricus, through a Latin translation published by Henri Estienne in 1562. Montaigne placed ten quotations from Sextus on the walls of his library, and his own mildly skeptical spirit was obviously strengthened by their inspiration. Essay III defines philosophy as the science of doubting. Death is a remedy against all evils and the most voluntary death is the fairest. Essay VIII on education is reminiscent of his own boyhood, condemning violence and advocating that fathers be companions to their children. He inserts a quotation from Thales, which was later picked up by Bacon to the effect that "young men should marry not yet, old men not at all." Essay X "On Books" finds Boccaccio and Rabelais enjoyable and scorns the romantic stuff of the *Amadís*. Virgil, Lucretius, Catullus, and Horace are admired. Ariosto is considered wretched compared with Virgil, fluttering as he does from tale to tale. Cicero's philosophy is good but his style is tedious. Montaigne confesses that he is "wonderfully curious to know the mind, soul, and judgment of our authors." Essay XI calls cruelty the worst of vices and notes that the cannibals are not as bad as some who persecute the living. Essay XII, the "Apology for Raymond Sebond," whose *Theologia Naxuralis* (*Natural Theology*) Montaigne had translated before his retirement, is the most outstanding single essay. Subtitled "The Vanity of Human Reason," this is not only an attack on the attempt to substantiate Christianity by reason but also a skeptical undermining of the validity of reason itself. In a long discourse which spreads forth the long record of human idiocies, credulities, and contradictions, he concludes that there are no truths or principles unless revealed by Divinity, and compares animals with civilized man to the disadvantage of the latter. In the course of the essay he remarks that we are Christians as we are Germans or Frenchmen, and are truly Christian only by works, not by oral professions. He discusses the folly of war, the pettiness and vanity of man, the absurdities of scholastic learning, and approaches very close to Rousseau in throwing out the suggestion that animals may possess more than five senses, implying that ultimate knowledge comes "instinctively" or by a natural response to divine principles. In Essay XVI "Of Glory," he reasserts his basic integrity: "I care not so much what I am with others, as I respect what I am in myself." In Essay XVII which laments the human habit of ignoring substance and grasping at shadow, he singles out as "great" Boëtie and his "daughter by alliance," Marie de Gournay. Essay XIX, pleading for liberty of conscience, notes that "Christianity has done more harm to learning than pagan flames." Essay XXVII calls cowardice the mother of cruelty. In Essay XXXI he exalts Seneca over Cicero, and in Essay XXXII praises Seneca and Plutarch as philosophers who teach virtue. Essay XXXVI singles out Homer as the greatest poet. Essay XXXVII, which is singularly the fruit of personal experience, is a diatribe against the absurdities and superstitions of contemporary medicine.

VOLUME III: The third volume indicates a far greater degree of maturity, displaying fewer enthusiasms and more carefully weighed judgments. Relying also much less on quotation and much more on personal experience, it may be taken as a kind of final statement of the results of Montaigne's researches into the nature of man. Essay II, in connection with "Repentance," discusses the corruption of the age and opines that repentance is not something that can be purchased, but can be effective only through actions. The true worth of the mind, he adds, is not in high but in orderly thinking. Essay VII again attacks scholarship as the art of bewildering through entanglement of speech, and questions the validity of all final judgments. Essays IX and X are composed of highly personal reminiscences of his visit to Rome and his career as Mayor of Bordeaux. In Essay XII he comes back again to the precept of following nature. Nearly all opinions, he says, are based on authority, which may be good enough in so weak an age. Yet many examples of goodness may be found among those utterly ignorant of Aristotle or Plato. The peasant is often better adjusted than the scholar and is less concerned about dying. Finally, in Essay XIII, he concludes that there is a kind of all-inclusive universal reality of which all individuals are a part. The only certainty in life is variety and diversity. The measure of man is, in a sense, the common denominator or average of all mankind. Therefore, "know thyself," for "sit we upon the highest throne of the world, yet sit we upon our own tail."

IMPORTANCE

As in the case of Rabelais, the value of Montaigne lies in the whole and in the spirit of his writings rather than in any individual pronouncement. Here the humble, questing spirit, refusing to be awed by authority, forages through the maze of opinions which the learned have uttered, and finds only endless contradiction. He knows for a certainty only that man is a most variable and unstable creature. He notes that the average man is what nationality, customs, and circumstance have made him, and that final, definite reality is unattainable. Yet he arrives at the same kind of all-inclusive acceptance of his world that characterizes Rabelais and Goethe. In the very nature of this variable creature there is a kind of guiding star, possessed alike by the savage and by that savant who cuts through the maze of scholarly logic-chopping to feel the spirit of goodness, generosity, nobility, love of truth, and love of man. This spirit is somehow closely connected with nature; it is a gift of the Creator of the Universe. The ultimate pleasure in reading Montaigne springs from the infectious influence of this spirit and also from the sheer pleasure of following his investigations of the thoughts and behavior of the human race. It has been remarked that Montaigne is for the mature and the old, not for the young. It is certain that he possessed one of the most mature minds of Europe, and that he writes particularly for those who are more interested in the variety of life than in pat conclusions regarding it.

Travel Journal

Montaigne's *Journal du Voyage* or *Travel Journal* (published posthumously in 1774) is a fascinating picture of Renaissance Italy. In Montaigne's spirit of amused curiosity, the book (written in Italian) describes the baths, customs, monuments which he saw; notes the statue of Ariosto at Ferrara, the wonderful gardens and fountains at Florence; and admires the pageants, fireworks, and chariot racing observed there. A visit to the pope is described with very little reverence, and Rome impresses mainly by its cosmopolitanism, its processionals, ceremonials, and courtesans. The book reflects his inquisitive and tolerant attitude.

MINOR WRITERS

Henri Estienne (1528–1598)

Montaigne's interest in man as a social animal is an indication of that growing concern for patterns of behavior that was to mark French Neoclassicism in the seventeenth century. The concurrent determination to break away from dependence on Italian models had its own forerunner in Henri Estienne, who was more of a Greek scholar than an original writer but who fought for an independent French literature and the cultivation of the French language which, he said, was innately superior to Italian in beauty and power.

François de Malherbe (1555–1628)

The outstanding rebel against Italian influence and the preciosity of the imitators of the *Pléiade*, François de Malherbe became the determining factor in turning French poetry in the direction of purity, clarity, and exactness. Born in Normandy at Caen, he was educated for the law, but soon began a literary career by imitating the poets of the *Pléiade*. As a result of a kind of innate rugged honesty of character he soon became disgusted with the superficiality of his own creations and began to write careful, restrained, and meticulously correct verses. Made poet laureate in 1605, he became a kind of literary dictator, warning against undisciplined imagination and insisting on universal subjects and rigid laws of rhyme. He also made of the Alexandrine (the six-foot line) a cadence that was to become standard in the seventeenth century. His own poetic productivity is small and undistinguished except for his sensitive ear for the words and cadences in which the commonplaces of his thought are clothed.

Honoré d'Urfé (1568–1625)

The last noteworthy Renaissance work of France, *L'Astrée* is a blend of Italian Neoplatonism and the Italian pastoral with the romantic influence of the Spanish *Amadís*. Its author, Honoré d'Urfé, was brought up in a rural region near Lyons, the scene of his pastoral, was educated at the Collège de Tournon, and after several violent years during which he was engaged in the current civil wars, he retired to the peace of Annecy in Savoy to devote himself to literature. His principal work, the *Astrée* (1607), is made up of five books totalling over five thousand pages, which describe in narrative, dialogue, and verse the loves and trials of seven pairs of lovers. The setting, supposedly in a third century countryside where shepherds and shepherdesses are still living in the golden age, is entirely in the pastoral tradition, as is the sophisticated speech of the pseudo-shepherds headed by Celadon, who is loved by the nymph Astrée. But the adventurous involvements of plot and the tone of high nobility are much closer to the *Amadís*, while the concept of love, "the desire for immortality in beauty," is pure Neoplatonism. This colossal work continued to be popular in court circles throughout the first half of the seventeenth century, being enjoyed for its soft harmonious style, its forty interwoven love stories, its elevated sentiments, and the pleasant contrast provided by the character of Hylas who jests at the ideals of love.

7
THE RENAISSANCE IN SPAIN, PORTUGAL, AND HOLLAND

THE RENAISSANCE IN SPAIN

After a stormy medieval history made up of Moslem conquests and the division of the Iberian peninsula into warring kingdoms, the final defeat of the Moors and the discovery of America, both in 1492, marked the beginnings for Spain of a glorious age of national unity and prosperity. Imitations and emulation of the Italian Renaissance which appeared early in the fifteenth century gradually developed into a full-fledged literary movement with distinctive Spanish characteristics: the retention of regionalism or the local cultures of the various parts of Spain, a strong sense of independence, a love of dreamy romanticism and, right beside it, that delight in the earthy realities of low life which made Spain the home of the *picaro* or rogue, who flourished as hero of what is known as picaresque literature.

The Amadís de Gaula

The strong Spanish penchant for romanticism produced the most romantic of all romances, the *Amadís de Gaula*. The story of Amadis of Gaul probably originated in Wales, was connected with the Arthurian legends, and was known in Spain and Portugal in the fourteenth century. The version which became so widely popular throughout all of Europe was composed around 1500 by Garci Rodriguez de Montalvo, who revised an earlier text and added a final section of his own invention. The background, place, and time of the story is much more vague than in other traditional romances, and the Arthurian mingling of heroism and love reaches its height in Amadis himself, the quintessence of knighthood. Amadis is punctilious in honor, absolute in fidelity, unequalled in courage, and both tender and passionate as a lover. Falling in love with Oriana at first sight, he engages in a long series of remarkable adventures, destroys natural and supernatural adversaries, and wins to his resolutely faithful mistress at last. As in the other romances, the central story is complicated by the introduction of many lesser figures and events. Although without any marked distinction in its composition, the *Amadís* clearly appealed to the Neoplatonic tone of ennoblement and perfectionism throughout Renaissance Europe and spawned a host of imitations, particularly in Spain.

Miguel de Cervantes Saavedra (1547–1616)

At the height of Spain's Golden Age, a somewhat prolific and not particularly noteworthy writer happened upon an idea that was to make him the most widely known of Spanish authors. For Cervantes' *Don Quixote*, which is one of the most praised and best-loved books in world literature, has come to be regarded as the prime expression of all that is most uniquely Spanish and as a universal symbol of the precarious balance held by all mankind between ennobling idealism and the necessary acceptance of vulgar reality.

For such a celebrated author very little dependable biographical information exists. Miguel de Cervantes Saavedra was born probably in Valladolid in 1547, the fourth child of a physician of rather meagre means. As a student at Madrid he showed an interest in writing, and in 1569 he was at Rome apparently in the service of a churchman. In 1571 he fought in the Battle of Lepanto where he was seriously wounded and lost the use of his left hand. After some months of hospitalization he returned to soldiering until 1575 when he was captured by pirates and carried off as a slave to Algiers. After several unsuccessful attempts to escape, he was finally ransomed, and returned to Spain in 1580. He was married in 1584 and apparently turned to writing as a means of livelihood, publishing his pastoral *Galatea* in 1585 and composing between twenty and thirty plays. In 1587 he bcgan to supplement his income by services to the state as commissary and revenue collector. His pay was small, and he seems to have been in almost perpetual trouble. He was excommunicated for requisitioning cereals belonging to the Church and was in prison at least twice because of irregularities in his accounts. Meanwhile, out of the bitterness of a degrading and irritating career he was somehow distilling the rare humor of *Don Quixote*, the first part of which was published in 1605. In the same year the death of a young nobleman near Cervantes' home in Valladolid threw him again into prison for a few days on suspicion. Soon after, he apparently went to Madrid where he continued to write and publish (the second part of *Don Quixote* appearing in 1615) until he died of dropsy in 1616.

His first long work, the *Galatea*, is a pastoral in the usual tradition, employing contemporary figures as models for the artificial shepherds who pursue their loves in prose and verse in the fashion made popular in Italy. His twelve *Exemplary Stories* (*Novelas Ejemplares*) (1613) are on the order of the Italian *novella*. Some of them are ingenious in theme and handling; the best of them are made effective by the inclusion of realistic details and by the personal viewpoints of the author.

Don Quixote: In comparison with the generally undistinguished nature of Cervantes' other works, the uniqueness of *Don Quixote* seems all the more remarkable. Unlike these other literary efforts, *El Ingenioso Hidalgo Don Quixote de la Mancha* (*The Ingenious Gentleman Don Quixote of La*

Mancha), was begun as a satire on the large number of popular romances that had followed on the heels of *Amadís*. His purpose, in his own words, was "to expose to the contempt they deserve the extravagant and silly tales of chivalry." As a literary satire *Don Quixote* accomplished its purpose by bringing to earth with a resounding thud the cloudland of chivalric romance. That it went far beyond the limits of its intention, transcending satire by striking basic chords of human behavior, is entirely the result of Cervantes' own broad and deeply human sense of reality and sense of humor. It is entirely possible that Cervantes was led into this infinitely richer subject by the sheer accident of the creation of his two leading characters as a basis for the ridicule of chivalry. But, however it happened, the popular appeal of the mad knight and his doltish companion was as immediate as it has been continuous. The *First Part* ran through ten editions in the first fifteen years. The publication of a *Second Part* in 1614 by an anonymous imitator forced Cervantes to write and publish his own *Second Part*, at the end of which the death of the hero brings the complete work to a definite close.

The story of this famous pair of madmen begins with the description of Alonzo Quixano of La Mancha, a poor retired gentleman whose mind has become befuddled by reading quantities of chivalric tales. Determining to revive the age of chivalry he assumes the name Don Quixote de la Mancha, puts on an old suit of armor inherited from his grandfather, mounts a decrepit old nag called Rosinante, and sets out on his adventures. Meeting a company of merchants not far from town, he challenges them to a passage at arms. Convinced that he is mad, they beat the poor old gentleman and leave him to make his way home to recuperate. A priest and a barber, his neighbors, burn his library in an attempt to cure him of his hallucination but succeed only in convincing him that the powers of darkness have spirited away his books.

Refusing to be so turned from his appointed mission, he sets out again, now accompanied by a page Sancho Panza, a moronic peasant who goes along on his ass Dapple in the vague belief that Don Quixote intends to make him governor of an island. Don Quixote, aware that he still requires a mistress as an object of his devotion, selects at random an earthy peasant girl noted for her skill in salting pork. Thereafter he fights for the honor of his Dulcinea del Toboso.

The basis for the satire is now complete, and the remainder of the book is filled with the invention of episodes in which the incurably romantic nature of Don Quixote leads him into one predicament after another, aided not at all by the heavy stupidity of his companion. On one adventure the knight runs at tilt against a group of windmills, mistaking them for giants, whence the common phrase "tilting at windmills" to describe a furious attack upon a trivial or nonexistent object. Don Quixote's avowed aim is "to give drink to the hungry and to feed those who are thirsty." From the most benevolent of motives he commits all kinds of absurdities. He attempts to rescue a lady from her proper escort, believing her to be a captive princess. He frees from a chain gang some of the worst criminals in Spain. He interferes with a meeting of lovers and is beaten for his pains. He snatches a basin from a poor barber, believing it to be the golden helmet of Mambrino (the helmet stolen by Rinaldo in *Orlando Furioso*). He tortures himself for love of Dulcinea but the lady is both indifferent and uncomprehending. Endless tricks are played upon him, including very elaborate ones as his fame becomes noised abroad, but he ascribes all his misfortunes to the power of magic. As a result of one such planned imposition upon him, wherein the village student Carasco, attired as a Knight of the White Moon, defeats him in combat and orders him to return home, Don Quixote retires from adventure and, approaching death, comes to his senses sufficiently to comprehend the nonsense of chivalry.

IMPORTANCE

For sheer inventive genius, *Don Quixote* is a masterpiece of storytelling, the incidents following one another with unfailing variety and ingenuity. The humor is occasionally slapstick but is often very delicate and always turns on the solid core of character represented by the Don and his squire. Don Quixote alone is interesting enough in his complete unworldliness; but the contrast between his soaring imagination and the utter absence of that quality in Sancho Panza sharpens both the humor and the absurdity. To Don Quixote Dulcinea exudes an aromatic sweetness too sublime for description. Sancho finds no difficulty in describing it as a "masculine smell resulting from her being in a sweat from too much work." Neither the Don nor his squire is capable of seeing the truth, but Sancho's mental image of life is degrading and dull while Don Quixote's is ennobling and inspiring.

Figured in the dreamer and the rogue, two of the dominant characteristics of all Spanish literature are here united in a single book. In the author's vision of a world that exists somewhere between the two lies a sane and sober evaluation of reality, which is, after all, always somewhat elusive even at best. In Cervantes' easy, natural style of writing there is an invitation to the reader to abandon pretentiousness and yet rise above the vulgarity of the commonplace. And if madness is inescapable, better the noble madness of Don Quixote than the dull idiocy of Sancho Panza. Badly equipped, poorly horsed, wretchedly attended, Don Quixote has won a place in the hearts of all who admire generosity and the stubborn courage to serve an ideal without assistance and in the face of derisive laughter. Like Shakespeare's Falstaff he is one of those rare literary creations that can be laughed at and loved at the same time.

Lope Felix de Vega Carpio (1562–1635)

Renaissance drama in Spain parallels that of Elizabethan England in the copiousness and fertility of invention that marked its playwrights. Its principal difference from the drama of Shakespeare and his contemporaries is in its failure to develop character or depth of any kind, placing its emphasis on plot and theatrical effects.

The most prolific of all the Spanish playwrights was Lope Felix de Vega Carpio, who was born at Madrid of a family belonging to the minor provincial nobility. Studying under the Jesuits he displayed amazing precocity and a passionate love of poetry. On leaving college, he was attached to the household of Don Geronimo Manrique, Bishop of Avila, in whose service he apparently began to write his first plays. After a short time he left the Bishop to enter the University of Alcala where he acquired the degree of Bachelor in Arts. Becoming secretary to the Duke of Alva he married Isabel de Urbina around 1584 but was compelled to leave his home shortly thereafter as a result of a duel. He found refuge at Valencia, and there he became the head of a school of poets. He returned to Madrid two years later, where his wife died in childbirth in 1588. He joined the Invincible Armada, returned to pursue his career of being secretary to members of the nobility, and married a second wife Juana de Gardio. He had two children by her and two other children by a mistress. When his second wife died in 1612, he took orders as a priest, being already acknowledged as the dictator of Spanish literature and founder of the Spanish theater. As a churchman he had another child by a married woman but spent his last years in severe penance for his worldliness. Dying in 1635 he was nationally mourned by both nobility and commoners.

Although he was the author of twenty-one volumes of epics, pastorals, odes, and sonnets, defender of the vulgar tongue and of the Castilian octosyllabic line, he is best known for his dramatic writings. Not considering play writing as anything but hackwork to please the multitude, he frankly discredited his art in his *Arte Nuevo de Hacer Comedias* (*New Art of Composing Comedies*) (1609) as being a simple device of inventing ingenious plots, maintaining suspense, and putting off the dénouement as long as possible. Using such a formula and writing comedies of everyday life, plays concerning the nobility, and religious plays, Lope de Vega produced upwards of two thousand dramatic works of which more than four hundred are extant.

His best plays are the comedies of common life in which intrigue is the principal ingredient in the presentation of love affairs complicated by the involvement of a point of honor—not honor as we know it but honor as related to the public reputation of an individual, a very touchy subject in Spanish literature of this period. A sample play is the *Punishment Without Vengeance* (*El Castigo sin Venganzo*) (c. 1610) in which a loose-living duke has an illegitimate son, marries, and goes off to the wars leaving the son in the care of his new wife. Upon his return the duke discovers that his son and wife are in love. He binds his wife, enjoins his son to kill a traitor, calls witnesses to the murder committed by his son, and thus ensures his son's death as a murderer without personal participation in it. Meanwhile his adopted daughter, who has also been in love with his son, marries another duke to bring about a happy ending.

Using such contrived and melodramatic plots, Lope de Vega is notable principally for having created a solid dramatic structure of three parts—exposition, involvement, dénouement—and of having grasped the very essence of the dramatic art of conflict, surprise reversals, and rapid motion.

Juan Ruiz de Alarcón Mendoza (c. 1581–1639)

Alarcón, born in Mexico but educated in Spain, added depth to Spanish play writing by his own idealism and by his sense of reality. Using melodramatic materials with great moderation, he attempted to make his plays more human and natural, creating character studies and criticisms of behavior on the basis of the comedy of intrigue. His *Walls Have Ears* (*Las Parades Oyen*) (c. 1622) is a reproof of slander and a defense of honesty. *El Examen de Maridos* (*The Examination of Husbands*) (c. 1625) exalts the unselfishness of friendship. His best play, *La Verdad Sospechosa* (*Truth Suspected*) (1628), which combines comedy of character and comedy of intrigue, was the model for Corneille in his composition of *Le Menteur* (*The Liar*).

Pedro Calderón de la Barca (1600–1681)

The last and in many respects the most effective dramatist of the Spanish Renaissance was Pedro Calderón de la Barca, who pushed the point of honor to fanatical extremes and created a series of plays, some of which are painfully memorable by the very extravagance of the events depicted in them. He was also the possessor of a highly poetic imagination which, in spite of constant infractions of good taste, lends a haunting quality to his plays of a religious nature.

Born in Madrid in 1600, educated at Salamanca, he led an entirely uneventful life as retainer of various noblemen. Having begun his dramatic career in 1622, he attracted the attention of the court and was employed by King Philip IV in 1636 to furnish entertainment. He was knighted in honor of his services, but in 1651 he entered the Church and turned his attention mainly to religious plays until his death in 1681.

Of his many plays based on the point of honor, the outstanding are *El Médico de su Honra* (*The Physician of His Own Honor*) (c. 1630), in which a suspicious husband forces a surgeon to cut the veins of his innocent wife so that he may dip his hand in her blood to wash away the stain on his scutcheon, and *El Pintor de su Deshonra* (*The Painter of His Own Dishonor*) (c. 1630), in which an artist is required by his prince to paint the portrait of his unfaithful wife. His religious plays combine poetic insight and otherworldly philosophy. *El Magico Prodigeoso* (*The Wonder-Working Magician*) (1637) revolves about the Faustian situation of the surrender of a human soul to the devil, and concludes with the inability of the powers of darkness to control the soul wedded to Christian purity and the virtue of God.

La Vida es Sueño (*Life Is a Dream*) (1635) describes death as the great awakening. Prince Sigismund, beguiled to a life of bestiality, is redeemed by reason, implying that man has within himself the power to better his own nature, that life is a dream, but that good deeds performed in the dream count in one's favor upon awakening. All of these plays, ingenious and sometimes near profundity in theme, are marred by affectation in composition and the introduction of extraneous characters and episodes.

Minor Writers

Among the lesser figures of the Spanish Renaissance, mention should be made of Fernando de Rojas (c. 1475–1537), who probably composed part if not all of the extraordinary novel *La Celestina*, which is written in dramatic form and in twenty-one long acts relates, with considerable emphasis on the realism of low life, the love story of the noble Calisto and Melibea. The brief anonymous *Lazarillo de Tormes* (1554), life of a folklore personage who is the first picaresque hero, contains much realistic satire on the clergy and on pretentiousness in general. Spain's Golden Age ends with the affectations of Góngora, assumed name of Luis de Argote (1561–1627), who was not satisfied to be the foremost song writer of the nation but preferred to use his talent in the creation of an artificial occult style intended only for the elect. "Gongorism" as a result has come to be synonymous with obscurity and artificiality, closely allied in nature to Marinism in Italy and Euphuism in England. Quevedo (Francisco Gomez de Quevedo Villegas, 1580–1645) was Spain's greatest satirist and wit. Brilliant and cynical, he fought Gongorism in behalf of simplicity of style. His outstanding composition is the picaresque novel *La Vida del Buscón* (*The Life of Buscón*), which is a bitter commentary on the heartlessness of humanity and is difficult to understand in spite of its sharp clear-cut style because of its faithful reproduction of the obscure colloquialisms of the gutter inhabitants who fill its pages.

THE RENAISSANCE IN PORTUGAL

Portugal, whose Renaissance history and characteristics are scarcely distinguishable from those of Spain, produced two writers of sufficient magnitude to be included in a survey of world literature. One of them, Jorge de Montemayor (1520–1561) borrowed from Italy the idea of the pastoral novel and wrote one of the most popular of its type in his *Diana*, parts of which were reproduced in Shakespeare's *Two Gentlemen of Verona* and in Honoré d'Urfé's *Astrée*. Alluding as usual to contemporary characters and events, the essentially simple love affair of the shepherd Sireno and the shepherdess Diana is filled with obstacles, and continued by the interruption of subplots and the customary interspersing of songs. Its great appeal can be ascribed to the freshness and simplicity of its subject and style in contrast to the absurdities of the current romances.

Luiz de Camoens (1524–1579)

Portugal's epic poem *The Lusiads* (*Os Lusiadas*) was the work of Luiz de Camoens, a widely travelled and adventurous gentleman-poet who took Vasco da Gama's voyage to India as a fitting subject for the glorification of Portugal. Luiz de Camoens was born at Lisbon in 1524 and educated at the University of Coimbra where he became interested in literary pursuits. He was engaged at the court until his attentions to a lady, who was a favorite of the king's, brought about his exile to Santarem. There he began his epic poem, *Os Lusiadas* (The Lusitanians or Portuguese) to celebrate in ten books the journey to India of Vasco da Gama in 1497. Upon being restored to Portugal, Camoens joined the army in its conflict against the Moors, lost an eye in patriotic service, and, receiving little gratitude at court, adventured into India in 1553 where he amassed a considerable fortune before his return to Portugal in 1569 with his completed epic. The work was published in 1572, won him a small pension and little renown, and Camoens died in poverty in 1579.

The Lusiads: The strength of this epic lies in its patriotic feeling and in the realistic descriptions of the emotions and experiences which give this single exploit both national and human significance. Its obvious weaknesses result from over-dependence on classical machinery and the interpolation of pagan traditions into an essentially adventurous story.

BOOK I: Jupiter directs the gaze of the gods to the ships of Vasco da Gama on their voyage to India, Bacchus vows that Portugal shall not rob him of his own country, but Venus and Mars beg Jupiter to favor the Lusitanians who are the descendants of Rome. Jupiter sends Mercury to guide the voyagers to Madagascar where they land, but Bacchus incites the natives against them. Cowed by Da Gama's artillery, the natives offer to provide a pilot to guide him to India, treacherously intending to land him at Quiloa where all Christians are killed. Mars and Venus prevent Da Gama from landing at this port.

II: The pilot makes a second attempt at the destruction of the Portuguese by leading them to Mombaça. When Venus blocks the entrance to the harbor, the pilot realizes that the gods are ensuring the Christians' safety and drowns himself. Venus, triumphant, arranges for the safe guidance of the explorers into the harbor of Melinda.

III: Visited on shipboard by the King of Melinda, Da Gama entertains him with an account of the history of Portugal. He describes how Portugal resisted both Romans and Moors and became independent of Spain.

IV: Continuing the historical narrative, he describes other repudiations by Portugal of foreign alliances and the visions granted to early kings predicting the conquest of India.

V: Bringing history up to date, Da Gama explains that he is the last of many explorers who have sought out India and describes his leavetaking of Portugal and the events of his voyage.

VI: The King of Melinda is so favorably impressed by Da Gama's narrative that he commissions a pilot to guide him safely to Callicut, aided by Christian prayers and the guidance of Venus.

VII: A Moorish prisoner in Callicut offers to act as an interpreter for Da Gama in his audience with the native prince and his prime minister.

VIII: On the way to the interview Da Gama passes a temple, carved on three of its sides. Upon asking why the fourth side is bare, he is told of a prediction that India will be conquered by foreigners whose deeds will be sculptured on the empty side. At the ensuing interview, the Prince is favorably disposed to consider a trade treaty with Portugal, but the next night Bacchus assumes the disguise of Mohammed and stirs up enmity against the Portuguese. Da Gama is therefore emprisoned, but his fleet has been forewarned to take action in any such event.

IX: The formidable appearance of the armed ships is enough to cause the Prince to change his mind. Da Gama is released, loaded with gifts, and sent safely on his way home with the interpreter Monçaide, who is converted to Christianity during the voyage.

X: In reward for their exploits, Venus leads the voyagers to the Island of Joy, where they are entertained by a prophecy of the future and where Da Gama is treated to a vision of the universe. After the added attraction of a recounting of the life of St. Thomas, the apostle of India, the Portuguese return home with the brides they have won on the island of Venus. The poem concludes with an account of their glorious reception at Lisbon and a final glorification by Camoens of Portugal's King.

THE RENAISSANCE IN HOLLAND

Desiderius Erasmus (c. 1466–1536)

In Holland where the full effects of the Renaissance were not to appear until late in the sixteenth century, there was born at Rotterdam around 1466 that sturdy independent citizen of the world, Desiderius Erasmus. Left at the age of thirteen to the care of three guardians, Erasmus was persuaded to enter monastic life. When he became disgusted with the ignorance and coarseness of his fellows, he was fortunate to secure liberation by an appointment as secretary to Henri de Bergues, Bishop of Cambray. Supported and encouraged by his new patron, he studied at the University of Paris and at Oxford, after which he carried on a kind of one-man crusade for the return of Christianity to the simple teachings of the gospels. Travelling all over Europe, supported by gifts and pensions in recognition of his writings and his mission, he became an internationally known figure who was admired and welcomed by a constantly increasing intellectual audience. After an amazingly active life and massive literary editorship and personal productivity, he died at Basle in 1536.

The Latin works of Erasmus live not as models of style or composition but as the expression of a personality. His *Colloquies* (1519), apparently intended as lessons in Latin phrasing, contain many pungent remarks breathing the spirit of both Reformation and Renaissance. He voices hatred of cruelty, of force, or of restriction in any form. He berates the avarice of both Church and State and the superstitious nature of the multitude by which they are imposed upon. He advocates freedom of mind, the spirit not the letter, devotion to God rather than to the saints, and the natural exercise of human instincts. Christ, he says, brought freedom and the Church invented monasteries.

This essential spirit of Erasmus is present in all his works, but his most engaging and most widely-known work is his *In Praise of Folly* (*Encomium Moriae*) (1509). Probably inspired by the immensely popular *Ship of Fools* (*Das Narrenschyff*), published in 1458, in which the German satirist Sebastion Brandt described every conceivable variety of folly, Erasmus sets out in a mocking vein to prove the superiority of folly over wisdom. After a series of extraordinary arguments delivered in a bantering, irresponsible tone that quite disarms the reader, Erasmus supports his thesis by parading one by one all the kinds of professional and nonprofessional people who make folly their god, proving his point by revealing the manifold follies of medicine, law, and lesser vocations. His principal attack is upon the absurdities of the Church, for "what can be said bad enough of others, who pretend that by the force of such magical charms, or by the fumblings over their beads in the rehearsal of such and such petitions...(which some religious impostors invented, either for diversion, or what is more likely for advantage), they shall procure riches, honor, pleasure, health, long life, a lusty old age, nay, after death a sitting at the right hand of our Savior in His kingdom; though as to this last part of their happiness, they care not how long it be deferred." Such neat turns and such invidious sarcasm, displaying both a corrosive wit and a magnanimous liberal spirit, made Erasmus the leading inspiration for the humanism of the Renaissance.

8
THE THEATER TO 1800

CLASSICAL INFLUENCES

The first major period of drama for which we have records today is that of fifth century Greece. This period lasted roughly one hundred and fifty years, and spanned the lives of two great Greek dramatists, Aeschylus (525 B.C.–c. 455 B.C.) and Aristophanes (448 B.C.–385 B.C.). Though the origins of Greek drama remain unclear, the influence of Egyptian culture is speculated. Greek drama was a very serious and highly perfected art form, and playwrights entered competitions in which their plays were judged and prizes awarded. Though Greek tragedy is perhaps the most remembered form of Greek theater, writers of light farce and comedy such as Aristophanes (*Lysistrata*) and Menander (*The Grouch*) were also quite popular.

Greek drama is essentially a celebratory art, as it was born from the festivals inspired by Dionysus, the Greek god of fertility and wine, symbolic of the life force. Greek amphitheaters, which often seated in excess of ten thousand people, had at their centers an orchestra where the actors and the all-important chorus performed. In the Greek conception of drama, tragedy possessed a societal function, purging the spectator of fear through catharsis, according to Aristotle. Among the most important Greek dramatists are Sophocles, whose *Oedipus* cycle is perhaps best known to the modern reader; Euripides, who wrote *Hippolytus* and *Elektra;* and Aeschylus, famed for his cycle of plays on Orestes. The dramatic art was well established in Greece by the third century B.C., when Rome began importing both dramatists and actors from Greece. But Rome never developed the high level of drama attained in Greece.

MEDIEVAL DRAMA

When Rome's vast empire crumbled, Europe was plunged into what some refer to as the Dark Ages. Though somewhat of a misnomer, this period, which lasted from the fall of Rome in 476 through the tenth century, saw no light cast on the texts of the Greek playwrights. Instead, drama was effectively dead for several centuries, until it began to grow, slowly at first, from the darkness of medieval cathedrals in the form of liturgical drama. The dramatic art, with the help of the strong oral tradition of literature brought by the minstrels and troubadours, finally spread into the streets and among the common people. The Roman Catholic Church was an all-powerful force during the Middle Ages, and although secular drama was considered a profane art form, the Church itself put on small plays, called *tropes,* as part of the Mass. Soon these grew into larger pieces representing whole scenes from the Bible, and by the twelfth century the theater had moved outside the church entirely.

The two main forms of medieval drama were mystery plays and morality plays. Mystery plays, usually several short pieces making up a larger cycle, were performed throughout Europe in association with the feast of Corpus Christi. Though these plays took their plots mainly from the Bible, many of the details of each story were actually invented by the actors, thus shedding new light on otherwise ambiguous biblical text. Mystery plays can be dark but also extremely witty and entertaining, as is evidenced by one of the most famous examples of the genre, *The Second Shepherd's Play.* Other well-known mystery plays include *Noah* (part of the Wakefield Cycle), *The Fall of Lucifer,* and *The Slaughter of the Innocents.* Morality plays do not draw on the Bible for plot, but rather use personification and allegory to spin tales of good and evil, always with a clear moral message. As in the French romances of the twelfth century, such as the *Roman de la Rose,* these fourteenth and fifteenth century plays personified feelings and values, using them allegorically as characters of the play. *Mankind, Everyman,* and *Wisdom* are among the morality plays preserved today.

THEATER OF THE RENAISSANCE

The rebirth of culture during the Renaissance drew literature and the stage together again. Italy's improvisational *commedia dell'arte,* a rough and tumble comic form complete with Pulcinellas and Harlequins, spread across Europe. This genre dated from the improvisations in the mid-1500s of theater companies, especially the Gelosi ("Jealous Ones"). It became their practice to include within their repertoire of comedies a new, improvisational form based on a slender thread of plot and stock characters. Actors demonstrated their creativity and expertise by their ability to conjure passable comedy from these bare materials—hence the name, *commedia dell'arte* ("comedy of the profession"). Stock characters included the beautiful young maiden, the handsome but poor suitor, the foolish merchant, the pedant doctor, the braggart captain, and the servants. Of the servants, the most notable for future developments in theater and literature was the stock figure of a manservant, Arlecchino, who were a patchwork costume of many colors and was, in fact, the predecessor of the harlequin tradition in many national literatures since. Another stock character, Pulcinella, has a large nose and even larger appetite; he lives on in the Punch and Judy shows of puppet theater. Popular throughout Europe for hundreds of years, the *commedia dell'arte* proved influential on later dramatists such as Moliere, Goldoni, and Gozzi. At the same time, many dramatists sought a reconception of classical drama, and the texts of Sophocles and Aeschylus were revived through the Italian *commedia erudita*. A true renaissance of the dramatic art came in part as a result of the collision of these two forms.

The first great age of English drama began near the turn of the sixteenth century. The Elizabethan drama was born in part from the genius of several authors, all contemporaries, who produced a vast body of comedies, tragedies, and historical plays for the reinvented Elizabethan stage. Among these writers were Ben Jonson (1572–1637), Christopher Marlowe (1564–1593) and William Shakespeare (1564–1616), and the lesser-known Thomas Kyd and Inigo Jones. Inspired both by the revival of classical drama and the new period of geographical discovery and religious reformation, these dramatists also owe their success as artists to what is now seen as a highly enthusiastic, if not always polished, group of theatergoers. Elizabethan audiences were astounding in their diversity, and even more astounding was the ability of the Elizabethan playwrights to please them all.

Although more complex and much less obvious than the medieval morality plays, Elizabethan drama still possessed a moral basis. Yet Shakespeare's plays, still eminently readable today, remain so in part because of the implicit and often malleable nature of any moral lesson one may take from them. Macbeth, for example, can be viewed existentially as being ultimately responsible for his own undoing, or classically as a victim of his fate and the gods or devils that control it. Are the three witches real, or are they but a creation of his distorted mind?

As the greatest playwright of the English language, Shakespeare was a master craftsman in all genres of theater. His tragedies include, in chronological order, *Hamlet, Othello, King Lear,* and *Macbeth.* His most famous comedies, which frequently found their origins in the Italian *commedia,* are *The Taming of the Shrew, A Midsummer Night's Dream, Much Ado About Nothing, Twelfth Night,* and *Measure for Measure.* He is also responsible for a number of historical dramas, less often performed and studied today. Other important Elizabethan plays include Marlowe's *Edward the Second, Massacre at Paris,* and the formidable tragedy *Doctor Faustus.* Johnson, mainly an author of comedy and farce (*Bartholomew Fair, The Alchemist*), also contributed to the Elizabethan masque, a Dionysian and celebratory form of theater entertainment which included a very basic plot and much merry-making.

The years just before the Elizabethan period saw an explosion of dramatic activity in both Spain and Portugal. Spain's Golden Age of theater began at the end of the fifteenth century, with Juan del Encina as its founder. In the years from 1570 Spanish drama grew in popularity, with masters such as Calderon de la Barca, Lope de Vega, author of the masterpiece *El Cid* along with as many as one thousand other plays (over seven hundred of which survive), and Miguel Cervantes. Spanish drama developed out of the same religious traditions of the Middle Ages and the Italian revival of classical theater, but its staging took a freer form than the French or Italian plays of the period. Spanish plays were performed in enclosed courtyards or *corrales,* and usually mirrored the staging conventions of the Elizabethan theater. The founder of the theater in Portugal is Gil Vicente (1465–1537), who wrote both farce and drama, as well as highly complex allegorical plays. Many of his works, including several tragedies and for the most part comedies, are still performed regularly in both Portugal and Brazil. His work has been translated, notably *Farces and Festival Plays, The Soul's Journey, Ship of Hell,* and *The Carriers.*

EUROPEAN NEOCLASSICAL AND EIGHTEENTH CENTURY DRAMA

The Golden Age of French theater is without a doubt the seventeenth century, and especially the early years of the reign of Louis XIV, who ruled from 1661 to 1715. The first great Neoclassical dramatist in France was Pierre Corneille (1606–1684). Corneille's plays include *Horace, Le Cid,* a rewriting of the Spanish play, and one of his early plays, a rewriting of Sophocle's *Oedipus Rex.* In the middle of the century and at the height of his popularity, a man thirty years his junior, Jean Racine (1639–1699), became his chief rival and competitor. Racine, who alongside Molière is today viewed as France's greatest playwright, was the author of seven tragic masterpieces, including *Andromaque, Bajazet, Britannicus,* and his final secular work, often hailed as his finest, *Phaedra.*

Corneille and Racine both took their plots directly from classical authors and works, mainly Greek but also Roman. The strength and beauty of their work lies not so much in its subject matter, but in its great poetic artistry. Nearly every line of Racine's entire theater is a perfect Alexandrine (a line of 12 syllables) in rhyming couplets. Although this high style of speech can appear overdone or forced, it does add to the dramatic intensity that always surrounds Racine's characters. This intensity in turn is born of the strict limitations that Racine put on his drama. The action of Racine's plays follows the three classical unities: unity of time, usually twenty-four hours; a unity of place; and unity of action, all borrowed from the theories of classical playwrights, and from Aristotles *Poetics.* Racine finished his career as a dramatist with several religious plays, and he became, near the end of his life, the official historiographer of Louis XIV.

French comedy in this golden age also had its master, Jean-Baptiste Poquelin, who is known by his pseudonym, Molière. Molière (1622–1673), who began his career as an actor in a family theater group, soon became the group's artistic director as well as its main source of scripts. The company won favor in the court of Louis XIV, as Molière wrote, directed, and acted in his comedies, which include *The Bourgeois Gentleman, The School for Wives, Tartuffe,* and *The Imaginary Invalid.* Though influenced by the Italian *commedia dell'arte,* these plays owe much of their greatness to Molière's own comic genius.

The middle of the seventeenth century was a rather dim period for theater in England, as the Puritan-ruled parliament closed the theaters to stop this art form, which they viewed as immoral. But the end of the century did see somewhat of a revival in the form of the comedy of manners, which, like the plays of Molière, mocked contemporary society. These comedies were light and rarely moralizing, and they enjoyed making light of the faults of society. By the end of the century, the stage had become an artificially lit indoor theater, much like ours today. The major playwrights of this period were William Congreve (*The Way of the World*), Aphra Behn (one of the first female playwrights in England and author of *The Rover*), and Richard Brinsley Sheridan (*School for Scandal*).

The theater continued to be a popular form of entertainment in the eighteenth century, as the older comedy of manners slowly evolved into what is known as sentimental comedy. Like its predecessor, sentimental comedy relied largely on farce and satire of society, but also contained an element of drama—truly the beginnings of melodrama. Both the Neoclassical tragedies of this period and the sentimental comedies were largely based on English, French, and Italian models from the past, and though these plays were usually revamped to suit contemporary mores, they often contain little originality. As a result, few plays from the eighteenth century are read or performed today. They are, however, an excellent source for anyone interested in the popular culture of the day.

In England, the main dramatists of the early eighteenth century include Richard Steele, Joseph Addison, and Colly Cibber. French drama included such writers as Marivaux, whose *Le jeu de l'amour et du hasard (The Game of Love and Luck)* is a wonderful example of the light and bantering wordplay of the sentimental comedy. Voltaire, today known essentially for his philosophical and satirical writings, was in his day considered a great dramatist. His plays appear to modern scholars and audiences as nearly unreadable and highly derivative. In sum, the drama of this period is often not playable by virtue of the length of its speeches and the obscurity of its themes.

REVIEW QUESTIONS

THE RENAISSANCE

Multiple Choice

1. _____During the Renaissance, intellectual authority came from
   a. the classics
   b. the Church
   c. city patrons
   d. the Ottoman Empire

2. _____The unique culture of the Renaissance derived from
   a. Christian influences
   b. pagan influences
   c. classical influences
   d. all of the above

3. _____Petrarch is most famous for
   a. his religious piety
   b. the sonnet
   c. his comprehension of classical literature
   d. his patronage of poets

4. _____Petrarch's life exemplified the conflict between
   a. church and state
   b. Latin and vernacular languages
   c. mortal pleasures and the promise of heaven
   d. marriage and sensual love

5. _____Humanists of the fifteenth century
   a. wrote in classical Latin
   b. emphasized secular leaning
   c. emulated the Greeks and Romans
   d. all of the above

6. _____Machiavelli wanted to
   a. write the best love sonnets possible
   b. return literary leadership to France
   c. unite Italy
   d. return Latin to its classical form

7. _____The political philosophy in Machiavelli's *The Prince* states
   a. that a successful leader must be moral
   b. that a successful leader must love his people
   c. that it is better to have an evil prince than no prince
   d. that a successful leader must have mercy

8. _____One of the ideas in *Gargantua and Pantagruel* is that
   a. man is the only animal that can laugh
   b. Catholicism is the only true religion
   c. allegory is the only true literary form
   d. Latin is the only true literary language

9. _____Erasmus desired to
   a. return Holland to the rituals of Catholicism
   b. return religion to a simple teaching of the gospels
   c. return to the monastery where he believed the only truly educated men lived
   d. control the passions of mankind

10. _____La Pléiade was
    a. a university in Spain
    b. a poet from Italy
    c. a school of classical poets in France
    d. the object of devotion for Montaigne

True or False

11. _____During the Renaissance, most intellectual energy was focused on spiritual rather than secular matters.

12. _____The interest in exploration was evidence of the new intellectual attitudes of the Renaissance.

13. _____Class distinctions became more important than nationality during the Renaissance.

14. _____In the Renaissance, life was to be endured, not enjoyed.

15. _____During the Renaissance, Italy took the leadership in literature away from France.

16. _____Plato was the guiding philosopher of the Renaissance because he validated the worship of earthly beauty.

17. _____Petrarch wanted only to imitate classical poets.

18. _____*The Decameron* was written as a consolation to women suffering from unrequited love.

19. _____Rabelais believed that laughter was man's best defense against misery.

20. _____Michel de Montaigne wrote discursive familiar essays about the absurdities of mankind.

Fill-in

21. The failure of the autocracy of _____ is the most definite clue of the new direction of the new period in history, the Renaissance.

22. Renaissance societies tried to emulate what they believed to be the elegance of _____.

23. _____ expressed his appreciation of the game of courtly love in his poetry written for his mistress Fiametta.

24. A member of a remarkable Florentine family, _____ was a skilled statesman, writer of love sonnets, and founder of the Platonic Academy.

25. _____, patronized by Lorenzo de' Medici, brought about the transition from religious to secular drama.

26. _____ is a work by Machiavelli that earned him a reputation as a shrewd and cynical political analyst.

27. _____ wrote the book that was destined to be a guide for elegant deportment for several centuries.

28. Lodovico Ariosto's _____ came to be the supreme example of a romantic epic about knightly exploits and courtly love.

29. Luiz de Camoens' epic poem, *The Lusiads,* is the best example of Renaissance literature from _____.

30. _____ is a Spanish writer who is best known for his plays employing a dramatic structure of exposition, involvement, and denouement.

Matching

31. _____ Laura	a.	patron of the arts
32. _____ Boccaccio	b.	"handbook for dictators"
33. _____ Petrarch	c.	*Don Quixote*
34. _____ Lorenzo de' Medici	d.	*The Decameron*
35. _____ Cellini	e.	wrote romantic epics
36. _____ Cervantes	f.	Petrarch's symbol of earthly beauty
37. _____ *The Prince*	g.	handbook of manners
38. _____ Lodovico Ariosto	h.	*Gargantua and Pantagruel*
39. _____ *The Courtier*	i.	*Autobiography*
40. _____ Rabelais	j.	first humanist

Answers

1.	a	12.	t	23.	Boccaccio	31.	f
2.	d	13.	f	24.	Lorenzo de'	32.	d
3.	b	14.	f		Medici	33.	j
4.	c	15.	t	25.	Poliziano	34.	a
5.	d	16.	t	26.	*The Prince*	35.	i
6.	c	17.	f	27.	Castiglione	36.	c
7.	c	18.	f	28.	*Orlando*	37.	b
8.	a	19.	t		*Furioso*	38.	e
9.	b	20.	t	29.	Portugal	39.	g
10.	c	21.	the Church	30.	Lope	40.	h
11.	f	22.	Rome		de Vega		

Part 4

NEOCLASSICISM

WORKS AT A GLANCE

Gottfried Wilhelm Leibniz

1671	*Hypothesis Physica Nova*	1697	*On the Ultimate Origin of Things*
1868	*Discourse on Metaphysics*	1714	*Monadologia*

Giambattista Vico

1720–1721	*Scienza Nova*

Molière (Jean-Baptiste Poquelin)

1655	*The Blunderer*	1666	*The Misanthrope, Doctor in Spite of Himself*
1656	*The Lovers' Quarrel*		
1659	*The Ridiculous Precious Ladies*	1668	*The Miser*
		1670	*The Would-Be Gentleman*
1660	*Sganarelle*		
1661	*The School for Husbands*	1672	*The Learned Ladies*
		1673	*The Imaginary Invalid*
1662	*The School for Wives*		
1665	*Don Juan*		
1665, 1667, 1669	*Tartuffe*		

Pierre Corneille

1629	*Mélite*	1643	*The Liar*
1636	*Le Cid*	1644	*Rodogune*
1640	*Horace, Cinna*	1652	*Pertharite*
1641	*Polyeucte*		

Jean Racine

1664	*La Thébaïde*	1672	*Bajazet*
1665	*Alexandre*	1673	*Mithridate*
1667	*Andromaque*	1674	*Iphigénie in Aulide*
1668	*The Litigants*	1677	*Phaedra*
1669	*Britannicus*	1689	*Esther*
1670	*Bérénice*	1691	*Athalie*

Jean de la Fontaine

1664, 1667, 1671	*Tales*	1668, 1679, 1693	*Fables*

Nicolas Boileau-Despréaux

| 1666 | *Discourses* | 1674 | *The Art of Poetry* |
| 1673, 1683 | *The Lectern* | | |

Blaise Pascal

| 1656 | *Letters Written to a Provincial* | 1670 | *Thoughts* |

François, Prince de Marcillac, Duke de la Rouchfoucauld

| 1662 | *Memoirs* | 1665 | *Maxims* |

Jean de la Bruyere

| 1687 | *Characters* |

Charles de Marguetel de Saint-Denis, Seigneur de Saint-Evremond

| 1705 | *Works* |

Madame de la Fayette

| 1678 | *The Princess of Cleves* |

Madame de Sévigné

| 1725 | *Letters* |

Madame de Maintenon

| 1719 | *Letters* |

Louis de Rouvroy, Duke de Saint-Simon

| 1839 | *Memoirs* |

Jacques Benigne Bossuet

| 1681 | *Discourse on Universal History up to the Time of Charlemagne* |

François de Lalignac de la Mothe-Fénelon

| 1699 | *Telemachus* |

Voltaire (François-Marie Arouet)

1718	*Oedipus*	1748	*Zadig*
1730	*Brutus*	1751	*Epoch of Louis XIV*
1732	*Zaïre, The Death of Caesar*	1752	*Micromégas*
1734	*English Letters*	1756	*The Essay on the Manners*
1736	*Mondain, Alzire*		*and the Spirit of Nations*
1738	*Elements of Newton's*	1759	*Candide*
	Philosophy, On the Nature	1760	*Tancred*
	of Fire	1763	*The Treatise on Tolerance*
1740	*Mahomet, or Fanaticism*	1764	*Philosophic Dictionary*
1743	*Mérope*	1772	*The History of Russia under*
1745	*The Princess of Navarre*		*Peter the Great, A*
1746	*Babouc*		*Summary of the Age of*
1747	*Memnon*		*Louis XV*

Charles de Secondat, Baron de Montesquieu

1721	*The Persian Letters*	1748	*The Spirit of Laws*
1734	*Reflections on the*	1750	*Defence*
	Causes of the Great-		
	ness and the Decline		
	of the Romans		

Jean le Rond d'Alembert

1751–1759	*Encyclopedia*	1775	*Eloges*
	(edited)		

Denis Diderot

1749	*Letter on the Blind*	1759–1781	*Salons*
c. 1750	*Grimm's Leaves*	1760	*The Nun*
1751–1772	*Encyclopedia*	1762	*Rameau's Nephew*
	(edited)	1766	*Jack the Fatalist*
1757	*The Natural Son*		
1758	*Discourse on*		
	Dramatic Poetry,		
	The Father of the		
	Family		

Bernard Le Bovier de Fontenelle

1686	*Conversation on the*	1708–1719	*Éloges*
	Plurality of Words		

Pierre Bayle

1686–1687	*Historical and*
	Philosophical Dictionary

Abbé de Saint-Pierre

1713–1717   *A Project for Perpetual Peace*

Georges-Louis Leclerc de Buffon

1749	*Natural History*	1753	*Discourse on Style*

Pierre Carlet de Marivaux

1722	*Love's Surprise*	1735	*The Upstart Peasant*
1731–1742	*The Life of Marianne*	1737	*False Confidences*
1734	*The Game of Love and Chance*	1740	*The Proof*

Caron de Beaumarchais

1775	*The Barber of Seville*	1792	*The Guilty Mother*
1784	*The Marriage of Figaro*		

Alain René Le Sage

1707	*The Limping Devil*	1715–1735	*Gil Blas*

Abbé Prévost

1726–1732   *Memoirs of a Gentleman of Quality*, includes *Manon Lescaut*

Jean François Marmontel

1767	*Bélisaire*	c. 1785	*Memoirs*
1778	*The Incas*		

Giuseppe Parini

1763–1803   *Il Giorno*

9
NEOCLASSICISM IN FRANCE

ORIGINS OF NEOCLASSICISM

Neoclassicism was the prevailing mode in the world of art from the time of the beginnings of scientific investigation early in the seventeenth century to the very brink of the French Revolution at the end of the eighteenth century. It was a movement that was both an extension of the Renaissance and a reaction against it. From the Renaissance, Neoclassicism inherited the worship of the Latin and Greek classics as models of perfection to be copied and imitated. But Neoclassicism was also a rejection of the extreme individualism in which the Renaissance had resulted; writers of this movement had little sympathy with purely personal emotional problems. For them interest centered on discovering ideal social conduct, the common basis for reasonable relationship between members of a society possessed of good sense.

The seventeenth century, which saw the establishment of Neoclassicism throughout Western Europe, was the period in which rationalism in philosophy and experimentation in natural science made their first great strides. At the opening of the century Francis Bacon, in England, had heralded the new scientific method of investigation, and by 1645 a number of his countrymen were meeting regularly for the purpose of reading scientific papers. In 1662 Charles II granted them the charter for what became the Royal Society in that country. In Italy, Galileo's students set up the first scientific academy in 1657 at Florence. In France, Descartes, Pascal, and Gassendi met with similar groups. It was the century of the telescope, the reflector, the thermometer, the barometer, the pendulum clock, the astronomical observations of Kepler and Galileo, Newton's law of universal gravitation, Descartes' invention of analytical geometry, the development of calculus, Halley's study of comets, Swammerdam's invention of the science of entomology—to mention only a few of the scientific exploits of the time.

Step by step with this study of the laws of nature, philosophy advanced and changed. The *Essays* of Montaigne, widely read in France and other countries, spread a new gospel of detachment in judgment and tolerance for the beliefs of others. According to the great French essayist, philosophy should teach one not what religion to espouse but how to live intelligently. Self-examination, as it had been with Socrates, was with him the very basis of the search for truth. After him, René Descartes (1596–1650), one of the greatest of all mathematicians, applied the methods of mathematics to philosophical speculation. All truth, he insisted, must be proved, not accepted from "authorities." Beginning with the one axiom he could accept, "I think, therefore I must exist" (*Cogito ergo sum*), he proceeded to build intellectually his universe on purely mechanical grounds, from which he exempted only God and man's soul.

Arguably the most important western philosopher of the last millennium, Descartes maintained that the body, which he explained based on purely mechanistic principles, is entirely distinct from the soul (and mind), the veritable matter of human existence. Two major philosophical texts, the *Discourse on Method* (1637) and the *Meditations,* gained recognition for Descartes during his own time. The former, which is the most widely read today, outlines the *cogito* and the famous mind-body split as the integral parts of Descartes' philosophical method, which is quite empirical in nature. Cartesian thought has greatly influenced almost every field of science and philosophy, and many Neoclassical writers deal implicitly with the Cartesian system in their work.

Thomas Hobbes (1586–1679) in his *Leviathan* (1651) made perhaps the most revolutionary of all attempts to found a philosophy on our knowledge of natural science. He allowed no exceptions in applying mechanical principles to mind and matter. "All that exists," he said, "is body; all that occurs is motion." He is, thus, the father of mechanical empiricism.

Few philosophers have ever exercised the influence that John Locke (1632–1704) maintained over thinkers in the eighteenth century. His *Essay Concerning the Human Understanding* (1690) was the first searching examination into the origin of ideas. Locke repudiated the Platonic doctrine that man at birth is already supplied with certain fundamental concepts (the doctrine of "innate ideas"), and insisted that man's mind at birth is like a blank tablet (*tabula rasa*) on which experience is to write. From experience alone come the "materials of reason and knowledge," he said. Reflection, beginning with such a premise, naturally led next to an examination of social institutions, their merits and defects, and the conditions by which society can satisfactorily operate. For if experience is the source of ideas for every man, then human institutions, customs, and morals become of the gravest importance. Here we have, too, the inspiration for that "study of Mankind" (to quote the English poet Pope) which was, at the end of the century, to foment a revolution in France against the old order.

Gottfried Wilhelm Leibniz (1646–1716)

Leibniz was born into a Germany laid almost in ruins by the Thirty Years' War. Self-educated in his father's extensive library, Leibniz eventually entered the University of Leipzig as a law student in 1661, where he became fascinated with the discoveries and implications of the "new science" as conceived by Galileo, Francis Bacon, Thomas Hobbes, and René Descartes. Toward the end of his legal studies in 1666, he authored an important epistemological treatise, "On the Art of Combination," which sets forth some of the theoretical bases of modern computing.

After being refused the degree of doctor of law due to his young age, Leibniz left Leipzig for Nurnberg, where he not only obtained his doctor's degree but quickly became involved in the court of the archbishop of Mainz, Johann Philipp von Schönborn. Under Schönborn's sponsorship, Leibniz pursued his philosophical interests, publishing his early theories of space and movement in 1671 under the title *Hypothesis Physica Nova*. When the archbishop died in 1673, Leibniz was thrown onto his own resources to find support for his future studies and investigations. He constructed what he described as a "calculating machine" and presented it to the Royal Society in London in 1673. Encouraged by the interest of this prestigious group, Leibniz went on to lay the foundations of both integral and differential calculus by 1675. In opposing Cartesian theories of motion, Leibniz set forth the alternate theory of dynamics, including the concept of kinetic energy.

Eventually in 1676 Leibniz obtained an income-producing position as librarian and councillor to the Duke of Hanover. A German da Vinci, Leibniz worked on a wide variety of projects and proposals for the Duke, including schemes to build submarines, windmills, and water pumps. His work in mathematics continued, and in 1679 he perfected the binary system used in contemporary computing and proposed the outlines of the branch of mathematics now known as topology. His deeper search, however, was for a theory of knowledge that metaphysically related the mind of God to the mind of man (described in his *Discourse on Metaphysics*, 1686). In a later work, *On the Ultimate Origin of Things* (1697), Leibniz attempted to refute the implications of Cartesianism by showing that the ultimate origin of things must rest necessarily in God. In the last decades of his life, Leibniz went on to several positions in the court of Russian Czar Peter the Great, under whose patronage his published *Monadologia* (1714), his final formulation of the relations between theology, philosophy, and science.

Giambattista Vico (1668–1744)

Giambattista Vico, a philosopher and early forerunner of cultural anthropology, came from the humblest of roots in a mud-floored Naples apartment that doubled as a bookstore. Largely self-taught, the young Vico eventually attended a Jesuit college and accepted a position thereafter in the home of an Italian duke near Salerno. Vico secretly fell in love with his pupil, Giulia, and was devastated by her death at twenty-two years of age. He returned to Naples, where he obtained a chair of rhetoric at the University of Naples. He married during this relatively tranquil period of his life. Stung by a contemptuous review of his scholarship in a journal, Vico set about his greatest work, the *Scienza Nova,* which appeared first in outline in 1720–21. In this work, which continued to grow in complexity over the following decades, Vico describes an evolution for human society, beginning with what he termed the "bestial" stage and progressing through "the age of the gods," "the age of heroes," and "the age of men." In this last stage Vico prefigures much the Marxist concept of class conflict. For Vico, the progress of human history depended much more on belief systems such as religion than upon technological change.

After Vico's death, Goethe visited Naples and received a copy of *Scienza Nova* from students still enthusiastic about its implications. Goethe was deeply influenced by the theoretical richness of the work and praised its "prophetic insights." Similar influence was acknowledged in following centuries by Michelet, the French historian, the philosopher August Comte, and by Karl Marx.

As these concepts were disseminated through Western Europe, such rationalistic and scientific thinking engendered in men a desire to understand life rationally, to interest themselves in the real and the contemporary rather than in the world of the imagination. It is this desire that is fundamental to Neoclassicism.

THE NATURE OF NEOCLASSICISM

This "Neo" (new) classicism, like its progenitors, the classics of Greece and Rome, aimed above all at clarity, lucidity, and simplicity. The mark of genius was no longer exalted inspiration, but rather restrained good sense. A typical Neoclassicist was likely to be dignified rather than impassioned, clever rather than ardent.

Since clarity was desired, form became of great consideration to him. Through firmly molded form he could curb the exuberances of purely personal enthusiasms or dissatisfactions. Since he was seeking the common denominator for all intelligent readers of his tongue, he respected conventions and standards. Correctness of style, of conduct, of ideas, and of values became paramount in his thinking. His intelligence became critical. He was on the alert for deviations from the norm of good sense in style, conduct, ideas, and social values. Hence, satire became in this age the most popular vehicle of literary expression.

The concern for form degenerated, in the hands of some neoclassicists, into an endless preoccupation with "rules." Aristotle's *Poetics,* which was devoted to the principles, not the rules, of dramatic composition, became now mistakenly the authority in the stipulation among dramatists for "the three unities." The Neoclassical dramatist insisted that a play take place in one physical location, on one day, and be confined to one plot. Aristotle had, indeed, required that a drama have unity of action; but he had had nothing to say at all about unity of place; as for the unity of time, he did no more than observe that many plays deal with events that occupy about twenty-four hours. It was the commentators on the *Poetics* who were responsible for spinning out the doctrine of "the three unities." But in the Neoclassical age, these unities were beyond challenge. Sometimes, as in the case of the time element in Corneille's *Le Cid*, the results are a strain upon credibility.

The Neoclassical avoidance of the particular and the individual even affected the very language of literature. Diction became formalized in its effort to avoid vulgarity, and generalized in its effort to avoid the particular.

Household words were considered too inelegant, and the names of characters in drama and fiction were transformed into florid Greek names for men and women alike.

Elegance, polish, wit—these were the new attractions that Neoclassicism offered. The appeal of writers being to the intellect, rather than to the emotions, good taste and judgment were valued far more than profundity or great originality. Life was seen as a whole, not in moments. A man's character was delineated in terms of outstanding traits universally recognizable, not with any nuances or shadings which might mark him as peculiarly himself. It was not the writer's business, said one sturdy English Neoclassicist, Samuel Johnson, to number the streaks of a tulip. Human nature was interesting only in its universal aspects.

Another distinguishing trait of the Neoclassical school was the didactic purpose with which men wrote. They wrote to entertain, to be sure, but they entertained in order to teach. Such an objective was, of course, closely connected with their social-mindedness, their predilection for satire, and their interest in the universal rather than the particular.

Finally, it may be said of them that their interests were essentially urban. Nature, which was to be the nurse and teacher of the Romantic movement, had little charm for the Neoclassicist. Paris and London, to Frenchman and Englishman, were the focus of life. It was a misfortune to be compelled to live in the country, they felt, for in town there were people to talk to, to observe, to exchange ideas with. The Neoclassicists were very fond of posing "nature" as the criterion for all values, but by that word they always meant *human nature*. Wild landscapes bored them; trees and gardens were charming only when laid out in symmetrical rows, clipped in geometric shapes, and approached by easy walks.

Neoclassicism in France

France, or, more precisely, Paris, was the capital of Neoclassicism. There are many reasons why this should have been so, but no reason is more basic than the fact that the French are classicists by temperament. The French have always delighted in logical discussion, and have always tended to intellectualize their emotions. They are naturally a critical people. Their very language reflects their passion for fine distinction and precision. It is not surprising that in this period France should have, therefore, achieved her golden age of literature. Montaigne (who was a precursor of Neoclassicism), Corneille, Racine, Molière, La Fontaine, Pascal, La Bruyère, Bossuet, Boileau, Voltaire, La Rochefoucauld, Mme de Sévigné—these are among the very greatest names in French literature, and they all belong to this period.

Louis XIV, who reigned from 1643 to 1715, the Grand Monarch, the Sun King, had much to do with the conscious realization of French genius in his time. Under him and his absolute monarchy, France first emerged as the leading nation on the Continent. The Court became the center of national life; even the critical intelligence of Molière accepted without question the finality of the King's judgments in all matters. Louis indulged his taste for luxury, pomp, and elegance to the full. His costly palace at Versailles, with its miles of formal gardens, fountains, beautiful galleries, became the envy and model throughout Europe of royal living at its best. He gave employment to the best architects and artists of the time, and was the personal patron of some of its writers. Molière was his chief entertainer; Racine and Boileau his appointed historians; Bossuet the chaplain to his court.

MOLIÈRE (JEAN-BAPTISTE POQUELIN) (1622–1673)

The greatest writer of classic comedy in Europe was born Jean-Baptiste Poquelin, but he is known to the world by his stage name of Molière. The family Poquelin was well-established as prosperous merchants of furniture. In 1631 Molière's father bought the post of "royal upholsterer," a title that conferred much honor on this middle-class family. The boy was educated by the Jesuits at the fashionable Collège de Clermont, where his enthusiasm for Latin made him familiar with the works of the Roman comic dramatists. Some biographies are of the opinion that on leaving school, Molière studied law and practiced it for a time; it is true that his plays indicate considerable knowledge of legal matters. At any rate, it was not long before he fell in love with the stage and, discarding the reversion of the office of "royal upholsterer" and all the bright prospects therewith connected, he joined the Béjart family to form an acting troupe. They had their troubles in finding a theater; Molière, moreover, proved highly unsuited to the heavy tragic roles he had assumed. Before long the elder Poquelin was rescuing his son from debtor's prison.

With the Béjarts, nevertheless, the young man was determined to throw in his lot. For thirteen years they toured the provinces, wandering from town to town, enduring every kind of hardship. But the experience proved invaluable to Molière's art as actor and playwright. The first of the plays that can be definitely ascribed to him, *The Blunderer* (*L'Étourdi*) was presented at Lyons in 1655. This play and *The Lovers' Quarrel* (*Le Dépit Amoureux*) of the next year, were both written in the style of the Italians. At last acquiring the interest of the King's brother, Molière was able to realize his dream of returning to Paris. In 1658 his company presented a play of Corneille's and *Le Dépit* before the King at the Louvre. Within a week the players were granted the use of the Hôtel du Petit-Bourbon, a theater adjoining the King's palace. Here it was that Molière enjoyed his first great success, *The Ridiculous Precious Ladies* (*Les Précieuses Ridicules*) in 1659. It was the right moment for the satire, and Molière's genius may be said to have come into its own with this hilarious ridicule of affectation and false elegance. At the salon of Mme. de Rambouillet a group of elegant ladies and gentlemen had been exerting themselves to purify the French language of coarseness and vulgarity. Much of what they achieved is to their credit. But they had their inept imitators who were pushing their phraseology to the point of the absurd. It was this sham elegance which Molière pilloried in *Les Précieuses*. The satire was so brilliantly handled that it is applicable to affectation of speech in any era.

Cathos and Madelon, the heroines of *Les Précieuses*, two silly girls of the upper middle class, have had their heads turned by these false ideas of elegance. They cannot even bear their names, which they think too commonplace, and change them to Aminte and Polixène respectively. Two excellent young gentlemen are their suitors, but the girls think them too plain in speech to be truly cultivated. Whereupon the exasperated lovers send their valets to pay court to the young ladies under the titles of the Marquis de Mascarille and the Viscount de Jodolet. The valets ape all the empty elaborateness under the spell of which the girls have fallen, and one of them reads some idiotic verses of his own composition, submitting them to the judgment of Aminte and Polixène. Then the young masters enter, and show up the valets for what they are. The two damsels learn to their chagrin how little they know of the ways of the world of fashion.

Sganarelle (1660), a farce, introduces a favorite character of the dramatist, the cowardly man of the title. He reappears in *The School for Husbands* (*L'École des Maris*) in 1661. Here Sganarelle and Ariste, his older brother, have the guardianship of Isabelle and Léonor, two orphans. Sganarelle, who thinks well of himself, expects to marry Isabelle, and keeps her under lock and key. Bored to death with such a life, she outwits him and marries Valère instead.

The School for Wives

In 1662 Molière contracted a most unfortunate marriage with Armande Béjart, twenty-one years his junior. She was a sister of Madeleine Béjart of the troupe, and proved a heartless coquette.

In the same year he wrote one of his most important comedies, *The School for Wives* (*L'École des Femmes*), a fine study of incompatibility in marriage. Arnolphe, the hero, has his own elaborate theories on the education of women. He has Agnès brought up in a convent in the country, where she has never learned of the differences between men and women, and has never been taught anything about the relationship of the sexes or the conventions of sex. The result is that she is too much the "child of nature." She behaves with the men she meets as though they were fellow students at the convent, has no fear of their intentions, and kisses them freely. Before he knows it the middle-aged Arnolphe is acting unknowingly as a go-between for Agnès and Horace, the son of an old friend. Agnès at length decides to escape from Arnolphe. Luckily for the young lovers it is revealed, upon the appearance of their fathers, that they have been betrothed as children. The play ends happily for them but bitterly for Arnolphe, who by this time has become almost a tragic character. His denunciation of Agnès, to whose wishes he bends because of his genuine love for her, occurs in one of the finest scenes Molière ever wrote.

In honor of his mistress, Mlle. de la Vallière, Louis XIV arranged a festival at Versailles. For the occasion Molière presented the first three acts of the masterpiece, *Tartuffe*. But his enemies had summoned their powers, and the play was forbidden further performance. He next wrote *Don Juan* (1665), an attack on hypocrisy. After some fifteen performances the censor authorized the stopping of the play. Then, after *Love the Doctor* (*L'Amour Médecin*) appeared *Le Misanthrope* (1666).

Molière's genius achieved its highest expression in *The Misanthrope* and *Tartuffe*. It is part of the paradox of genius that in these two masterpieces the playwright who could fill the stage with such healthy merriment as finds its equal only in Shakespeare, should have been so near the borderline of heart-rending tragedy. For as much as one may be amused by the satirical lines in *The Misanthrope* or *Tartuffe*, no one with a heart is provoked to laughter by either comedy. The truth they present is too bitter, too universal, too near the realm of tears.

The Misanthrope

The Misanthrope has been called "the French *Hamlet*,"—though it is hard to understand on what grounds unless the comparison is based upon their preeminence in their respective literatures. Molière was never closer to reality than in his portraits here: the incorruptible but unreasonable hero, Alceste; the bewitching but self-centered coquette, Célimène; the insincere man of fashion, Oronte; the urbane but affectionate friend, Philinte; the sensible, good woman, Éliante; and the pretender-to-virtue, mischievious Arsinoë.

ACT ONE: The action of *The Misanthrope* takes place in the home of Célimène in Paris. Alceste (the Misanthrope) is upbraiding his close friend Philinte for being a hypocrite like the rest of the world, just because Philinte doesn't go around telling everyone exactly what he thinks. Philinte pleads for more tolerance for the weaknesses of human nature. Oronte enters, assuring Alceste of his great affection for him, and then, despite his receiving no encouragement, reads him a stupid lyric of his own composition. He then pleads for an honest criticism. Philinte, knowing his man, praises it lightly. But Alceste is brutally frank, and urges Oronte not to publish anything so silly. Oronte leaves in a huff, and Alceste renews his attacks on Philinte's "dishonesty."

ACT TWO: The act opens with the entry of Célimène. Alone with her, Alceste accuses her of encouraging everyone's attentions, and confesses he wishes he didn't love her so passionately as he does. She mocks him for the strangeness of his gallantries. Two noblemen, Acaste and Clitandre come in with Éliante (Célimène's cousin) and Philinte. The nobles begin to gossip about their various friends with sarcasm. Célimène outdoes them all in the mercilessness of her satire. Alceste is enraged to see the girl he loves behaving like this, and blames her friends for encouraging her. He asserts that she must choose now between these admirers and him. But just then an Officer appears to tell Alceste that the Marshal's office wants to see him on account of his recent disagreement with Oronte over the verses. He goes out swearing he will never pretend to like the poem.

ACT THREE: Clitandre and Acaste decide to find out which of them is Célimène's favored lover; the unlucky one, they agree, will quit the field. Arsinoë, the prude, proud of her reputation for virtue, enters as they leave. Arsinoë tells Célimène that everyone is gossiping about the number of admirers she allows to surround her. Célimène answers that Arsinoë must not blame her if the latter has no admirers at all; she's not responsible for Arsinoë's advanced age. When Alceste returns, Célimène leaves him to Arsinoë's wiles. Arsinoë, as everyone knows, is smitten with Alceste, but he is not at all interested in her. She tries to flatter him on his unrecognized talents, but makes no impression. She ends by telling him that if he will accompany her home, she will prove to him that Célimène is unworthy of his love.

ACT FOUR: Philinte is telling Éliante how the difficulty between Alceste and Oronte was settled. They are unhappy about his love for Célimène, and know he must be eventually hurt by it. Philinte, guessing Éliante's unreturned affection for Alceste, tells her that once her feelings for his friend have been liberated, he himself would be honored if she would consent to marry him. Alceste comes in, in a rage because of a letter Arsinoë has given him, a letter written to Oronte with affection by Célimène. He asks Éliante to help him revenge himself upon her faithless cousin by marrying him. Before the girl can reply, Célimène enters. Proudly and defiantly she refuses to explain the letter, and tells Alceste he may believe whatever he chooses, since her assurance that she loves only him isn't enough. Alceste's servant comes in to announce that a friend has left a letter for Alceste at his home, warning him to flee Paris for his life.

ACT FIVE: Alceste is telling Philinte that his enemy in a lawsuit that has been pending, has won the case by pulling political wires, even though the world knew justice was on Alceste's side. He has now made up his mind to run away from all society, and has come to learn Célimène's decision. Oronte enters, also determined that she must make a choice. But she refuses to answer him on the grounds that it would be too indelicate to do so. Éliante, entering, agrees that the men have a right to know where they stand. Now Acaste, Clitandre. Philinte, and Arsinoë are also present. The noblemen both have letters from Célimène in which the characters of each other, as well as of Oronte and Alceste, are slandered. The other three suitors leave. Arsinoë upbraids her on Alceste's behalf, but he tells her to mind her own business. She goes out angrily. Despite the revelation of her perfidy, Alceste is willing to marry Célimène if she will go off with him to a desert. She flatly refuses to marry him, unless it means staying in town. He now rejects her absolutely as vile. Half-heartedly he offers himself to Éliante. But he is too late: she has already accepted Philinte's love. Poisoned against humanity, he runs off, beside himself with rage. Philinte and Éliante, constant in their love for him, will try to dissuade him from becoming a recluse.

Doctor in Spite of Himself

In 1666 Molière also presented a deliriously funny play, *Doctor in Spite of Himself* (*Le Médecin malgré Lui*), an attack on the incompetence of the medical profession. It was based on one of the old French *fabliaux*, and was itself the source in modern times for Anatole France's rollicking farce, *The Man Who Married a Dumb Wife*.

In Molière's play we meet Sganarelle again, this time in the role of a drunken woodcutter who abuses his wife, Martine. When some people come looking for a doctor to treat Géronte's daughter, Martine sees the opportunity to revenge herself on Sganarelle. She pretends that her husband is really a great doctor, but that he will not admit his profession unless he is soundly thrashed. Sganarelle is thereupon whipped, and to end his torture agrees to call himself a physician. At Géronte's home he talks a great deal of high-sounding nonsense, and gives his diagnosis of the sickness of Géronte's daughter Lucinde. Actually the loss of speech which the girl has suffered is only a trick she is playing on her father for his refusal to accept Léandre as a son-in-law. Sganarelle, learning the state of affairs, makes a pact with Léandre, who is now able to visit Lucinde in the disguise of an apothecary. The lovers elope, and Géronte is ready to murder Sganarelle in his fury. But the young couple return with the announcement that Léandre is the heir of a rich uncle, and Géronte removes his objections to the marriage.

The Miser

The Miser (*L'Avare*) was acted in 1668, and is one of its author's important plays. Its powerful study of the most obnoxious of all mental sicknesses has made its hero's name, Harpagon, synonymous with the disease itself. He is a fabulously rich man who, while adding to his store by usury, refuses to part with a penny of his hoard. His son, Cléante, is so impoverished that he borrows money where he can at an exorbitant rate of interest. His daughter, Elise, is to be married off without a dowry to an old nobleman, Anselme; but she is resolved to marry Valère, her father's steward. Cléante is in love with the young Mariane, but his miserly father intends to marry her himself. Harpagon is convinced that everyone is out to rob him, and at last this act does take place. La Flèche, Cléante's valet, to aid his young master, robs Harpagon of a casket of coins. Harpagon is beside himself with anguish. When La Flèche agrees to return the casket on condition that Harpagon renounce all claims to Mariane, the miser chooses to have his money back. At the end it develops that Valère and Mariane are both children of old Anselme; and so Harpagon agrees to the marriages of both his children. He is left with his beloved cash-box.

Tartuffe

Tartuffe, the first three acts of which had been presented only once and then banned, was tried again in 1667 as *The Impostor*, with the title part changed from a clergyman to a layman, but the dramatist was no more successful in gaining the right to performance for his work. Finally in 1669 it appeared in its present five-act form under the original title. No play has been more universally admired. Satire is at its most intense in this unmasking of a religious hypocrite; few characters evoke more hatred from an audience than Tartuffe. Molière's dramatic skill is nowhere greater than here; he cunningly delays presenting his villain until the third act. We can hardly wait to meet the wretch, and yet we anticipate the encounter with dread and loathing. His deluded victim, Orgon, is depicted with biting satire too, but for him we have only pity. There is no mirth in the smiles this play evokes; we can be only bitter at the follies of human nature which the poet has so convincingly shown us. But even here, in the bitterest of his comedies, Molière never loses his basic sanity. The good sense of Orgon's brother, children, and wife reminds us throughout that humanity is not to be despaired of. The picture of their well-to-do middle-class family life is beyond praise in its realism.

At the opening of *Tartuffe* we are introduced to Orgon's family. His second wife, Elmire, is much younger than he, and is deeply in love with him; she is on the best of terms with her two stepchildren, Mariane and Damis. But Orgon's mother, Mme. Pernelle, whose headstrongness her son unfortunately inherits, does not at all approve of the household Elmire runs. She rebukes what she considers an extravagant and frivolous mode of life—such is her interpretation of the innocent amusements of her daughter-in-law. She alone seconds Orgon's new infatuation with Tartuffe. This creature Orgon first came upon in church, where the beggarly scoundrel was making a great display of his humbleness of spirit and his piety. Orgon had insisted that his saint come to live with them.

Once entrenched there, Tartuffe began to work havoc in the family relationships. Insisting, with Orgon's and Mme. Pernelle's agreement, on a Puritanical severity of life for everyone, Tartuffe has already intervened in the love affair of Mariane. She is engaged to Valère, but Orgon has been easily persuaded to break the engagement; he has every intention of marrying her to his pious Tartuffe. Despite Valère's dependence on her rebellion, Mariane is afraid to oppose her father, and stands weakly by, leaving Elmire and the old servant Dorine to battle for her.

Dorine, a saucy, plain-spoken woman, detests both Tartuffe and the latter's valet, Laurent, who is aping his master; she does everything she can to make her master see his folly, but her efforts are vain. At her account of Elmire's ill health, he is interested only in the well-being of Tartuffe. He is prepared to disinherit his son for objecting to the sainted man, and he quarrels with his brother, Cléante, because Cléante tries to defend Orgon's wife and children against the usurpations of Tartuffe.

Elmire is convinced that she must do something to bring her husband to his senses. She suspects that underneath his mask of piety Tartuffe is a lecher, and that he is so sure of victimizing Orgon that he anticipates little trouble in winning the favors of his benefactor's wife. She therefore allows Tartuffe to compliment her on her beauty, and even to lay his gross hand on her knee. Unfortunately, the hot-headed Damis, who knows nothing of Elmire's purposes, is an unseen witness to all this, and ruins her plan by declaring that he will reveal what he has heard to his father. But Tartuffe has Orgon so much under his thumb that the latter refuses to believe his son; indeed, he orders him to apologize to Tartuffe. When Damis refuses, Orgon, enraged, disowns him and bids him leave home.

To make up to the saint for this indignity, he signs over to Tartuffe the management of his estate, so that he himself can be free of worldly matters. He also, to everyone's horror, announces his intention of marrying Mariane to Tartuffe.

In desperation, Elmire resolves to try unmasking Tartuffe, even though it means a gross indignity, as well as a great risk, for her. She persuades Orgon to conceal himself under a table while she proves to him what a scoundrel Tartuffe is. He agrees only because he is sure she will fail. When Tartuffe comes in, he is at first afraid that this is a new trick. But when he is convinced that they are alone, he boldly asks her to give herself to him, assuring her that her husband is too stupid to know. He goes on to show his contempt for her husband's credulity.

Orgon, overwhelmed with disillusionment, comes out from under the table, upbraids Tartuffe, and orders him to leave. Tartuffe, to Orgon's horror, sneeringly reminds him that he is now master of the estate by Orgon's own design.

As Tartuffe quits the room, a new matter rises in Orgon's mind to cause him uneasiness. An exiled friend of his had committed to Orgon's care a casket containing important state papers. This casket Orgon has foolishly entrusted to Tartuffe. The contents of the casket, once known, would mean death for the friend, and a charge of treason against Orgon. Disgusted with his experience, Orgon assures Cléante that he is through with pious people. Cléante reminds him that he is rushing to extremes again: religion is not to be open to suspicion just because a scoundrel was masquerading as a saint.

Mme. Pernelle arrives, and angers her son by refusing to believe his story against Tartuffe. But a sheriff's officer comes on the scene to dispossess Orgon and his family from their home. Now she too is convinced. Tartuffe has also taken the casket to court, and orders have been issued for Orgon's arrest. But at the last minute, the King's justice is revealed. Orgon's unquestioned loyalty and service now repay themselves. The King has voided the document in which Orgon had handed over his property to Tartuffe, and Orgon is pardoned for having held the casket. Tartuffe is sent to jail as a felon.

The Would-Be Gentleman

In 1670 Molière performed his merriest play, and his most popular, The Would-Be Gentleman (Le Bourgeois Gentilhomme). For the ballet scenes, the distinguished composer Lully wrote the music. The Turkish entertainment with which the piece concludes was very much in the mode; there was a new passion in Paris for everything Turkish.

The hero of the play, M. Jourdain, the son of a wealthy cloth merchant, is eager to escape from the shopkeeper class into which he was born, and become a man of rank. In order to learn the manners pertaining to the gentry, he hires the services of a music teacher, a fencing master, a dancing master, and a teacher of philosophy. In his lessons on the use of language, he makes the great discovery that he has been talking prose all his life. A cheat by the name of Dorante is also filching money from him under the pretence of bringing Jourdain to the attention of the King. Jourdain has also decided that his daughter Lucile may not marry any man unless he is of the nobility. Cléante loves Lucile, and therefore causes his own valet, Covielle, to invent a burlesque to deceive his sweetheart's father. Covielle introduces Cléante to Jourdain as the son of the Grand Turk, who has come to France just to marry Lucile. To make this royal match possible, they elevate Jourdain to the rank of "mamamouchi." Highly flattered at his new "rank," Jourdain gives Lucile to the disguised Cléante.

The Learned Ladies

After several other less important works, Molière produced *The Learned Ladies* (*Les Femmes Savantes*) in 1672. This great comedy is a kind of elaboration of the theme first exploited by the dramatist in *The Ridiculous Precious Ladies*.

Chrysale, a solid member of the middle class, has Philaminte to wife, and by her two daughters, Armande and Henriette. Philaminte is an enthusiast for the new pedantry in learning, and maintains what she hopes is a fine salon. Among its frequenters are her sister-in-law, Bélise, and a ridiculous poet, Trissotin; her daughter Armande is an ornament of the collection too. Clitandre has been in love with Armande, but as a result of her requiring him to wait for three years, has fallen in love now with her sister Henriette. But the mother of the girls has decided that Henriette is to marry the silly poet—an arrangement that Chrysale disapproves of entirely. The parents quarrel over the issue.

At first Chrysale gives in and Trissotin seems likely to triumph. At the salon he wins acclaim for his idiotic lines, and introduces his pedant-friend Vadius. Just when Henriette's marriage to Trissotin appears inevitable, Ariste, Chrysale's brother, makes the painful disclosure that the family is now bankrupt. The announcement has the effect of terminating Trissotin's interest in Henriette, and he leaves. It is then made known that the disclosure was only a ruse to expose the mercenary purposes of the poet, and the girl's mother, awakened from her spurious intellectualism, consents to Clitandre's suit. In this play, Molière expresses his conviction that nothing is more unbecoming to women than pretentiousness, and that they are at their best only when truly womanly.

The Imaginary Invalid

The Imaginary Invalid (*Le Malade Imaginaire*), a comedy-ballet produced in 1673, was Molière's last play. It is another satire at the expense of the medical profession.

Argan is an imaginary invalid. His only interest in life is his own health; he has a loving concern for every imagined ache and symptom of disease. He is anxious, too, to marry his daughter to the son of a doctor. His second wife, Béline, has complete dominance over him, and is able to persuade him to sacrifice the rights of his children by making out a will in her favor. But his brother Béralde foils her plans, and succeeds in making Argan see how he has been victimized. Argan at last consents to the marriage of his daughter to the man she loves. At the end, however, he decides to become a doctor himself.

Ironically, while enacting the title role of his last play, Molière became mortally ill. He managed to finish the performance, but had to be carried home, where he died. He was refused the last rites of the church, and was nearly denied Christian burial.

IMPORTANCE

The French do not hesitate to place Molière even above Shakespeare as the world's greatest writer of comedy. It is true that he lacks Shakespeare's wealth of poetic imagination and endless variety. But on almost every other ground he has no superior. The boundless sanity of Molière is matched only by his unfailing wit and easy grace. Boileau called him "the great observer." For Molière knew how to penetrate to the very roots of human absurdity. Despite the complexity of some of his plots, his plays are comedies of character rather than of situation. The large gallery of portraits he has left us is a tribute both to his genius and his humanity. His portraiture of human foibles, his understanding of the human character are everywhere true to the facts of life.

There is one trait that distinguishes him from nearly all writers of comedy: the fact that he is consistently a moralist. He rarely wrote a play that was not concerned with the improvement of manners. He castigated hypocrisy, pretentiousness, dishonesty, excess, folly, perverted values, injustice in family relationships wherever he found them. He is so great an artist that he never seems to be in the pulpit, but at the core of every one of his major works is great moral earnestness. Although some of his critics objected to the almost colloquial ease of his lines, there is no writer of the period who has more natural elegance or who more insistently advocates the classic love of moderation in all things. His plots are constructed with admirable fluency; incident follows incident with an air of naturalness. Nothing is strained, nothing seems improbable. Most remarkable of all, even his most farcical stories are elevated by his intelligence to the plane of high comedy.

PIERRE CORNEILLE (1606–1684)

Pierre Corneille, the first of the great tragic writers of the era, has been surnamed "the Great," not only to distinguish him from his brother (who also wrote plays), but, as Voltaire remarked, to distinguish him from the rest of men as well. He was a Norman, born at Rouen on June 6, 1606, the son of a lawyer. He proved an excellent student at the Jesuit college in his native city, studied law, practised it without success or enthusiasm, and obtained several legal positions.

His first comedy, *Mélite* (1629), having been well received at Rouen, he took it to Paris, where it had some success. For a while he worked in the play-factory of the Cardinal de Richelieu, but did not long enjoy that subordination. When he left, he seems to have incurred the enmity of the Cardinal.

Beginning with his great play, *Le Cid* (1636), Corneille produced a series of masterpieces: *Horace* (1640), *Cinna* (1640), *Polyeucte* (1641)— all tragedies—and the comedy, *The Liar* (*Le Menteur*) (1643). *Rodogune* (1644) is generally considered the climax of the period of his greatest achievement. After a series of other plays, his *Pertharite* (1652) was damned by the public.

Corneille was so deeply wounded by his failure that he ceased writing for the stage for some years. When he returned to playwriting in 1659 with *Œdipe,* he was at first successful. But there was a falling-off thereafter in his dramatic power. Racine, a man of great genius, had become his formidable rival, and Corneille was not able to hold his own against him. He continued to write until 1674, but nothing he produced was worthy of the author of his earlier masterpieces.

His last years seem to have been spent in the midst of considerable financial worries. He was not adept in playing the sycophant at Court, and he himself has said that he found more praise than profit there. He seems to have had too little personal charm—to have been, indeed, too timid—to do well in material ways in an age when influence at Court was essential to a writer. His contemporaries were struck with the discrepancies between the personal limitations of the man and the grandeur of the poet.

Le Cid

For *Le Cid* (1636) Corneille took his subject from the Spaniard de Castro.

Rodrigue, the son of Don Diègue is in love with the daughter of Don Gormas, Chimène. Both families have consented to the union. But suddenly a quarrel breaks out between the fathers; Don Gormas strikes the older man, Don Diègue, who is too enfeebled to take up the fight. Don Diègue calls upon his son to avenge his honor.

Torn between love and duty, the noble-minded Rodrigue can choose only the latter. He provokes Chimène's father into fighting with him, and kills him. He informs his sweetheart that he cannot regret his deed, since it was an act of duty. Chimène is forced to agree with his view, and, adopting it, demands punishment against her father's murderer.

But just at this juncture the Moors are planning an attack on Seville. Rodrigue is sent to combat them, and he wins a complete victory. Although he returns triumphant, Chimène still asks for his death. The King arranges a combat between Don Sanche, appointed champion for Chimène, and Rodrigue. Rodrigue is the victor. The King declares that she ought to feel that her honor has been satisfied; after a suitable period of mourning, it is suggested, Chimène and Rodrigue will marry.

The play was a great success with the public, but provoked great enmity for its author. A now celebrated quarrel began over *Le Cid*. Scudéry, a rival dramatist, accused Corneille unjustly of plagiarizing the Spanish, and violating Neoclassical rules. The matter was submitted to the newly formed French Academy for its decision; its patron, Richelieu, had not forgiven Corneille, and the Academy in an historical publication of its *Sentiments* on *Le Cid* upheld Corneille's enemies. Hurt, the dramatist produced nothing for almost four years. *Le Cid*, however, remains his best-known play in France.

Horace

Horace (1640), a polished tragedy of great dignity, returns to the subject of the conflict between duty and love.

In the contest between the cities of Alba and Rome, three Curiaces are to represent Alba, three Horaces to represent Rome. One Horace is married to a sister of the Curiaces; one of the Curiaces is betrothed to a sister of the Horaces. Nevertheless, with the warriors honor comes first. The father of the Horaces learns that two of his sons have been killed, and that the third has run away from battle. He curses his coward-son, and is determined to kill him on his return. But it turns out that the flight was only a ruse by which the young Horace has triumphed. When the hero returns victorious, his sister Camille curses him and Rome for the death of her betrothed. Outraged, her brother kills her. For this crime, after the King has heard the pleas of the old Horace, the young hero is forced only to go through a purifying ceremony.

Other Plays

Cinna (1640) is another tragedy on the heroism of human will. The Emperor Augustus proves in it his great nobility by pardoning the conspirators against his life—all of whom have been treated by him as good friends—when their treachery is discovered. He proves that he is not only ruler of the world, but of himself too.

Polyeucte (1641) has been called the greatest of Christian tragedies. Its theme is duty in religion. In it the Christian martyr Polyeucte teaches his wife, by his example, to rate duty higher than passion; she comes to put her older love for another man behind her, and to love her husband for his nobility. In the end she becomes a Christian too, and by her noble example wins other converts.

IMPORTANCE

Corneille's plays are not likely ever to have the vogue in the English-speaking world that they have in France. To us they seem too rhetorical, too full of talk, too far removed from the issues of common experience. Their appeal is almost entirely intellectual. Though love plays an important part in all Corneille's masterpieces, it always serves only as a basis for the conflict which most interests him—that between passion and duty. The necessity of subjugating passion to reason (which, according to Corneille, sees duty as our first obligation) is always the fundamental issue of his great plays.

The men and women whom he conceives as the most heroic are those of almost superhuman will. They never know human weakness in themselves. If their act of duty destroys their happiness, they have no regrets for what they have done. They say, with Rodrigue to Chimène, "I should do it again, if I had to choose." This is the heroic quality for which Corneille's has been esteemed: his conception of human dignity must evoke our admiration, even if we cannot warm to the heroism of his *dramatis personae.*

Corneille must also be credited with having shaped a drama that, when he came to the theater, was at best crude. In his hands French tragedy achieved its adulthood. As for his comedy, *The Liar,* Molière cheerfully acknowledged his indebtedness to it.

What is not so plain to readers of Corneille's in translation: he is one of the best of French poets. There is a remarkable firmness in his lines, and a fine robustness and virility in his verse. His abstract vocabulary, entirely alien to the best in English tradition, is perfectly suited to his ideas. At climactic moments there is a resounding crash in his diction which is stirring to hear.

JEAN RACINE (1639–1699)

Racine is by general consent described as the greatest writer of tragedy France has ever had, as well as one of her finest poets. In him the virtues of Neoclassicism are seen at their best. In his relation to Corneille as a writer, there is a certain resemblance to the Englishman Pope's relation to Dryden. Both Racine and Pope took over the heritage of their precursor and gave it elegance, polish, mellowness, wit, and brilliance.

The details of Racine's biography are not so edifying as his accomplishment as a dramatist. He was a man vain of fame, jealous of the success of others, and capable of astonishing ingratitude.

He was born near Soissons at La Ferté Milon on December 21, 1639—more than three decades after Corneille. His family held official positions in their district, and were connected with the Jansenist Movement. The Jansenists, a religious order with headquarters at Port-Royal, had for a while been subject to some persecution because of their extreme views on the doctrine of original sin. They were accused of virtually espousing the heresy of predestination, which is contrary to the Church's doctrine of the freedom of the will. Both of Racine's parents were dead by the time he was four, and he was raised by his Jansenist grandmother. By her he was sent to the Jansenist college at Beauvais, and from there to a Jansenist school near Port-Royal. He became equally proficient in reading the Greek of Euripides and in acquiring the severe religious precepts of his Jansenist teachers. He finished his studies at the college of Harcourt. His family was anxious that he take holy orders, and with this object he went to the country for a few years. But by 1663 he was convinced that poetry was his true vocation and he returned to Paris. An ode written on the recovery of the King from illness brought him a large present from the monarch.

His first plays were *La Thébaïde* (1664), on the rivalry between the two sons of Œdipus, and *Alexandre* (1665), on Alexander the Great. Both were produced by Molière and his troupe, who were responsible for procuring Racine his first public successes. For no good reason Racine played Molière the highly unethical trick of giving the *Alexandre* to the rival company, so that the tragedy was presented at both theaters at once. Racine was also responsible for persuading Molière's best actress to join the rival company. As a result, Molière was naturally very angry; thus ended what might have proved a productive friendship.

Racine's friends and relatives at Port-Royal were very much worried about his increasing wordliness, and looked upon his writing for the theater as ungodly work. His answer, despite all he owed to the Jansenists, was a brilliantly witty attack upon them in the form of a public *Letter*. He was about to follow this with a second attack when Boileau pointed out to him that he was attacking people already sufficiently persecuted.

With *Andromaque* (1667) he came into his own as the greatest dramatic poet of his age. For the next ten years he composed a series of tragic masterpieces which are the glory of the French stage: *Britannicus* (1669), *Bérénice* (1670), *Bajazet* (1672), *Mithridate* (1673), *Iphigénie in Aulide* (1674), and *Phaedra* (1677). He also wrote the delightful comedy satirizing the legal profession, *The Litigants* (*Les Plaideurs*) in 1668. In 1673 he had entered the French Academy, and in 1664 he had been appointed to a post at Court.

The success of *Andromaque* inevitably made Racine a challenger of Corneille's position as the leading dramatist; he was popular at Court, and sought after by everyone. But he was sensitive to the least criticism, and often responded with prefaces that were remarkable for their bitterness. At last his enemies succeeded in routing him from the stage. A powerful woman of the nobility encouraged a second-rate writer to do a play also on the theme of *Phaedra*, bought up the tickets for both houses, and saw to it that Racine's play was attended only by a hissing clique.

This failure was only temporary and very brief. But it proved enough to turn Racine from the stage. He took it as a judgment from God for his ingratitude towards his Jansenist friends. Returning to Port-Royal, he made his peace with his old friends, and was ready to enter a cloister. His spiritual adviser, however, counseled him to marry. He did so, and raised seven children. His last years (1677–1699) were devoted to his family and to the King as Royal Historiographer. With the years he became more and more deeply devout and confirmed in his Jansenist views.

His period of great creativity, therefore, ended in his late thirties. But his withdrawal from creative activity was not due, as he was to prove, to any diminution of powers. In 1689 he suddenly turned to dramatic composition at the instigation of Mme. de Maintenon for her pupils at St. Cyr, when he wrote *Esther.* Two years later he wrote his last and, perhaps, his greatest tragedy, *Athalie* (1691), to be performed before the King at Versailles without scenery or costumes. When he died he was buried at the Port-Royal cemetery. The Parisian public did not see *Athalie* until more than fifteen years after his death.

Andromaque

In *Andromaque* (1667) we find Andromache, the widow of Hector, living in captivity with her son Astyanax, after the Trojan War, at the court of Pyrrhus. Orestes, sent by the Greeks to claim Astyanax, arrives at Epirus. Orestes is in love with Hermione, the betrothed of Pyrrhus, and desires Andromache to accept Pyrrhus' suit for her hand. Pyrrhus, who at first has refused to surrender Astyanax, angered at Andromache's refusal of him, is determined to marry Hermione instead, and give up the boy to Orestes. Whereupon, Andromache, who secretly intends killing herself, agrees to marry her captor. Instigated by the jealous Hermione, Orestes kills Pyrrhus. Hermione commits suicide by her dead betrothed's side, and Orestes loses his reason.

Britannicus

Britannicus (1669) is concerned with the unfolding of criminality in Nero's character. Nero's mother, Agrippina, through intrigue and murder has secured the throne for him. Nero, beginning to act independently of his mother, has had Junia, the betrothed of Britannicus (the legitimate heir to the crown), carried off. When Nero refuses to account to his mother for this act, Agrippina threatens to support the claims of his rival. Corrupted by the evil advice of his counsellor, Narcissus, Nero has Britannicus poisoned. Junia takes refuge with the Vestal Virgins, and Agrippina foresees her own downfall and much catastrophe to Rome.

Middle Plays

Bérénice (1670) has the simplest of all of Racine's plots. It contains almost no physical action, dealing, as it does, with the renunciation of two royal lovers, Bérénice and Titus, for political reasons. The laws of Rome forbid the emperor to marry a foreigner; after passionate hesitation, both tragically separate.

Bajazet (1672) is Oriental in setting, though, as usual with Racine, there is no attempt to bring in local color. The Sultaness, Roxane, has been ordered by the Sultan, Amurat, to kill his younger brother, Bajazet, during the Sultan's absence. Roxane loves Bajazet, and offers to save him if he will marry her. But he is in love with Atalide. When Bajazet is offered the choice of Atalide's death or his own, he is indignant. Roxane has him killed, and then Atalide kills herself.

Phaedra

Phaedra (1677) is generally considered to be the masterpiece of French classic tragedy. The title role has been sought after by the greatest actresses of the French stage. Racine's play was inspired by Euripides' *Hippolytus.*

Having slain the Minotaur, the hero Theseus has married Phaedra, daughter of the King of Crete. She, despite her own will, has fallen in love with his son by an earlier marriage, Hippolytus. To conceal her passion she has been cold and hostile to the young man. At last—and here the play opens—Hippolytus decides to leave Troezen and go in search of his long-absent father. He confesses to Theramenes, his tutor, that he wishes to avoid both his stepmother and the Athenian princess, Aricia, whose family has good reason for hating anyone connected with Theseus. Phaedra confesses to her nurse, Œnone, that she has an ungovernable passion for Hippolytus, and explains the reason for her spiteful conduct towards him.

Rumor reaches Troezen that Theseus is now dead. Hippolytus, a just youth, assures Aricia that he will second her claims to the throne of Athens. Œnone urges Phaedra to support the claims of her own son to the kingship of Athens over those of Hippolytus. Hippolytus thinks that he ought to inherit Troezen, Phaedra's son Crete, and Aricia Athens. He admits to Aricia his love for her, but fears the gods will never sanction such a marriage.

Hippolytus goes to Phaedra to tell her his hopes; she abandons all pretense of hostility, and admits her passion for him. He is horrified at her revelation, and repulses her. She threatens to take her own life. But the people of Athens choose Phaedra's son rather than Aricia.

There are rumors now that Theseus is not dead. Hippolytus is anxious that his father's whereabouts be found. Phaedra, now bitter at her loss of dignity and deeply regretting her honesty with Hippolytus, cannot nevertheless control her feelings. She offers him the kingdom only so that she may keep him near.

Rumor now reveals that Theseus is approaching home. Œnone, fearing the worst, counsels Phaedra to hide her emotion, and even to charge Hippolytus before Theseus of attempting her honor. When Theseus arrives he is chagrined at what he finds: Hippolytus asks to be allowed to leave Troezen, and Phaedra tells him she is no longer fit to be his wife.

Œnone now tells Theseus that his son has attempted to violate Phaedra's honor. He threatens Hippolytus, accuses him, and refuses to listen to his denials. He banishes the young man from Troezen forever. Hearing that his son loves Aricia, Theseus calls upon Neptune to wreak vengeance on his son.

Urged by Aricia to prove his innocence, Hippolytus refuses, knowing that Theseus could not sustain hearing the truth of Phaedra's passion for the young man. The two lovers agree to escape from the land. After an interview with Aricia, Theseus' suspicions are aroused, and he sends for the nurse.

Fearful of the encounter, Œnone commits suicide. At the seashore Hippolytus is destroyed by a monster sent by Neptune. Hearing of the young man's death, Phaedra confesses her guilty passion, tells the whole truth, and drinks poison. Theseus is glad that his wretched queen is dead, and seeks out Aricia to comfort her.

In returning to drama after a long absence, Racine in *Esther* (1689) pushed his love for Greek drama further by employing a chorus in the work. The story has to do with the Jewish Esther who has married Ahasuerus, King of Persia. Not knowing his wife to be Jewish, the King, under the influence of his minister Haman, has ordered the extermination of all Jews in his kingdom. When her uncle Mordochai urges her to do so, Esther confesses her religion to the King, and asks freedom for her people. The King grants her request, and orders Haman hanged.

Athalie

Athalie (1691) also deals with a Biblical story. Athalie, desiring to seize all power to herself, has arranged to have all her children and grandchildren killed. Young Joas, however, has escaped, and has been brought up by the high priest Joad and his wife Josabeth in the temple. At the opening of the drama, Joad informs his wife that he means to have Joas crowned that day, so that Athalie can be dethroned. The Queen, because of a dream, comes to the temple, speaks to the young prince, and attempts to take him away with her. She is not successful in this ruse, and Joas is crowned. The Levites, the priestly caste, are prepared to defend his claims with arms. When Athalie comes to the temple she is murdered.

IMPORTANCE

In Racine we find neoclassic tragedy at its best. The three unities, which had been something of a restriction to Corneille's talents, Racine found thoroughly comfortable for his purposes. It has been said that the three unities almost seem to have been invented for Racine's use. If this statement is true, it is because Racine always reduces the plot to a minimum. (Nowhere in his work is there such a succession of incidents as we find in *Le Cid*, for instance.) Racine always centers his tragedy on a single moral crisis. There is always a sense of great simplicity and artistic purity in his plays. His defense of his method in the preface to *Bérénice*, states his position well:

> Some think that this simplicity is a sign of little invention. They forget that, on the contrary, real invention consists in

making something out of nothing, and that a multitude of incidents has always been the recourse of poets who never owned a genius rich enough to maintain their audience's interest through five acts by a simple action, sustained by the passions, the beauty of the ideas and the elegance of the expression.

Racine has depicted with depth and subtlety the passion of political ambition (Agrippina in *Britannicus*, Haman in *Esther*, Athalie in the play named after her), of religious exaltation (Joad in *Athalie*), of court intrigue (Narcissus in *Britannicus*), and of maternal love (Andromaque in the play named after her)—but above all he is the dramatist of the passion of love between man and woman. Such love is the recurrent theme at the basis of most of his masterpieces. Despite his elegance, Racine's women of passion seem to talk with the violence of life itself; Phaedra and Hermione achieve the heights of tragic dignity by the naked truth of their emotions. The very absence of complications in plot only serves in Racine's plays to emphasize each shade of feeling in the characters.

Racine's style is equally remarkable for its precision and restraint. His simplicity is the result of a consummate artistry that everywhere achieves harmony between what is meant and what is being said. Voltaire suggested that on every page of Racine should be inscribed: "Beautiful, sublime, wonderful."

FRENCH POETRY OF THE SEVENTEENTH CENTURY

In the field of nondramatic poetry, the man who has been credited with having introduced Neoclassical practise into French verse is François de Malherbe (1555–1628). He reacted strongly against the Renaissance traditions of Ronsard's school, and ridiculed their language and metres. It was through his efforts that poetry was brought nearer to the realm of prose. For him the highest virtue of poetry was not imagination but clarity. He stipulated for a purely French (as opposed to Italianate or pedantic) diction, polished the Alexandrine line (the twelve-syllable line later employed by Corneille, Racine, and Molière), and set the style for elegance of expression. His poetry is not of a very high order, but his influence was considerable on his successors. As a critic he prepared the way for Boileau. Among his immediate disciples were Racan (1589–1670) and Maynard (1582–1646). A man of far greater gifts, Régnier (1573–1613), a brilliant satirist, continued the older traditions of French poetry; Cyrano de Bergerac (1619–1655) also resisted the new tradition in his eccentric verses.

Outside of the drama, the two most notable poets of the century in France were La Fontaine and Boileau.

Jean de la Fontaine (1621–1695)

La Fontaine was born at Château Thierry but became eventually a confirmed Parisian. Among his friends were Boileau, Molière, and Racine. He was elected to the French Academy at the same time as Boileau (1684). His simplicity of character, impracticality, and absent-mindedness were legendary already in his own times. Nevertheless, the quantity of his writing is astonishing, considering his easygoing nature. In addition to a number of unsuccessful plays, a romance, and miscellaneous works, he is author of two collections for which he will always be read: the *Tales* (*Contes*) and the *Fables*—both of which appeared in series at various times.

The first part of the *Tales* appeared in 1664, the second in 1667, and the third in 1671; the first part of the *Fables* appeared in 1668, the second 1679, and the third in 1693. The two works complement each other. The best qualities of each are common to both: raciness of language, easy flow of narrative, and pointedness of satire. But the *Fables* are kept within the vocabulary and morals of young people; while the *Tales* are very sophisticated, and intended for an urbane and worldly audience. For the *Tales* he took stories from Boccaccio, the old French collection of *Cent Nouvelles Nouvelles*, Rabelais, the *Heptameron*, and some of the Italian *novella* writers. It cannot be denied that intermixed with the wit there is a looseness of moral values in the *Tales*. Nevertheless, they are remarkable for their variety and vividness; and even the worst of prudes will have to grant them their vivacity and grace as verse.

The *Fables* have been universally admired. They are full of good humor and charm, and in them la Fontaine reveals a deep understanding of human nature. Taking his subjects chiefly from Æsop and Phaedrus, he has transformed his little moral tales into little dramatic episodes in verse in which the animal characters and the human characters are painted to the life in gesture and language. He managed to convey every status of human life from the courtier to the peasant in these amusing allegories. They are all interesting, and where the level of excellence is so high it is impossible to single out individual pieces.

As he says himself, "Everyone speaks in my work, even the fishes." In an epigrammatical remark of one of his characters, he is able to sum his moral. Thus, in "The Grasshopper and the Ant," when the improvident Grasshopper comes begging for food in winter, he tells the Ant that all summer long he has been singing; "Very well, then," says the Ant, "dance now."

Nicolas Boileau-Despréaux (1636–1711)

Boileau was born at Paris, was educated at the colleges of Harcourt and Beauvais, and was at first destined for the clergy. Disliking theology, he was allowed to study for the law, and for a while practised the legal profession. The death of his father in 1657 left him free to renounce that too, and his substantial income now enabled him to devote himself to poetry. He took the name of Despréaux after the name of an estate his father owned. In 1660 he wrote his first satire, and in 1663 published his first collection of poems, none of which rises above mediocrity. But his real abilities were being exploited in his satirical poems, which were already being appreciated in the salons. A poor pirated edition of these appeared in Holland during 1666, and Boileau therefore issued an authentic one in Paris during the same year. Boileau was soon a great favorite of the King's, and Louis XIV saw to it that sinecures and pensions were liberally awarded to the satirist. Boileau also numbered Molière, Racine, and la Fontaine among his good friends by this time.

His satires, which were entitled by him *Discourses*, continued as he wrote them to attack poets whom posterity has forgotten, and to defend others whom posterity reveres. For this reason it was some time before his enemies in the French Academy could be placated enough to admit him to their numbers. When he was admitted in 1684, it was only through Louis XIV's influence. All his life he suffered from poor health, and in his later years his contemporaries found him rather arrogant and morose in temper. By the time of his death all his close friends were dead; nevertheless, at his funeral the attendance was so large that someone said, "He had many friends, this man who attacked everyone!"

Boileau's works consist of twelve satires, twelve epistles, *The Art of Poetry* (*L'Art Poétique*), *The Lectern* (*Le Lutrin*), a translation of Longinus, a few miscellaneous poems and epigrams, a few short critiques, and some letters. Nearly all his poetry is written in imitation of Horace. His satire is witty but malicious and very personal, and he was not above substituting the name of a new enemy for an old one in a piece of invective he had already finished. However justified he has been by time as a result of the neglect that has been accorded the minor poets he attacked, his own two odes are beneath contempt in quality. Nevertheless, with one exception, his critical judgments were sound. The exception was the great Corneille, already advanced in years when Boileau came to the fore; against Corneille he directed some of his satire because Boileau was anxious to exalt his own disciple Racine at the expense of the older man.

The Lectern (1673, 1683), in which the author burlesques a trivial quarrel about the placing of a lectern in a church by writing about the dispute in the epic style, we find Boileau at his most engaging. The verse is polished and easy, the sarcasm delightful. But it was his *Art of Poetry* (1674) that brought him to the height of his reputation, and vastly increased the number of his enemies. Its influence has been a lasting one on French literature, and for a century and a half its wisdom was hardly questioned. Because of it Boileau has been called "the Lawgiver of Parnassus." It is written in epigrammatic Alexandrine lines (which much influenced the Englishman Pope), the product of much polishing, and it is clear and smooth. But it lacks almost all the qualities which one expects of even good poetry—not to speak of the great.

The Art of Poetry tells us that the poet must found his ideas on nature, and must learn to love reason. Reason will teach the poet perfect diction, variety, nobility of language, polish, and true versification. Boileau then proceeds to give a highly uninformed history of French poetry. Nothing good, according to him, was written before Malherbe, since Malherbe was the first to limit his muse by the rules. In the Second Canto of *The Art of Poetry* we are given the various classifications of poetry: the eclogue, the ode, the elegy, the sonnet, the epigram, and the satire. These are all good, having been perfected by the ancients. The old medieval French forms are bad from the standpoint of art and reason. The Third Canto deals with tragedy, comedy, and the epic. Here Boileau is chiefly indebted to Horace's *Art of Poetry.* He allows no deviation from the unities: "one place, one day, one dramatic fact." He discusses the technique of managing exposition of past events through narrative in drama; the preparation for the catastrophe; the catastrophe itself. Tragedy, he says, must avoid the familiar and the trivial, and must obey the dictates of decorum. The writer of comedy must learn from nature; that is the quality, he says, which makes Molière a great writer. Comedy and tragedy should never be mixed in the same play. Reason must be the guide to comic action, and there must never be any jests at the expense of reason.

Here we have summed for the times the essentials of Neoclassical faith. In the ninth *Epistle*, Boileau adds one more fundamental: "Nothing is beautiful but the true." (Logical truth, not imagination, is thus the foundation for Neoclassical art.)

IMPORTANCE

Boileau's range was very narrow, but he was strong within his limitations. He is the first great critic of his age, and the first to insist upon the importance of *taste*, and simplicity. His importance, indeed, has not been at all as a poet, but as a critic. Despite the prosaic quality of his verse, his influence on his age and his country has been second to none. He looked upon himself as the guardian of classical standards, and his times accepted him at his own valuation. His name will always figure large in histories of literature because of his influence.

FRENCH MORALISTS OF THE SEVENTEENTH CENTURY

The literary and popular success of Montaigne's essays did much in the seventeenth century to stimulate the writing of short prose compositions. The flourishing of salons, gathering places of wits and men of learning, also encouraged this kind of writing to match in prose the poetic effusions of sonneteers and epigrammatists. Moral ideas were on everyone's lips, and the emergence of prose types like the Character, the Maxim, and the *Pensée* (thought) gave rise to some important literature of this period.

Blaise Pascal (1623–1662)

Pascal was a man of genius trapped by the conflicting traits of his interests. He belongs to the science of physics: when he was still a boy he invented an adding machine; his famous experiment with the barometer was conducted when he was only twenty-five; all his brief life mathematics was his chief recreation. His writings give him place also in philosophy and theology, as well as in belles lettres. He was by temperament a mystic, but strove valiantly to conform to the dictates of reason, as his age prescribed. In his early twenties he was converted to Jansenism. But his scientific experiments brought him into association for a while with freethinkers in religion; what he heard said in their company was probably the inspiration for his religious meditations in the *Pensées*. In 1654 a miraculous escape from death in an accident was responsible for his second conversion to Jansenism, and the next year he retired to Port-Royal to join the Jansenists. In 1656 he was called upon to defend the order publicly; the result was his major literary work, *Letters Written to a Provincial* (known as *Les Provinciales*), which appeared in that year. For the rest of his days Pascal was busy collecting materials for an apology for the Christian religion; these scattered thoughts, found among his papers, were published after his death as the *Pensées* (1670). To the end, however, his religious reflections were interrupted by his still lively interest in scientific questions and practical invention. The work of these last years was carried out in the midst of painful ill health.

Les Provinciales was issued under a pseudonym, and is an attack on the Jesuits, the great enemies of the Jansenists. In the letters which make up the book Pascal is revealed as a master of elegant irony. Despite their religious contents, the sceptic Voltaire greatly admired them and asserted that they were as lively as the best of Molière. What Pascal believed to be the sophistries of the Jesuits he exposes with the lightest and most perfect of sarcasm. As one critic has put it, he seems to be smiling throughout. His steady stream of polite satire, in which he has never had a master, to this day holds place as the leading criticism of the Jesuits.

The *Thoughts* (*Pensées*) reveal the other side of their author. As an honest man Pascal was affected by the growing skepticism of the Age of Reason. But, temperamentally, he found religious skepticism a source of the most intense personal spiritual agony. The *Thoughts* are a record of the struggle between the mystic in Pascal's nature and the doubts which were the product of his brilliant rational intellect. Here we find no satire, no levity, though the charm of the style is everywhere worthy of the author of *Les Provinciales*. The *Thoughts* also have the advantage over *Les Provinciales* of being unlimited by a purely contemporary issue, the controversy between the Jesuits and the Jansenists. The subjects of the *Thoughts* are of permanent interest. His mind is fascinated by the dilemma of man's insignificance in the face of the infinite. Man, he says, is "a cipher in comparison with infinity, a middle place between nothing and everything." Man's senses can operate only within "fixed limits; too loud a sound stuns, too much light blinds, too great or too small a distance hinders sight." Man yearns to find "a fixed base on which he may build a tower to pierce the infinite, but the foundation trembles, and the earth yawns in an abyss."

François, Prince de Marcillac, Duke de la Rochefoucauld (1613–1680)

La Rochefoucauld was descended from one of the noblest of French families, relatives of kings. At court he became involved in the intrigues against Richelieu, and, after the latter's death, those against Mazarin. He made a reputation for himself for his fearlessness, and was a good friend of Madame de Sévigné, the celebrated letter-writer. He was a man of melancholy temper, fond of the company of women, and rather reckless about his affairs. His two important books are his *Memoirs* (1662) and his *Maxims* (1665). His *Memoirs* is an objective account of his own failures at the court. It is the *Maxims* by which he is best known. These pithy sentences were a product of the stimulating conversations of the salons. He spent years polishing his little gems, and after the slender volume appeared he continued to improve on them in new editions.

La Rochefoucald's *Maxims* reveal him as a cool skeptic. He had no illusions about human nature. "Nobody merits praise for doing good unless he also possesses the capacity for doing evil," he has said. He did not believe men capable of disinterested benevolence. "Our virtues are lost in selfishness as rivers are lost in the sea." "Love of justice is only the fear of experiencing injustice." "If we succeed in overcoming our passions, it is more because they are weak than because we are strong." "Virtue could not go so far if vanity did not bear it company." At the basis of all human endeavor he saw only self-love.

It would be unjust to say that La Rochefoucauld attempts to justify this selfishness, which he finds the common denominator in all human beings. He merely observes and records what he sees. As a master of compression and precision he has never been surpassed. He is never unclear, never pompous, and never interested in mere cleverness. If his view of humanity is spiritually superficial, his is a healthy medicine against moral hypocrisy.

Jean de la Bruyère (1645–1696)

La Bruyère is a man whose biography is hardly known to us. He was born in Paris, and seems to have come from a family associated with the law. He was well-educated and apparently possessed a good income. In 1687 he published his *Characters* (*Les Caractères*). This, in addition to his translation of Theophrastus, is his only important book. In 1693 he was elected to the French Academy. He was very much liked by his contemporaries for his good nature and his lack of pedantry.

Theophrastus (B.C. 372?–287), a philosopher of the Peripatetic School, was the leading botanist of antiquity. His *Characters* were unknown to Christian times until unearthed by the French scholar Casaubon (1592); they are a collection of sketches in which, to quote their author, Theophrastus set down "the manners of each several kind of men both good and bad...and the behavior proper to them." In the seventeenth century the Character became a literary type intimately connected with the development of the Essay. In England it had already flourished in the hands of Hall, Overbury, Feltham, and Earle. Unlike Theophrastus, who dealt largely with abstract qualities, la Bruyère modelled his portraits on people he knew and whom his readers could recognize in transparent disguise. His subtitle, "the Manners of This Century," indicates his purposes. The plan of the work is fluid, and gives the impression almost of a collection of thoughts and observations recorded in a diary. We find moral maxims, personal observation, portraits, literary criticism, and moral criticism following one another with ease and without formal arrangement. He may be read on any page as a beginning, and laid aside at any page. His book lacks the tight manner of the *Maxims* or the *Pensée*, and exhibits him as a man of great taste and shrewd observation. If less sharp than la Rochefoucauld, his style is admirable for fluency and grace. There is also a notable absence of skepticism in his moral view. The *Characters* appeared in new enlarged editions in 1688, 1689, and 1696—the last a Ninth Edition.

Charles de Marguetel de Saint-Denis, Seigneur de Saint-Evremond (1613–1703)

Saint-Evremond, a Norman, was educated by the Jesuits and took the opposing side in Pascal's controversy with them. Incurring the King's displeasure, he went to England with the returning court of the Stuarts, and spent the remainder of his life chiefly in London as a friend of the Restoration courtiers. He was buried in Westminster Abbey. His works are nearly all the product of transient issues and occasions, but display acute and well-informed literary taste. His criticism of French drama as compared with the drama of antiquity is excellent, and his comparative studies of Corneille and Racine are full of good sense. His particular brand of wit is said to have greatly influenced Voltaire. It was not until after his death that his *Works* were published (1705). These contain letters, critiques, portraits, discourses, etc. Sainte-Beuve considered him the most distinguished courtier-writer of his time.

WOMEN WRITERS

The selection and grouping of women writers in this section is not intended to depict them as a gender subgroup viewed apart from male authors by their culture or, for that matter, by themselves. Our intent here is simply to highlight the contributions of several women who, like the Brontë sisters in England, shared the burden of prejudicial judgments made against them solely because of their gender.

In the writings of several distinguished women of this age we catch the tone of the lively play of wit fostered in the salons.

Madame de la Fayette (1634–1693)

A devoted friend of la Rochefoucauld, Madame de la Fayette was the author of *The Princess of Clèves* (*La Princesse de Clèves*) (1678), a good example of the neoclassical novel. It has been called "*Polyeucte* without the religion." The story tells of a noblewoman who finds herself not in love with her husband; she asks him to protect her against herself; thinking falsely that his wife is faithless, her husband dies; free to love whom she chooses now, the widow prefers to live in seclusion. The psychology, the delicacy and charm of sentiment, and the loveliness of style are captivating in this book.

Madame de Sévigné (1626–1696)

Madame de Sévigné has preserved a vivid picture of her century in her *Letters* (1725), which run to many volumes. She was a woman of great wit and extraordinary sincerity. Though connected with the most prominent families and personages of her day, she managed to steer clear of intrigue and affectation—both of them a trap for countless of the nobility in her day. In 1651 she found herself a young widow with a daughter and a son to raise. In 1677 she purchased the now celebrated Hôtel Carnavalet in Paris (now a museum), and there received visits from a brilliant company of friends for the rest of her life. Most of her letters are addressed to her daughter, Madame de Grignan, in the provinces. She thus carefully and wittily retailed all the latest news, and has reflected, as in a clear mirror, her age for posterity. Her correspondence shows her as an entirely charming and balanced woman of the world.

Madame de Maintenon (1635–1719)

Born a Protestant, Madame de Maintenon was raised in a convent and converted to Catholicism. After the death of her husband Scarron, she was given the position of governess to the children of Madame de Montespan and Louis XIV. By degrees the King made her his confidante, and after the death of the Queen, he secretly married Madame de Maintenon (1684). She made it her duty to bring him back to the Church. Under the influences of Jansenist education, she founded Saint-Cyr for the daughters of the indigent well-born. It was for her that Racine returned to the drama to write his two last plays, *Esther* and *Athalie.* She is the author of various religious works, but is best remembered for her *Letters* (1719), where her reasonableness and her naturalness are evident. Without the sprightliness of Madame de Sévigné's correspondence, her letters have an admirable directness and forthrightness.

SEVENTEENTH CENTURY FRENCH MEMOIRS

Few countries have produced a completer picture of the times recorded in memoirs than did France in the seventeenth century. Henri de Rohan (1579–1638) gives a vivid account beginning with the year 1629. We have already mentioned la Rochefoucauld's *Memoirs*, which give a lively view of intrigue at court under Richelieu. Madame de Motteville (1621–1689) has left us a straightforward account of Anne of Austria's affairs, in whose suite she was from 1643 to 1666. Madame de la Fayette, the novelist, has left fragments from the years 1688 and 1689, interesting for their psychological analysis of Louis XIV's relations with James II of England. Madame de Caylus (1673–1739), a niece of Madame de Maintenon, has provided vivid narratives of her aunt and the school at Saint-Cyr. Cardinal de Retz (1614–1679), an inveterate conspirator, left memoirs containing colorful portraits, racy anecdotes and pointed maxims. But no collection of memoirs has been read with more interest than that of Saint-Simon.

Louis de Rouvroy, Duke de Saint-Simon (1675–1755)

Saint-Simon came of a very distinguished and ancient noble family. He was very prominent in Court circles, and constantly irritated Louis XIV by his being an intransigent stickler for his rights of precedence at court. With a handful of peers, his place was second to none except the royal princes. His memoirs were too personal to be published during his lifetime. After his death, they were published in excerpt; but it was not until 1839 that they were issued in their entirety. These records are certainly more vivid and real, and more full of anecdote, than any other memoirs in existence. Stylistically they suffer from their rapid composition and his unconcealed hostilities. But they give a picture unrivalled in detail of the complicated life at the Court of Louis XIV.

FRENCH THEOLOGIANS OF THE SEVENTEENTH CENTURY

In this century French theologians made significant contributions to literature. The dominance in politics, first of Richelieu, and then of Mazarin, gave importance to church affairs. Moreover, Louis XIV almost equalled the laxity of his private morals with the strict orthodoxy of his religious views.

Jacques Benigne Bossuet (1627–1704)

Bossuet was the leading theological writer of his times. Educated by the Jesuits, he soon proved himself as a fine orator and skilled controversialist. He became tutor to the Dauphin, member of the French Academy, and Bishop of Meaux. As an apologist for the rights of the Crown he was untiring, and naturally won the gratitude of Louis XIV. In addition to many other works, he wrote an analysis of Catholic dogma and a history of the different Protestant sects. But his most important work was his *Discourse on Universal History up to the Time of Charlemagne* (*Le Discours sur l'Histoire Universelle*), which has been called the first attempt at a philosophy of history. His purpose was to arrive at "a theology of human progress," beginning with Adam.

The First Part of the *Discourse* gives a chronology of history to the time of Charlemagne; the Second Part, *On Religions*, exhibits Providence guiding the world through His chosen peoples; the Third Part, *On Empires*, traces the Roman Empire up to the time of the Holy Roman Emperor. His approach is rational. It is as a stylist that Bossuet is now read; his command of language was superb, and his rhetorical effects are often magnificient; he is never pompous, never overstrained in his majestic utterance.

François de Salignac de la Mothe-Fénelon (1661–1715)

Fénelon, Bossuet's adversary, was a man of deeper learning and humanity. He devoted much of his time to the poor and was much interested in education. Late in his thirties he became Archbishop of Cambray. Certain of his observations attracted the attention of Bossuet as being probably heretical, and Fénelon found himself violently attacked by the King's favorite theologian. Naturally, Bossuet had the King's backing, and later the Pope's too; and Fenelon submitted to the Papal decision. The publication of his *Telemachus* (1699) completed the public disgrace of the gentle Fénelon, and he was banished from court. His last years were spent in attempting to alleviate the sufferings of the victims of the War of the Spanish Succession.

Telemachus, modelled chiefly on the *Odyssey* and the *Æneid*, shows the son of Odysseus going through adventures similiar to his father's, with a Circe-like nymph, Calypso, many voyages over the sea; and a descent to the infernal regions. The style is a compound of Homeric phrases and classical allusions, but contains much charm and simplicity; it is considered a classic now for young people and beginners in French.

But Fénelon's purposes were to instruct the Dauphin in a moral life. Bossuet, for all his orthodoxy, never made any attempt to correct the immorality of Louis XIV's life. Fénelon was anxious to teach the Prince another way of living, and thus indirectly was criticising the King. The Dauphin is warned against the life of gallantry and love-conquests, against luxury, and even against desiring absolute power. No wonder Louis XIV was angered! Though not a writer of the highest gifts, Fénelon's personal charm comes through his prose, and he is skillful at telling a direct story. He is at his best in dialogue. What is not least admirable in his book is his courageous objections to war and absolute monarchy.

FRENCH NEOCLASSICISM IN THE EIGHTEENTH CENTURY

Neoclassicism in the eighteenth century retained the basic bias of the seventeenth in favor of a rationalistic approach to life; it was equally concerned with achieving clarity, simplicity, wit, elegance, perfection of form, and it was equally didactic in its literary intentions. But in France (as in England) one important change is to be observed in the new century. The splendor and absolutism of the Court had made the royal house and its retainers the focus of interest in seventeenth century literature. In the eighteenth century the audience became instead the general reading public. Learning, science, philosophy, and wit became the proprieties for the well-to-do citizen with the leisure to develop his taste and knowledge.

Historical Perspective

Louis XIV had already lost much of his prestige among his people before his death in 1715. The bigotry and sombreness of his last years alienated the devotion of the public. The Regency of the Duke of Orléans (1715–1723) was a period of reaction against the moral ostentation of Louis XIV's court—a period of license and frivolity, even, some would say, of libertinism. Louis XV during his reign (1715–1774) showed little aptitude for and less interest in ruling the country; the destinies of the nation were settled according to the whim and caprice of a succession of his mistresses, from the Marquise de Prie through Madame de Pompadour to Madame du Barry—to mention only the leading ones. The extravagance and expenditures of the Court were steadily ruining the country. Louis XV was not unaware that his successor would have to pay the penalty. "After me, the deluge," he said prophetically. Louis XV followed his own pleasures, and was indifferent to the political divisions of his court. The real influences of the time in the world of letters emanated not from the Court but from the salons.

In the days of Molière the fashionable gatherings at the salons were guilty of preciosity, and the great dramatist had suitably castigated them in his comedies. But in the eighteenth century a series of brilliant women made their homes the centers of truly philosophic and literary conversation. It has been said that the literature of eighteenth century France was all spoken before it was written. In these salons writers and cultivated readers met on an equal footing. The elegant ladies who were queens over their coteries afforded real help, politically, financially, and intellectually, to writers. Madame de Lambert (1710–1733), Madame de Tencin (1730–1749), and Madame Geoffrin (1749–1777), as their dates of influence indicate, succeeded one another in eminence. Holding rival court to these ladies was the Marquise du Deffand (1740–1780), and Mademoiselle de Lespinasse (1763–1776). In various of these gatherings could be found men like Voltaire, Fontenelle, and Montesquieu; distinguished foreigners like the Englishmen Horace Walpole and Lord Chesterfield, and the German Grimm; and artists like Greuze and Van Loo. Madame Geoffrin's success shows the growing power of the middle class whence she came; at her salon the philosophers were particularly at home. The general effect of these gatherings on literature was to make it witty, polished, and agreeable. The sciences were deprived of technicality; knowledge became lucid and impersonal.

This was the period when the admiration of England and English literature developed almost into a mania. Voltaire discovered Shakespeare, the philosopher Locke and the Deists, and the poet Pope. Montesquieu celebrated the liberalism of the English constitution. Both Voltaire and Montesquieu were powerfully affected by their visits to England. Diderot was influenced by the English novelists and the philosopher Shaftesbury; even the *Encyclopedia* was modeled on an English original. Rousseau was indebted to Locke, to Richardson and to many other English writers. Many translations from the English were made, during this period, into the French. The force of this Anglomania was to augment the growing restlessness in French political affairs. While half of France was living in starvation and political oppression, England seemed to liberal Frenchmen to be holding aloft the beacon of liberty.

The period of Louis XV was, therefore, a period of contradictions. The Court continued its old parade of splendor, but actually was losing hold over the people. Outwardly life in Paris and Versailles was more charming and attractive than ever; as Talleyrand said, "Whoever hasn't lived before 1789 knows nothing of the sweetness of living." But the lower classes, of whom literature for a while took little cognizance, were becoming tired of all this pretty gallantry and the artifices which made vice appear graceful.

The reign of Louis XVI (1774–1792) and his queen Marie Antoinette saw the final dissolution of this world of charming artificiality. Had Louis XVI been capable he might have led the Revolution instead of becoming its victim. But he and his queen, though privately morally superior to their predecessors, were wholly unfitted to direct the political turbulence which at last erupted. The Revolution, which Voltaire, Rousseau, and Diderot had unknowingly done much to prepare, was destined to alter the political life not only of France, but of the whole western world.

The life of the western world was undergoing radical change because of another basic factor: the growth of scientific invention. The eighteenth was the century of the spinning jenny, the flying shuttle, the water frame, and the steam engine. Mechanical invention led to the steady increase of industry and the emergence of urban powers as the directing forces of nations. Money began to assume an importance it had never possessed before. Great wealth and great poverty began to appear for the first time in Europe in glaring disparity.

Unlike their predecessors in Neoclassicism, the leading writers of the eighteenth century, therefore, instead of placing themselves under the sheltering favor of the Court, became increasingly concerned over the issues of justice, equality, and "the rights of man." Their social idealism, indeed, often brought them into conflict with the government, for their arguments were profoundly disruptive of the status quo. Voltaire illustrates this tendency perfectly; he has often, because of his tone of bantering disillusionment, been charged with cynicism. And how unjustly! For Voltaire penned almost a library of books with the sole purpose of improving social conditions. He and his fellow writers fervently believed that their literary labors could bring about a more decent life for posterity, and in that faith alone they wrote. With an almost religious reliance on the curative power of reason, so characteristic of the neoclassical era, they were convinced that an untiring criticism of social evils must cause a gradual improvement in society. Some of these men actually believed that the exercise of reason would make society perfect eventually.

(Against this faith in reason the great heretic was Rousseau, in some respects far more influential than any of his rationalistic confrères. Him we consider, more suitably, later in connection with the growth of the Romantic movement.)

VOLTAIRE (FRANÇOIS-MARIE AROUET) (1694–1778)

François-Marie Arouet was born of sturdy middle-class stock in Paris, November 29, 1694, the son of a well-established notary. Educated by the Jesuits, at the celebrated Louis-le-Grand College in his native city, the boy developed considerable skill in the art of controversy. His deep-rooted enthusiasm for literature made him view with distaste his father's determination to have him practice law. To satisfy the elder Arouet, young François went for a time to The Hague as a secretary to the Ambassador there. Back in Paris as a law-clerk, young Arouet began to write satirical verse, and to work on his earliest writings, the epic *La Henriade* and the tragedy *Œdipus*. A lampoon against the Regent, however, caused him to be exiled for a while; soon thereafter another satire on the reign of Louis XIV resulted in his being imprisoned in the Bastille for eleven months in 1717. In 1718 his *Œdipus* was performed at the Théatre Français to much applause. It was at this time that he took the name of "Voltaire."

The next seven years found Voltaire much pampered and admired by the Court for his witticisms and light pieces. It was a lucky catastrophe that changed the whole course of his life. Without it, he might have been satisfied to be a minor versifier for Court circles. It chanced, however, that because of a gibe he made at the Opera at the expense of the stupid Chevalier de Rohan, Voltaire was beaten by the Chevalier's lackeys; Voltaire, enraged, challenged the nobleman to a duel, and for his insolence he was again shut up in the Bastille. To save appearances for the Chevalier, Voltaire was released on his promise to leave for England (1726).

At the age of thirty-two, therefore, Voltaire found himself in England, a country of which he was a sincere admirer because of its achievements in science and in political liberty. He had already mastered English while incarcerated in the Bastille, and was fully equipped to make the most of his exile. Indeed, he reveled in it. These three years in England proved to be the most formative years of his career. With Bolingbroke, who at that time had the repute of being a great philosopher, Voltaire already had had some acquaintance. He now became his intimate. The exile also was frequently to be seen at the homes of Walpole, Lord Hervey, the Duke of Newcastle, and the Prince of Wales. He met Congreve, attended Newton's funeral, visited Pope at Twickenham, and was elected a member of the great English scientific body, the Royal Society. He saw performances of Shakespeare and Dryden, read Bacon and Locke, and came to know the language well enough to think and write in it. Above all, he became saturated with a devotion to that religious and political freedom which he beheld Englishmen enjoying, and was resolved to be its champion in France. As Lord Morley has put it, "He left France a poet, he returned to it a sage."

After three years' exile he came back to his country, and produced several plays showing the influence of Shakespeare, notably: *Brutus* (1730), *Zaïre* (1732), and *The Death of Caesar* (1732).

The English Letters

But the chief fruit, at this time, of his visit to England was the publication of his *English Letters* (*Lettres Anglaises*) (1734)—also known as *The Philosophic Letters*. This work, his earliest adventure into philosophy, contains the germ of all his important ideas, later to be exploited in many volumes; it is also written in that witty, ironic style which is most associated with Voltaire's name.

The book is largely a series of comparisons between the tolerance and liberties which Englishmen knew and the arbitrary oppression to which Frenchmen were subjected. The most important chapters are those on "Parliament," on "Commerce," on "Vaccine," on "Locke," on "Descartes and Newton," on "Tragedy," on "Comedy," and, a kind of supplement, on "The *Pensées* of Pascal."

Issued anonymously, the volume was condemned by the government, seized, and burned. Nevertheless, five editions of it were sold the year of its appearance. The publisher was thrown into the Bastille, and Voltaire thought it wise to leave Paris for Cirey, where a fellow Newtonian, Mme. de Châtelet, invited him to stay at her chateau.

Later in the century Condorcet wrote of *The English Letters* that it was the work which must be considered "the starting-point of a revolution; it began to call into existence the taste for English philosophy and literature, to give us an interest in the manners, politics, and the commercial knowledge of the English people." And, it should be remembered, that for Frenchmen an interest in the English meant an interest in achieving liberties comparable with theirs.

Another historian, Texte, finds *The English Letters* important in another respect. He dates from it "the commencement of that open campaign against the Christian religion which was destined to occupy the whole of the century." He finds also that with it begins "that new spirit . . . critical, eager for reform, combative and practical, which concerned itself rather with political and natural science than with poetry and eloquence."

Voltaire at Cirey

Under the sympathetic eye of his hostess, Voltaire wrote busily at Cirey (1734–1749). But he was by no means a recluse. He made a number of quick visits to Paris, and with Mme. de Châtelet, who was the best of intellectual comrades, he traveled to Brussels, Lille, Lunéville and other places.

Among the most notable works of this period are poems and philosophical tragedies. *Mondain* (1736) is a very witty poem defending a theory that Voltaire never abandoned: that there is progress in human affairs when the latter are viewed in perspective; because of this book, however, Voltaire fled to Holland for a while to escape the police. *Alzire* (1736) is a tragedy laid in Peru, and was performed with great success. *Mahomet, or Fanaticism* (1740) is a philosophical tragedy that attacks religion; Voltaire makes Mohammed typical of the founders of all religions—an impostor and fanatic, who causes much evil in the world. The play was the source of much unpleasantness to its author. When produced in Paris in 1742, it was enthusiastically applauded; but Voltaire's enemies lost no time in charging him with "infamous blasphemy." To avoid the wrath of the government, Voltaire had to quit Paris again. He had the audacity to dedicate this piece to the Pope, nonetheless, and the Pontiff, not lacking a sense of humor, gracefully accepted the honor. *Mérope* (1743), Voltaire's most classical tragedy is based on a story similar to that of Racine's *Andromaque*. At the instance of Richelieu, Voltaire wrote a comedy-ballet for Court performance, *The Princess of Navarre* (*La Princesse de Navarre*) (1745).

In addition to other works, of a minor nature, during this period Voltaire also wrote his *Elements of Newton's Philosophy* (1738), and a treatise *On the Nature of Fire* (*Sur la Nature du Feu*). At this time, too, he began his monumental *The Epoch of Louis XIV* (*Siècle de Louis XIV*).

Voltaire's celebrated correspondence with Frederick the Great, who at the beginning accepted the role of a humble disciple, commenced in 1736. The two came to admire each other sincerely. Their meeting in 1740 was in all respects satisfying to both. During the ensuing decade Voltaire several times took on the responsibility of diplomatic missions to Frederick from the French Court. Each time Frederick urged Voltaire to remain as his guest, but he was unable to persuade him.

Touching Voltaire's correspondence, we ought now to remark that there are in existence some ten thousand of his letters, and these are said to be not half of what he wrote. It would appear that most of the notable people in Europe of his day corresponded with him.

Among his warmest intimates, judging by his letters, were the Count d'Argental; Cideville, Councillor to the Rouen Parliament; the Abbé Moussinot; Thiériot. Among his closest female correspondents were Mme. de Graffigny, a well-known novelist; Mlle. de Lespinasse; Mme. du Deffand; the Duchess of Choiseul; Mme. Denis, Voltaire's niece; Mme. Necker, mother of Mme. de Staël; Mlle. Quinault, an actress, sister of a man who often enacted leading roles in Voltaire's plays; Mlle. Clairon, an actress who took over some leading parts in Voltaire's dramas.

The list of his philosopher-correspondents is even more imposing: d'Alembert, Diderot, Marmontel, Duclos, La Harpe, the Abbé Dubois, Vauvenargues. Among his foreign friends were Lord Harvey, Keeper of the Seals in England; Horace Walpole, celebrated son of a celebrated English Minister; Count de

Schouvaloff, Chamberlain to the Empress of Russia; De Soumarokoff, a Russian noble; Goldoni, the great Italian writer of comedy. Among the princes and princesses who were glad to write to him were Frederick the Great; Catherine II, Empress of Russia; the Duchess of Saxe-Gotha; King Stanislas; the Duchess of Maine.

These names include but a few of his regular correspondents. The letters of Voltaire are well worth the reading today. They reveal their author in all the charm, enthusiasm, and anger of which he was capable. Some of his most hastily composed letters are among his best pieces of prose.

The "Cirey period" of Voltaire's life was one of accomplishment, intellectual stimulation, and great annoyance. *Mondain*, as we have seen, had sent him off in flight from the police; *Mahomet* had caused him to leave Paris hastily because of the authorities; his election to the French Academy in 1746 reawakened the zeal of his enemies, and he had to flee Paris again. Moreover, during these years Voltaire was the victim of unremitting ill-health. Finally, the greatest blow he ever sustained terminated the days at Cirey: Mme. de Châtelet died in the late summer of 1749.

For nearly a year Voltaire tried his fortunes in Paris once more. He attempted running his own theater and began to circulate, to the delight of the literary world, a number of his Tales. Every one of these racily written stories had a purpose—moral, political, social, or theological. Of these the best known are: *Babouc* (1746), *Memnon* (1747), *Zadig* (1748), and *Micromégas* (1752). *Zadig* is a tale crowded with episode, conversation, and adventure; it illustrates the uncertainty of human experiences. *Micromégas* (the title is a combination of two Greek words meaning, respectively, *small* and *great*) has as its hero an inhabitant from the star Sirius who travels through our world, and proves that all values are merely relative.

Voltaire and Frederick

Frederick the Great was insistent in his invitations to Voltaire to come to stay at his court (1750–1753). Finding himself disappointed of all his expectations in Paris or at Versailles, Voltaire at last procured the permission of Louis XV to go to Prussia. He arrived in Berlin in July 1750.

At first Frederick was delighted with his distinguished guest, and lodged him near the palace at Potsdam. Voltaire, on his part, took great pleasure in the freedom of conversation and the exchange of ideas encouraged by this "Solomon of the North," as he called Frederick. But Voltaire and Frederick were both too sensitive and too fond of being the leader to put up with each other long. Frederick began to think that he was purchasing at the price of too high a pension Voltaire's services, which consisted chiefly in the Frenchman's adding lustre to the Prussian court and correcting the German monarch's French verses. Frederick unfortunately said to La Mettrie, the physicist, "I shall need him a year more at the most; one squeezes the orange and then throws away the skin." La Mettrie did not fail to report the remark to Voltaire. Voltaire, on the other hand, was getting into financial difficulties, and then had the indiscretion to pen a deliriously funny attack on Frederick's favorite, Maupertuis, President of the Berlin Academy. To appease the monarch's anger, Voltaire surrendered his decorations and his pension early in 1753. There was a brief reconcilement, but the friendship was at an end. On his way out of the country, he was arrested and forced to give up a poetical effusion of Frederick's that he was smuggling out of the country; it was his intention to use it to make Frederick the laughingstock of the European world of letters. Frustrated in that laudable intention, Voltaire was at last allowed to leave in peace. At the age of sixty he was unwelcome in every kingdom of the western continent.

The Epoch of Louis XIV

The most significant work produced by Voltaire during his residence in Prussia is *The Epoch of Louis XIV* (1751). It is a history of thought during one of the periods of great intellectual enlightenment and almost equal intolerance. Beginning with a description of "the state of Europe before Louis XIV," Voltaire discusses the foreign policies of Louis XIV and his ministers, and their plans of military operations. The first part of the work concludes with a picture of Europe from the Peace of Utrecht to the death of Louis. The next chapters are devoted to the state of commerce, justice, the police. and public finances. Then follows a discussion of science, painting, sculpture, and music in Europe of Louis XIV's time. One chapter contains Voltaire's judgments on all the great seventeenth century writers. The work concludes with a discourse on the condition of religious affairs during Louis XIV's reign; here the author demonstrates his disgust with narrow theological disputation; his satirical comment on seventeenth century religious fanaticism implies everywhere the superiority of his own era.

The importance of *The Epoch of Louis XIV* lies in its being the first attempt at writing a history of a civilization. Voltaire's point of view is that reason, not religion, is the true guide to civilized values. But he also recognizes, throughout, the power of chance as often playing a decisive role in human events. In addition to being one of the most finished histories of its century—for as historian, Voltaire was never on more solid ground than here—*The Epoch of Louis XIV* has the added charm of its author's witty, graceful, and direct style. Everything, no matter how innately complicated, is made easy to understand.

The Sage of Ferney

After leaving Germany, Voltaire went to Geneva. Nearby he bought a summer house, which he called "Les Délices." There he presented plays at his own little theater. But first the Council of Geneva objected to them on religious grounds, and then Rousseau attacked the performances. Voltaire therefore decided to make his home just across the Swiss border on French soil. He bought the estate of Fernex (which he spelled *Ferney*). This became his favorite residence. He built a chateau and converted it into a kind of court where men of letters and great noblemen came to pay their respect to the veteran of letters and to take part in his endless theatricals. It is said that Voltaire often entertained as many as fifty guests at a time. Luckily his income was now large enough to enable him to live in this handsome style.

Though over sixty when he came to Ferney, it was now (1754–1778) that he began to work harder than ever. It was these last years of his life that saw the production of some of his greatest works, notably the one book by which he is best known to the world, *Candide* (1759). He wrote many plays, including one of his best tragedies, *Tancred* (1760). His work as historian was continued with *The History of Russia under Peter the Great* (*L'Histoire de la Russie*) (1772) and *A Summary of the Age of Louis XV* (*Le Précis du Siècle de Louis XV*) (1772). But the crowning glories of this period were his philosophical writings; these include *The Essay on the Manners and the Spirit of Nations* (*Essai sur les Moeurs et l'Esprit des Nations*) (1756), *The Treatise on Tolerance* (*Traité de la Tolerance*) (1763), the *Philosophic Dictionary* (*Dictionnaire Philosophique*) (1764), and, of course, *Candide.*

The Essay on the Manners and the Spirit of Nations is a kind of universal history beginning with Charlemagne and continuing to the reign of Louis XIII. Voltaire is unnecessarily contemptuous of the Dark Ages, but he is able at last to do some justice to the civilizing force of religion at certain epochs. His description of Mohammedan culture in Spain, his account of late medieval manners and commerce, his discussion of Renaissance art, and his review of the reign of Louis XIII—these are the high points of the book. The unifying theme is progress—progress in the arts and sciences, and progress in human well-being. The style is Voltaire's at its most energetic.

His *Treatise on Tolerance* will ever be a monument to the nobility of Voltaire's ideals. It was the product of a series of interventions on Voltaire's part in behalf of the politically maltreated. Calas, a quiet Protestant merchant of Toulouse, had been legally murdered for the crime, of which he was obviously innocent, of killing his son; this gross injustice had been perpetrated to satisfy the superstitions of a Catholic community. Sirven was a Huguenot similarly persecuted. The young Chevalier de la Barre was put to death for his irreverance towards religious images. In all these cases, and in others, Voltaire intervened to rehabilitate the good name of the victims of injustice and intolerance.

To Voltaire tolerance "is the consequence of humanity. We are all formed of frailty and error; let us pardon reciprocally each other's folly. . . . It is clear that the individual who persecutes a man, his brother, because he is not of the same opinion, is a monster."

These remarks are made in the article on Tolerance in the *Philosophical Dictionary*. The *Philosophical Dictionary*, one of his most characteristic works, is a series of such articles arranged in alphabetical order. One finds essays on the Soul. Beauty, Glory, War, etc. Most of the articles are attacks on Roman Catholicism, particularly Catholic dogma—questions of ritual, prerogatives of the clergy, etc. Orthodox Catholic dogma he finds irrational, and often immoral and inhuman. He is also contemptuous on the subjects of miracles and visions, for Voltaire utterly denied the possibility of supernatural manifestations. And, everywhere, his attack is levelled against intolerance. He finds that all religions have common beliefs; these alone are the credible, and hence the valuable, portions of all religions.

Though Voltaire was no friend of revolution, the *Philosophical Dictionary* became a kind of revolutionist's guide. By the time it appeared Voltaire's reputation was universal, and no man of letters in Europe was more vastly admired. At Ferney he was busy dictating twenty letters a day.

Candide

But it is *Candide* (1759) that has always been quite justly the favorite among Voltaire's many dozens of volumes. Probably no book has ever been written containing within a comparable number of pages so much devastating wit. It is perhaps the world's masterpiece of skepticism. But it is short-sighted to accuse it of being a work of easy cynicism. Not only its never-failing laughter, but also the moral earnestness of its conclusion, make such a charge utterly fallacious.

The satire is levelled at many things. The chief butt of the mockery is philosophic optimism—"This is the best of all possible worlds," as Leibnitz put it. A man who believed, as much as Voltaire did, in the need of social reforms could hardly endorse any doctrine that encouraged satisfaction with the way things are. The dogged optimism of Pangloss in *Candide* is painted as merely idiotic.

In *Candide* Voltaire also attacks the follies of war, the injustices of religious persecution and of governmental persecution, the stupidity of ambition, the avarice of men. Above all, he condemns those who expect to find great happiness in life, for such a search is vain. The best answer he can give to the quest for contentment is, "Cultivate your garden." In the end, those characters in *Candide* who are able to lose themselves in useful work such as is ever ready at hand, no matter what their earlier errors and misfortunes have been, find a measure of peace.

At the opening of *Candide* we learn that our honest hero was brought up in the castle of the Baron Thunder-ten-Tronckh in Westphalia. The boy is in love with the Baron's daughter Cunegonde. His teacher, Doctor Pangloss, believes that this is the best of all possible worlds and that everything that happens is good. Candide is expelled from the castle when found in innocent love-making with the Baron's daughter. He is seized by two men, bound, and forced into military service for the King of Bulgaria.

Escaping from the army, he reaches Holland, where he is succored by an intelligent and noble-hearted Anabaptist. He comes upon his old teacher again, now covered with scabs, his nose half-eaten away; from Pangloss Candide hears that Cunegonde and all the Baron's family have been murdered by the invading Bulgarian army. The young man takes Pangloss to the Anabaptist, who cures the philosopher, causing him to lose no more than one eye and one ear. Pangloss insists throughout that this is the best of all possible worlds.

The good Anabaptist takes them along on a voyage to Lisbon, but himself perishes in the sea in an attempt to save the life of a brutal sailor. The ship is wrecked, and all drown except the sailor, Candide and Pangloss.

The lad and his tutor arrive in Lisbon just in time for a great earthquake which causes general ruin. Because Pangloss attempts to prove that all their misfortunes are actually blessings, they are both handed over to the Inquisition as heretics. Pangloss is hanged and Candide whipped for heresy, while other unfortunates are burned at the stake for their errors.

An old woman comes to Candide's rescue. She leads him to a secret house, and there he finds his Cunegonde. She was not killed after all. After being carried off by a Bulgarian captain, she was sold to a Jew who brought her to Portugal, where her person is shared between him and the Grand Inquisitor. She has been at the *auto-da-fé* and seen Candide whipped. It was her servant who has brought the young man to her home. At this point the Jew enters, flies into a jealous rage, attacks Candide, but is killed by him. The Grand Inquisitor also arrives, and Candide kills him too.

Candide, Cunegonde and the old woman escape to Cadiz, where he enlists in the army going to Paraguay. They all cross the ocean. En route, the old woman tells her story which proves that she, once a Princess, and the daughter of a pope, has been through much worse misfortunes than the two young people.

At Buenos Aires the Governor has designs on Cunegonde. Since the constabulary arrive from Europe to arrest the murderer of the Grand Inquisitor, Candide is forced to flee, leaving Cunegonde behind.

He goes to Paraguay with his faithful black valet Cacambo, to fight for the Jesuits. There he finds that the Commandant is none other than his boyhood friend, Cunegonde's brother, alive too. They are deeply moved at the meeting until Candide announces his intention of marrying Cunegonde. Outraged that a plebeian can dare to aspire so high, the Jesuit attacks Candide, who kills him in self-defense. Our hero reflects sadly that for a peaceful young man he has killed an astonishing number of men. Cacambo helps him to escape in the garb of the dead Jesuit.

They are next taken by savages, who are about to eat them until it is proved that Candide is not really a Jesuit. They now visit the wonderful country of El Dorado, where the pebbles on the road are precious gems. There they are magnificently entertained in a land where there exist no priests, monks, nor Church or prisons, no court of justice—for none of these is needed. But Candide yearns for Cunegonde, and departs from this land of felicity, laden with treasures.

In Dutch Guiana he and Cacambo witness the misery of black slaves. Cacambo, it is decided, is to go off alone to Buenos Aires to rescue Cunegonde, while Candide makes for Venice, where they are all to meet again. But Candide is cheated of a good portion of his fortune by the treachery of a Dutch captain.

Finally he sets out for Europe again in the company of Martin, an impoverished philosopher whose beliefs are exactly opposite to Pangloss's. Martin is a complete pessimist, and is convinced that evil is the ruling principle in the world.

They land in France and go to Paris. Here they attend the Comédie Française, and listen to the criticisms of the audience. Candide next visits a gambling house run by a Marchioness, who seduces him. The Abbé who is conducting Candide around Paris, annoyed that he hasn't been able to appropriate any of the young man's treasure, has him arrested on a trumped-up charge, and then gets him off for a large fee. Paris has turned out to be a city of monkeys who behave like tigers.

Candide and Martin coast by England, and then make for Venice by way of the Mediterranean. There he finds a girl, once a servant of the Baron's, who is now living as a prostitute; her current lover is a friar who loathes his calling into which he was forced by his parents. They visit a Venetian senator who despises all art and literature, although he has a large collection of both; Milton is his special hate. Candide next dines at an inn with six deposed monarchs.

Cacambo at last turns up with the information that Cunegonde, no longer beautiful, is in Constantinople. They set out at once for that place. On the banks of the Propontis they see two galley slaves who turn out to be Pangloss and Cunegonde's brother, both still alive as if by miracle. Both explain how their lives were saved by chance. Candide ransoms them. They find Cunegonde and the old woman, and ransom them too, even though Cunegonde is now ugly and wrinkled. He is ready to marry her because of his old promise, but the Baron's son still objects on the grounds of rank. They therefore arrange secretly to send him back to the Jesuits in Rome. That accomplished, Candide has nothing left of his money now except just enough to buy a little farm.

Cunegonde grows uglier and more unbearable every day. One day they meet an old farmer who lives in great contentment with his family; the secret of his peace seems to be that he works hard and never troubles his head over the world's problems or metaphysical questions. In work his family has found salvation.

Candide, now joined by the friar and the former prostitute, and Cunegonde, Cacambo, Martin, and the old woman, all take the cue from the farmer. They start applying themselves to the tasks proposed by their little farm, and each discovers, despite his personal shortcomings, redeeming traits by persevering in his chosen work. Thus in cultivating their farm they find happiness at last.

Final Honors

A few years before his death a statue was erected to Voltaire in Paris, the city of his greatest triumphs and his greatest frustrations. In February 1778, moved by a great desire to see his native town again, the old man left Ferney and came to the metropolis. Louis XVI was on the throne now, many reforms had been instituted, certain liberal forces were in power—and Voltaire's tragedy, *Irene*, was being presented at the Théâtre Français. The moment seemed propitious for the return.

The visit proved an endless triumph. Every distinguished person in town, Frenchman or foreigner, hurried to see the patriarch at his lodgings. At the Academy he was elected Director, and outlined a plan for a new Dictionary, for which he undertook to write the letter A. Then, he attended the theater to see his play. An actor entered his box and placed a wreath of laurel on his head. During the intermission, Voltaire's bust was placed upon the stage and crowned by all the actors in turn, while the audience cheered.

The joy of this triumphant visit to Paris was too much for the feeble old man, and within a few weeks he died—it is said from excess of emotion. In 1791 the Revolutionists transferred his ashes to the Panthéon.

IMPORTANCE

Voltaire's shortcomings are obvious: his mind, though quick and sharp, was not profound; as an historian he was far too careless of fact; and as a philosopher he was not always patient enough to be logical. His dislike of all religion made him blind to the accomplishments of the Christian tradition, and he rarely wrote about the Church without deliberate prejudice. In political speculation he was limited. It would probably have horrified him to learn that his works were to be regarded by the French Revolutionists as having done much to prepare the way for revolution, for his thoughts were far from such volcanic change. As a matter of fact, he never thought through his political beliefs in terms of any consistent political philosophy; political reform meant to him largely the extension of private rights.

On the other hand, he was unquestionably the leading figure in European letters during his lifetime. No other man displayed so astounding a versatility. He was indefatigable in the writing of plays, stories, history, literary criticism, verse, philosophy, and the popularizing of science. In all of these departments, with the exception of his serious poetry, he achieved the highest rank of his day.

The incomparable ease and wit of his style has made him read in philosophy and history, science and metaphysics, when profounder writers have been ignored. His ready laughter removes the sting of his bitterness as a satirist. His stories still delight because of these same qualities and the speed of their action. Voltaire's prose exhibits the critical spirit so native to France in all its attractiveness and racy intelligence.

But it is the spirit of Voltaire's work—the sum-total of his career—which has left the deepest impression on humanity. *Ecrasez l'infâme!*—"Crush the infamous thing!"—was his watchword—and for him "the infamous thing" was superstition and intolerance. The more than seventy volumes of his collected works were all written, more or less, for that untiring war that Voltaire was conducting in behalf of freedom of thought. His fundamental belief has been popularly summarized in his attributed remark to his fellow-philosopher Helvétius: "I entirely disapprove of your opinions and will fight to the death for your right to express them."

It is perhaps too much to agree with Egon Friedell's tribute to Voltaire: "If our world today consists of no more than two-fifths villains and three-eights idiots, we have largely Voltaire to thank for it." But it is not too much to say that no one contributed more generously than Voltaire towards the emancipation of the human spirit from the barriers of authority and ignorance. For a generation his figure dominated Europe, and his restless mind kept Europe alert to every issue of intolerance and bigotry that crossed his horizon.

CHARLES DE SECONDAT, BARON DE MONTESQUIEU (1689–1755)

Charles de Secondat, Baron de la Brède et de Montesquieu, came of an old Gascon noble family, and was born near Bordeaux. He was educated to follow in the footsteps of his forebears and to become a leader, like them, in the legal profession. In 1716 he became President of the Parliament of Bordeaux. As a distraction from his duties he joined the Bordeaux Academy of Sciences, and contributed papers on various subjects in the science of physics. In 1721 appeared, anonymously, his first book, *The Persian Letters* (*Lettres Persanes*). It had an enormous success.

Disposing of his office as President, Montesquieu went to Paris, where he frequented the salons. Then in 1728 he embarked on three years of travel. He visited Vienna, Venice, Milan, Turin, Florence, Rome, Naples, cities along the Rhine, and Holland. From the Netherlands he accompanied Lord Chesterfield to England. He was so much impressed, as Voltaire had been a few years earlier, with the English constitutional monarchy, that he remained in England two years to study its workings. He concluded that Englishmen lived under the best government to be found in Europe.

Returning to France, he began to work on his magnum opus, *L'Esprit des Lois* (*The Spirit of Laws*). As a prologue to this he published first his brilliant *Les Considerations sur les Causes de la Grandeur et de la Decadence des Romains* (*Reflections on the Causes of the Greatness and the Decline of the Romans*) in 1734. This grave and dignified work explains the rise of Rome to the position of mistress of the world as due to her early love of liberty and her military discipline; and her fall to the loss of civic virtue, growth of inequalities, and the excessive extent of the Empire.

This work was warmly applauded, and Montesquieu, working assiduously at his last great task, sought relaxation and stimulation at the salons of Mme.

du Deffand, Mme. Geoffrin, and Mme. de Tencin. At last *The Spirit of Laws* appeared in 1748. Its success was both instantaneous and merited. Before long it was translated into many European languages. It had taken twenty years in the composition, and remained, except for a *Defense* of it (1750), his last work. When Montesquieu died in Paris in 1755, he was recognized as one of the greatest men his country had produced.

The Persian Letters

Many of the ideas later elaborated in *The Spirit of Laws* were originally expressed in the author's first literary triumph, *The Persian Letters* (1721). Montesquieu was much admired in the salons for his fine irony, aristocratic air, and keen observation; it was not long, therefore, before his authorship of the anonymous work that exhibited these very traits, was recognized. Its satire is an admirable commentary on the follies of the time, and the literary public was enamored of its direct and witty criticism of social institutions and manners. The Church party, however, infuriated at Montesquieu's mockery of its abuse of power, saw to it that his election to the Academy was delayed many years.

The Persian Letters was undoubtedly influenced by the Englishman Addison's social satire in *The Spectator.* But Montesquieu was also following a recent tradition in giving his book an Oriental tone. The first great impetus towards this new Orientalism was given Western Europe by the French scholar Antoine Galland's translation (1704) of *The Arabian Nights.* This newly unearthed treasure house of Oriental lore and atmosphere took European imagination by storm. Addison himself wrote a number of his essays in an Oriental framework. By 1713 four editions had appeared in England of Galland's French translated into English. Thereafter, the Oriental disguise became a favored one of French eighteenth century writers who wished to satirize powerful institutions like the Church without incurring the wrath of the authorities. Voltaire's *Mahomet* and *Zadig* have already been cited. Montesquieu's immediate influence was Dufresny's *Amusements Serious and Comic of a Siamese Gentleman* (1707).

The plan of Montesquieu's book is very simple. Three Persians, Rica, Usbeck, and Rhedi, set out for Europe to study its manners. Rhedi stops at Venice while the other two go to Paris. *The Persian Letters* consists of a series of lively letters exchanged between the visitors at Paris and the one at Venice, and from all three to Usbeck's harem at home. This scheme enabled Montesquieu to incorporate much of the brisk criticism and intellectual revolt which the best minds of the salons were expressing against the status quo of Europe in general, and France in particular. The naïve logic and unsophisticated astonishment of the Persian visitors underline the oppression and injustices they witness in France. It is, indeed, rather remarkable, considering the alertness of eighteenth century censorship, that *The Persian Letters* was allowed to circulate. The portrait of French royalty, for example, is bold in the extreme:

> The King of France is old. We have no instance in our history
> of a monarch who reigned so long. . . . He likes to gratify those
> who serve him, but he pays as liberally for the attentions, or
> rather the idleness of his courtiers, as for the toilsome campaigns
> of his captains; often he prefers a man who attends upon his toi-
> let or who hands him a napkin when he sits at table to some
> other who captures cities or gains battles for him.

The Persian Letters contains "characters" in the manner of La Bruyère; Parisian gossip; pictures of life at the theater and the cafés; and discussions on the coquetry of women, ignorant magistrates, gambling, theological disputations, divorce, literary types, convent libraries, etc. In the midst of much wit and light-ness, Montesquieu's seriousness of purpose often appears. Throughout he is to be seen as a bold critic of injustice and a man of the most liberal political views. The author of *The Spirit of Laws* can be glimpsed in the more sober passages.

Montesquieu set a fashion which D'Argens followed in his *Chinese Letters*, D'Ancourt in his *Turkish Memoirs*, and Oliver Goldsmith in his *Citizen of the World*.

The Spirit of Laws

The Spirit of Laws (1748), Montesquieu's profoundest work in political phi-losophy, has won for its author the title of father of comparative ethics. He maintains that all ideas of good and evil arise from the conditions which exist in any given society. Those conditions, he argues, are largely the result of climate and geography.

From Plato, through Aristotle, Cicero, Aquinas, and Bossuet, writers on law had discussed legislation ideally, in terms of abstract and moral defini-tions. Montesquieu's method was empirical. "I first examined men, believing that in their infinite diversity of laws and morals they were not altogether led by fancy," he says. From the outset he accepted the necessity of this diversity among various peoples. "Laws ought to be so peculiarly proper to the peo-ple for whom they have been made, that it is doubtful if the laws of one country could do for another." Laws should be made with consideration to "the physical conditions of the country, to a cold, hot, or temperate climate; to the nature of the land, its situation, its extensiveness; to the kind of life people lead, whether farmers, shepherds, or hunters."

Like Voltaire, he looked upon England's as the ideal government. It is to be feared, however, that Montesquieu had seen more of what he wished to see in England than was actually there. The English legislative and executive powers in practice are interlocked. In Montesquieu's ideal government the judicial, the legislative, and the executive powers of a government are to be kept independent of one another. This conception, because of the prestige of Montesquieu's name, impressed the founding fathers of the United States as being the correct one for a functioning republic; it was in the forefront of their thoughts while they were framing the American Constitution. In England, Edmund Burke was largely a disciple of Montesquieu.

IMPORTANCE

Montesquieu's variety and exactitude of knowledge are astounding. He has a firm view of the march of history. He did not, like Voltaire, fall victim to the eighteenth century idea that the Middle Ages were merely barbaric. Nor was Montesquieu, as were so many of his contemporaries, merely destructive in his social criticism. It has been said that his ideas of limited monarchy could have been put into practice in the generation in which he wrote without too much civil trouble. As a stylist he is a master of lucidity and proportion; *The Spirit of Laws*, devoid of ornamentation or ideological involvement, is a triumph of prose. The French consider it as one of their greatest books.

THE *ENCYCLOPEDIA* (1751–1772)

In 1727 an *Encyclopedia of Arts and Sciences* was published in London by Chambers. (The word "encyclopedia" means "the circle of education in the arts and sciences.") The French bookseller Le Breton wished to have the English work translated around 1745, but discovered that it was already dated. He therefore commissioned the Abbé de Malves, Diderot, and d'Alembert to undertake the writing of a new encyclopedia. These three divided the work and also asked the collaboration of others. Diderot published a prospectus of the projected work in 1750. The next year d'Alembert published the first volume, which was devoted to a survey of the progress of knowledge and a general classification of the sciences and arts. The government seemed to favor the undertaking, and the public was more than interested. But when the second volume appeared in October 1751, the work was suddenly forbidden, largely because of a scandal raging over the opinions of one of the theological collaborators, the Abbé de Prades. Through the patronage of the Count D'Argenson, however, the prohibition was lifted, and three censors were appointed to read the manuscript before publication. Thus, Volumes Three to Seven appeared without difficulty. But in 1757 because of the stir of political events, the *Encyclopedia* was attacked from all sides, and d'Alembert, to avoid being embroiled, resigned from the project. It began to appear that the other volumes would have to be printed abroad; but luckily some of the eager subscribers were men of influence. The difficulty was solved by a deception to which all parties agreed: the books were to be published in Paris but to bear a title page implying they were published in Switzerland; then they were to be shipped to the provinces, and to be sent to Paris from there. Thus the complete work was issued at last in 1772; it consisted of seventeen volumes of text, four supplementary volumes, and eleven volumes of illustrations.

The editors of the *Encyclopedia* were well aware of the dangers they faced, and so they cleverly maintained an air of innocence throughout. By a brilliant device of cross-reference, however, they were able to annihilate the effect of an orthodox view in one article with the arguments expressed in another article to which the reader was referred. Officially, for example, the *Encyclopedia* was orthodox. But its arguments in favor of Catholic dogma were based exclusively upon "faith," which, the editors declared, has nothing to do with reason. Moreover, their praise was so extreme in favor of such doctrines as that of eternal damnation that it required little alertness to catch their mocking intention. On the other hand, when for reasons of objectivity they presented the arguments against Catholic dogma, their intense earnestness was obvious. They opposed belief in miracles as contrary to the laws of nature, and they indicted religious intolerance and persecution as contrary to the laws of humanity.

From Montesquieu came the leading ideas on government presented by the *Encyclopedia*. The editors registered no objection to monarchy as such, only strongly defended civil liberties and the right of commerce to expand. The attack in politics they leveled chiefly against the nobility and its prerogatives. The Encyclopedists also demanded reform in legal and moral matters. They gave considerable attention to science, a knowledge of which they were anxious to diffuse. The physics of Newton was throughout the work enlarged upon and expounded; biology, agricultural developments, and economics also received elaborate discussion. The *Encyclopedia* in its criticism of eighteenth century literature expressed weariness with Neoclassical rules, and demanded more significant subjects for literary consideration.

The importance of the *Encyclopedia* has been described by historians as awakening the reading public of France to the claims of "nature, reason, and humanity." As one writer says, "A reasoned humanitarianism is perhaps the greatest contribution of the Encyclopedists."

Voltaire tells an interesting anecdote as to how even the King was won over to the *Encyclopedia*. The publisher had been required to give to the government a list of his subscribers; whereupon a royal order was sent to the subscribers ordering them to surrender their copies to the police. At one of the King's "little suppers" at Trianon a discussion began on the chemical composition of gunpowder. Mme. de Pompadour remarked that she had no idea how her silk stockings or her rouge were made. The Duke de la Vallière sighed his regrets that the King had confiscated their encyclopedias, which could have settled all these questions. The King answered that he had been advised that the *Encyclopedia* was dangerous; but he now decided to see for himself, and sent for a copy. Three servants finally arrived staggering under the weight of the twenty-one volumes by then issued. Everyone present looked up the information he sought, and the King then ordered that the confiscated copies be returned to the subscribers.

The contributors to the *Encyclopedia* included Condillac, Helvétius, the Abbé Morellet, Daubenton, d'Holbach, Turgot, Quesnay, Marmontel, de Jaucourt, Rousseau, Voltaire, and Montesquieu. But, as Voltaire said, the Atlas and Hercules of this world were d'Alembert and Diderot—and, we might add, the Atlas was Diderot.

Jean le Rond d'Alembert (1717–1783)

D'Alembert, the illegitimate son of Mme. de Tencin by an unidentified father, was picked up on the steps of the church of Saint Jean le Rond as a foundling by the wife of a glazier. He lodged with his foster parents until he was fifty years of age. He received a fine education at Mazarin College, and early showed a genius for mathematics. At the age of twenty-four he was elected to the Academy of Sciences. He was a man of retired habits, a charming talker, and engaging in manner. Through the influence of Mme. du Deffand, whose salon he frequented, he was elected to the French Academy (1754), and later became its secretary.

He first came into literary prominence by a series of extremely polished obituary notices, his *Eloges*, in which it was said he praised the dead only that he might make satirical allusions to the living. Most of his other writings outside of the *Encyclopedia* were in science or polemics. His chief claim to immortality, however, rests upon his sharing with Diderot the early arduous labors in editing the *Encyclopedia* from 1751 to 1759. When he did retire from the undertaking, it was because of disgust at the apparently endless obstacles thrown in their path. Without Voltaire's brilliance or Diderot's unquenchable enthusiasm, d'Alembert had more dignity than either of them, and preferred his own studies to the tempting offers of Frederick the Great or Catherine of Russia to come to their courts as an honored guest.

Surprisingly enough, however, he hated religion more than any of his collaborators, and carried his detestation of it to the point of fanaticism. His celebrated review of the sciences, which constitutes the first volume of the *Encyclopedia,* is, nonetheless, a remarkable achievement. D'Alembert did much to add to exactness in thinking and style among the "philosophers" of his day.

Denis Diderot (1713–1784)

Diderot, a man whose memory has been cherished, despite his failings, because of the spontaneity and generosity of his character, was born at Langres the son of a cutler. A brilliant student, he refused to enter either the church or the legal profession. His father insisted that he choose a "regular" mode of living, so he decided to become a writer on his own, and lived precariously by all sorts of hack writing for a time. In 1743 he married a laundress and was thereby in greater need of money than ever. He made translations, wrote stories, issued pamphlets; he was interested in and enthusiastic about everything—literature, the fine arts, the theater, archeology. A man of tempestuous nature, like Rousseau he seems out of place in his rationalistic generation. In philosophy he was a bold materialist and atheist; yet his works abound in tributes to beauty, goodness, and love.

His marriage proved unsatisfactory because of his wife's shrewishness and Roman Catholicism. He formed a lifelong attachment to Sophie Valand, and his letters to her are the most vivid account we possess of daily life among the Parisian "philosophers." There is a curious contrast, despite the parallelism, between his English contemporary Samuel Johnson's pontifical leadership of a literary coterie weekly in London at the Turk's Head Tavern, and Diderot's mad declamations at the weekly dinners in Paris at the Baron d'Holbach's. For Diderot was a great and fascinating talker. His friends record of him that he was often truly inspired in his extempore discourses.

His first important piece was his *Letter on the Blind* (1749), a keen work on man's dependence on his senses. It is interesting to note, in passing, that Diderot is so far ahead of his times as to suggest the possibility of teaching the blind to read through the sense of touch. The authorities disliked the work enough, however, to imprison the author for three months.

It was the editorship of the *Encyclopedia* (1751–1772) that he made his lifework. For twenty years, from the very beginning to the trying end, Diderot saw the gigantic task through, despite every discouragement, frustration, and personal danger. Though he was miserably underpaid, the position made him a leader in the intellectual world. It was Diderot who persuaded the publisher not to issue merely a translation of the English Encyclopedia, but to make theirs a completely new and all-embracing publication. It was he who persevered through years of persecution, plots of enemies, and defection of friends. It is he, therefore, to whom the chief honor of the accomplishment belongs.

With characteristic generosity Diderot assisted his friend Grimm in an elaborate correspondence with the rulers of Germany and Russia—a series of letters intended to keep Frederick and Catherine informed on the current Parisian intellectual world, towards which all Europe was looking. In *Les Feuilles de Grimm* (*Grimm's Leaves*) (1750) Diderot proves himself a remarkable critic of literature and art; his insight gave these pages a quality quite beyond the reach of their reputed author. Many of these short pieces are hurriedly written reviews of contemporary literary works; here Diderot is found breaking with Neoclassical precedent. He judged books not according to rules and the laws laid down for each species of writing; instead, he evaluated each work according to its author's intentions and the general laws of esthetics. Quite as remarkable are Diderot's *Salons,* also written for Grimm. These are a series of criticisms of the biennial exhibitions of paintings in Paris. It is said that these art critiques were imitated as models for the next hundred years. Here again Diderot did not follow the lead of the classics in art criticism. Rather than describe the paintings, Diderot recorded the impressions created in his mind by the various pictures; the works of art that he criticized are recreated for us by the power of suggestion and association.

In dramatic criticism Diderot was an innovator too. He had no taste for the old kind of comedy and tragedy. An enthusiast for the sentimental novels of Richardson and Sterne, he more or less created a new type of drama, the bourgeois play—otherwise known as the "sentimental comedy." His theories are to be found in the Preface to his first play, *Le Fils Naturel* (*The Natural Son*) (1757), and in a *Discourse on Dramatic Poetry* (1758) addressed to Grimm. His second play was *Le Père de Famille* (*The Father of the Family*) (1758). Both plays are inferior in importance to the theory that sponsored them. Diderot reasoned that between tragedy (which makes us weep) and comedy (which makes us laugh)—that is, between high passions and absurd ones—there is room for the play representing ordinary, everyday life; to show not princes, but average men in their common walks of life and normal social relationships, was, Diderot felt, to open up a new field of interest in drama. As a matter of fact, it is the kind of play he favored which has been ever since the early nineteenth century the typical play to be enacted on the boards.

In the field of the prose tale, Diderot issued a number of polemical works. *La Religieuse* (*The Nun*) is an attack on convent life (1760). *Jacques le Fataliste* (*Jack the Fatalist*) (1766), influenced by Sterne, is the story of the adventures of a servant traveling with his master; many tales are told within the framework of this plot. One of Diderot's most interesting works is *Neveu de Rameau* (*Rameau's Nephew*) (1762), written in the form of a dialogue between the author and a man at the fringe of "society"; here the follies and corruptions of the time and of the human animal generally are masterfully exposed; it is one of its versatile author's best achievements.

During his later years Diderot was the recipient of a gracious favor at the hands of Catherine of Russia. Learning that he was in financial straits, the Empress bought Diderot's library, and then appointed him to the post of librarian of it. In 1773 he traveled to Russia to thank her. One of his last works was an elaborate plan for a Russian university.

POPULARIZERS OF KNOWLEDGE

The *Encyclopedia* was symptomatic of the eighteenth century's thirst for knowledge in science, philosophy, and social matters. The French critical spirit played restlessly over all subjects. The scientific writers may not have been too accurate; the philosophers had little that resembled a philosophical system; social criticism turned its attention to sundry matters in a haphazard style—but the reading public was increasing, and increasingly avid for more facts. And these writers were supplying an important demand. This popularizing of knowledge is one of the most salient characteristics of the century. To this general dissemination of popular learning may directly be credited the frame of mind which made possible the French Revolution.

Among the writers who contributed their share to the effects which larger figures like Voltaire, Montesquieu, Diderot, and Rousseau were chiefly responsible for, were men like Fontenelle, Bayle, La Motte-Houdard, the Abbé de Saint-Pierre, and Buffon.

Bernard Le Bovier de Fontenelle (1657–1757)

In a hundred years of living, Fontenelle played many roles. He was a professional wit, a frequenter of the salons, a brilliant conversationalist, a writer of tragedy and of opera libretti, and secretary of the Academy of Sciences. A man of the world, his watchword was, "Everything is possible, and everyone is right." He has been called the last of the *précieux*. His *Entretien sur la Pluralité des Mondes* (*Conversation on the Plurality of Worlds*) (1686) considers, in an entertaining easy style, the theories concerning the inhabitation of other planets; the scientific learning, artfully concealed, is solid, and the author's intention, despite his wit, is very serious.

Fontenelle's *Éloges* (*Eulogies on the Academicians*) (1708–1719) is frankly in earnest. His object was to expound the scientific teachings of Leibniz, Newton, Cassini and other scientists, to the general reading public. Here he speaks with authority on physics, biology, medicine, and related subjects.

Pierre Bayle (1647–1706)

Bayle is chiefly remembered for his *Historical and Philosophical Dictionary* (1686–1687). Though writing in the seventeenth century, Bayle belongs to the eighteenth because of his skeptical spirit. His *Dictionary* (*Dictionnaire*) is the most important precursor of the *Encyclopedia*. An enemy of Christianity, he gathered together all the skeptical opinions of men like Montaigne and Gassendi, and by a clever manipulation of references exerted himself to undermine the dogma and authority of the Church. His chief contribution is an insistence on the historical method. Nothing is accepted by him as worthy of credit unless historical fact or documentation can prove it. His chief weakness is that his intelligence was largely destructive. He had no theory, no definable purpose in his attack on orthodoxy. But he has been often called the father of eighteenth century skepticism.

Antoine La Motte-Houdard (1672–1731)

La Motte-Houdard was closely associated with Fontenelle. With the latter he participated in the lively discussion on the comparative superiority of the ancients and the moderns, both defending their contemporaries. He is also remembered for his adaptation of Homer and a number of critical works on Tragedy, the Ode, etc.

Abbé de Saint-Pierre (1658–1743)

The Abbé de Saint-Pierre, a gentle soul, was expelled from the Academy (1718) for his severe literary judgment on Louis XIV. His celebrated work is *A Project for Perpetual Peace* (1713–1717), one of a number of "Projects" that he spent his life formulating, in quest of universal peace and social amelioration. He was singularly sensitive to the miseries of poor people, and he tried to solve the problem of the basis for periodic financial depressions. He contributed to the *Encyclopedia*, and is credited with the invention of the word *benevolence* (in French, *bienfaisance*), which was so popular with the early romantic writers. His concern over the possibility of improving society has caused him to be called the father of the idea of Progress, which so much agitated the French romantic philosophers whom we consider in the next chapter.

Georges-Louis Leclerc de Buffon (1707–1788)

Buffon, after a brief residence in London, at the age of twenty-six was already associated with the Academy of Sciences. In 1740 he translated a treatise of Newton's. The year before he had been appointed director of the Botanical Gardens in Paris (formerly called *Jardin du Roi,* now known as the *Jardin des Plantes).* It is to this position that we owe his thirty-six volumes of *Natural History* (*Histoire Naturelle*), the first attempt during the Christian Era to present a systematic, exhaustive account of the physical world. The work was enormously popular. The modern reader will be repelled by the highly rhetorical style in which Buffon wrote. But it should be remembered that his grandiose manner was born of a desire to raise natural science to the eminence already accorded arts and letters.

He is the author of the phrase *Le style c'est l'homme* (The style is the man) and no one has ever more unfortunately exhibited the validity of that statement. Buffon was an extraordinarily pompous man, disdainful of his literary superiors; and his style is a perfect reflection of his own pomposity. On the other hand, his knowledge of science was remarkable for his century, his enthusiasm sincere. The *Natural History* begins with an account of the earth's becoming detached from the sun, then revolving around it, and by degrees cooling off. Organic matter appears on its surface. The intermediary steps between mineral and vegetable life are traced, and then those from vegetable to animal. Buffon's theories have in many instances been accepted in toto by modern science. But considering man as set apart from the rest of animal life because of man's ability to think, speak, and progress, Buffon believed in a Creator and in Divine Providence. He thus rejected the materialism and skepticism of his age.

Buffon's *Discourse on Style* (*Discours sur le Style*) (1753), addressed to the Academy, is a French classic. The author advocates orderliness in composition; style is only the movement of thought, and the first requirement for a good style is clear thinking.

10
EIGHTEENTH CENTURY DRAMA, FICTION, AND LITERARY CRITICISM

DRAMA IN FRANCE

As we have seen, the theater was the constant love of Voltaire during his entire life, though it cannot be said he ever achieved anything like great excellence in his plays. In addition to Voltaire, the chief writer of tragedy of the century was Crébillon (1673–1762), whose plays abound in tragic horror; *Rhadamiste and Zenobia* (1711), a melodrama, had the longest life of any of his dramas.

In comedy there were a number of writers carrying on the traditions of Molière. Regnard (1655–1709) was the author of twenty-two comedies and comic operas; the best of them are *The Player* (*Le Joueur*) (1696), a character study of a gambler; and *The Legatee* (*Le Légataire*) (1708), a satire on the law. Dancourt (1661–1725) is remembered for *The Chevalier à la Mode* (1687), its sequel *The Bourgeois of Quality* (1700), and *The House in the Country* (*La Maison de Campagne*) (1688). Dufresny (1648–1724) was the author of *The Spirit of Contradiction* (*L'Esprit de Contradiction*) (1700) and *The Double Widowhood* (*Le Double Veuvage*) (1702). Le Sage (1668–1747), well-known for his romance *Gil Blas,* is also the author of a comedy in this school, *Turcaret* (1709). Piron (1689–1773) wrote *Metromania* (1738). And Gresset (1709–1777) is the author of *The Wicked Fellow* (*Le Méchant*) (1747).

The two most important writers of comedy in eighteenth century France were Marivaux and Beaumarchais.

Pierre Carlet de Marivaux (1688–1763)

Marivaux was a novelist as well as a dramatist, and a frequenter of the salons. In comedy he showed considerable originality by deliberately breaking with the traditions of Molière. Whereas the element of love was often present in the comedies before Marivaux, he made love the subject of his plays. Before him, in the French theater, love had been the central theme only in tragedies. Marivaux is particularly skillful in presenting the most delicate shadings in the sentiments lovers feel because of their pride or timidity. He never laughs at the expense of sincere love. As he stated his purposes, "I have penetrated into the human heart as far as those shelters where timid love hides itself." Unlike Molière, the central characters of his plays are always feminine.

His best plays are *Love's Surprise* (*La Surprise de l'Amour*) (1722), *The Game of Love and Chance* (*Le Jeu de l'Amour et du Hasard*) (1734), *False Confidences* (*Les Fausses Confidences*) (1737), and *The Proof* (*L'Épreuve*) (1740). Marivaux's style is dramatic rather than satirical, and animated rather than witty. It is particularly to be admired for its delicacy.

Caron de Beaumarchais (1731–1799)

Beaumarchais is beyond question the most important French dramatist of the eighteenth century. He was born in Paris the son of a clockmaker, and for a while was a clockmaker himself. Well-trained in music, he came to know the life of the nobility as a result of his teaching music to the ladies. Later he entered the field of diplomacy, and was elevated to the nobility himself. Having accumulated a vast fortune, Beaumarchais lost it all during the Revolution. An exile for a while, he returned at the end to France, and died in extreme poverty.

His chief plays are the three that form a trilogy: *The Barber of Seville* (*Le Barbier de Séville*) (1775), *The Marriage of Figaro* (*Le Mariage de Figaro*) (1784), and *The Guilty Mother* (*La Mère Coupable*) (1792).

When *The Barber of Seville* was first performed, it was hissed. The dramatist cut off the fifth act, announced to the audience that he had deleted the act to please them, and the play became a great success. It has been a success ever since. Later, Rossini wrote his best music for it, and made it one of the world's favorite operas. The basis of the plot is conventional enough: the efforts of Count Almaviva to steal Rosine from the watchful eyes of her scheming guardian. But it is the personality of the barber Figaro that lifts the play far above the realm of the commonplace. This good plebeian, full of salty wit at the expense of the nobility even while he is serving the purposes of Count Almaviva by duping the jealous guardian (Bartholo) and the dull-witted priest (Basile), seems to sense the approaching revolution by the independence of his spirit. The style of the dialogue is racy, full of dash and sparkle.

The Marriage of Figaro, out of which Mozart soon made his most enchanting opera, "sounds the tocsin of the Revolution," as one critic has said. Beaumarchais could not get it produced for three years after he had written it. When finally presented in 1784, through the good offices of the Count d'Artois, the public heard Figaro speak out boldly against the nobility, scorning their vices and privileges, and plainly denouncing them as superfluous parasites. It is amazing, particularly when one reads Figaro's soliloquy in the last act, that the play was allowed performance. In this play the characters of *The Barber* appear again. Some time has elapsed, and Count Almaviva is now weary of his wife, and desires Figaro's own betrothed. The story reveals a bitter Figaro outwitting the intended seduction and making a dupe this time out of the monstrously ungrateful nobleman whom he once aided so much. One of the delights of this comedy is the character of Chérubin, a callow lad in love with every woman he meets.

The Guilty Mother seems hardly the work of the same man. It has neither verve nor wit. We find Figaro an old man, and the Countess a prey to remorse.

The great success of Beaumarchais was owing to two elements in his play: the boldness and courage of Figaro's criticism of the nobility, and the personality of the author, which shines through the lines. The audience understood that Figaro was Beaumarchais himself. The success was well merited. Beaumarchais is a perfect craftsman in his two great comedies, and second only to Molière in his wit. He set a fashion in comedy which French dramatists have followed ever since. Scribe and Sardou are among his followers.

FRENCH NEOCLASSICAL FICTION

In the general enthusiasm for prose during the Neoclassical period, the novel was of course not overlooked. Indeed, as French prose achieved a kind of perfection in the Age of Reason, to the increasing neglect of verse, it was perhaps inevitable that the novel should begin to displace the drama as a popular form of literature. This phenomenon is certainly true of English prose as well; in England the novel had almost no history before the middle of the eighteenth century, but with Richardson and Fielding it began a tradition that very soon made that form the most significant vehicle for storytelling. In France, many of the leading writers tried their hands at the novel.

During the eighteenth century the French novel took on all kinds of tone: frivolity, deep earnestness, fancifulness, realism. Sometimes a novel went into many volumes; sometimes it occupied only seventy-five pages. Voltaire and Diderot, as we have seen, wrote a number of pieces of prose-fiction. Rousseau's *The New Eloisa* had enormous influence. Among Voltaire's contemporaries, the most significant novelists were Le Sage, Marivaux, Prévost, and Marmontel.

Alain René Le Sage (1668–1747)

Le Sage, whose comedy we have already referred to, is known in France particularly for his *Le Diable Boiteux* (*The Limping Devil*) (1707), and all over the world for his *Gil Blas* (1715–1735), one of the most widely read of books.

Le Diable Boiteux is imitated from the Spanish, and tells how the demon Asmodeus carries a Don over the roofs of Madrid and shows him all that is occurring in the homes of the city. Through this simple device Le Sage was able to depict contemporary manners.

Gil Blas: The setting is again Spain. The hero Gil is a rogue, and the novel is one of the earliest to have as its characters thieves, vagabonds, and common people. Actually the tone suggests Breton, rather than Spanish, life. Though filled with disconnected episodes, the novel is often dramatic, and racily written.

Gil is the son of a retired warrior and a chambermaid; his uncle is the town canon, and from this fat little clergyman the boy receives his education. Gil is sent at the appropriate age to Salamanca for his studies; his wealth, at starting out, consists of forty pistoles and a mule. After some initial misadventures Gil encounters some underworld characters in a forest, where they hide from the law. He joins the gang in their robberies and murders.

But one day, after Gil has joined in a general massacre of coach passengers, he resolves to rescue the sole survivor, a beautiful lady of rank. While the robbers sleep, he binds the cook, and escapes with the beauty. The lady, Donna Mencia, in gratitude rewards him with fine clothes and gold. He continues his travels. Presently he meets Fabricio, a former fellow student turned barber.

On his old friend's recommendation, Gil enters service as a lackey, and reveals extraordinary talents in flattery and intrigue. One of his employers is Doctor Sangrado, whose remedy for all diseases is water and bleeding. By degrees Gil is allowed to take care of poorer patients. He proves equal to his master in ability: during an epidemic, all of their patients die.

Gil soon is working for another employer, Don Matthias, who lives the high life; Gil particularly enjoys this new life and its intrigue, the banqueting and drinking. Aspiring to procure a mistress for himself, Gil masquerades in his master's clothes; his efforts are rewarded by his introduction to a great lady who is anxious for an affair. He is disillusioned, however, when, accompanying his master to the home of an actress, he discovers his own fine lady to be a servant too.

After Matthias' death in a duel, Gil enters the service of the virtuous Aurora, who is neglected by Lewis, whom she loves. On Gil's advice Aurora disguises herself as a young man, takes lodgings in the same house with her lover, and makes his acquaintance. The love affair ends happily, and Aurora and Lewis are married.

Gil again goes off, and saves the life of Don Alphonso from the snares of a gang of robbers. Gil soon is working for an archbishop, who counts on him to let him know when his sermons fall off in quality. When Gil does offer such a criticism, he is discharged by the angry prelate.

Gil next becomes the private agent of the Prime Minister. In this post of influence, he sells favors, and as his success at court increases he grows increasingly greedy. Soon he has a servant himself, and eventually he is able to procure the governorship of Valencia. But because he undertakes the role of pimp for the crown prince, he is arrested when found leading the prince to a bordello.

Gil sickens in prison. On his release, he is exiled from Spain; but Don Alphonso in gratitude for his old bravery gives him an estate at Lirias. There Gil and his servant settle down to country life. Gil marries a farmer's daughter, but he loses her and her child at the confinement.

Gil sets out again for adventure. The prince is now King of Spain, and Gil succeeds in winning the favor of the new Prime Minister. But he gets into difficulties again, and returns to his estate. There he contracts a second marriage with a girl named Dorothea. The novel ends with Gil contemplating his wife's bearing him children to comfort his old age.

The novel is a lively picture of eighteenth century manners in various ranks of society.

Pierre Carlet de Marivaux (1688–1763)

We have already discussed the comedies of Marivaux. His best-known novels are *The Life of Marianne* (*La Vie de Marianne*) (1731–1742) and *The Upstart Peasant* (*Le Paysan Parvenu*) (1735). It is generally believed that the first English novel, Richardson's *Pamela,* was inspired by *Marianne.* In Marivaux's novel, too, the heroine writes her own story—the tale of a poor but good girl and her adventures. At the age of two, Marianne, travelling with her family to Paris by coach, is suddenly orphaned when all the passengers except her are killed by robbers. Protected by a country curé, whose sister educates her, she is later placed in a school. The rest of the story of her life (by the time she writes it, she is a Countess) is told with wit and verve. This has been called the first analytical novel. Marivaux is very good at describing a considerable variety of characters in modest walks of life.

The Upstart Peasant is the story of the fortunes of a young peasant and the adventures he encounters in his search for success. The pictures of life here are quite realistic.

Neither novel was actually completed by Marivaux. All that seems missing, however, are the concluding installments, the tendency of which is plain enough to the reader anyhow.

Abbé Prévost (1697–1763)

Prévost is the author of a celebrated novel, *Manon Lescaut,* which provided the story for the operas of Puccini and Massenet. His own life was as romantic as one of his own novels. He was first an army officer, then a member of the Benedictine order of monks. Leaving the monastery without permission, he was in consequence exiled, and lived for a time in Holland and later in England. During his absence from France he turned to novel writing under the influence of English romance writers; a number of his pages draw their materials from English life and manners.

Allowed to return to France, he began to edit a paper, *For and Against.* In 1734 he was appointed chaplain to the Prince de Conti. Apparently untiring in energy, he produced over a period of thirty years almost a hundred volumes.

From 1726 to 1732 appeared his eight-volume *Memoirs of a Gentleman of Quality (Mémoires d'un Homme de Qualité),* the seventh book of which contains his celebrated novel, *Manon Lescaut.*

Manon Lescaut: This is one of the masterpieces of what the French call "the literature of passion." Some critics have gone so far as to say that *Manon Lescaut* is the first piece of French fiction that can properly be called a novel, since its predecessors were all episodic romances loosely strung together; this book has a unified and fairly well-knit plot. The story deals with the love of the Chevalier Des Grieux, the narrator in the novel, for the beautiful Manon.

Des Grieux and his close friend and fellow student Tiberge first see Manon Lescaut as she alights from a coach at Amiens. Smitten, Des Grieux presents himself and discovers that she is about to be forced into a convent. He is determined to rescue her from such a fate; after they get rid of her escort, he takes her to an inn, where he makes his plans for an escape to Paris with her, despite Tiberge's dissuasions.

The lovers manage to reach Paris. For a time theirs is a life of bliss, until Des Grieux learns that Manon has been betraying him with another man. With all his sorrow at this discovery, the young man dotes on her so much that he forgives her. At this point his father has him brought home forcibly, and does what he can to make the young lover agree to terminate the affair. When words avail nothing, the senior Des Grieux locks his son in his room.

There Tiberge visits the prisoner and tells him that fickle Manon has gone back to her other lover. Des Grieux feels himself cured of his passion, and begins his studies in divinity at Paris. His concentration soon results in his doing brilliantly at the seminary. But Manon appears again; they kiss; and Des Grieux renounces this new career.

Penniless, he quits school, and it is Manon who must pay the bills when they go to live in the suburbs, at Chaillot. The joy of their reunion urges them to recklessness and lavish expenditures, and when Manon's soldier brother turns up, he comes to live with them too. They are at the end of their resources when a fire burns up all they still own. Seeing no other way out, Des Grieux embarks upon the career of a professional cardsharp. He prospers at the game, and their finances are improving; suddenly a pair of servants steal the lovers' money.

Manon's brother has been urging her to capitalize on her beauty; therefore, to meet this crisis, she becomes the mistress of old M. de G—— M——. Unable to do other than cooperate with her, Des Grieux allows himself to be introduced to the wealthy nobleman as Manon's brother. When Manon has acquired many jewels and much money from M. de G—— M——, the lovers make off with the booty, but are overtaken by the police, and placed in different prisons.

In order to effect an escape, Des Grieux parades his enthusiasm for theological study, and provokes the interest of the man he has helped rob. But his excitable nature ruins his scheme. When M. de G—— M—— comes to see him, Des Grieux becomes nearly insane on learning that Manon is in prison too, and almost chokes the life out of the old man. Procuring a gun from Manon's brother, Des Grieux breaks jail, not without having to kill a keeper first.

Free, he procures Manon's liberty through bribery. Disguised in men's clothing, Manon joins her lover once more. Unhappily, just as they are to meet her brother, the latter is shot by a soldier he has ruined in a card game, and the lovers are once more compelled to run away lest they be held responsible for the crime. Tiberge comes to the inn where they are hiding, and lends his old friend some money.

Accident brings the son of M. de G—— M—— to their place of refuge, and he becomes as enamored of her as his father has been. When he offers in turn to become her protector, the young lovers decide to revenge themselves against the entire family. Manon agrees to accept gifts from the young M. de G—— M——; they intend to cheat the young man of his expected enjoyment by having him bound by ruffians. But old M. de G—— M—— has learned of their whereabouts, and the police arrive and take them into custody.

Des Grieux exercises himself in his son's behalf, and procures his son's release, but Manon is sentenced to exile in Louisiana. Unable to save her, Des Grieux goes with her into exile. In New Orleans, in wretched surroundings, they live as man and wife. At last Des Grieux finds a job, and thinks it high time the law set its seal upon their union. He asks the governor to sanction a marriage, but is met with a refusal. The latter's nephew is taken with Manon. He and Des Grieux fight a duel over her.

Once more the lovers are in flight. But Manon dies in a deserted countryside from sickness and heartweariness. Des Grieux is in despair. Faithful Tiberge seeks his friend in the New World and together they leave for their fatherland, the embittered Des Grieux hoping to find some consolation in religion.

The characterization in Prévost's novel is natural and skillful throughout. Des Grieux's inability to cease loving his immoral sweetheart despite his awareness of her perfidy is quite moving and subtly portrayed. Manon's faithlessness, on the other hand, is convincingly based upon her need for luxury and expensive pleasures. Tiberge is well painted as the constant friend, as is Manon's brother as a ne'er-do-well.

IMPORTANCE

Prévost's influence through this novel has been great in France, particularly during the ensuing romantic period. Rousseau's *The New Eloisa* follows in its school. Prévost also translated *Pamela, Clarissa Harlowe,* and *Sir Charles Grandison,* the three novels of the first great English novelist, Richardson. These translations which Prévost made of Richardson's sentimental novels did much to bring about their vogue in nineteenth century France.

Jean François Marmontel (1723–1799)

Marmontel was a dramatist, critic, and novelist. His *Memoirs* (c. 1785) has familiarized the world with his autobiography; he was, plainly, a pleasant mediocrity. Most of his stories now make very dull reading, though his historical novel, *Bélisaire* (1767) achieved some notice because it was con-demned by the Sorbonne for a passage on tolerance. *The Incas* (1778), deal-ing with the conquest of Peru, shows the increasing interest in the primitives of the New World, and has some well-written local color; it protests against the barbarous treatment by the Spaniards of the Peruvian natives, and expresses great indignation against slavery.

LITERARY CRITICS IN FRANCE

Literary criticism continued to be throughout the eighteenth century an important occupation of all the leading writers. Voltaire, Montesquieu, Diderot, Buffon, as we have seen, wrote considerably in the field of literary criticism. Other specialists, worthy of mention, are La Harpe and Fréron.

La Harpe (1739–1803)

La Harpe was brought to the attention of Voltaire, who thought well of him. Himself a writer of tragedy possessing some quality, La Harpe was a busy critic of other writers. His good judgment is often warped, however, by touches of pedantry and a recurrent bad temper. His tastes were purely Neo-classical; he is therefore at his best on Molière, Corneille, Racine, and Voltaire. His opinions are to be found in his lectures on literature; in them he seems to outdo Boileau in his addiction to rules.

Fréron (1719–1776)

When Fréron was twenty-seven, he began a critical periodical that experi-enced various vicissitudes. Eventually named *L'Année Littéraire* ("The Literary Year") in 1754, it became both celebrated and notorious for its bitter attacks on Voltaire and his fellow philosophes. The Encyclopedists did all they could to have it suppressed, but in vain. Despite the superior genius of his ene-mies, Fréron, a man of cool judgment and witty pen, held his own. He was a lively defender of orthodoxy in religion and literature—a merrier Samuel Johnson. He defended Neoclassical precedent on all occasions.

EIGHTEENTH CENTURY ITALIAN NEOCLASSICAL LITERATURE

Out of the main stream but affected by the trends of the period, Italian literature experienced a slight revival during the Age of Reason, a revival in the direction of throwing off the artificiality which had been a besetting sin and turning to a closer and more honest scrutiny of reality. Encouraged by English, French, and German examples, a new school of writing came into being which attempted to revive the simplicity, directness, and honesty of fourteenth century Italian writing.

Carlo Goldoni (1707–1793)

The ablest of the new writers was Carlo Goldoni, who engaged for a time in a career as a lawyer but became fascinated by the theater and turned his attention to the writing of musical dramas, tragedies, and comedies, which he produced at high speed for a fixed stipend paid him by theatrical companies. After a great number of such made-to-order plays in the traditional mode, he began to take stock of himself and decided that his natural bent was for comedy and that common sense was a better guide than the classical rules of composition. He objected to the plays of his most famous contemporary, Vittorio Alfieri (1749–1803), whose emphasis was on a rigid concern for form and a careful observance of the dramatic unities.

The result was the creation of comedy of character where the plot is simple but provides a good situation for the revelation of personality traits. Goldoni turned out a long series of such comedies, all of which are too superficial to have had enduring value but which educated the public to comedies of manners based on reality and won him recognition and applause. Goldoni's ideas ran into head-on collision with those of the reactionary Carlo Gozzi (1722–1806), who also desired to be popular but wanted to restore the fantastic world of Ariosto.

Giuseppe Parini (1729–1799)

The outstanding poet of the age was Giuseppe Parini, who exhibited in his life and poetry that self-contained poise and dignity that was an eighteenth century ideal. Believing in propriety and morality, he implies rather than preaches these guides of virtuous living in a series of poetic compositions. His masterpiece, *Il Giorno* (*The Day*) (1763–1803), which is reminiscent of Pope's *Rape of the Lock*, reveals the empty pomposities of society by describing its commonplaceness in terms of solemn grandeur.

Tragedy

The eighteenth century in Italy also saw reforms in the theater, particularly in the realm of tragedy. The movement away from melodramatic opera-like renderings of tragic themes began with Francesco Maffei's *Merope* in 1713 and continued toward more explicitly Shakespearean handling of tragedy in Antonio Conti's several Roman tragedies written in blank verse. The trend toward a more spare, emotionally direct enactment of tragedy was assured, however, by the vast success of Vittorio Alfieri's *Saul* in 1782. Like their Greek predecessors, Alfieri's works are harsh in both language and theme. Basing most of his works on classical or Biblical themes, Alfieri (as he reveals in his autobiography) sought to return Italian tragedy to grandeur of emotion and patriotic commitment.

Periodicals

Similar in many ways to the frequenters of the coffeehouse salons of eighteenth century England, groups of upper middle class Italians deemed it fashionable to meet in social setting for animated discussions of social and political topics. A new form of journalism reflected this movement, as voiced in such publications as Pietro Verri's periodical *Il Caffe* (*The Coffeehouse*). The contributions to such publications could rise to eloquence on serious social subjects, as in Cesare Beccaria's pleas for an abolition of the death penalty. *L'Osservatore,* a similar periodical, focused more on the lives of Venetian socialites. By contrast, Giuseppe Baretti's *La Frusta Letteraria* (*The Literary Whip*) sought out and castigated those Baretti decided were bad writers.

REVIEW QUESTIONS

NEOCLASSICISM

Multiple Choice

1. _____Montaigne believed that the purpose of philosophy was
   a. to decide what was the true religion
   b. to answer the great mysteries of the universe
   c. to understand how to live intelligently
   d. to explain which culture was superior

2. _____Neoclassicism was
   a. an extension of the Renaissance
   b. a reaction against the Renaissance
   c. a rejection of individualism
   d. all of the above

3. _____The *Essays* of Montaigne spread the idea of
   a. detachment in judgment
   b. comparing the values of different societies to find a morally superior code
   c. judgment based on one system of Christian ethics
   d. truth as conceived by a higher authority

4. _____During the seventeenth century, Neoclassicism established
   a. rationalism in philosophy
   b. experimentation in natural science
   c. scientific methods of investigation
   d. all of the above

5. _____Thomas Hobbes is considered the father of
   a. tolerance
   b. mechanical empiricism
   c. self-examination
   d. mathematical philosophy

6. _____Neoclassical writers valued
   a. clarity and lucidity
   b. simplicity and conciseness
   c. dignity and cleverness
   d. all of the above

7. _____François de Malherbe is credited with
   a. putting Neoclassical practice into verse
   b. using Neoclassical methods in his orations
   c. writing serious Neoclassical treatises
   d. injecting Catholicism into Neoclassical theories

8. _____*The Persian Letters* by Montesquieu is
   a. a series of observations about Persia
   b. a critique of Persian government
   c. a social satire about Paris
   d. a book that was banned for many years
9. _____The *Encyclopedia*
   a. was written solely for the intellectuals of Italy
   b. expressed cleverly disguised controversial ideas
   c. had the approval of the French church and state
   d. was based on an earlier Greek encyclopedia
10. _____When he said, *"Écrasez l'infame,"* Voltaire meant
    a. crush superstition and intolerance
    b. spread knowledge
    c. trust in a higher authority
    d. keep the common man ignorant

True or False

11. _____Neoclassical writers focused on personal emotional problems.

12. _____*Manon Lescaut* was intended to reverse the movement toward "the literature of passion" in the mid-1700s.

13. _____Neoclassical writers valued a standard form and style for their works, which sometimes degenerated into an obsession with rules.

14. _____The Neoclassical genius exalted inspiration over common good sense.

15. _____During the Neoclassical era, satire was the most popular form of literary expression.

16. _____*Tabula rasa* refers to the concept of the human brain being at birth a blank slate upon which experience will write.

17. _____Molière's play *Tartuffe* is a satirical unmasking of a religious hypocrite.

18. _____Racine always centered his plays on multiple moral crises.

19. _____Saint-Simon is famous for the posthumous publication of his personal memoirs.

20. _____Diderot was imprisoned for three months when he suggested that the blind could read by the sense of touch.

Fill-in

21. The main interest of Neoclassical writers was to define ideal _____ between reasonable members of society.

22. The _____ was a group of English intellectuals who read scientific papers and who were given a charter by Charles II in 1662.

23. Montaigne believed that _____ was the basis of the search for truth.

24. René Descartes applied the methods of _____ to philosophical speculation.

25. Together with Fontanelle, _____ participated in lively literary debate over the comparative superiority of the ancients versus the moderns in art and literature.

26. Jean Racine is considered France's greatest writer of _____.

27. Voltaire's masterpiece of skepticism, _____, levels its satire at many things, including philosophical optimism.

28. The _____ was a collection of seventeen volumes of text that spread new ideas about nature, reason, humanity, and religion.

29. One of the most important characteristics of this century is its popularization and spread of _____.

30. _____ was an Italian playwright who believed that common sense was a better guide to writing than the classical rules of composition.

Matching

31. _____ Hobbes	a.	*Le Cid*
32. _____ Locke	b.	tolerance for the beliefs of others
33. _____ Descartes	c.	"All is for the best in the best of all possible worlds."
34. _____ Montaigne	d.	*The Limping Devil*
35. _____ Molière	e.	the origin of ideas
36. _____ Corneille	f.	*The Barber of Seville*
37. _____ *Candide*	g.	"All that exists is body; all that occurs is motion."
38. _____ Diderot	h.	"I think, therefore I am."
39. _____ Le Sage	i.	editor of the *Encyclopedia*
40. _____ Beaumarchais	j.	*The Miser*

Answers

1. c	12. f	22. Royal Society	31. g
2. d	13. t	23. self-	32. e
3. a	14. f	examination	33. h
4. d	15. t	24. mathematics	34. b
5. b	16. t	25. La Motte-	35. j
6. d	17. t	Houdard	36. a
7. a	18. f	26. tragedies	37. c
8. c	19. t	27. *Candide*	38. i
9. b	20. t	28. *Encyclopedia*	39. d
10. a	21. social	29. knowledge	40. f
11. f	conduct	30. Goldoni	

Part 5

NON-EUROPEAN LITERATURE

Clearly, the main focus of this history of world literature is Western European literature. Yet the last three decades have seen a dramatic increase in both the translation and study of non-European writers, and the importance of writers of European and African ancestry in both South America and the West Indies can no longer be overlooked. What in fact we may be witnessing as we near the turn of the century is a globalization of literary studies, as more and more scholars cross both linguistic and cultural boundaries to discover what is common to all literatures of the world, as well as what makes these varied forms of human artistic expression different and unique.

This short survey of literature outside of Europe is by no means comprehensive, and this text remains primarily a guide to students of Western literature. In presenting an outline of some of the major trends, authors, and periods in Asian, Latin-American, African, and Caribbean letters, the authors wish to inform and inspire readers in the hopes that they will pursue in greater depth and detail the works and writers mentioned here.

WORKS AT A GLANCE

LATIN AMERICAN LITERATURE

Cabeza de Vaca

1542   *Narrative*

Inca Garcilaso de la Vega

1616   *Royal Commentaries*

THE LITERATURE OF CHINA

Pre-Han Dynasty

Confucius	*Ching, Analects*	Lieh tzu	*Lieh tzu*
Lao tzu	*Lao tzu (The Book of Faith and Virtue)*	Chuang Chou	*Chuang tzu*
		Chu Yuan	*Suffering in Exile*

Han Dynasty (206 B.C.–220 A.D.)

Confucius	*The Annals of Spring and Autumn*	Ssu-ma Hsiang-ju	*Tzu-hzu Fu*
		Anonymous	*The Peacock*

Post-Han Dynasty (221–618)

Ko Hong   *Shen-hsien chuan*

Tang Dynasty (618–907)

Liu Tsung-yuan   *Shui ching chu*

Sung Dynasty (960–1279)

Chou Tun-yi   *Fundamental Treatise*

Ming Dynasty (1368–1644)

Anonymous	*The Romantic Tale of the Three Kingdoms*	Ts'ao Hsueh-ch'in	*The Dream of the Red Chamber*
Anonymous	*The River Bank*		
Anonymous	*Novel of the Gods*		

THE LITERATURE OF JAPAN

The Nara Period (710–784)

Yasumaro   *Record of Ancient Matters, Chronicles of Japan*

The Heian Period (784–1185)

Anonymous	*Kokinshu*	Sei Shonagon	*The Pillow Book*
Murasaki Shikibu	*The Tales of Genji*		

The Kamakara Period (1185–1332)

Kamo no Chomei   *Chronicle of a Ten-Foot Hut*

The Nambokucho and Muromachi Periods (1332–1603)

Anonymous	*History of the True Succession of the Divine Emperors*	Kenko	*Materials for Dispelling Ennui*

The Edo Period (1603–1868)

Kaibara Ekiken	*Schooling for Women*	Motoori Noringa	*Explanation of the Kojiki*
Ohashi Junzo	*Hekizasoron*		

THE LITERATURE OF INDIA

Vedic (1200–200 B.C.)

Anonymous   *Rig-Veda, Sama-Veda, Yajur-Veda, Athara-Veda, Upanishads*

Epic (200 B.C.–400 A.D.)

Anonymous	*Mahabharata*	Valmiki	*Ramayana*

Classical (400–Present)

Jayadeva	*Gitagovinda*
Gunadhya	*Brhatkatha*
Hemacandra	*Lives of Sixty-three Distinguished Persons*

11
LATIN-AMERICAN LITERATURE

As seen in previous chapters, one of the great periods of literature in both Portugal and Spain was the Renaissance. Whether one speaks of the drama of *El Cid* or the masterful poet Luís de Camoens, the colonial era was truly an apogee of literary creation on the Iberian peninsula. The first European explorers to reach the New World—Pedro Vaz de Caminha, Vasco de Gama, Amerigo Vespucci, and of course Christopher Columbus—brought with them not only the customs, laws, and religion of Europe, but also its vast literary history. These explorers themselves have left us many fascinating and often chilling accounts of their conquest of the Americas, and in so doing they unknowingly sewed the seeds for what would become one of the richest literary traditions of the modern world.

Due mainly to censorship imposed on artists by the colonial government authorities, one finds that the vast majority of Latin-American writing before 1800 is classified as nonfiction; that is, writers would cloak their often highly fictional works beneath the protective names of memoirs or chronicles. This is not to say that fiction was not produced, but simply that the lines between factual and fictional writing were much more blurred than they are today. Publishing a novel, if its contents came under the disapproving and scrutinizing eyes of the colonial censors, frequently led its author prison or exile. Thus colonial authors, happily for historians and literary scholars alike, produced a large corpus of historical works that explore and describe a time that appears almost mythical, both in their eyes and in those of the modern reader.

Despite these efforts, many works that are now seen as fundamental to colonial literature were never printed during the lifetime of their authors. This was also caused by the relative lack of printing presses and publishing houses in the new cities of Latin America. Not until the nineteenth century and the independence of all Latin-American nations were some of the most important texts finally printed, and even today it seems that each new anthology or study of Latin-American literature includes a new and never-before-published text that dwelt in relative obscurity for centuries and now appears of high literary merit. This constant revision of the corpus of Latin-American literature is both exciting and refreshing, and tends to give a sense of constant renewal and discovery to its study.

Among the varied themes and styles taken by colonial writers, scholars often point out the singular sense of marvel and astonishment experienced by the explorers as they stumbled, almost blindly, upon such wonders as the

Aztec and Inca temples, and the vast expanses of the Amazon. One is struck, in reading early colonial writings, by the magic of the land, as well as by the horrors of the conquest. Later writers would certainly demystify the Utopian ideal of the New World.

As the European population of the New World grew and soon out-stretched that of its ruling homelands, differences in the new cultures being created began to separate and divide the people. It is important to recognize that the literature of Latin America, already bilingual (Spanish and Por-tuguese), by no means represents a cohesive or integrated society. In fact, the question of integration, and especially a cultural integration that could unite the diverse political factions of postcolonial Latin America, plagued these burgeoning republics through most of the nineteenth century. Much as one finds today in postcolonial Africa, the politics of Latin-American nations after independence was a constantly changing battlefield of factions and infighting. If the political base was weak, thought many writers and artists, then the cultural base must be strong in compensation. Cultural integration was in fact a goal for authors as diverse in origin and work as Antônio Gonçalves Dias, Andrés Bello, and José Joaquín Fernández, and continues to be so for modern giants such as Octavio Paz.

One of the difficulties of such an integration was the cultural border that divides Spanish Latin America from its Portuguese counterpart, mainly Brazil (the largest country in South America with a population nearing 155 million). Although the movements and trends in the literature and art of these two groups do mirror each other more often than not, one must nonetheless con-sider their important linguistic and cultural differences before speaking of them in the same breath. This survey, following the tradition set out by oth-ers, will also tend to overlook this important distinction, but at a more pro-found level one must be conscious and aware of it.

OF STYLE AND THEME

The colonial literature in Latin America was marked by the baroque style, both in secular and religious poetry and prose. Writers of the Latin-American baroque borrowed this style from sixteenth century European writers, reworking and reexamining it to fit their own expressive needs. The period immediately following independence—that is, after 1810—saw the somewhat belated arrival of the Romantic movement, as much from the Anglo-Saxon world as from Germany and especially France. Although the precise date of its arrival in the New World is the subject of endless debate, it is obvious that the movement reached Latin America after it had essentially run its course in Europe and was reaching the end of its creative fire, with the premature death of both Keats and Shelley, in England. Among the names mentioned in association with Latin-American Romanticism are Andrés Bello, José de Olemedo, Esteban Echeverría and the Brazilian Antônio Gonçalves Dias.

As one can well imagine, the volatile political situation in Latin America at the time of independence lent itself not only to a revolutionary idealism in political thought, but also to a Romantic idealism in literary expression. A Latin-American poet of the time would likely identify with revolutionary Byronic verse more easily than with the lyrical but ultimately conservative poetry of Wordsworth—although one finds glimmers of both poets in the works of Latin Americans. The influence from the French school of Romantics, and especially the two great epic Romantic poets Alphonse de Lamartine and Victor Hugo, is undeniable, and both were widely read, usually in French, in Latin America. Though Romanticism was by no means short lived, prose writers in the latter part of the century began to gain importance, introducing both Realism and Naturalism.

EXPLORATION AND COLONIZATION

Though not usually thought of in terms of his literary talents or production, Christopher Columbus wrote abundantly, both in journals and correspondence, about his voyages and the discovery of the New World. Today the air of heroism that long surrounded this most renowned explorer has, with the coming of multiculturalism, all but faded, and even the historical validity of his accounts are somewhat in question. Nonetheless, his writings and the legends that they inspired influenced writers for generations to come, and the writings of Columbus are basically responsible for the birth and propagation of the European ideal of the New World and its people. He paints the latter as timid yet kind and intelligent and in great majority peace loving, the image of the gentle or noble savage who, as history unfolded, was to meet a violent death at the hands of the conquistadores.

Roughly a decade after Columbus, the Portuguese explorer Pedro Vaz de Caminha joined with the *Cabral* voyage, which discovered and claimed the territory of Brazil for the Kingdom of Portugal. Although the letters of Columbus were widely circulated among European scholars (both Voltaire's magical El Dorado in *Candide* and Thomas Moore's *Utopia* took inspiration from them), the letter of Caminha remained unpublished until the nineteenth century, when it became an important addition to the literature of discovery.

Two recent films document the lives of two explorers. Along with a film on Columbus, the astonishing life and times of Alvar Cabeza de Vaca have also been dramatized in a film that takes the explorers name as its title. The film is based on Cabeza de Vaca's *Narrative*, which describes, to the reader's endless amazement, the long series of adventures and hardships that befell his captain, Narvaez, and their group of explorers. Upon his arrival in the supposed Edenesque paradise of the New World, Cabeza de Vaca was taken prisoner by the Indians and enslaved. This role reversal was, needless to say, a brutal shock to the cultured and pious European. Eventually gaining respect and freedom from the Indians, Cabeza de Vaca traveled widely in North and South America, and nearly all of his voyages are documented in his *Narrative*.

Both Columbus and Vaz de Caminha wrote in descriptive terms, with a tone of either praise or ambivalence toward their native hosts. The following generation of explorers, however, were to witness not the discovery but the conquest and murder of huge numbers of Indians and documented the terrors of colonization. Among these texts, those of Bartolomé de las Casas stand apart as powerful testaments to the bloody war of conquest waged by the Spaniards and the Portuguese. Las Casas himself, who traveled to Latin America not long after Columbus, began his life-long battle against the injustices of the conquest with his pen in hand. His style is highly readable even today, and the best of his writings appear not as anticonquest propaganda but rather as heartfelt condemnation of what he perceived to be fundamentally inhuman behavior on the part of his countrymen. Las Casas became a Dominican priest and fought with true religious zeal and conviction to prevent the slaughter of the indigenous peoples of the continent.

The son of one of Peru's first conquistadores, Inca Garcilaso de la Vega took his Spanish name from his father and kept the name Inca as a tribute to his mother, an Incan princess. Because he was one of the first great prose artists born in Latin America (Peru, 1539), he is frequently recognized as a quintessential figure in the birth and genesis of a distinct literature in Latin America. Garcilaso's chef d'oeuvre is without a doubt his *Royal Commentaries* (1616), a historical (or historiographic) account of the Incan empire through the time of the discoveries. Garcilaso, having lived in Peru until the age of twenty an then moving to Spain to pursue his fortune and his education, spoke both Spanish and the Incan language, and he was intimately familiar with the myths and legends of the Incan religion. At the same time, he was a devout Catholic and a Spaniard, an apparent true believer in the natural right and obligation of the Europeans to impose their creed on the Indians.

Yet perhaps the spirit of his Incan mother never truly left him, for he tells of the grandeur of Incan civilization, discrediting some of the earlier historical accounts of this fascinating society. Garcilaso further nuances his narrative with stories and anecdotes culled from his own memory and those of friends, both Indian and Spanish, which praise Incan culture and seem to capture some of its glorious heritage. Today, this text is of great value to anthropologists and historians alike, but at the time the colonial regime did not look kindly upon it, and it suffered at the hands of the censors, to be published and widely read only at the time of independence.

THE BAROQUE IN LATIN AMERICA

Giambattista Marino and Luís de Gongora, of Italy and Spain respectively, were the two European masters of the post-Renaissance style of poetry known as the Baroque. Writers of verse that mirrors an elaborate and ornate style of architecture, these two men greatly influenced the colonial poetry of Latin America. As with the Romantic movement, this style of poetry was slow to arrive in Latin America, but once it had, it truly captured the imagination of an entire generation of writers. The baroque in poetry is seen in its greatest abundance in the work of a half-dozen Mexican poets, including Miguel de Guevara, Bernardo de Balbuena, the dramatist Juan Ruíz de Alarcon, and Sor Juana Ines de la Cruz. If Garcilaso is the father of Latin-American prose, then Ines de la Cruz (1651–1695) is certainly the mother of its poetry. Little is known of her life. She was born of a noble family and became a nun at the age of sixteen (and is thus often referred to as "Sor Ines"). The influence of Gongora is clear in her work, especially in her finely crafted earlier erotic poems. In her later work, she explored several philosophical themes, never losing the elaborate and rich constructions from which she took her first literary inspirations.

Another of the baroque poets was the Brazilian Gregório de Matos, whose career spanned the latter half of the seventeenth century. As is frequently the case, little of his life was documented and even his poetic works were never printed during his life, due in part to his raucous lifestyle and his neglect of his writings (the first edition of his poetry appeared in the 1880s). De Matos was adept in many styles of poetry, and he wrote songs of both secular and religious nature, as well as many works in the classical baroque tradition. But the genre that he preferred was a popular ballad verse, which sang of his and others' vices and misadventures among drunkards and prostitutes. His themes are not dissimilar from those of the French playwright Jean Genêt, and though he does in some respects show the high caliber of serious baroque poetry of his time, the writings of De Matos also perfectly reflect the oral tradition of literature in colonial Brazil.

12
THE LITERATURE OF CHINA

To trace the general lines of literary developments in China requires several preliminary remarks. First, one must recognize that, as one of the world's most ancient civilizations, the literary history of China extends back twenty-five centuries. This short essay will treat both the beginnings of literature and philosophy in China and the periods paralleling those of our study of European literature; that is, in terms of Chinese chronology, from the beginning or the Tang dynasty (618) to the modern era. Second, and quite unlike the literary giants and their respective movements in the West, classical Chinese writers and philosophers alike were repulsed by the idea of originality or uniqueness in thought in their work. This is not to say that stagnation or banality reigned in the literature of China, but rather that its development was founded on advances in style and expression rather than in theme or idea.

Third, it is worthwhile to note the vast difference that exists between the monosyllabic, phonetically simple spoken Chinese and the highly abstract ideographic written Chinese. The written language, which differs both grammatically and lexically from its spoken counterpart, highlights the disparity between lower forms of literary expression, such as the novel, and the high art of Chinese *wen*, or literature. And finally, one must note the innate difficulty that people accustomed to Western names find in distinguishing among the family name, surname, courtesy name, and personal name by which one author may be alternately known. For this reason, our study does not focus on names, but rather on the larger structures of movement and style that will be, hopefully, an ideal introduction to the rich literature of China.

The Chinese word *wen* expresses, in Western conception, several distinct ideas, including drawing, writing, general civilization, and, of course, literature. It thus becomes immediately problematic for Western scholars to attempt to classify Chinese literature according to our categories of poetry, drama, and so on. In fact, Chinese academics classify the *wen* in much broader groupings, which stretch beyond our usual boundaries of literature, into what we might call history or philosophy. The four main divisions are (1) anthologies and collected works of poetry and fiction; (2) the historical writings that describe the development of the twenty-four Chinese dynasties; (3) the works of Confucius and other philosophical classics, including critical studies and commentaries; and (4) other non-Confucian philosophical works, writings on the sciences, and the vast collection of encyclopedias that have over the years meticulously preserved works of literature, classifying them by style.

GENERAL CHARACTERISTICS OF CHINESE POETRY AND PROSE

The graphic representation of Chinese poetry and prose differs in several ways from the print representation of Western literature. Because the characters of Chinese script depict symbolic images (unlike our alphabet characters), the written version of Chinese literature claims a visual aesthetic component. By contrast, a Western poet rarely places much value on the visual images conveyed by the printed poem. And because the individual graphs in the Chinese writing system do not indicate specific sounds but instead can be pronounced in a number of variant dialects, the corpus of Chinese literature has over the centuries remained available to all Chinese people, no matter what dialect they speak. Western languages, bound by the relation between graphic letters and sounds, have not maintained this accessibility. Chaucer's Middle English, for example, is virtually a foreign language for most present-day speakers and readers of English.

Like Greek poetry, Chinese poetry was originally accompanied by music and performed in a sung or chanted manner. Although most of the original musical scores for such poetry have been lost, the cadences and tonalities of the music remains. To this day, Chinese poetry is more often chanted than simply read by native speakers of Chinese. But unlike their Greek equivalents, Chinese poems are quite brief and compact. The Chinese poet typically attempts to mark the height of ecstasy or sorrow in verse rather than the progress to or departure from those states. Unnecessary parts of speech such as conjunctions and pronouns are often omitted. The remaining core words are richly embued with layers and levels of denotation and connotation, making both interpretation and translation difficult. Most Chinese poems rely upon end rhyme and repeated cadences for unity.

The line between poetry and prose is not drawn sharply in Chinese literature. The *fu*, for example, is a form roughly translated as prose poem or rhapsody by Western interpreters. This literary mode uses rhyme and cadence freely in the midst of a general prose format and method of exposition. Another genre of mixed poetic and prose elements is *p'ien-wen* ("parallel prose"), in which rhyme is replaced by constructions of antithetical paired lines that are parallel in tonal pattern. The effect is not unlike that of the Biblical psalms.

Classical or literary Chinese prose (*ku-wen*) rigidly follows the rhetoric, grammar, and models of ancient Chinese masters. The language of literature is thus far removed from the language of speech. Because this form of literary language was emphasized for centuries in the Chinese education system, it became the primary linguistic mode for Chinese writers through the twelfth century and continues as a tradition among many Chinese writers to this day. In contrast, the vernacular form of prose (*pai-hua*) was based on the living language spoken by the common people. Not until the thirteenth century was it adopted by Chinese novelists and playwrights as an acceptable language for literary expression.

FROM THE BEGINNINGS TO THE HAN DYNASTY

The basis for many stylistic and conceptual aspects of the great eras of literary art in China was the pre-Han literature. These philosophical classics (*Ching*) of Confucius (551 B.C.–479 B.C.) and others preached a humanistic doctrine, claiming only, as Confucius himself stated, to mirror the works and ideals of the ancients in their own writings. Confucius spent his time, much as Western philosophers from Aristotle to Neitzsche did, teaching. It was subsequent generations of scholars who recorded the teachings of Confucius in writing, for he never wrote anything down. All of the work of Confucius served to communicate and further the teachings of the ancients. It is in the Confucian *Analects* that one will find the clearest expression of Confucian philosophy. The *Ching*, or *Classics*, are the canonical Confucian works upon which the subsequent centuries of Chinese scholarship and philosophy are based. Knowledge of the *Ching* was literally the key to success as a scholar in China—a sought-after position that garnered much respect and security. The Confucian tradition stayed with China through both royal and imperial dynasties, and only in the modern era have a large number of scholars and writers broken with the basic precepts about Chinese culture and civilization set out in the *Ching*. Serving as the basis of pedagogy in China, the *Ching* were a reference guide to proper conduct in the smallest aspect of private life, as well as to the largest philosophical inquiry. Though the *Ching* did shape the minds and morals of the Chinese people for almost two thousand years, extolling the virtues of humanism while repudiating vulgar activity, it is important to recognize that they were taken as revelatory or divine, and never attained the pure power or authority of dogma. The *Ching* are, however, responsible in part for the extraordinary stability of Chinese culture.

The *Ching* is made up of roughly a dozen books, depending on the era one is studying. Among these the most widely read in the West are the *I ching*, a book of divination containing a group of sixty-four hexagrams and their interpretations. The *Shih ching* is a book of classical poetry and songs in the *shih* style (musical), while the *Lun-yu* contains the famed aphorisms and maxims of Confucius. Other books treat such varied topics as government administration, description of rites and rituals, Chinese language and grammar, and an assemblage of anecdotes about moral questions. The *Ching*, which has no formal author, thus appears as a collective work, not ignoring original thought but rather passing along the original thoughts of humankind.

Another philosophical doctrine that gave rise to an entirely distinct vein of thought and literature, Taoism differs greatly from Confucianism. Taoist philosophers of the fourth and third centuries B.C. proposed a philosophy based on individualism and free will, and were openly disdainful of the high moral tone of the *Ching* and its insistence on the sharp division between good and evil. Taoist thought tends to stray from traditional social conventions, concerning itself with dialectical reasoning and the contemplation of paradoxes. Although the basic framework of Taoism was later incorporated, under the influence of Buddhism, into a religious doctrine, it was at the outset a highly secular school of thought.

The three books from which modern scholars, often with much difficulty, have interpreted the tenets of Taoism are the *Lao tzu* (*The Book of Faith and Virtue*), the *Lieh tzu*, a book of fables and anecdotes, and the *Chuang tzu*, written by Chuang Chou and one of the true treasures of Chinese prose.

A slightly more minor philosophical figure and a contemporary of Confucius, Mo Ti was the leader of the *Mo tzu* school, which produced a collection of texts dealing mainly with morality and logic. Mo Ti and his followers were concerned with some of the same questions as the so-called Legalists of the pre-Han period. The Legalists were quite radical in their thought and advocated moving away from the precepts of the *Ching*. Taking on a somewhat Machiavellian air, the Legalists saw men as naturally inclined to evil and only controllable through fear. Mo Ti and his followers, while they saw the same difficulties with government and control, advocated a more peaceful solution and proposed a government based on universal respect and love, and also frugality.

Among the wide variety of pre-Han literary styles, it is worth singling out at least two. The first is a prose style, characterized mainly by short narratives, called *Hsiao Shuo*. Composed mainly of what we would call fantastic or mythical literature, some of these works are quite long and could even be considered novels. Of course, this popular type of literature did not hold the cultural weight or importance of works such as the *Ching*, but fragments of these texts, which were also richly illustrated, were preserved by the philosophers of the Confucian tradition.

Second, there exists a whole body of poetic works distinct in style and theme from Shih poetry. Known as *Chu-tzu*, this short assembly of poems represents the work of the poet Chu Yuan (340 B.C.–275 B.C.) and his disciples. Something of a romantic figure, Chu came from the southern part of China and, having offended the northern Prince with his foreign customs, he was banished to the south, at which point he composed a long and highly allegorical lament called the *Li sao* (*Suffering in Exile*). Chu Yuan also wrote a group of religious poems called the *Nine Songs*, which, along with the *Li sao*, stood as a model for the rhythm and versification of most of the Chu-tzu poetry.

THE HAN DYNASTY

The reign of China's first emperor, Chin Shin Huang-ti, signaled the end of the feudal period and brought unfortunate consequences for Chinese literature. Having adopted the somewhat extreme and dogmatic ideals of the Legalists, Chin Shin ordered the burning of many of the books written before his empire, and especially of the Confucian works of literature (excepting the *I-ching*). However, the books in the royal library were conserved and when the Han dynasty (206 B.C.–220 A.D.) was restored and the ban lifted (190 B.C.), Confucian scholars began the arduous task of reconstructing the literary and philosophical works that had been lost.

Because the scholars of the Han dynasty remained almost exclusively in the Confucian tradition, many of the ideas of other philosophical schools slipped into obscurity. The Taoist tradition was among the few that survived. Although scholarship was not particularly valued in the early part of the Han dynasty, some knowledge of the *Ching* soon became required of all government administrators and officials. This measure assured the literacy of all officials, and coincided with the founding of the first Confucian schools by the Emperor Wan. Out of this early imperial era was born much of the difficulty that modern scholars find in their attempts at historical or textual criticism of the *Ching*. The dubious objectivity of the Confucian scholars who reconstructed the *Ching*, coupled with the growing conflicts between the two divergent schools of Chinese script (the *Chin-wen*, or modern script, and the *Ku-wen*, both more ancient and less widely read) rendered objective attempts at interpretation very problematic.

Two of the greatest Confucian scholars of the Han dynasty were Tung Chung-shu (c. 100 B.C.) and Cheng Hsuan (125–200 A.D.). Tung, who advocated the *Chin-wen* or modern script of the *Ching*, showed through his interpretations the absolute power of the Chinese emperor over his people. He was also instrumental in the empire's decision to adopt Confucianism as the official philosophical doctrine, with the *Ch'un-ch'iu (The Annals of Spring and Autumn)* at the head of the Confucian canon, holding the key to Confucian philosophy.

Cheng, nearly three centuries later, witnessed the end of the long-standing division between the two styles of script. By incorporating both the *Chin-wen* and the *Ku-wen* in his work, he effectively eliminated the dispute. Both works were set into stone in the first few centuries A.D., and the Han period, in general, continued the Confucian tradition of recording, preserving, and distributing the wisdom and words of the ancients.

Perhaps the most renowned poet of the Han period was Ssu-ma Hsiang-ju, who lived near the end of the second century B.C. and wrote poetry in the *Fu* style, an imitation of the earlier *Chu-tzu (Chu Elegies)*. This style of verse was characterized by its attention to detail and the richness of its highly erudite vocabulary. Ssu-ma's poems, though they do not ignore the political and philosophical themes popular during the Confucian Han period, tend more toward descriptions of nature, and especially the gardens and land of the Emperor. As a poet of the Imperial Court, Ssu-ma won praise for his poem *Tzu-hzu Fu*, which paints a detailed picture of a landscape in the Chu province.

Ssu-ma was also responsible in part for the birth of another style of poem, the *Yueh-fu*. This poetry takes its name from the Imperial Office of Music established under Emperor Wu. Originally this government office sought to preserve the popular music of the time. Some original pieces also came from this period, including the sacrificial hymns of the dynasty. Ssu-ma, in addition to his other writings, composed several of these religious songs, from which in turn came the profane poetry of the *Yueh-fu*.

Near the end of the Han dynasty, which was a period of transition in literature, politics, and culture, a stronger sense of individualism began to emerge in both poetry and prose; but it was certainly in poetry that the greatest advances came. One of the warlords during the fall of the Han dynasty, Tsao Tsao (155–200), and his two sons, Tsao Chih and Tsao Pei (the future Emperor Wen), were among the greatest Chinese poets of the time. In their works, these three men established many of the conventions of style, tone, and theme that influenced poetry for centuries to come. Their poetry followed the tonal rules of Chinese, and thematically they wrote of the primary subjects of Chinese poetry of this period and those to come: raucous stories and anecdotes of debauchery, laments on the hardships of war, and descriptions of nature and landscapes.

Other works of this period include a wonderful epic poem written by one of the rare women poets, Tsai Yen. This poem is an emotional description of her abduction by the Huns and the misfortunes she survived during the decade in which she was forcibly kept. As the Han empire began to crumble under increasing strain from foreign invasions and internal crises in agriculture and the economy, some of the poets, including Tsao Tsao and a group he patronized called the Seven Poets, wrote of the sadness and helplessness they felt. One of these poems, whose author is unknown, is the *Kung-chia tung nan fei* (popularly translated as *The Peacock*), which is a tragic poem about a couple who choose death over separation.

THE POST-HAN PERIOD

This period, which lasted from the end of the Han dynasty to the beginning of the Tang (618), saw both political and social strife divide the country many times. The era of the Three Kingdoms (221–265) was followed by the somewhat unified but short-lived Chin (265–420) and Sui (581–618) dynasties. The voyages of Chinese explorers to India brought the influence of Buddhism to China, without a doubt the most important cultural event of this long period of instability. As translations of Buddhists texts became more frequent, so an interest developed on the part of the Chinese in the syntactic and phonetic structure of their own language. The advent of Buddhism also greatly decreased the influence of Confucianism, and many scholars lost their place in the rigid hierarchy established by the Han emperors. Poetry was in turn influenced in theme by this Indian religion, especially by numerous Buddhist folktales.

In literature, the *Fu* style of poetry continued to be written, under the title *Wen fu*, into the seventh century. Poets of the time, such as Lu Chi (c. 260–300) and his predecessor the Emperor Tsao Pei, concerned themselves primarily with the search for aesthetic, beautiful poetic structure. The individualist ideas first proposed by the poet Tsao Tsao were continued by the poet Chuang tzu, who sought both originality and spontaneity in his work and refused to abide by the old doctrines. But the style of the *Tzu-fu* was the predominant influence on writers of the time. Poems contained a seemingly inordinate number of allusions and syllogisms, and poetic form and structure were put ahead of philosophical insight or clarity of expression.

Aside from poetry, the later part of the period in question produced many collections of ancient stories or tales, the *Hsiao Shuo* (also known as novels). The best of these tales were written by two authors, Kan Pao and Ko Hong. The writings of Kan Pao are best classified as short stories or folktales, and in the collected anthology of these works one often reads of the fantastic or the supernatural. Ko Hong (283–343) wrote the *Shen-hsien chuan*, which tell of the lives of many of the immortal Taoist figures of ancient times. In addition to his short stories, Ko Hong was a respected scholar, doctor, and alchemist; a Renaissance man before the fact who appears today as an important figure in the overall history of Chinese philosophy.

THE TANG DYNASTY

The new stability found in the Tang dynasty (618–907) brought back the Confucian *Classics*, or *Ching*, as the basis of Chinese morality and philosophy. A definitive text of the *Classics* was established, and all of the ancient Confucian writings were reexamined with the goal of creating an official interpretation of the *Ching*. As in previous dynasties, the new version of *Ching* decided, somewhat arbitrarily, on the "correct" meaning of the five books of the traditional *Ching* (the *Li chi, Chun-chiu, Shih ching, Shu ching,* and the *I-ching*). It was during this era that the study and interpretation of the *Ching* became more rigorous and objective. Furthermore, the ancient interpretations of the *Ching* were put to close scrutiny by writers and scholars. Concurrently, the central texts of the Taoist tradition were also studied and interpreted, but most of these writings do not survive today.

The Tang period was truly an apogee of creation in Chinese art and letters. In prose a radically new style emerged, with the writer Han Yu (768–824) as its principal inventor. This narrative style, misnamed *ku-wen*, was less rigorous in rythmic constrictions, which dominated prose in past eras, and more exacting in its word choice and syntactical precision. Another writer in this tradition was Liu Tsung-yuan (773–819), whose *Shui ching chu* describes walks the author took in the beautiful countryside of the Hunan province. Liu can also be credited with introducing the fable into Chinese letters.

The short story took on greater literary importance during the Tang dynasty, and the precise narrative style adopted by writers appears today as a window into the lifestyle of people of the time. In addition, the *Hsiao Shuo* genre, which corresponds somewhat to our conception of the novel, was further developed and vivified by the Tang writers. Inspired by the increasing wealth of their country and the arrival of more foreign actors and comedians, these writers, including Li Chao-wei, Tu Kuang-ting, and Chen Hung, wrote fantastic, highly stylized, rich prose, which often presented a moral about life, relationships, or success.

Although innovative, the prose of the Tang dynasty cannot compare to its brilliant poetry. The great number of Tang poets, who were adept especially at the craft of form and style, were also influenced by the new openness enjoyed in China to the outside world. If the rules governing prose form became looser, those that dictated poetic style became much more strict. The poetry of the Tang, known generally as the New Style (*Hsin-ti*), is traditionally divided into several subgroups: the *cheuh-chu* is poetry with stanzas of four lines, with a meter that varied from five to seven feet; the *lu-shih,* a style characterized by its strict attention to meter and stanzas of eight lines; and the *pai-lu,* a more lengthy type of *lu-shih*. Among the self-imposed complexities of the Tang poets were rules governing rhyme and tone, both of which gave an eerie phonetic symmetry to these poems.

Three of the best poets of the Tang dynasty were Tu Fu, Li Po and Wang Wei. Tu Fu is known for his four-lined *cheuh-chu*, which are stylistically simple yet beautifully crafted. On the whole his work is quite formal and studied, but certainly not lacking in inspiration. Like his friend the poet Li Po, Tu Fu spent his early years in the court of Hsuan-tsung, which became in the Tang dynasty a center for poetry and the arts. Li Po, who is perhaps the most famous Chinese poet in western eyes, led a life that in some ways parallels that of the great French poet François Villon—that is to say, raucous and full of debauchery. He was not original in his themes (wine, friendship, and the passage of time), but his poetry contains both great verve and enthusiasm, while at the same time showing a sparse and economical style. Li Po expressed much with very few words. Finally, the poet, painter and musician Wang-wei, who found inspiration in the Taoist philosophy and the humanism of the Buddhists, wrote with great precision on a number of formidable themes, including quiet contemplation of our infinite universe.

THE SUNG DYNASTY

Despite the instability that marked the turn of the millennium in China, order was reestablished under the Sung dynasty (960–1279), and once again a great period for Chinese literature, the arts, and philosophy was born. Tracing the history and development of the Confucian doctrines, one finds that in the Sung dynasty Confucian scholars took a more critical approach to commenting on and interpreting the *Classics*, moving further away from the Han tendency toward conservative preservation and seeking the true meaning held in these now-ancient texts. The interpretive method of the time stressed above all objectivity, and writers combined theories culled from Taoism, Buddhism, and Confucianism in their commentaries. Chu Hsi (1130–1200) was among the most prolific commentators on the *Ching*, and also wrote a great number of literary works—for the most part essays and poetry. The clarity of his style was rarely matched in his or any other time, and he was also a scholar of considerable importance, writing a complete history of China, along with numerous philosophical essays in which he expounded some of the ideas later found in *Tai-chi* (such as the essential morality of Nature and the universe).

Another philosophic movement, based on the conception of the *Tai-chi* or *Supreme Pinnacle*, came to light in the eleventh century. The philosopher Chou Tun-yi (c. 1019–1075), and the brothers Cheng Hao and Cheng Yi were all instrumental in its conception and dissemination. In his *Fundamental Treatise*, Chou gives a step-by-step accounting of the genesis and evolution of the universe, founding his account on historical cosmogony.

The poetry of the Sung dynasty was characterized by a new and somewhat lyrical style, the *tzu*. This musical form of poetry, which resembled somewhat the ancient sacrificial hymns of the Empire, used verse written specifically for a tune composed by a musician. Again, as in the Tung dynasty, the *tzu* poetry had to follow very strict rules of meter, rhythm, and rhyme. In many cases, more vulgar popular songs were adapted into more aesthetically pleasing poetic works. Today, the rhythmic bases for nearly one thousand different *tzu* poems survive, along with the restrictions one must impose on their meter. The musical melodies, unfortunately, were lost centuries ago.

Tzu were composed over a long period stretching from the end of the Tang dynasty to the final years of the Sung, and the poetic form changed gradually, lengthening into what is called *man-tzu* and losing its musical accompaniment. Among the most renowned *tzu* poets were Wen Ting-yun, the first *tzu* poet; Liu Jung, author of the longer *man-tzu*, and Su Shih, who saw to the transformation of what was a strict musical form into a freer spoken structure. Finally, the female poet Li ching-chao wrote some of the finest and most masterful *tzu* poems, with a heavy touch of melancholy from the loss of her husband.

Lucidity of expression was the rule in Sung period prose. In a return to the ancient prose style of the *ku-wen*, authors often dropped altogether the formalities of written Chinese and, in part surely to facilitate reader comprehension, wrote in the spoken idiom. As Confucianism finally triumphed as the doctrine that had seen China through over fifteen centuries, so did the clear and practical prose style of the *ku-wen*. The two best prose writers of the period were Su Shih, mentioned above for his poetic works, and Ou-yang Hsiu (1007–1072). Ou-yang was an essayist who wrote on nature, and also a poet and historian. Su Shih was a masterful *tzu* poet and wrote many beautiful descriptive essays, and is often seen as the quintessential Sung writer.

YUAN THEATER

One of the literary styles of importance to emerge from the otherwise culturally bleak reign of the Mongols in China (the Yuan dynasty, 1280–1368) was *Yuan* theater. Its origins can be found in one of the first forms of dramatic expression in China, the religious ceremonies and liturgical dances spoken of in the *Shu ching*. *Yuan* drama is on the whole very formal, with a group of traditional roles, a structure in four acts, and strict attention to the poetry and rhyme of the monologues. Each act presented the audience with one or more of the characters, or roles, and contained at least one musical piece. A chorus of actors repeated the lines sung by the principal characters. From this new poetic form spring a style of poetry that preempted the *tzu* style. Known as the *chu*, or *san-chu*, these were poems with a very loose structure, written in the vernacular language, and quite free in their rhyme and meter.

THE MING DYNASTY

The Ming period (1368–1644) was another dark age, at least so far as philosophical advances were concerned. The Confucian scholars began to take their positions for granted and the rigorous system of government examinations began gradually to deteriorate. At the same time, the Emperor ordered a new interpretation and commentary on the *Classics*. What was produced was insignificant by any stretch of the imagination, as many scholars depended on the Han commentaries as their only source of knowledge, while others neglected study altogether in favor of what they believed to be their innate knowledge.

However, this period's literature should not be overlooked, as it was yet another great age for Chinese drama and the novel. The Ming drama, or drama of the South, differed in many ways from the *Yuan*, or Northern drama. The form had changed, and authors had more freedom to make their characters speak their minds—and this for as long as needed, for the number of acts in a Ming play was unlimited. Another important addition to this dramatic form was the prologue, which outlined the general plot of the piece in one or more songs.

What Western scholars would truly label novels were unknown in China before the Ming dynasty, the period that produced what are still often seen as China's best novels. A great many of these novels, which were printed and widely read and distributed amongst all the classes, were historical in content. Of these, the *San-kuo-chih yen-yi (The Romantic Tale of the Three Kingdoms)* was by far the most famous. This lively tale is not particularly well crafted, but it nonetheless conveys with much exuberance the popular historical characters of Tsao Tsao, Liu Pei, and others. Nearly the whole history of the Chinese people was available in print by the end of the Ming dynasty. Other forms of the novel included a realistic style which, like the work of Balzac, Flaubert, or Stendhal, worked from a base of historical fact to create highly imaginative and enthralling tales. Among these is *The River Bank*, again by an unknown author, which tells of the picaresque adventures of a band of robbers. Still other novels, such as the *Feng shen yen yi (Novel of the Gods),* have a fantastic, somewhat mythological tone. Finally there were novels that we may call naturalistic that described the mores and morals of Ming society.

The novelistic traditions of the Ming period led to great popularity for the genre in the following century. By far the most profound and aesthetically advanced of these later novels was *The Dream of the Red Chamber (Hung lou meng,* c. 1760), by Ts'ao Hsueh-ch'in (c. 1715–1763). This work, reminiscent in some ways of later novels of Galsworthy, traces the decline in fortunes of the large, aristocratic Chia family. The novel was unique in its time for its depth of characterization and vividness of detail.

13
THE LITERATURE OF JAPAN

There has been some debate as to how and when the Japanese Empire was originally founded. Tradition says that it was founded by the chief of a tribe from Kyushu, named Jimmutenno, who settled in Yamato and became the first emperor of Japan. A document created in the Nara period in 712 A.D. recording the imperial chronology of Japan states that his reign began in 660 B.C. but that date has been hotly debated. From the beginning until 710 A.D. is known as the Archaic period in Japanese literary history. During that time both Buddhism and handwriting were brought to Japan from India and China respectively by Koreans, who remained as interpreters of Chinese literature and thereby greatly influenced Japanese culture and literature. The strength of Japanese identity is evident in that both Buddhism and handwriting soon had a distinctively Japanese interpretation. Despite the many outside influences that came to Japan over its history, the uniqueness of Japanese culture has always been maintained.

The Archaic period was a time of continuous social upheaval, so social progress was slow. The only surviving literature from this period is primitive songs sung by soldiers and ritual prayers to Shinto gods, which are also highly developed poems. In both cases these works were probably passed down verbally for many generations but were not recorded until the eighth or ninth century.

THE NARA PERIOD

The Archaic period was superseded by the Nara period. The Nara period, from 710 A.D. to 784 A.D., was a time when Japanese society finally accepted a central authority. With the new stability that resulted, Japan had a chance to make great social progress. For example, the Nara period produced the two oldest pieces of Japanese literature in existence: the *Kojiki* (*Record of Ancient Matters*) and the *Nihongi* or *Nihonshoki* (*Chronicles of Japan*). Both of these were compiled by Yasumaro, whose contribution was similar to that of a medieval scribe rewriting classic manuscripts. The *Kojiki* was compiled from the imperial archives. It relates the Shinto myths and history from the creation of the world to the reign of Empress Sui-ko in 628. Historically it has little value because it does not record any major political events and merely records the dates of death for the emperors in its chronology. The *Nihongi* was compiled from a variety of other, more ancient texts, which no longer survive. Its chronology records precise details that unfortunately contradict both itself and the *Kojiki*. It is important to note the alphabet in which these were written. An entirely Japanese alphabet had not yet been developed, so the *Kojiki* was written in Chinese characters, which translated into the Japanese language either ideographically or phonetically. The *Nihongi* was written completely in Chinese.

The eighth century is considered Japan's golden age of poetry. In the Nara period, poems, written primarily by women, were refined, elegant, and delicate works. The structure of poetry in that period, called *tanka*, was strict, alternating lines of five and seven syllables. The length of a poem was flexible, but the content was highly controlled. For example, a poem would always begin with a commonly used metonym, which was always followed by a double entendre. Since these poems were written by the poets for their own entertainment, only a few were published when new governments published the best of the previous emperor's reign.

THE HEIAN PERIOD

The Nara period was succeeded by the Heian period (784–1185), which is considered the classic poetry of Japanese literature. At this time there emerged a growing leisured class and an accompanying growth in intellectual and artistic pursuits. A gap developed between the kinds of literature produced by men and women. Men remained the masters of Chinese literature, while women wrote and developed the Japanese language and alphabet. Japanese was considered a more feminine language, best suited to the poetry and stories that were also considered women's domain. Because of those women's contributions to literature, the Japanese language became more sophisticated, and two new types of wholly Japanese writing were fully in use by the end of the ninth century— *katakana* and *hiragana*.

The indomitability of Japanese culture was once again illustrated by the publication at this time of the first prose literature in Japanese. This work, the *Kokinshu*, was the first of many things in Japan. It was also the first literary criticism and the first philosophical argument. Other prose works that were published during this era were diaries written by women and the first pieces of Japanese fiction. An example of these novels is the *Genji monogatari (The Tales of Genji)*. This is a fifty-four chapter novel written by a woman who used the court pseudonym Murasaki Shikibu. The book was intended to be a critique of women through the description of a series of women that Genji, the princely protagonist, either falls in love with or admires. Other types of literary works that began to be published during this time are historical novels, which were partly fictional, and a collection of short tales by Sei Shonagon called *Makura no soshi* or *The Pillow Book*.

Several anthologies of poetry were published during this time, many showing the influence of Buddhism, which by this time was distinctly Japanese.

Kobo-daishi, the inventor of *hiragana*, also originated a new type of poetry, *iroha-uta*, which was as strict in structure as the *tanka*. An *iroha-uta* poem uses all forty-seven syllables in the Japanese language, but repeats none of them. Another type of poem from that period is the *imayo-uta*, which has four groups of two stanzas containing the usual alternating five- and seven-syllable lines.

THE KAMAKARA PERIOD

The Kamakara period lasted from 1185 to 1332 and was a time when military matters took precedence over intellectual ones. Japanese society became generally more masculine, and women virtually disappeared from art and literature. Since Japan's was machine often disrupted relations with China, Chinese literature lost its privileged place in Japanese culture. Peaceful Buddhist monks, called *Bonze*, were the only ones who continued intellectual pursuits like writing, so literature from this period has strong Buddhist overtones. Diaries were still published, but often they were written by Buddhist hermits and other religious figures who were recording their spiritual reflections. The best example of this would be the delicately written *Hojoki* or *Chronicle of a Ten-Foot Hut*, which was written by the hermit Kamo Chomei. Outside of these Buddhist treatises, literature tended to be historical or military accounts.

THE NAMBOKUCHO AND MUROMACHI PERIODS

The next periods, the Nambokucho (1332–1392) and the Muromachi (1392–1603), brought great changes to Japanese society. The monarchy finally succeeded in regaining power from the militaristic Hojo, only to be split into two dynasties, which divided Japan into the North and South. The fifty-six-year struggle between these rival factions was followed by another power struggle between the Emperor Go-Komatsu and the shoguns. Also during the Muromachi period, the first Europeans came to Japan. The Portuguese arrived in 1542, and, by 1587, Christianity was being aggressively resisted by the government.

These two periods are placed together here because of the continuity of their literature. Historical stories continued to be the most common prose works produced during these periods. One of these, *Jinno-Shotoki (History of the True Succession of the Divine Emperors)*, is significant because it is the first work to interpret history rather than just relate events. It was written as political propaganda to justify the legitimacy of the Southern dynasty. In fiction it is a collection of observations and anecdotes by *bonze* Kenko that stands out as the most significant addition to Japanese literature of that time. The collection is called *Tsure-Zure-gusa* or *Materials for Dispelling Ennui*. It is an intriguing insight into the personality of the author and is as readable today as the day it was written.

Kenko was also a successful poet. The predominant poetical style was still the *tanka* although those of this period were not as sophisticated as those of earlier periods. It was during this era that the *haiku* was developed. This type of poem is an interpretation of the *tanka* form but consists of only three lines of five, seven, and three syllables and often has a comic element. In the Muromachi period poetry made its greatest strides in the form of lyrical dramas. These dramas are called *no* and were performed for the elite of that period. They are highly expressionistic dramas, which are reminiscent of their origins in dance. A *no* consists of only a few players, usually two, and a small chorus that explains the action and sometimes includes a small accompanying orchestra. The plots resemble those of Greek tragedies. Characters are usually masked and mime their action, and actors are exclusively male. The cultured elite in Japan still patronize *no* theaters, which draw from the original two-hundred-fifty-play repertory of this period.

THE EDO PERIOD

The Edo or Tokugawa period (1603–1868), which followed the Muromachi period, was very peaceful. The social stability of the shoganate government allowed for a great many social and artistic advances. This was also the period when the Japanese closed their doors to outsiders. Their isolation lasted until foreign pressure forced them to trade internationally. This period of exclusion allowed for a more complete development of Japanese culture. In fact, their isolation inspired fervent nationalism, which created divided camps in literature between the *kangakusha* and the *wagakusha*. The *kangakusha* were scholars who studied and wrote in the Chinese style of literature and who remained faithful to Chinese traditions. The *wagakusha* were nationalistic scholars who believed that the study of Japanese literature should take precedence over Chinese literature. They also managed to restore respect for Japanese literature, which had been considered less artistic than Chinese literature.

The *kangakusha* frequently wrote serious educational and intellectual treatises. For example, Kaibara Ekiken was revered for his moralistic books, primarily his *Onna daigaku* or *Schooling for Women*. This book was used as a standard guide for raising girls for generations. Arai Hakuseki was a typical *kangakusha* author. He wrote hundreds of historical books about Japan during his long career. Other *kangakusha* authors wrote political works like *Hekizasoron*, by Ohashi Junzo, which was an anti-Europe proisolationism book.

An offshoot of the *kangakusha* was a literary movement called *kogakusha*, which focused on the teachings of Confucius. This movement included authors like Togai, Ogyu Sorai, and Dazai Shuntai. Togai's father, Ito Jinsai, was the founder of the movement.

The *wagakusha* authors generally held political beliefs that supported imperial power rather than shoganate power. This movement resulted in a renaissance of Japanese literature and even threatened the power of the shoguns. Much of this literature was political commentary exalting Japanese traditions and culture and proposing the elimination of Chinese literary and linguistic influence. Motoori Noringa was the master of this movement. His most influential work was *Explanation of the Kojiki (Kojikiden)*, which praised all aspects of indigenous Japanese culture including Shintoism and obscure grammatical constructs. He spawned many disciples who carried on his work. The *wagakusha's* proimperialist standpoint did not ingratiate them to the shoganate government. One of Motoori's disciples was eventually exiled for his views.

Besides these three rather high-brow literary movements was one that appealed to a less elite and educated audience. The prosperity of this period created a large educated middle class who hungered for more approachable literature. A novel whose themes focused on love and dramatic moments was introduced for this audience. The originator of this movement was Ibara Saikaku who produced realistic stories about common subjects from daily life. Other books published for this audience were novels with risqué subjects. In fact, these novels became so popular that the shoganate government had to ban them several times. The shoganate had to work hard to try to keep control of all the books published for this new audience. They were also offended by the war novels written about real military heroes that took liberties with the facts of their careers. Those too were banned as disrespectful to the military heroes. Despite the restrictions placed on common novels, there were still many to choose from, including a category of book in which the text was subordinated to the illustrations. These books were usually romantic tales or epics. Japan's first great novelist was Kyokutei Bakin. His adventure stories are still very popular today.

There was a corresponding demand for theater for common people. *No* theater was still being produced for the elite, but the new wealth and leisure of the middle classes created a need for accessible dramas. *Kabuki* theater was born during this time, created by a dancer-priestess named O-kuni who ran off with a samurai to Kyoto, where she and a group of women began performing song-dances called *Kabuki* in Japanese. It was not long before the shogunate banned women from performing in these dramas for moral reasons. *Kabuki* theater eventually lost popularity to *Joruri* theater and had to reinvent itself. *Joruri* theater evolved from the combination of storytelling accompanied by music and puppet shows. These shows by a performer named Takemoto Gidayu were so popular that his name became interchangeable with his style and respected dramatists sometimes wrote scripts for him.

Popular poetical styles of this period were still the *tanka* and *haiku*. The *haiku*, because of its light style and accessibility eventually gained the larger audience. The rigidity of the *tanka* may have diminished its popularity, but the *wagakusha* were faithful to it. They continued producing that classic Japanese poem. Recognized *haiku* masters included the famous Basho, who took his name from the banana tree growing outside of his home. His disciples became the group known as the *jittets*, or the Ten Sages. *Haikus* went out of favor after Basho died, but regained favor with an impressionistic school of poetry that came about in the eighteenth century. The comic possibilities of the *haiku* reflects a movement in Japanese poetry during this time. Other popular poetical styles included mad poetry, *kyoka*, and mad verse, *kyoku*. These two styles were a part of the many comic and ridiculous poems produced then. These poems were absurd and delightful in their language and content and even achieved respect in the eighteenth century.

THE DIFFICULTY OF READING JAPANESE LITERATURE

Because the Japanese language lacks syllabic stress (accent) and meaningful end rhyme (all Japanese words end with one of five common vowels), the sound and shape of a Japanese poem often strike a Western ear and eye as unfamiliar. Only the number of syllables, in fact, distinguishes a line of poetry from a line of prose. Poetry typically appears in alternating lines of five and seven syllables. But even that distinction, if it is not accompanied by the emotionally intense and suggestive use of language, is insufficient to distinguish poetry from prose. Genres within Japanese poetry are similarly defined by number of syllables and line construction. A *haiku* traditionally has seventeen syllables and a *tanka* thirty-one syllables.

Historically, Japanese poets have nurtured the resources of what they consider the "pure" Japanese language—that is, the concrete, native words that existed before the abstracting and generalizing influence of the Chinese language reached Japan. Although such an elemental vocabulary is inadequate for expressing abstract intellectual concepts, it is superb for capturing a fleeting emotion, a glimpse of truth, a momentary whim, or, for that matter, a lasting verity of nature. Japanese poets have refined this art over the centuries to the point that much poetry (and literary prose) of the last four hundred years seems at first view to be a literary code of sorts available only to the initiated. In part, this linguistic movement toward condensation of language can be attributed to Japan's isolation from other nations through the eighteenth century. Japanese writers could direct their works to an audience with a predictable common set of cultural referents. To that extent, poetic language came to center on shared cultural meanings that could often be signaled or nuanced in a single word. Later readers who no longer share these cultural reference points inevitably find much Japanese poetry impenetrable.

14
THE LITERATURE OF INDIA

The oldest and most extensive body of literature in India is that of the Hindu Sanskrit tradition, with the earliest hymns and other religious poetry dating from the time of the arrival of the Indo-Aryan tribes in India about 1500 B.C. This literature can be divided into three general periods: Vedic, to 200 B.C.; Epic, to 400 A.D.; and Classical, to the present.

VEDIC LITERATURE

Vedic literature consists of four collections of hymns, each known as *Veda*, which means "sacred knowledge". The *Rig-Veda* contains 1,028 hymns, each of approximately ten stanzas and arranged in ten books. The content of these hymns is praise and supplication to a variety of Hindu gods. The *Sama-Veda* is made up of 1,549 stanzas used in religious chants and of songbooks that provide instructions for these chants. The *Yajur-Veda,* written in prose and poetry, is a manual intended to help Hindu priests prepare for their roles in sacrificial rituals. The *Athara-Veda* consists of 730 hymns in both stanzaic and prose forms focusing on personal prayers, charms, and spells that can be used to bring good fortune or ward off evil. Together, these four parts comprise the religious literature believed to be most authoritative by Hindus.

Attached to the *Vedas* are several forms of theological commentary written over the centuries by Hindu priests and scholars. The most famous of these are the *Upanishads*, India's oldest philosophical works. A mixture of folk tale, parable, dialogue, and lyric poetry, the *Upanishads* deal in rich, mystical language with the relationship between the individual soul and the surrounding cosmos.

EPIC LITERATURE

Epic literature in Sanskrit is made up of the *Mahabharata,* an episodic collection of tales stemming from several centuries of folk materials, and *Ramayana,* a shorter epic written primarily by one man, Valmiki, and dealing with court politics. Like the Arthurian legends in England, these epics have been the source of material for a wealth of Indian literature in the centuries since their compilation.

CLASSICAL LITERATURE

Classical Sanskrit literature is distinguished by its conformation to the grammatical rules set down by Panini and others in the period 350 to 250 B.C. One popular form within this division of literature is the *kavya*, a rhetorically complicated epic poem celebrating a famous religious or secular event. Two particularly well-known *kavyas* are those dealing with Buddha's life and the conversion of his half-brother. Prominent authors of *kavyas* in the period 400 to 500 A.D. were Kalidasa and Bharavi.

The most important achievement of Classical Sanskrit writers, however, came in the drama. From its early roots in religious rites and puppet plays, Indian drama blossomed in the fourth to sixth centuries A.D. It differs substantially from Western dramatic traditions in that it has no tragedy, and death is never enacted on stage. The status levels of different characters are indicated primarily by the language they speak: Sanskrit for kings, Brahmans, and educated women and varieties of Prakrits for less prestigious characters. A regular feature is the buffoon or jester. Most action takes place in prose, with poetry used for the description of scenery and the emotions of characters. Classical Indian drama aims to evoke one of nine moods in its audience: erotic, heroic, comic, pathetic, wondrous, odious, furious, peaceful, or terrible. Important dramatists in this tradition are Bhasa, Kalidasa, King Harsha, King Sudraka, Visakhadatta, and Rajasekhara.

The lyric is yet another important Classical Sanskrit genre. Both secular and religious in nature, the lyric consists typically of a series of stanzas describing the beauties of nature and the paths of earthly and divine love. In the twelfth century, the poet Jayadeva wrote some of the most celebrated Indian lyrics in his *Gitagovinda*.

Classical Sanskrit literature also abounds in prose tales, romances, and fables. The *Brhatkatha* by Gunadhya dates from about 600 and collects a wide range of tales within a frame story, much after the fashion of Chaucer's *Canterbury Tales*. The biographical mode was popularized in India by Hemacandra (1089–1173), who wrote the *Lives of Sixty-three Distinguished Persons*. From the twelfth through the seventeenth centuries, Indian literature underwent a vernacular Renaissance, with both secular and religious tales, hymns, and aphorisms being written throughout the land.

REVIEW QUESTIONS

NON-EUROPEAN LITERATURE

Multiple Choice

1. _____One of the greatest difficulties faced by colonial authors in Latin America was
   a. the lack of printing presses
   b. limited subject matter
   c. censorship
   d. lack of readership

2. _____It is generally true of Latin-American literature that it
   a. represents a unified ideal of Latin America
   b. shows the great diversity of Latin America
   c. is monolingual
   d. is less popular now than it once was

3. _____Which of the following best describes the *Tales of Genji*?
   a. a short narrative work
   b. the first Japanese novel written by a man
   c. the first work of Japanese philosophy
   d. a lengthly novel that critiques women

4. _____Japanese literature of the Heian period
   a. was written in large part by women
   b. consisted mainly of prose works
   c. included no historical novels
   d. is mainly concerned with philosophy

5. _____The *Kangakusha* and the *Wagakusha* were
   a. two great poetic works of the Edo period
   b. two opposing camps of scholars
   c. the first Japanese novels
   d. the two main types of *haiku*

6. _____In the Edo period, the popular poetic styles included
   a. *haiku*
   b. *tanka*
   c. *kyoka* and *kyoku*
   d. all of the above

7. _____The clearest, simplest expression of Confucian philosophy can be found in the
   a. *I-Ching*
   b. *Analects*
   c. *Lun-Yu*
   d. *Shih-Ching*

8. _____The Tang dynasty brought
   a. a general rejection of literature
   b. a more subjective approach to literary interpretation
   c. new perspectives on the *Ching*
   d. a lull in artistic production

9. _____The origins of *Yuan* theater can be found in
   a. Confucian philosophy
   b. the religious ceremonies described in the *Shu-Chi*
   c. Taoist rites and rituals
   d. the themes of early Chinese novels

10. _____All of the following played important roles in Chinese literary history except
    a. the early Han emperors
    b. the Tang poets
    c. Confucius and his disciples
    d. Ming dynasty philosophers

True or False

11. _____The literature of Spanish- and Portuguese-speaking Latin America show parallel but separate development.

12. _____Latin-American authors contributed greatly to the growth of the Utopia myth.

13. _____In the Nara period, Japanese was considered a more feminine language, suited to the woman's domain in poetry and stories.

14. _____The form of the *No* drama resembles that of Greek tragedy.

15. _____The content of *tanka* poems was highly controlled, though the length remained flexible.

16. _____The *haiku* has a very loose form and resembles the *hiragana* style.

17. _____There was much stylistic innovation in the writings of Confucius.

18. _____Poetry was the greatest contribution of the Tang dynasty writers.

19. _____Taoists sought to uphold the sharp distinctions between good and evil proposed by the followers of Confucius.

20. _____Literature in general fared well during the Han empire.

Fill-in

21. In his famous narrative, _____, the Spanish explorer, wrote about his adventures as a captive of the Indians.

22. The Dominican priest _____ inveighed against the evils of colonialism.

23. The most famous Buddhist treatise, _____, was written during the Kamakara period.

24. The observations and anecdotes of Kenko, entitled _____, remains a highly readable text.

25. The Chinese word _____ refers to literature, drawing, and history.

26. The three philosophies of the greatest importance in Chinese literature are _____, _____, and _____.

27. The pre-Han narrative style, called _____, later came to mean "tale" or "novel."

28. India's oldest philosophical works are called the _____.

29. The Indian *kavya* is a rhetorically complicated type of _____ poem.

30. A more accessible type of drama than the elite *No* theater was the _____.

Matching

31.	_____ Sor Ines	a.	nationalistic Japanese scholars
32.	_____ Kamakara period	b.	ornate baroque verses
33.	_____ Li Ching Chao and Su Shih	c.	collection of hymns
34.	_____ Jayadeva	d.	rise of masculine literature
35.	_____ Wagakusha	e.	son of an Inca princess
36.	_____ Carcilas de la Vega	f.	Indian lyric poet
37.	_____ Ssu-Ma Hsiang Ju	g.	Tang poetry
38.	_____ Vedic literature	h.	Tzu poetry
39.	_____ Taoism	i.	Fu style
40.	_____ *Hsin-ti*	j.	dialectical reasoning; individualism

Answers

1.	c	15.	t	27.	*Hsia-Shuo*
2.	b	16.	f	28.	*Upanishads*
3.	d	17.	f	29.	epic
4.	a	18.	t	30.	*Kabuki*
5.	b	19.	f	31.	b
6.	d	20.	f	32.	d
7.	b	21.	Cabeza de Vaca	33.	h
8.	c	22.	Bartolome de las	34.	f
9.	b		Casas	35.	a
10.	d	23.	*Hojoki*	36.	e
11.	t	24.	*Tsure-Zure-Husa*	37.	i
12.	t	25.	*wen*	38.	c
13.	t	26.	Taoism, Buddhism,	39.	j
14.	t		and Confucianism	40.	g

GLOSSARY

Allegory: A literary device, in prose or poetry, in which a literal character, event, or object also possesses a symbolic meaning. Thus an allegory may illustrate a philosophical idea, or a moral or religious principle. A work of literature is said to be allegorical if it has more than one level of meaning. (Examples: the *Romance of the Rose*, La Fontaine's *Fables*, Kafka's *The Penal Colony*, Orwell's *Animal Farm*)

Alliteration: The repetition of a sound, especially an initial consonant, in a line of poetry or prose. (Example: "Walking in a Winter Wonderland")

Allusion: An indirect or explicit reference to a well-known place, event, or person. Allusion in literature often takes the form of a figure of speech. (Example: In Keats' "Ode to a Nightingale," the phrase "and Lethe-wards [I] had sunk." The poet alludes to Hades, the underworld.)

Archetype: In literature, archetypal criticism examines types of narrative, character, and image that occur in a large variety of texts. Literary archetypes, like the Jungian archetypes of the collective unconscious, are said to reflect a group of elemental and universal patterns that trigger an immediate and profound response from the reader.

Assonance: The repetition, in a line of prose or poetry, of similar or identical vowel sounds.

Consonance: The repetition of consonant sounds, with a change in the vowel that follows or is between the consonant. (Example: give-gave)

Chivalric romance: A genre of narrative developed in twelfth century France, similar to the epic in form but treating the themes of courtly love and chivalry. This form of romance spread through the courts of France as oral literature provided by troubadours and minstrels.

Fabliau: A satiric or comic tale and a common literary form in the Middle Ages, the fabliaux both mocked and reveled in the obscene and vulgar elements in lives of both middle- and lower-class persons. Many of Chaucer's *Canterbury Tales* are perfect examples of the fabliau form, including the "Miller's Tale."

Genre: A French word meaning type, kind, or form; in literature the term is used to designate different literary forms, such as *tragedy, satire, epic*, and more recently *novel, biography*, and so on.

Irony: A figure in which the implicit meaning of a statement or action differs drastically from its implicit meaning. Types of irony include dramatic irony, verbal irony, and structural irony.

291

Lyric: A short poem, usually nonnarrative, in which the text expresses the speaker's emotional or mental state. A lyric is often written in the first person, and may be associated with songs and other musical forms.

Meter: This term designates the recognizable and repeated rhythms and stresses created by verse form. Iambic pentameter is the most common meter of English poetry.

Metonomy: A figure of speech in which a literal term for or attribute of one thing comes to represent another to which it has a contiguous relation. (Example: the use of "crown" to mean king)

Mimesis: A Greek word meaning imitation, mimesis is the active or dynamic copying or representation of a literal (sensual) or metaphysical (spiritual) reality in a work of art or literature.

Motif: A thematic or structural element used and repeated in a single text, or in the whole of literature. A motif may be a literary device, an incident, a formula, or a reference. (Also "leitmotif" or guiding motif)

Ode: A lyric poem of high and formal style, usually rhymed, which often addresses itself to a praised person, object, or quality. (Example: Wordsworth's "Ode: Intimations of Immortality")

Personification: A figure of speech or rhetoric in which inanimate objects or abstractions are given human qualities, or represented as having human form. (Example: "that lazy old sun")

Satire: A work of literature that attacks society's vice and folly through irony and wit.

Scansion: The analysis of verse or poetry to uncover its meter and rhythmic patterns.

Sonnet: A fourteen-line lyric poem with a formal rhyme scheme, originated in the thirteen century by Sicilian court poets influenced by troubadour poetry. In Italy, it reached its zenith in the sonnets of Petrarch. He wrote a sonnet cycle of 317 sonnets, his *Canzoniere*, to his idealized love, Laura. In so doing, he established his sonnet form as one of the two dominant sonnet schemes (the other being the English or Shakespearean sonnet).

The Petrarchan sonnet, used frequently by Milton, is divided into an octave (eight lines) and sestet (six lines), rhyming *abbaabba* and *cdecde* (or *cdccdc*) respectively. Typically, the first eight lines in a Petrarchan sonnet pose a problem or ask a question of some kind. The last six lines resolve the problem or question.

Synecdoche: A figure of speech in which a part of something is taken to represent the whole. (Example: "ten sails on the horizon," meaning ten ships)

Theme: An idea presented and expanded upon in a literary work. A theme can be explicit or implicit, and it is usually suggested by the narrative action.

SUGGESTED READINGS

General

Bermel, Albert. *The Genius of the French Theatre*. New York, 1961.

Bishop, Morris. *A Survey of French Literature*. New York, 1955.

Bloch, R. H. ed. *A New History of French Literature*. Cambridge, MA, 1989.

Bradley, R. F. *Eight Centuries of French Literature*. New York, 1951.

Brereton, Geoffrey. *A Short History of French Literature*. Baltimore, 1954.

Brown, Harcourt. *Science and the Human Comedy*. Toronto, 1976.

Butler, K. T. *A History of French Literature*. New York, 1966.

Charvet, P. E., ed. *A Literary History of France*. New York, 1967.

DeJean, J. E. *Fictions of Sappho, 1546–1937*. Chicago, 1989.

Daniel, G. B. *The Development of the Tragedie Nationale in France from 1552–1800*. Chapel Hill, NC, 1964.

Edelman, Nathan. *The Eye of the Beholder*. Baltimore, 1974.

Fowlie, Wallace. *French Literature: Its History and Its Meaning*. Englewood Cliffs, NJ, 1973.

France, Anatole. *The Latin Genius*. New York, 1971.

Gill, Austin, ed. *Life and Letters in France*. London, 1970.

Glasser, Richard. *Time in French Life and Thought*. Manchester, 1972.

Harvey, Paul. *The Oxford Companion to French Literature*. Oxford, 1959.

Hatzfield, H. A. *Literature Through Art*. New York, 1952.

Hawkins, F. W. *Annals of the French Stage*. Detroit, 1968.

Howarth, W. D. *French Literature from 1600 to the Present*. London, 1974.

Jordanova, L. J. *Languages of Nature: Critical Essays on Science and Literature*. New Brunswick, NJ, 1986.

Knapp, B. L. *Dream and Image*. New York, 1977.

Latham, A. G. *The Oxford Treasury of French Literature*. Oxford, 1940.

Levine, George, ed. *One Culture: Essays in Science and Literature*. Madison, WI, 1987.

Lockert, Lacy. *The Chief Rivals of Corneille and Racine*. Nashville, TN, 1956.

Mason, Germaine. *A Concise History of French Literature*. New York, 1969.

Partridge, Eric. *A Critical Medley*. New York, 1969.

Peyre, Henri. *Historical and Critical Essays*. Lincoln, NE, 1968.

Poulet, Georges. *The Interior Distance*. Baltimore, MD, 1959.

Roaten, D. H. *Structural Forms in the French Theatre, 1500–1700*. Philadelphia, PA, 1960.

Smith, H. E. *Masters of French Literature*. New York, 1969.

Stambolian, George. *Homosexualities and French Literature*. Ithaca, NY, 1979.

Steele, A. J. *Three Centuries of French Verse, 1511–1819*. Edinburgh, 1961.

Street, J. S. *French Sacred Drama from Beze to Corneille.* London, 1983.

Wilson, D. B. *Descriptive Poetry in France from Blason to Baroque.* Manchester, 1967.

Wright, C. H. *A History of French Literature.* New York, 1969.

Medieval Literature

Crosland, J. R. *Medieval French Literature.* Oxford, 1956.

Ferrier, J. M. *Forerunners of the French Novel.* Manchester, 1954.

Fox, J. H. *The Middle Ages.* London, 1974.

Kelley, Douglas. *The Art of Medieval French Romance.* Madison, WI, 1992.

Le Goff, Jacques. *The Medieval Imagination.* Chicago, 1988.

Mandel, Oscar. *Five Comedies of Medieval France.* New York, 1970.

Muir, L. R. *Literature and Society: the Mirror and the Image, 1100–1500.* New York, 1985.

Poirion, Daniel, ed. *Contexts: Style and Values in Medieval Art and Literature.* New Haven, CT, 1991.

Rickard, Peter. *Britain in Medieval French Literature, 1100–1500.* Cambridge, 1956.

Ryding, W. W. *Structure in Medieval Narrative.* London, 1971.

Vitz, E. B. *Medieval Narrative and Modern Narratology.* New York, 1989.

Sixteenth Century

Cave, Terence. *The Cornucopia Text: Problems of Writing in the French Renaissance.* Oxford, 1979.

Coleman, D. G. *The Gallo-Roman Muse: Aspects of Roman Literary Tradition in Sixteenth Century France.* New York, 1979.

Conley, Tom. *The Graphic Unconscious in Early Modern French Writing.* New York, 1992.

Daniel, G. B., ed. *Renaissance and Other Studies in Honor of William Leon Wiley.* Chapel Hill, NC, 1968.

Graham, V. C. *Sixteenth-Century French Poetry.* Toronto, 1964.

Griffiths, R. M. *The Dramatic Technique of Antoine de Montchrestien: Rhetoric and Style in French Renaissance Tragedy.* Oxford, 1970.

Haggis, D. R., ed. *The French Renaissance and Its Heritage.* London, 1968.

Jeffrey, Brian. *French Renaissance Comedy, 1552–1630.* Oxford, 1969.

Jondorf, Gillian. *French Renaissance Tragedy: The Dramatic Word.* Cambridge, 1990.

Kritzman, L. D. *The Rhetoric of Sexuality and the Literature of the French Renaissance.* Cambridge, 1991.

La Charite, R. C. *From Marot to Montaigne: Essays on French Renaissance Literature.* Lexington, KY, 1972.

Langer, Ullrich. *Divine and Poetic Freedom in the Renaissance.* Princeton, NJ, 1990.

Levi, A. H., ed. *Humanism in France at the End of the Middle Ages and in the Early Renaissance.* Manchester, 1970.

Maskell, David. *The Historical Epic in France, 1500–1700*. London, 1973.

McFarlane, I. D. *Renaissance France, 1470–1589*. London, 1974.

McFarlane, I. D. *Renaissance Studies: Six Essays*. London, 1972.

McGowan, M. M. *Ideal Forms in the Age of Ronsard*. Berkeley, CA, 1985.

Richmond, H. M. *Puritans and Libertines: Anglo-French Literary Relations in the Reformation*. Berkeley, CA, 1981.

Rouillard, C. D. *The Turk in French History, Thought, and Literature*. Paris, 1940.

Schutz, A. H. *Vernacular Books in Parisian Private Libraries of the Sixteenth Century*. Chapel Hill, NC, 1955.

Smith, P. M. *The Anti-Courtier Trend in Sixteenth Century French Literature*. Geneva, 1966.

Stabler, A. P., ed. *Four French Renaissance Plays*. Seattle, 1978.

Stone, Donald. *Four Renaissance Tragedies*. Cambridge, MA, 1966.

Stone, Donald. *France in the Sixteenth Century*. Englewood Cliffs, NJ, 1969.

Stone, Donald. *French Humanist Tragedy: A Reassessment*. Manchester, 1974.

Tilley, A. A. *The Literature of the French Renaissance*. New York, 1959.

Weinberg, Bernard. *French Poetry of the Renaissance*. Carbondale, IL, 1964.

Seventeenth Century

Abraham, C. K. *Enfin Malherbe: The Influence of Malherbe on French Lyric Prosody, 1605–1674*. Lexington, KY, 1971.

Adam, Antoine. *Grandeur and Illusion: French Literature and Society, 1600–1715*. New York, 1972.

Atkinson, Geoffrey. *The Extraordinary Voyage in French Literature*. New York, 1969.

Bannister, Mark. *Privileged Mortals: the French Heroic Novel, 1630–1660*. Oxford, 1983.

Baldner, R. W. *Bibliography of Seventeenth-Century French Prose Fiction*. New York, 1967.

Beasley, F. E. *Revising Memory: Women's Fiction and Memoirs in Seventeenth-Century France*. New Brunswick, NJ, 1990.

Benichou, Paul. *Man and Ethics: Studies in French Classicism*. New York, 1971.

Boas, George. *The Happy Beast in French Thought of the Seventeenth Century*. New York, 1966.

Borgerhoff, E. B. *The Freedom of French Classicism*. Princeton, NJ, 1950.

Davidson, H. M. *Audience, Words, and Art: Studies in Seventeenth-Century French Rhetoric*. Columbus, OH, 1965.

Demorest, J. J. *Studies in Seventeenth Century French Literature*. Ithaca, NY, 1962.

Douthwaite, J. V. *Exotic Women: Literary Heroines and Cultural Strategies in Ancien Regime France*. Philadelphia, PA, 1992.

Edelman, Nathan. *Attitudes of Seventeenth Century France Toward the Middle Ages*. New York, 1946.

Farrell, M. L. *Performing Motherhood: the Sévigné Correspondence*. Hanover, NH, 1991.

Harth, Erica. *Ideology and Culture in Seventeenth Century France*. Ithaca, NY, 1983.

Horowitz, L. K. *Love and Language: A Study of the Classical French Moralist Writers*. Columbus, OH, 1977.

Kamuf, Peggy. *Fictions of Feminine Desire*. Lincoln, NE, 1982.

Krailsheimer, A. J. *Studies of Self-Interest: From Descartes to La Bruyère*. Oxford, 1962.

McBride, Robert. *Aspects of Seventeenth Century French Drama and Thought*. New York, 1979.

Michell, R. B. *French Literature Before 1800*. New York, 1936.

Moriarity, Michael. *Taste and Ideology in Seventeenth Century France*. Cambridge, 1988.

Nurse, Peter. *Classical Voices: Studies of Corneille, Racine, Molière, Mme. de Lafayette*. New York, 1971.

Showalter, England. *The Evolution of the French Novel, 1642–1782*. Princeton, NJ, 1972.

Spitzer, Leo. *Essays on Seventeenth Century French Literature*. Cambridge, 1983.

Tilley, A. A. *The Decline of the Age of Louis XIV*. New York, 1968.

Waith, E. M. *French and English Drama of the Seventeenth Century*. Los Angeles, CA, 1972.

Williams, R. C. *Bibliography of the Seventeenth Century Novel in France*. London, 1964.

Yarrow, P. J. *The Seventeenth Century, 1600–1715*. New York, 1967.

Eighteenth Century

Atkinson, Geoffroy. *Prelude to the Enlightenment*. Seattle, WA, 1970.

Atkinson, Geoffroy. *The Sentimental Revolution*. Seattle, WA, 1966.

Brooks, Peter. *The Novel of Worldliness*. Princeton, NJ, 1969.

Cardy, Michael. *The Literary Doctrines of Jean-François Marmontel*. Oxford, 1982.

Charlton, D. G. *New Images of the Natural in France*. Cambridge, 1984.

Davies, Simon. *Paris and the Provinces in Eighteenth-Century Prose Fiction*. Oxford, 1982.

DeJean, J. E. *Literary Fortifications*. Princeton, NJ, 1984.

Fellows, Otis. *From Voltaire to La Nouvelle Critique*. Geneva, 1970.

France, Peter. *Rhetoric and Truth in France: Descartes to Diderot*. Oxford, 1972.

Gearhart, Suzanne. *The Open Boundary of History and Truth: A Critical Approach to the French Enlightenment*. Princeton, NJ, 1984.

Green, F. C. *Minuet: A Critical Survey of French and English Literary Ideas in the Eighteenth Century*. New York, 1935.

Heroit, Angus. *The French in Italy, 1796–1799*. London, 1957.

Keener, F. M. *The Chain of Becoming.* New York, 1983.

Lynch, L. W. *Eighteenth Century French Novelists and the Novel.* York, SC, 1979.

Macary, Jean, ed. *Essays on the Enlightenment in Honor of Ira O. Wade.* Geneva, 1977.

Miller, N. K. *The Heroine's Text: Readings in the French and English Novel, 1722–1782.* New York, 1980.

Mylne, Vivienne. *The Eighteenth Century French Novel: Techniques of Illusion.* New York, 1981.

Niklaus, Robert. *The Eighteenth Century, 1715–1789.* New York, 1970.

Newman, L. L. *Ten Letter-Writers.* New York, 1968.

Northeast, C. M. *The Parisian Jesuits and the Enlightenment, 1700–1762.* Oxford, 1991.

Picard, Raymond. *Two Centuries of French Literature.* New York, 1970.

Saisselin, R. G. *The Literary Enterprise in Eighteenth Century France.* Detroit, MI, 1979.

Stewart, Philip. *Imitation and Illusion in the French Memoir-Novel, 1700–1750.* New Haven, CT, 1969.

Temmer, M. J. *Samuel Johnson and Three Infidels: Rousseau, Voltaire, Diderot.* Athens, GA, 1988.

Todd, J. M. *Women's Friendship in Literature.* New York, 1980.

Weinstein, Leo. *The Subversive Tradition in French Literature, 1721–1971.* Boston, MA, 1989.

Origen

Balthasar, H. U., ed. *Origen, Spirit, and Fire.* Washington, DC, 1984.

Ambrose

Peredi, Angelo. *Saint Ambrose: His Life and Times.* Notre Dame, IN, 1968.

Jerome

Clark, E. A. *Jerome, Chrysostom, and Friends.* New York, 1979.

Augustine

O'Donnel, J. J. *Augustine.* Boston, MA, 1985.

Ancius Manlius Severinus Boethius

Reiss, Edmund. *Boethius.* Boston, MA, 1982.

Eddas

Glendinning, R. J., ed. *Edda: A Collection of Essays.* Manitoba, Canada, 1983.

Chansons de Geste

Calin, William. *The Epic Quest: Studies in Four Old French Chansons de Geste.* Baltimore, MD, 1966.

Keller, H. E. *Romance Epic: Essays on a Medieval Literary Genre*. Kalamazoo, MI, 1987.

Song of Roland
Jones, G. F. *The Ethos of the Song of Roland*. Baltimore, MD, 1963.

El Cid
Fletcher, R. A. *The Quest for El Cid*. New York, 1990.

Aucassin and Nicolette
Martin, J. H. *Love's Fools—Aucassin, Troilus, Calisto, and the Parody of the Courtly Lover*. London, 1972.

Eleanor of Aquitaine
Meade, Marion. *Eleanor of Aquitaine: A Biography*. New York, 1977.

François Villon
Anacker, Robert. *François Villon*. New York, 1968.
Paris, G. B. *François Villon*. New York, 1975.

Dante Alighieri
Bergin, T. G. *A Diversity of Dante*. New Brunswick, NJ, 1969.
Chubb, T. C. *Dante and His World*. Boston, 1967.
Federn, Karl. *Dante and His Time*. New York, 1969.
Fergusson, Francis. *Dante*. New York, 1966.
Freccero, John. *Dante: a Collection of Critical Essays*. Englewood Cliffs, NJ, 1965.
Holmes, George. *Dante*. New York, 1980.
Jacoff, Rachel, ed. *The Cambridge Companion to Dante*. Cambridge, 1993.
Moore, Edward. *Dante and His Early Biographers*. New York, 1970.
Musa, Mark. *Advent at the Gates: Dante's Comedy*. Bloomington, IN, 1974.

Renaissance Drama
Beecher, Donald, ed. *Comparative Critical Approaches to Renaissance Comedy*. Ottawa, Canada, 1986.
Blistein, E. M., ed. *The Drama of the Renaissance*. Providence, RI, 1970.
Hathaway, Baxter. *The Age of Criticism: the Late Renaissance in Italy*. Ithaca, NY, 1962.
Murray, Timothy. *Theatrical Legitimation*. New York, 1987.
Piccolomini, Manfredi. *The Brutus Revival: Parricide and Tyrannicide During the Renaissance*. Carbondale, IL, 1991.

Francesco Petrarch
Bergin, T. G. *Petrarch*. New York, 1970.
Foster, Kenelm. *Petrarch: Poet and Humanist*. Edinburgh, 1984.

Robinson, J. H., ed. *Petrarch, the First Modern Scholar and Man of Letters.* New York, 1969.

Wilkins, E. H. *Life of Petrarch.* Chicago, 1961.

Giovanni Boccaccio

Branca, Vittore. *Boccaccio: the Man and His Works.* New York, 1976.

Cottino-Jones, Marga. *Order from Chaos: Social and Aesthetic Harmonies in Boccaccio's Decameron.* Washington, DC, 1982.

Deligiorgis, Stavros. *Narrative Intellection in the Decameron.* Iowa City, IA, 1975.

Lee, A. C. *The Decameron: Its Sources and Analogues.* New York, 1966.

Marino, Lucia. *The Decameron Cornice: Allusion, Allegory, and Iconology.* London, 1979.

Potter, J. H. *Five Frames for the Decameron.* Princeton, NJ, 1982.

Burckhardt, Jakob Christian. *The Civilization of the Renaissance in Italy,* rev. ed. New York, 1960.

Humanism

Barthes, Roland. *Empire of Signs.* New York, 1980.

Barthes, Roland. *Mythologies.* New York, 1972.

Bentley, J. H. *Humanists and Holy Writ.* Princeton, NJ, 1983.

Foucault, Michel. *The Archaeology of Knowledge.* New York, 1972.

Rabil, Albert, ed. *Knowledge, Goodness, and Power: the Debate over Nobility among Quattrocento Italian Humanists.* Binghamton, NY, 1991.

Wolfflin, Heinrich. *Principles of Art History.* New York, 1932.

Wolfflin, Heinrich. *Classic Art: an Introduction to the Italian Renaissance,* rev. ed. Ithaca, NY, 1980.

Vittorino da Feltre

Woodward, W. H. *Vittorino da Feltre and Other Humanist Educators.* Cambridge, 1940.

Lorenzo Valla

Camporeale, S. I. *Lorenzo Valla* [in Ital.]. Florence, 1972.

Lorenzo de' Medici

Hook, Judith. *Lorenzo de' Medici: An Historical Biography.* London, 1984.

Rowden, Maurice. *Lorenzo the Magnificent.* London, 1974.

Poliziano

Ehrman, S. H. *Three Renaissance Silhouettes.* New York, 1928.

Luigi Pulci

Gianni, Angelo. *Pulci.* Florence, 1967.

Count Matteo Maria Boiardo

Di Tommaso, Andrea. *Structure and Ideology in Boiardo's Orlando Innamorato.* Chapel Hill, NC, 1972.

Jacopo Sannazaro

Kennedy, W. J. *Jacopo Sannazaro and the Use of Pastoral.* Hanover, NH, 1983.

Novella

Picone, Michelangelo, ed. *The Novella.* Montreal, Canada, 1983.

Niccolò Machiavelli

Skinner, Quentin. *Machiavelli.* New York, 1981.
Tarlton, C. D. *Fortune's Circle: A Biographical Interpretation of Niccolò Machiavelli.* Chicago, 1970.

Baldassare Castiglione

Ady, J. M. *Baldassare Castiglione, the Perfect Courtier.* New York, 1973.

Michelangelo Buonarotti

Hibbard, Howard. *Michelangelo.* New York, 1974.
Liebert, R. S. *Michelangelo, a Psychological Study of His Life and Images.* New Haven, CT, 1983.
Morgan, C. H. *The Life of Michelangelo.* New York, 1960.

Ludovico Ariosto

Brand, C. P. *Ludovico Ariosto: A Preface to the Orlando Furioso.* Edinburgh, 1974.
Gardner, E. G. *The King of Court Poets.* New York, 1968.

Benvenuto Cellini

Pope-Hennessy, J. W. *Cellini.* New York, 1985.

Torquato Tasso

Brand, C. P. *Torquato Tasso: a Study of the Poet and of His Contribution to English Literature.* Cambridge, 1965.

Giovanni Battista Guarini

Perella, Nicolas, J. *The Critical Fortune of Battista Guarini's Il Pastor Fido.* Florence, 1973.

Giambattista Marino

Schaar, Claes. *Marino and Crashaw.* Lund, 1971.

Clement Marot

Smith, P. M. *Clement Marot: Poet of the French Renaissance.* London, 1970.

Marguerite of Navarre

Putman, Samuel. *Marguerite of Navarre.* New York, 1935.

François Rabelais

Chappell, A. F. *The Enigma of Rabelais.* Philadelphia, PA, 1973.
Frame, D. M. *François Rabelais: a Study.* New York, 1977.
Greene, T. M. *Rabelais: a Study in Comic Courage.* Englewood Cliffs, NJ, 1970.
Tetel, Marcel. *Rabelais.* New York, 1967.

John Calvin

Partee, Charles. *Calvin and Classical Philosophy.* Leiden, 1977.
Selinger, Suzanne. *Calvin Against Himself: An Inquiry in Intellectual History.* Hamden, CT, 1984.
Wallace, R. S. *Calvin, Geneva, and the Reformation.* Grand Rapids, MI, 1990.

The Pléiade

Castor, Grahame. *Pléiade Poetics: A Study in Sixteenth Century Thought and Terminology.* Cambridge, 1964.
Merrill, R. V. *Platonism in French Renaissance Poetry.* New York, 1957.

Michel de Montaigne

Frame, D. M. *Montaigne: A Biography.* New York, 1965.

François de Malherbe

Rubin, D. L. *Higher, Hidden Order: Design and Meaning in the Odes of Malherbe.* Chapel Hill, NC, 1972.

Miguel de Cervantes Saavedra

Duran, Manuel. *Cervantes.* New York, 1974.
Entwistle, W. J. *Cervantes.* Oxford, 1965.

Lope Felix de Vega Carpio

Hayes, F. C. *Lope de Vega.* New York, 1967.
Rennert, H. A. *The Life of Lope de Vega, 1562–1635.* New York, 1968.

Juan Ruiz de Alarcón Mendoza

Poesse, Walter. *Juan Ruiz de Alarcón.* New York, 1973.

Pedro Calderón de la Barca

Gerstinger, Heinz. *Pedro Calderón de la Barca.* New York, 1973.
Honig, Edwin. *Calderon and the Seizures of Honor.* Cambridge, MA, 1972.

Desiderius Erasmus

McConica, James. *Erasmus*. Oxford, 1991.
Schoeck, R. J. *Erasmus of Europe: The Making of a Humanist*. New York, 1990.
Trapp, J. B. *Erasmus, Colet and More: The Early Tudor Humanists and Their Books*. London, 1991.

Molière

Mander, Gertrude. *Jean-Baptiste Molière*. New York, 1973.
Walker, Hallam. *Molière*. New York, 1971.

Pierre Corneille

Cook, A. S. *French Tragedy: The Power of Enactment*. Chicago, 1981.
Pocock, Gordon. *Corneille and Racine: Problems of Tragic Form*. Cambridge, 1973.
Yarrow, P. J. *Corneille*. London, 1963.

Jean Racine

Abraham, C. K. *Jean Racine*. Boston, 1977.

Jean de la Fontaine

Mackay, A. E. *La Fontaine and His Friend: A Biography*. New York, 1973.

Nicolas Boileau-Despréaux

Clark, A. F. *Boileau and the French Classical Critics in England, 1660–1830*. London, 1965.
Pocock, Gordon. *Boileau and the Nature of Neoclassicism*. Cambridge, 1980.

Blaise Pascal

Davidson, H. M. *Blaise Pascal*. Boston, 1983.
Hazelton, Roger. *Blaise Pascal: The Genius of His Thought*. Philadelphia, PA, 1974.

François, Prince de Marcillac, Duke de la Rochefoucauld

Bergin, Joseph. *Cardinal de la Rochefoucauld: Leadership and Reform in the French Church*. New Haven, CT, 1987.

Jean de la Bruyère

Knox, E. C. *Jean de la Bruyère*. New York, 1974.
Michaut, G. M. *La Bruyère*. Geneva, 1970.

Louis de Rouvroy, Duke de Saint-Simon

De Ley, Herbert. *Saint-Simon Memorialist*. Urbana, IL, 1975.

Jacques Genigne Bossuet

Reynolds, E. E. *Bossuet*. New York, 1963.

François de Salignac de la Mothe-Fénelon

Little, K. D. *François de Fénelon: Study of a Personality*. New York, 1951.

Voltaire

Hearsey, J. E. *Voltaire*. New York, 1976.
Mason, H. T. *Voltaire: a Biography*. Baltimore, MD, 1981.

Charles de Secondat, Baron de Montesquieu

Loy, J. R. *Montesquieu*. New York, 1968.
Shackleton, Robert. *Montesquieu: a Critical Biography*. London, 1961.

Jean le Roud d'Alembert

Grimsley, Ronald. *Jean d'Alembert, 1717–1783*. Oxford, 1963.
Hankins, T. L. *Jean d'Alembert, Science and the Enlightenment*. New York, 1990.

Denis Diderot

Furbank, P. N. *Diderot: A Critical Biography*. London, 1992.

Pierre Bayle

Whelan, Ruth. *The Anatomy of Superstition: A Study of the Historical Theory and Practice of Pierre Bayle*. Oxford, 1989.

Georges-Louis Leclerc de Buffon

Fellows, Otis. *Buffon*. New York, 1972.

Pierre Carlet de Marivaux

Brady, V. P. *Love in the Theatre of Marivaux*. Geneva, 1970.

Caron de Beaumarchais

Sungolowsky, Joseph. *Beaumarchais*. New York, 1974.

Abbé Prévost

Haven, G. R. *The Abbé Prévost and English Literature*. New York, 1965.

Jean François Marmontel

Cardy, Michael. *The Literary Doctrines of Jean-François Marmontel*. Oxford, 1982.
Renwick, John. *Marmontel, Voltaire, and the Belisaire Affair*. New York, 1974.

Latin American Literature

Caracciolo-Trejo, Enrique. *The Penguin Book of Latin American Verse*. London, 1971.

Collazos, Oscar. *Literature of Revolution and Revolution in Literature*. Mexico City, 1971.

Stimson, F. S. *Literature of Hispanic America*. New York, 1971.

Chinese Literature

Bishop, J. L. *Studies in Chinese Literature*. Cambridge, MA, 1965.

Hightower, J. R. *Topics in Chinese Literature*. Cambridge, MA, 1966.

Mackerras, Colin, ed. *Chinese Theater: From its Origins to the Present Day*. Honolulu, HI, 1983.

Paper, J. D. *Guide to Chinese Prose*. Boston, 1973.

Scott, A. C. *The Classical Theatre of China*. New York, 1957.

Wells, H. W. *The Classical Drama of the Orient*. New York, 1965.

Japanese Literature

Aston, W. G. *A History of Japanese Literature*. New York, 1937.

Bowers, Faubion. *Japanese Theatre*. New York, 1952.

Kato, Shuichi. *A History of Japanese Literature*. New York, 1979.

Keene, Donald. *Japanese Literature: An Introduction for Western Readers*. London, 1953.

Kokusai, B. S. *Introduction to Classic Japanese Literature*. Westport, CT, 1970.

Komiya, Toyotaka. *Japanese Music and Drama in the Meiji Era*. Tokyo, 1969.

Konishi, Jinichi. *A History of Japanese Literature*. Princeton, NJ, 1984.

Lombard, F. A. *An Outline History of the Japanese Drama*. New York, 1966.

Martins, J. A. *Japanese and Western Literature: A Comparative Study*. Rutland, VT, 1970.

Putzar, Edward. *Japanese Literature: A Historical Outline*. Tucson, AZ, 1973.

Rimer, J. T. *Pilgrimages: Aspects of Japanese Literature and Culture*. Honolulu, HI, 1988.

Rimer, J. T. *A Reader's Guide to Japanese Literature*. Tokyo, 1988.

INDEX

Notes

Notes

Notes